HOME
FURNISHING

SECOND EDITION

ANNA HONG RUTT,
FORMERLY HEAD OF ART DEPARTMENT
NORTHWESTERN UNIVERSITY, EVANSTON, ILLINOIS

JOHN WILEY AND SONS, INC., NEW YORK
CHAPMAN AND HALL, LTD., LONDON

THIRD PRINTING, JUNE, 1949

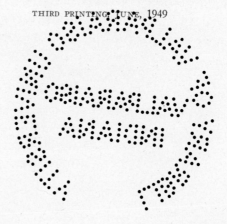

PRINTED IN THE UNITED STATES OF AMERICA

PREFACE

THIS BOOK has been written to serve as a textbook for classes in home planning and furnishing, as a practical book for homemakers, and as a book of general information for interior decorators. As a textbook it can be used for long or short courses. Lists of reading references and class problems are given at the end of each chapter. Additional class projects and bibliography lists are placed in the last chapter. A glossary is not included since a home furnishing classroom should have a copy of some dictionary of furniture terms, such as Joseph Aronson's *The Encyclopedia of Furniture*.

Unlike many books on home planning, decorating, and furnishing, this one treats the traditional and the contemporary styles with equal completeness. It includes chapters on designing a house and landscaping the grounds.

I am indebted for ideas to the artists, decorators, and craftsmen with whom I have worked, to the students in my classes, to the authors of many books on art which I have examined, and to the art teachers with whom I have studied in the United States and Europe. My special gratitude is due to the following persons who have read all or part of the manuscript of this book: Arthur Carhart, Marion Clark, Florence Spiehler Cook, Claire Cronenwett, Ellen Le Noir, Norman E. Rutt, the late Thomas E. Tallmadge, Ruth R. Tregenza, the late Rudolph Weaver, and William G. Whitford.

I appreciate the courtesy of Professor Ernest Pickering who supplied the drawings for the chapter on House Design. I am grateful to the many individuals and organizations that lent photographs to illustrate this book.

ANNA HONG RUTT

CONTENTS

CONTENTS

PART ONE

ESTHETICS OF HOME PLANNING AND FURNISHING

CHAPTER 1

OBJECTIVES OF HOME PLANNING AND FURNISHING

BEAUTY

The common problem, yours, mine, everyone's,
Is not to fancy what were fair in life
Provided it could be, but, finding first
What may be, then find how to make it fair
Up to our means: a very different thing!

—ROBERT BROWNING

Life provides few more challenging problems than that of making the home "fair up to our means." The solution of this problem, fortunately, is not too difficult for the average person. Almost every woman has some natural ability to recognize beauty and suitability in houses and their furnishings. This latent talent can be developed by study, observation, and experience in creative problems. Most women are eager to devote time and effort to this study, which will enrich their own lives in addition to making them better home makers.

The appearance of the home should be worthy of its high purpose, to provide a place for the promotion of the spiritual, intellectual, and physical growth of the family, as well as to furnish a shelter for it. Beautiful home surroundings constitute the most important factor in the development of visual good taste, for through daily contact with beauty a lasting appreciation of it evolves. Those fortunate families that live in dwellings of taste, no matter how simple, should have a higher understanding than others of the meaning of home. Their children should in turn be inspired to create homes that have beauty.

1

Beauty is not the only *objective* in planning and furnishing a home, however. In addition a home should be expressive of the personality of the owners and, most important of all, should function effectively. The ultimate goal to be attained in a home is the successful integration of the three objectives, *beauty*, *expressiveness*, and *functionalism*.

The home maker or interior decorator is concerned with the *meaning* of the term beauty as applied to the home. In this book the word beauty is freely used to describe all well-designed and pleasing things, although some writers refer to beauty as a precious quality rarely obtainable. One simple definition of beauty is "that combination of qualities that is pleasing to the trained eye or ear." Philosophers do not agree on the meaning of beauty, however, and neither do artists, especially those of different times and different lands. According to an Oriental proverb, "One man's beauty is another man's ugliness."

The philosophy of beauty is known as *esthetics*. Some of its guiding premises, which apply to the appreciation of art in the home, are presented here. They help to clarify vague ideas about beauty. Furthermore, acquaintance with the standard terminology of esthetics is necessary in order to understand others or to speak or write effectively about esthetic experiences.

Estheticians have studied objects made by man and, by determining what qualities are common to all beautiful things, have established certain *principles* that help us to recognize and appreciate beauty. These principles of art or design, which are proportion, balance, emphasis, rhythm, and repetition, are presented in Chapter 4 of this book.

Another basic factor in esthetics is the *elements* or components of art: line, form, color, texture, pattern, light, and space. Chapter 2 of this book consists of a study of the elements of art, except color, which is the subject of Chapter 3.

Study of the art elements and the art principles develops ability to judge the appearance of all man-made objects. This knowledge enables a consumer to distinguish between beauty and mere fashion, a valuable asset when new things appear and ideas change. Selection of articles that are fine in design is important financially, too, for others may be discarded before the budget warrants.

EXPRESSIVENESS

One way to approach the subject of selecting, decorating, and furnishing a home is to seek to express some *definite idea or theme* in it. The most interesting homes, large or small, are those that are consistent throughout. For this reason, the expressiveness of houses and their furnishings deserves careful study.

Similar terms are more commonly used than expressiveness, such as the character of a home, or the personality of a home. The word expressiveness is preferable, however, because it implies the power to excite emotional response that is lacking in the word character, and it avoids the suggestion of human attributes which is contained in the word personality. Talbot F. Hamlin uses the word expressiveness in regard to exteriors and interiors of houses in his book *The Enjoyment of Architecture*. He says, "All good architecture should have this gift of expressiveness. Every building, every well-designed room, should carry in itself at least one message of cheer or rest or power. . . . In the buildings which seem alive with some message the architect has succeeded; they are true works of art."

The following are some of the ideas that are expressed in homes, consciously or unconsciously: repose, animation, naturalness, sophistication, intimacy, formality, warmth, coolness, delicacy, strength, freshness, antiquity. Honesty and sincerity are expressed in the avoidance of dishonest things like imitation fireplaces, false flues, imitation coal or logs, imitation wood, stone, or plaster, and imitation flame on imitation candles.

Unfortunately one often sees an effect that is the result of expressing an unworthy idea in home decoration and furnishing. Some owners seek to impress others with their wealth or importance, and so select highly ornamented palatial furniture, not realizing that this is mere ostentation. Very often families of small means make the mistake of trying to imitate the furnishings of people of wealth and succeed only in being pretentious.

Since it is not possible to consider in detail all the themes that may be expressed in homes, four of the typical ones, *formality, informality, naturalness,* and *Modernism,* are presented here as examples. They are illustrated on pages 9 and 10.

Formality. A home that expresses formality usually also expresses dignity, strength, reserve, and impressiveness. Features that contribute to this effect in a house are unbroken lines, large spaces, and a symmetrical façade, that is, a house front in which the two vertical halves are alike. In an interior, formality results from symmetry and also from conservative color. The furniture is usually, though not necessarily, traditional in style and arranged with formal balance. The family that creates a home of this type generally lives a conventional, dignified, ordered life made possible by efficient service. A house which expresses dignity is not a mere lifeless representation of that quality but an active assertion influencing the emotions and behavior of all who enter it. See page 10 for an interesting illustration.

Informality. An outstanding characteristic of American life of today is informality. Casual clothes are favored and casual manners prevail. Naturally informality is desired in home surroundings also. Informality, unpretentiousness, friendly hospitality, and intimate charm are expressed through various means. Bright, warm colors and simple, comfortable furniture have these characteristics. Houses express informality through modest size, asymmetrical balance, and broken lines. See page 190 for examples.

Naturalness (Primitiveness). One type of informality is that which stresses naturalness or primitiveness. A house of this character may express the following themes: simplicity, handmade quality, sincerity, thrift, naïveté, playfulness, rugged force, unpretentiousness, originality, or protest against artificiality. Among the factors that contribute to the attainment of the natural effect are the use of native materials and native styles, handwork showing natural irregularities in structure, direct treatment, inexpensive materials, and peasant or primitive colors. Labored effects, fine finish, and imitations are avoided.

Natural or primitive houses are not numerous, but they are to be found in every part of the United States. See pages 74 and 75. Many families in the Southwest have shown their appreciation of the native art of that section by creating homes inspired by rather primitive American Indian, Mexican, and Spanish forms. Many ranch or farm houses in various parts of the United States are appropriately rustic and have simple, suitable furniture.

The meaning of the word primitive as it is used in interior decorating today should be explained. In the words of a dictionary primitive may mean "simple or crude, old-fashioned, characterized by the style of early times." The word crude in this connection is not used in a derogatory sense. It means merely "in a natural state, unrefined, unpolished, unfinished; showing lack of skill in workmanship." The words primitive and crude are used in describing the quality of sincerity that is today prized in many forms of art, from primitive sculpture to peasant wall painting.

Persons with highly trained taste often prefer articles of primitive or peasant construction because such products usually have satisfying realness, whereas the products of more highly organized society are too often artificial. The contrast between the beauty in the primitive textiles in museums and the lack of it in many of the textiles for sale in the shops of today is surprising. The unsophisticated artist does not usually imitate nature in his work. His feeling for suitable design is partly due to the fact that he alone is responsible for the entire object on which he works. Therefore he plans, makes, and decorates each article to suit the material that he is using. But his good taste is as unstudied and innate as his joy in his work.

The average home maker is not usually interested in a primitive or natural effect in her own home except in a cabin or some other rustic house. Some artists and other creative persons, however, have found that the simplicity and realness of this type of furnishing are expressive of their own ideas. They believe that the creative spirit does not thrive in luxurious surroundings or among sophisticated reproductions of other periods.

Modernism. The Modern home expresses the spirit of this machine age. Le Corbusier's famous definition of a house as "a machine for living in" indicates the importance of functionalism in a Modern house. See page 119. Speed and directness are expressed by stripping off all non-essentials in design. For a complete discussion of the twentieth-century style see Chapter 8. The families that choose Modern furnishings are usually young, courageous, experimental, impersonal, and logical. They are interested in a style which is expressive of their own day.

Owner's Personality. The personality of the owner determines the idea to be expressed in a home. Qualities sincerely characteristic of the family that is to live with it should be the basis for the home furnishing. An interest which has permanent significance, and not a mere passing fad, should provide the inspiration for a plan of decorating and furnishing.

If a family likes to do things in a formal way with careful regard for the conventions, that attitude should affect its choice in architecture and in home furnishings. On the other hand, if a family has an informal, domestic, stay-at-home attitude, it should select a more picturesque, but simple, type of house and garden and furnishings. A modern artist might create a distinctive effect by making his own furniture at small cost, using a plain type of furnishing corresponding to his own simple way of living.

A carefree and casual family that spends summer out-of-doors and lives in a remodeled stable in the winter wants heavy, indestructible, and rough furniture. A traveled lady of sufficient means and with a love of elegance may have her apartment done in a sophisticated French fashion. An old-fashioned bride might like the quaintness and simplicity of the Early American style as illustrated on page 102.

A certain writer of American Indian songs uses rather crude, simple furniture with Indian rugs, baskets, and pottery. One celebrated flower-lover has a vine-covered house that is close to the ground so that she can step right out among the flowers. The indefinite or capricious type of person generally has a collection of things that expresses her confused state of mind.

The fact that a family may contain several conflicting personalities may often make it necessary to effect a compromise as to the idea expressed in a home. Common sense is a good guide in this as in all other applications of theories. A house designed to satisfy the needs of both the boys and the girls in a family should be neither too delicate for the one, nor too rugged for the other.

It is not difficult for any family to decide whether it is more formal or informal in its tastes. Usually it is also easy to determine whether a family leans more towards natural, subtle, or Modern effects. With these decisions made, the selection of a suitable house and appropriate furnishings is simplified.

FUNCTIONALISM

The homes of today should function as well as the machines of today. They should give the maximum of service, comfort, and pleasure for the minimum of care. Those who are building new houses should make no compromises which sacrifice functionalism; however, other houses cannot be expected to function perfectly. Traditional styles which functioned well enough in their own time may not do so today.

Every phase of home planning and furnishing should be based on function. The number of rooms and their arrangement depend upon what will best serve the family. Outdoor areas, too, are divided according to function, with places to lounge, eat, play, exercise, and garden. Furniture is arranged in functional groups for study, reading, conversation, writing, and music. See page 425. Information on the best functional location for furniture and equipment, particularly in the kitchen, is available. From the utilities, the modern woman can expect perfect functioning. For example, an electric outlet every five feet in every room is now a necessity. Even air conditioning should soon be improved so as to function for general use.

The selection of individual articles should be governed by a critical judgment of how well they fulfil their functions. Some common mistakes in selection are lamps that throw light in the readers' eyes, vases that tip easily, and pitchers with spouts that do not pour well. All these mistakes are due to incorrect form. The right shape for any article is the one that will function best, and usually it is the shape that also looks the best. Ever since Louis Sullivan stated it, designers have used the slogan: *Form follows function.* Materials too should follow function. Garden furniture should be waterproof; upholstery fabrics should be durable.

A living room so fine that men of the house do not feel free to lounge in it or a room so cluttered with bric-a-brac that one has to be on guard against upsetting things is not serving its purpose. The home that does not permit its occupants to find peace, comfort, and relaxation is not functioning well. Function must, of course, sometimes be modified for the sake of appearance, the integration of beauty and function being the ideal.

PROBLEMS

A sufficient number of problems are listed so that choices may be made.

1. Analyze articles such as samples of fabrics, vases, dishes, and furniture.
2. Bring to class pictures of rooms or home furnishings expressing definite ideas.
3. Bring to class pictures of stars who are definite personality types of the stage or screen.
4. Analyze the students in the class as to personality appearance.
5. Make a list of things you have noticed that do not function well, and state how they could be improved.
6. Bring to class five definitions of the word beauty which could apply to homes.

READING REFERENCES

DEWEY, JOHN. *Art as Experience.* Minton Balch, 1934.

FAULKNER, RAY, ZIEGFELD, EDWIN, and HILL, GERALD. *Art Today.* Henry Holt, 1941.

READ, HERBERT E. *Anatomy of Art.* Dodd, 1932.

SOOY, L., and WOODBRIDGE, V. *Plan Your Own Home.* Stanford University Press, 1940.

STEIN, LEO. *A.B.C. of Aesthetics.* Boni and Liveright, 1927.

TEAGUE, WALTER D. *Design This Day.* Harcourt, 1940.

Informality and naturalness are expressed in the author's weekend house through the use of walls of wood and the short curtains. The owner's personality is revealed in her painting. The furniture is functional; the bed is pushed back under the home-made, enclosed shelves so that it is the right width to sit on. This is a comfortable spot for resting and reading by daylight. *Courtesy Anne Plettinger, photographer.*

The unusual room below, which is in an adobe house in Arizona, expresses natural or primitive quality in its adobe walls, rough wood ceiling, tile floor, hand-made furniture, and hand-woven fabrics, including the Indian rug. The leather chair and the rugged character of the room suggest a masculine personality. *Courtesy William Y. Peters, architect.*

Modernism is expressed in the picture above. The large window, the partial partitions between the dining, living, and study areas, the built-in furniture, and the emphasis on texture are all Modern features. *Courtesy Armstrong Cork Company.*

Formality, elegance, and conservatism are expressed in the dining room of traditional style which is pictured below. The bisymmetrical wall and the symmetrical arrangement of the furniture are formal. The serving table does not interfere with the landscape paper. The straight-legged Chippendale chairs and the Duncan Phyfe table look well together. *Courtesy Smyth, Urquhart & Marckwald, Inc.*

CHAPTER 2

ELEMENTS OF ART

The elements of art structure which are basic in all the visual arts are *line, form, color,* and *texture.* Three additional elements, *pattern, light,* and *space,* also apply to home planning and home furnishing. Pattern is not so distinct an element as the others, but it is an important component and is an essential term in a practical vocabulary of interior decoration. Light and space are not usually included among the elements of art, because general appreciation of them is recent.

Each of the basic elements is a well-defined and dissimilar feature of every art object. Each can be manipulated by the designer, who may focus his attention on different elements in turn as his work progresses. However, the effect of each element is considered only in connection with the other elements and in relation to the organic unit which is being constructed, whether it is a picture or a room.

The art elements serve as tools in conveying fundamental ideas in painting and in sculpture, and also in creating objects which meet material needs of mankind: architecture, home furnishings, handicrafts, and industrial, commercial, and related arts.

Although the use of the art elements, even according to the principles of design, does not insure the attainment of beauty, it can be stated that one who understands the relationship of all these factors is likely to reach that objective.

Elements		Principles	Objectives
Line	Pattern	Proportion	Beauty
Form	Light	Balance	Expressiveness
Texture	Space	Emphasis	Functionalism
Color		Rhythm	
		Repetition	

LINE

Line is a very important element in home planning and furnishing. Sometimes it is so much a part of form that it is difficult to consider separately. Lines have positive emotional significance, depending upon their direction and their quality. Man has associated definite elementary ideas with certain lines because positions of his own body have suggested these ideas. When he lies down, he is resting or sleeping; therefore the *horizontal line* naturally suggests repose, steadiness, and duration. Since, when he is standing, he is at attention and ready to act, *vertical lines* suggest life and activity. Because he bends forward to run or to pull things, a *diagonal line* suggests decided movement and force. In relaxation and play the body takes positions that are curved, so *curved lines* seem gracious and flexible.

In interior decoration *straight lines* are considered intellectual rather than emotional, classic rather than romantic, and sometimes severe and masculine. *Curves* are used to achieve a more joyful, subtle, and rich effect, but they must be carefully designed and well used or they tend to produce an appearance of weakness and instability. Diagonal lines are too active to be used much in the home, for they express decided restlessness.

FORM

The term form is generally considered to apply to two-dimensional areas or shapes as well as to three-dimensional volumes or masses. Form is the most important element in home planning. Without beauty of form, excellent color, texture, and decoration are of no avail. Even utilitarian articles may be so beautiful in form that they are able to inspire man much as the fine arts do.

Two essentials of good form should be mentioned here, although they are explained elsewhere in this book. These are that the form of an object should suit its *function*, and that the form of an object should be strongly influenced by the *material* from which it is made.

Harmony of form is essential in assembling home furnishings. A *dominance* of one kind of form or shape unifies the total effect. Even accessories are not too unimportant to conform to the shape that is emphasized.

TEXTURE

The word texture now generally refers to the tactile quality of the surface of any object, although originally it applied only to textiles. It refers also to the way small constituent parts are combined in a substance; for example, poor fudge may have a grainy texture and granite a granular texture. The pliability or rigidity of objects also has textural significance as it affects the quality of the surface. Sometimes the term texture is applied to effects which give an illusion of texture, such as streaked, or marbleized. In ordinary usage, however, texture refers to the qualities that are perceptible through the sense of touch. Although as children we first realize textural differences by feeling them, later we are able to perceive the tactile quality of an object without having to touch it. The following list enumerates some textures of interest to home planners and decorators.

airy	dull	jagged	prickly	sleek
bearded	dusty	lacy	quilted	smocked
blistered	faceted	leathery	raspy	smooth
bristly	feathery	level	reeded	solid
bubbly	filmy	lumpy	reticulated	splintery
bumpy	fine	marbled	ribbed	spongy
burnished	firm	meshy	ridged	striated
choppy	flexible	metallic	rigid	stiff
coarse	foamy	mossy	rippled	stratified
corky	frilly	nettled	rocky	thorny
corrugated	furrowed	nubby	rolling	tough
crackled	furry	peaked	rough	twisted
crepy	fuzzy	pebbly	rubbery	undulating
crinkly	glabrous	perforated	rutty	uneven
crisp	glassy	pierced	sandy	unpolished
crumpled	glossy	plaited	satiny	unyielding
crystalline	granular	pleated	scaly	velvety
curly	gritty	pitted	scratchy	warty
delicate	grooved	polished	shaggy	wavy
dense	hairy	porcate	shiny	waxy
dewy	harsh	porous	shirred	woody
downy	hob-nailed	powdery	silky	woolly

THE USE OF TEXTURE

Texture is an element of art that is valuable in giving character and beauty to objects, interiors, buildings, and landscape gardening. In some fields texture has been more or less ignored, but a great wave of interest in texture has now made it a prominent factor in all the visual arts.

Painters of the nineteenth century produced pictures which were as smooth as possible, expressing the refinement of the time. In the present century artists like Van Gogh used oil paint thickly, vigorously, and roughly. Some artists even apply it with a palette knife instead of a brush. Some use a variety of textures in one picture, and others, like Matisse and Marin, use spots and lines to suggest texture.

Sculptors are particularly concerned with texture, for the surface of sculpture is of vital importance in expressing an artist's meaning. The difference in texture between the sculpture that is modeled from wet clay and that which is chipped from stone or carved from wood is an important factor in the enjoyment of sculpture. Planned variety of treatment adds vitality and interest to surfaces. Sculpture should be felt as well as seen to be fully appreciated.

Architects make good use of the textural qualities of building materials. The physical composition of various substances produces tactile impressions which help to establish definite character. Similar textures are combined, such as rough bricks with rough timber, and sleek steel with sleek glass; many other characterful combinations are possible.

The roughness or smoothness of a material makes it absorb or reflect light; therefore its visual characteristics as well as its texture must be considered, both in exterior and interior architecture. Modern architectural schools stress the study of the textural aspects of materials. Research and experiment in this field indicate further development and employment of texture.

Landscape architects, too, employ texture as a valuable tool. Repetition of dominant plant textures unifies a plan, whereas contrast of texture at corners and focal points gives emphasis. The textures of the buildings, walks, trees, shrubs, and flowers that are combined should produce a unified total.

Interior decorators, both professional and amateur, are becoming more aware of the importance of texture. There is still great need for improvements in this respect, however, for many women know little about texture. A woman who would be shocked to see a wash dress, a fur coat, satin slippers, and a straw hat worn together might not even be aware that the rough bricks in her fireplace, her fine-textured rug, her ruffled Swiss curtains, and her iron lamp stands are equally inconsistent.

Even in a single article texture problems are present if more than one material is used, for only agreeable textures should be combined. For example, a metal chair looks well upholstered with a lacquered fabric, for both materials are sleek and waterproof.

Refinement in appreciation of texture suggests that a relation exists between color and texture. Coarse textures and dainty colors are not consistent, whereas fine textures and pastel tints are harmonious.

One of the first decisions to be made in furnishing a room or a house is the selection of the furniture wood or woods, for all other textures employed must be in harmony with the wood. Each kind of wood seems to produce a definite feeling in the observer. Pine, oak, and hickory suggest strength; mahogany and rosewood suggest elegance. Obviously, oak and mahogany furniture cannot be combined; walnut, however, is medium in texture and can be used either with mahogany or with a light type of oak. Mahogany requires delicate textures like fine silk, satin, velvet, roses, deep-pile rugs, and light-weight brass hardware to accompany it, whereas, with oak, coarser textures such as tapestry, rep, large-patterned linen, iron, and parchment should be used. In the study of texture it is helpful to analyze the significance of materials that have been combined in each of the great decorative movements.

Modern use of texture is creative. Rooms are now composed in which areas of various textures on walls, floors, and furnishings are organized to produce rich, subtle effects. The texture of any single article is not considered separately but as a contribution to the total effect of the room. When the full possibilities of this element are utilized, plastics, glass, metal, wood, cork, leather, and fabrics will be composed into a symphony of texture.

PATTERN

The term pattern here refers to any sort of extrinsic surface enrichment and applies to both two-dimensional and three-dimensional objects. In interior decoration it is well to use the word pattern rather than decorative design or ornamentation, because decorators, sales people. and the public understand the meaning of the adjectives patterned or figured as opposed to plain.

Surface pattern contributes liveliness and interest to a room. Many a dreary room owes its dullness to its lack of pattern, whereas a room that is restless and exciting usually has too much pattern. See page 24. Opinions differ on how much pattern is desirable in a room, but it is customary to use pattern on at least one-fourth of the total surface areas. If the walls and carpet are plain then the draperies and two-thirds of the upholstery fabrics may well be patterned. A large room can support more pattern than a small one. If a room is occupied but briefly it is permissible to use more pattern than otherwise.

The cost of an article is no indication of the quality of the decorative pattern used on it. The finest designers are employed chiefly for expensive goods; however, their designs are often adapted or imitated in inexpensive materials. It is desirable and often possible to buy patterned fabrics and other furnishings which have been designed and signed by famous designers. Manufacturers often underestimate the taste of consumers and make articles decorated with vulgar elaborate designs, which people buy because nothing else is available. This is particularly true of silverware, dishes, wall paper, drapery, and carpets.

Since so many patterns are poor, consumers should learn to discriminate. An elementary course in design, books and periodicals on design, and museum exhibitions all help the layman to judge patterns.

Beauty in surface pattern is produced by:

1. Excellent design in individual motifs or units.
2. Fine arrangement of the units in a repeat pattern.
3. Definite character or personality.
4. Honesty in technique.
5. Evidence of joy of the designer.
6. Harmony of line between an article and its decoration.

Units of Design. There are three general types of motifs or units of design: naturalistic, stylized, and geometric. See page 23 for examples.

Naturalistic motifs look like pictures, usually of flowers, fruit, animals, or scenes. Such motifs or pictures are seldom suitable for the decoration of utilitarian articles; for example, dishes decorated with pastoral scenes or realistic fishes are dubious backgrounds for food. Excellent naturalistic designs are to be found, however, but they are difficult for the amateur to recognize. Some of the best natural floral patterns are those in which the flowers are grouped in very definite stripes, blocks, or bouquets, sometimes confined in frame effects. Naturalistic designs are appropriate in some period rooms, some cottage rooms, and in some children's rooms, particularly in the draperies, upholstery, and wall paper. The present interest in naturalistic patterns is due mostly to a temporary Victorian revival but is also a reaction against pure functionalism and military severity.

Stylized motifs do not look like pictures of natural objects; usually the lines are simplified and conventionalized, sometimes they are distorted. The designer uses whatever degree of stylization the problem at hand requires, depending upon the material employed and the purpose of the article. Stylization alone does not insure high quality in design; however, in general, stylized designs are likely to be superior to the naturalistic. Color can be conventionalized as well as form; indeed an unnatural form suggests unnatural color. The most fashionable stylized motifs at present are ferns and other leaves. Patterns are sometimes made of a combination of stylized and geometric motifs.

Geometric motifs are based on the pure forms of the circle, rectangle, and triangle, although endless variations and combinations of them are used. Geometric motifs include stripes, dots, checks, and plaids, as well as many less usual forms. They are the safest designs procurable for untrained consumers. Modern designers prefer geometric motifs in the small amount of pattern that they use. The Greeks also realized the value of geometric form and developed it to a high degree. The Mohammedans, for religious as well as esthetic reasons, for a long time used no natural forms in their designs.

Arrangment of the Motifs. Beauty in pattern depends not only on having well-designed motifs but also on arranging them well. The units may be grouped in borders, stripes, checks, diamonds, ogives, or other regular or irregular plans. Arrangement is so important that the same unit may appear insignificant when used sparsely but distinctive when used in a compact scheme.

Definite Character. The most interesting patterns are those that have definite expressive quality. A design may have a feeling of dignity, quaintness, speed, restlessness, or whatever quality the able designer wishes it to have. The character of a pattern is determined by the direction of the lines and by the sizes, the shapes, and relation of spaces.

Honesty in Technique. Proper regard for the medium insures honesty in technique. For example, patterns for textiles should look clothlike. The process by which the pattern is applied to an article should also influence its design. A pattern to be carved in wood is necessarily bolder than one to be painted on silk.

Joy of the Maker or Designer. This quality is seen most commonly in the work of children, peasants, and primitive people. Their work often has naive charm, playfulness, directness, and apparent ease of execution. It is the opposite of work that appears to have been labored, overdone, and intellectually perfect, but dull, static, or lifeless. Gay peasant costumes are often expressive of the joy of the exuberant maker. Many designers of today produce results that speak of work done with joy. See page 59.

Harmony of Line. The lines of the pattern should usually follow the lines of the article that it decorates, for example, a circle fits better than a square on a round plate.

Pattern Agreement. In different articles used in the same room, the types of patterns should agree, whereas the sizes of patterns should vary. Highly stylized patterns are usually friendly with geometric patterns but not with naturalistic patterns. Large-patterned draperies should not have rivals of the same size in a room, patterns of medium size constitute foils and are better neighbors. See page 89. Inconspicuous stripes, texture patterns, and tweed-like mixtures are desirable accompanists for important patterns.

PATTERN SUMMARY

1. The decoration should be necessary for the beauty and expressiveness of the article; if it is not, it should be omitted.
2. The decoration should usually follow the same shape as the contour of the part upon which it is placed.
3. The motif should be in scale with the object decorated.
4. The parts of a design should agree in shape and scale.
5. The decoration should be placed at natural structural points on the object decorated.
6. The decoration should never interfere with function.
7. A design should suit the process used in its production. For example, fine detail should be avoided in a linoleum-block print.
8. The design should fit the material it decorates and should express the same idea. For example, fine detailed design is not proper on monks' cloth.
9. The design should be of the right historic period if the article is period in feeling.
10. A design should have definite character such as quaintness.
11. Decoration should be simple, not elaborate.
12. A design should appear to be a joyous expression of the creator, and not a labored, forced piece of work.
13. Casual, freehand effects usually result from skill of the artist, not from lack of skill.
14. The background spaces as well as the foreground motifs should make a fine pattern.
15. It adds interest to a design if background and foreground spaces interpenetrate so that the effect is reversible, with the background as definite in shape as the foreground.
16. The best designs are usually abstract or stylized.
17. Realistic, pictorial motifs are often poor.
18. The coloring should suit the design: for example, bold colors are best for bold patterns.
19. Out-of-the-ordinary designs are most desirable.
20. Consumers should became familiar with the work of the outstanding contemporary designers.

LIGHT

Light in an art element as well as a utilitarian element. It has a definite emotional effect. Light is stimulating; darkness is depressing. A sunshiny day makes us sparkle, and a dark day makes us dull. Those who are so unfortunate as to occupy only north rooms in the winter time realize the gloom that results from lack of sunshine. On the other hand, light that is too brilliant exhausts us physically and is as offensive esthetically as loud noise. In our homes we should have available, but under control, all the light that we can use.

The shadow element too is an important decorative factor both indoors and out. Architects use shadows for emphasis, in the front door, in overhanging eaves, under porch roofs, under siding boards, and on uneven surfaces such as stone or brick. In interiors, shadows assist decoratively, serving as a foil for light.

Daylight is such an important factor in the appearance of a room that no plan of decoration should be made without considering the exposure, the number of windows, the amount of sunshine that enters the room, the trees or vines that shut out light, and what season of the year the room is used most. As much daylight as is desired can now be procured by means of glass walls or large windows extending from floor to ceiling. Movable curtains should be provided, however, so that the quantity of light can easily be controlled to fit the needs of the occupants of a room.

Modern artificial light, particularly electric light, is not only a remarkable functional utility but also a marvelous flexible art medium. It should be used in a room as an artist uses light in a picture. Artificial light may produce unity by its diffusion through the entire room. It may show contrast and emphasis by bringing bright light to important areas while subordinate areas remain in the shadows. It can bring rhythm and continuity to a room's furnishings by linking together various points of emphasis. The subject of artificial lighting is thoroughly covered in Chapter 18.

American designers, particularly the Modern ones, have learned to employ artificial light with excellent results. Designers of lighting for homes became aware of the great potentialities of artificial light through its use in the modern theater.

SPACE

The importance of space as an element of art structure has been fully recognized recently; however, organization of space is basic in Modern architecture and interior decoration.

A sense of the beauty of space makes us want large undecorated walls and floors which bound space without disturbing its effect. Appreciation of space is the cause of our using a small amount of furniture and concentrating it in groups, so that we can have some empty silent spaces in our rooms.

The present trend is for space to become freer and less obstructed throughout a house. Indoor space seems increased by means of fewer partitions and larger openings between rooms. Indoor space seems also to connect with limitless outdoor space by means of glass walls, large openings, and porches. Interpenetration of outdoor and indoor space results from the use of wide overhanging eaves and extending free-standing walls which protect outdoor living areas.

The landscape designer, as well as the architect, utilizes this element of space. He may focus his garden on a bird bath or on a distant mountain peak, or he may project it into infinity. He organizes the space in the garden so that the result is livable, functional, and completely integrated with the house.

As our understanding of spatial organization increases we may expect to have better functioning and more beauty in our homes.

COLOR

Color is so important an art element that it is considered separately in the following chapter.

PROBLEMS

A sufficient number of problems are listed so that choices may be made.

1. Analyze the architectural lines of your classroom. (Related lines? Strong horizontals?)
2. Analyze the form of the furniture in your classroom.
3. Bring to class materials illustrating various textures (sandy, corrugated, crepy, etc.).
4. Classify fabric patterns (naturalistic, stylized, or geometric).
5. Select from fabric samples a desirable combination of harmonious patterns consisting of one dominant, one subordinate, and one innocuous pattern.
6. Make pleasing line arrangements of the notices on the bulletin board.
7. Make an abstract poster or wall plaque by using various textures such as sandpaper, tin foil, net, cord, thumb tacks, sand burs, and seeds.

READING REFERENCES

BOSSERT, HELMUTH T. *Ornament in Applied Art.* E. Weyhe, 1924.

DOW, ARTHUR W. *Composition.* Doubleday, 1928.

FRANKL, PAUL T. *Space for Living.* Doubleday, 1938.

GIEDION, S. *Space, Time, and Architecture.* Harvard University Press, 1941.

GROPIUS, WALTER A. *The New Architecture and the Bauhaus.* Museum of Modern Art, 1937.

LUCKIESH, MATTHEW. *Light and Shade.* Van Nostrand, 1916.

MOHOLY-NAGY, L. *The New Vision.* Norton, 1938.

The *naturalistic* pattern at the left has a suggestion of a vertical stripe arrangement. The plant material is unrestrained and recognizable. The central pattern is *stylized*, not representing any particular plant material. It is well adapted for printing. The pattern at the right is *geometric*. Here the pattern is produced by the process of weaving.
Courtesy Cincinnati Art Museum.

Beauty of line and form are qualities of the objects below. The use of decorative pattern is restrained. Rhythm is emphasized in the pleasing decoration of the bowl at the left. The pattern is created by depressed lines which are in shadow. The spoon is distinctive in design; the lines of the decoration follow the shape of the handle. The cookie jar is well decorated at structural points; the small stylized floral motif has curved lines suitable for a curved surface.

*Courtesy
Laura Andreson,
ceramist, U.C.L.A.*

*Courtesy
Lunt, Silversmiths*

*Courtesy Kenneth E. Smith,
potter, Newcomb College*

The amount, distribution, and quality of pattern in the room above are desirable. A bold drapery pattern necessitates unobtrusive upholstery and a plain carpet. Note pedestal for flower arrangement. The pictures are well framed and hung. *Courtesy Carson, Pirie, Scott.*

Confusion results where there is too much pattern. In the room below if the rug, wall paper, and draperies were entirely plain there would still be too much floral pattern. The plain lamps are a welcome note in this orgy of decorative pattern.

Interesting textures are featured in the room above. The bamboo furniture and linen rug are suitable for a sun room or even a living room in a semi-tropical climate. Close contact with the outdoors is felt here because the French doors and windows open on a garden. *Courtesy Louisiana State University.*

Consistent textures are combined in the room below. The dark green corduroy bedspreads suit the heavy furniture of ridged pine, the walls of wood, the pole ceiling, and the stone chimney. The total effect is suitable for a bachelor's house or a rustic house.

Space is the element emphasized in the room above. A movable window wall permits the spaciousness of the outdoors to become a part of this room. The uncluttered effect and the restraint in decoration help to produce quiet beauty. The architectural lighting is notable. The functional table is in proper scale. *Courtesy R. J. Neutra.*

Light is an important element in the Modern room pictured below. The reflected window wall provides daylight; the table lamps are for direct light; the floor lamps are for direct or indirect light, and the ceiling fixture for indirect light. The two phosphorescent murals glow when the other lights are turned out.

CHAPTER 3

COLOR

Appreciation of color, largely an emotional process, is felt by nearly everyone, whereas appreciation of line and form, a more intellectual process, is not common. Since color is a source of such universal pleasure, all families should have beautiful colors in their homes to delight them and fortify them against dullness elsewhere. Since the home maker should have some knowledge of color theory in order to employ color successfully a brief discussion of it is given here.

The Source of Color. *Light* is the source of color. Color is the impression received by the mind from certain stimulations of the retina. Color perception occurs because objects reflect or transmit light, which enters the eye, acts upon the optic nerve, and causes the sensation of light and color in the brain. Light rays or waves which vary in length and rate of vibration produce different sensations and appear as different colors. There is an optical instrument known as the spectroscope which breaks up or decomposes light and reveals the fundamental colors as arranged in the spectrum. At one end of the spectrum is violet, which has the shortest visible waves; at the other end is red, which has the longest visible rays. The other colors are produced by the intermediate waves. A glass prism or a diamond can also be used to throw sunlight on a white surface so that the complex beam of light is broken up much as in the rainbow.

Objects are usually able to reflect part of a light beam and absorb other parts. For example, if an object appears green it is absorbing all the other colors that make up white light and is reflecting only green. An object that appears white is reflecting all the colors that make up light. A black object is absorbing all the colors that make up light and reflecting none.

27

COLOR THEORIES

It is not within the scope of this book to present more than a few words about the theories of color used in the fields of physics, psychology, chemistry, and art.   Workers in each of these fields employ different color theories because they are concerned with different aspects of the study of color.

The figure below illustrates three different color theories, the pigment theory, the physicist's theory, and the psychologist's theory, and also the Munsell system of color notation.   Geometric figures other than the usual color circles have been used in order to emphasize the basic or primary colors, which are placed at the vertices (angles) of all the figures.   The secondary colors are shown in smaller type between the vertices.   The short lines inside the figures point out each pair of complementary colors, which are exactly opposite to each other on the figures.

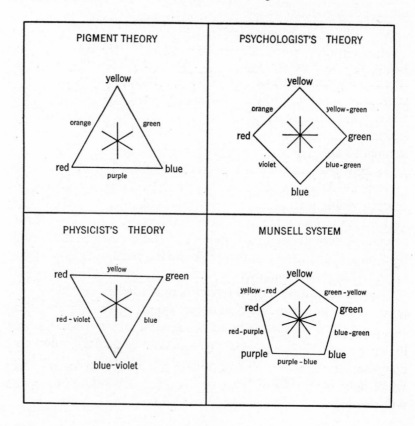

The Pigment Color Theory. (The Brewsterian theory.) A figure on page 39 and the color chart facing page 40 illustrate the pigment color theory. Red, yellow, and blue are the fundamental or primary colors, which can be mixed so as to form all the other colors but which cannot themselves be made by mixing any other colors. The secondary colors, orange, green, and purple, are made by mixing two primary colors; orange is a mixture of red and yellow, green is a mixture of yellow and blue, purple is a mixture of red and blue. A tertiary or intermediate color is made by mixing a primary color with its adjoining secondary color. The six colors, yellow, green, blue, purple, red, and orange, are called the standard colors.

The color chart facing page 40 shows six pairs of complementary colors, which are opposite to each other on the circle. When any pair of complements are combined equally, they neutralize each other and produce gray. In mixing paint one of the best methods of subduing a bright color is to add to it some of its complementary color. The pigment theory is the simplest basis for mixing paints.

The Psychologist's Theory of Color. The psychologist's theory is based on the visual perception of color. The four primary or fundamental colors are: red, green, yellow, and blue. The secondary colors are orange, yellow-green, blue-green, and violet. The complementary colors are opposite each other on the diagram. When a pair of these complements is twirled on a top, the top appears to be pure gray. A simple way to determine what color is complementary to another color, according to this theory, is to look for half a minute at a colored disk against a white background. When the disk is removed, a round spot of the color that is complementary to the one removed will appear as an after-image. The findings of psychologists have enabled them to develop color therapy to an important extent.

The Physicist's Theory of Color. In the physicist's scientific theory the primary colors in light are red (scarlet), green (emerald), and violet (blue-violet). The secondary colors, yellow (slightly orange), blue (cyan), and red-violet (magenta) are produced by combining two of the primary colors in light. The complementary colors will neutralize each other and look like white light if thrown on a screen together. The three primaries will also produce white light if combined.

The Munsell Color System. The Munsell color system is a system of color notation by means of which any color can be described in terms of its three dimensions: hue, value, and chroma. For example, R 4/10 is a symbol for a red that has a 4 value and 10 chroma (intensity, chromatic departure from gray), which happens to be the standard red. This system permits the entire visual color field to be mapped out in equal steps so that the visual difference between any two adjacent steps is always the same. Since the color solid assumes the shape of the sphere with white at the top, black at the bottom, and the various hues distributed around the sphere, it is usually demonstrated by a globe rotating around the center axis. The book *A Color Notation* fully describes the Munsell system.

In the Munsell system five equally spaced major hues—yellow, green, blue, purple, and red—and five minor hues spaced halfway between the five major hues form the basis of the Munsell decimal system dividing the hue circle. The complementary colors are yellow and purple-blue, green and red-purple, blue and yellow-red, purple and green-yellow, and red and blue-green.

Colored Light as Decoration. The modern decorator should understand the theory of colored light as well as the theory of colored pigment, for light is a flexible decorative medium with enormous potentialities. The modern theater has revealed the possibilities of colored light in obtaining desired effects. Changes of color schemes in homes may in time be made by the use of light rather than pigments. Pictures produced by colored light may replace painted pictures in later twentieth-century homes.

Mobile Colored Light. The time may come when color organs such as Thomas Wilfred's Clavilux will be available for homes. The person who plays the color organ can change at will the forms, sizes, and colors of the images which are thrown on a screen, so that an orderly, related succession of abstract figures can be produced, having themes, variations of the themes, and climaxes like musical compositions. Like music mobile color is most satisfactory when it is confined to abstractions. The colors employed in a composition may be of great intensity because they are of such brief duration. The field of mobile color may possibly be developed through television.

QUALITIES OF COLOR

Color has three qualities, hue, value, and intensity (or chroma), that can be measured with considerable exactness. These three are as distinct from one another as the timbre, the position in the octave, and the volume of a musical note.

Hue. The term hue needs little explanation beyond the statement that it indicates the name of a color and is practically synonymous with the word color itself. The color names used most are those of the spectrum colors. In addition to these some colors of dyes and paints are named for the materials out of which they are made, such as yellow ocher, terre-verte, madder, cobalt, indigo, cochineal red, chrome, and gamboge. Popular color names that are in no sense scientific, such as the names of fruits or gems, are nevertheless useful in describing colors.

Value. Value refers to the amount of light or dark in colors, regardless of hue. The lightest value is white and the darkest is black, but there are as many degrees between them as you choose to consider. In painting a value scale of a color, the normal or spectrum color may be placed at the center of an upright scale. White is added to make the *tints* which are lighter than the normal value, and black is added to make the *shades* which are below normal value. Water is mixed with water color paints to make tints. Of the spectrum colors, normal yellow has the lightest and normal purple the darkest value. Color values can be compared best by squinting at them, as nearly closing the eyes helps to shut out color and emphasize value. Tints are sometimes called high values and shades are called low values.

Intensity (or Chroma). Intensity refers to the brightness or dullness of colors. Most colors used in home decoration are somewhat neutralized or dulled. In painting color schemes there are several methods of neutralizing an intense color. The best way is to add its complementary color to it; however, black may be added, or any opposite color or colors. Complementary colors completely neutralize each other when properly mixed. Colors are sometimes described as one-fourth, one-half, or three-fourths neutralized. The popular term for light colors that have been reduced in intensity is soft colors.

Colors may differ from one another also in apparent warmth, distance, weight, and acidity. These qualities in general have no firmer basis than our feelings about them.

Warmth or Coolness. One of the most important qualities of color to be considered in interior decoration is its warmth or coolness. Colors that contain much yellow or red are considered to be warm; those that contain a preponderance of blue are regarded as cool. Green and purple are each made up of both a warm and a cool color. A yellowish green is likely to be warm; a blue-green is cool. A red-purple may be warm and a blue-purple cool.

We probably attribute warmth or coolness to colors because of their associations with objects that have warmth or coolness. Yellow and red seem warm to us because they are the colors of sunshine, artificial light, and fire. Blue and green suggest coolness because we associate them with skies, water, ice, and foliage.

In any color scheme either the warm or the cool colors should *dominate*, equal amounts of each being unpleasant. All the warm colors are harmonious with one another because they belong to the yellow-red family, and the cool colors are friendly with one another because they are all related to the blues.

Some decorators believe that the exposure of a room should influence its color scheme; for example, a north room should employ yellow to produce a feeling of sunshine. Other factors such as seasonal use and climate also affect the selection of color schemes.

Heaviness or Lightness. Studies are being made by psychologists concerning the apparent weight or lightness of colors. Colorists agree generally that blue and purple are the lightest in weight of all colors. Green seems a little less heavy than red and yellow, which are the heaviest. When the colors are grayed they tend to become alike in weight. In home decoration it should be realized that heavy colors seem to belong to the lower part of a room, to the base. Reds, greens, and browns therefore tend to be desirable colors for carpeting. Heavy colors are good for a man's room or a library; lighter-weight colors are usually better in children's and women's rooms, depending, of course, on personal taste and coloring. Heavy colors are usually appropriate for heavy furniture, whereas light weight colors have a soaring quality that makes them more suitable for furniture of smaller scale.

Advancing or Receding Colors. Advancing and receding qualities in colors are a reality, as psychologists have proved. The warm hues seem to advance and the cool ones to recede. The most strongly advancing color is yellow, then orange, red, green, violet, and last blue. Artists who paint in a logical way make use of this knowledge by keeping the yellow and red objects in the foreground of their pictures and blue things in the distance.

In interior decoration, advancing warm color makes a room seem smaller, whereas cool, pale color makes the walls appear to recede and apparently enlarges the room. This idea also applies to dress, for cool colors make a woman appear smaller and warm colors larger. Intense colors advance more than grayed ones.

A simple experiment proves that certain colors appear relatively to advance or recede. Select two squares of cardboard large enough to be seen clearly at a considerable distance. On one card paint a frame of blue around the edge, and a small square of yellow in the center. Then paint the space between the yellow center and the blue frame with other bands in this order from the center: orange, red, green, and violet. On the other card paint the colors in reverse order, making the outer frame yellow and the central square blue. When viewed from a distance the first card will appear to have a center which protrudes; the second will appear to have a hollow center. Colored paper may be used for this experiment instead of painted paper.

Earth or Acid Colors. In the spectrum a rather arbitrary division might be made between earth and acid colors, but it probably would be somewhat a matter of personal opinion. Earthy colors are those made from earth, such as umbers, siennas, and ochers, and also most of the reds, yellows, and sap greens. Vegetable dyes have the earth character. The so-called acid colors made by chemical means, usually from aniline, are magenta, blue-green, carmine, cyan blue, and certain violets. Inherent in them is the idea of artificiality or sophistication in contrast with the primitive appeal of the earth colors. These qualities should be considered by the decorator in her use of colors. She can find many fine earthy color schemes in museums, as, for example, the ivory, brown, dark blue, Indian red, yellow, and green which were combined by the ancient Egyptians.

THE EMOTIONAL EFFECT OF COLOR

Our emotional reactions to certain colors are partly due to the symbolic meanings that have become associated with them. In the early Christian churches colors were used to convey definite ideas to the people who were unable to read. White was employed for innocence, black for evil or death, gray for penitence, red for love or martyrdom, blue for sincerity or hope, and the other colors for equally definite ideas. The color symbolism instituted by the church has been carried on by the theater up to the present time.

Color, because of its emotional effect upon us, is largely responsible for the atmosphere of a home. It is capable of soothing or irritating, cheering or depressing, charming or boring, welcoming or repelling. A color changes in emotional value if its hue, value, or intensity is changed. To illustrate: pure blue will have a different effect from greenish blue, which is unlike it in hue, or from baby blue, which is different from it in value, or from grayish blue, which does not agree with it in intensity. An important thing for a decorator to know is how to use color for its emotional effect. Different colors excite different emotional responses, and, too, some persons are more sensitive and more stimulated than others.

Yellow, which is the color of the sun and artificial light, has an effect of cheerfulness, gaiety, buoyancy, optimism, exultation, sympathy, and even prosperity. It almost sings and shouts. For centuries it was considered a sacred color in China.

In home decoration yellow is indispensable, because more than any other color it gives the effect of light. It supplies sunshine, even on a gray day. The modified yellows, such as buff, cream, ivory, beige, ecru, pale lime yellow, and pale banana yellow, are useful wall colors because they have the happy faculty of pulling together and harmonizing colors used in draperies, carpets, and upholstery. Yellow is a friend to the person with a limited income because it has the power of making inexpensive cottons, linens, and woolens look beautiful. Accessories of yellow are usually needed in north rooms. Gold, which is a type of yellow, is also useful; for example, a gold screen would add cheer to a dull room of the more elegant type. Yellow is also being used effectively for exterior house trimming, especially for shutters.

Orange is the most vivid hue that exists. It possesses the qualities of both red and yellow, and in its pure state it is so warm that it should be used only in small quantities. It expresses energy, spirit, hope, courage, and cordiality. Neutralized forms of orange such as peach, rust, cedar, and copper which are often used in home decoration radiate hospitality and cheer. They should be featured in autumn decorations.

Brown, that most useful of colors, is being recognized again after a period of unpopularity. The brown or mission period was a reaction against the ugly reds and greens of the Victorian era, but the reformists carried their crusade so far that walls, woodwork, carpets, upholstery, and draperies became brown, and so naturally the color fell into disfavor. Brown walls are now effectively used with natural wood furniture and light beige rugs, or with one striking color such as turquoise or cherry red. Chocolate, burnt cinnamon, or other red-browns are more usable than yellow-browns. Brown is traditionally associated with ideas of humility, tranquility, and gentleness.

Red is the color of fire and blood. It is expressive of primitive passion, war, vigor, power, movement, aggression, boldness, and force. Red is one of the most beloved of colors. An explanation for this may be that red is the color of fire, and, since for untold years the fire at the mouth of the cave of primitive man was his protection and comfort, his descendants may have inherited some of his feeling of pleasure in its color.

In decoration, red gives the impression of splendor, warmth, hospitality, and exhilaration. It is cheerful, but not restful, and so must be used discreetly. Cool reds like American Beauty roses (magenta) harmonize with blues and purples. Warm reds like tomatoes or firecrackers harmonize with yellow, salmon, orange, and chartreuse. Reds are usually grayed, but cherry red and Chinese red are used without modification. Certain rich reds are used freely in Italian and Spanish rooms. Dark, dull, raspberry red has proved to be a successful color for carpets. Pink, one of woman's favorite colors, should usually be grayed if used in large quantities. Shrimp pink, which has warmth and character, is delightful in chair coverings and other small areas. If pink and blue are used together the pink should be slightly orchid and the blue should have a violet cast.

Purple is made of red and blue, which possess quite opposite characteristics and when mixed cancel each other's effect, so that purple is somewhat gentle and vague. It suggests mystery, dignity, reflection, mourning, philosophical musing, and twilight. Originally, the pigment came from certain shellfish and was so rare that only royalty used the color—hence the term royal purple. Some artists avoid purple and the common diluted purple known as lavender.

Blue is the color of clear skies and deep water, and so is associated with coolness. It expresses distance, spaciousness, loftiness, dignity, calmness, serenity, reserve, formality, restraint, lack of sympathy, and coldness. In decoration it acts as a check or an antidote for too much warmth. Blues are not so friendly with one another as other colors are and therefore have to be selected with additional care under both daylight and artificial light.

Blue is a very important decorative color as it is usable in large areas. Since blue is not an aggressive color it does not have to be neutralized as much as some of the others. Modified or Prussian blue walls are now used with light Modern furnishings, especially in bedrooms and dining rooms. Pale slate blue or pale grayed turquoise blue are refreshing wall colors which seem to add spaciousness to small rooms. Medium blue and white combine well in a two-tone scheme.

Green is the color of grass, leaves, and vegetables and naturally suggests rest, cool shade, and refreshment, all pleasant things. Green is considered beneficial to the eyes, nerves, and disposition. Some colorists say that green has negative qualities as well as positive ones and that it suggests envy, jealousy, and ill health. It is composed of yellow and blue and appears warm if yellow predominates or cool if blue is preponderant.

The restored colonial homes of Williamsburg, Virginia, have demonstrated the beauty of green walls. Vigorous greens combine well with knotty pine and other natural woods. The most usable greens are those that have been reduced in intensity and made subtle. Greens must be used with caution, however, for green ceilings and walls may reflect an unbecoming color on the persons in the room. Greens that are employed on the exteriors of houses or on garden furniture or fences should be warm in quality so that they will harmonize with the color of the foliage.

The neutral colors are black, white, and gray. The term neutral, however, usually refers not only to these but also to all the tans, beiges, sand colors, natural wood color, and brown, which have no very definite color of their own. Such colors are most valuable in home furnishing, for large background areas are usually neutral in color.

Black suggests mystery, wisdom, or sophistication and in decoration can be employed to create dramatic or other extreme effects. To a decorative scheme of dark colors it adds spirit and interest, but in a light color scheme it gives too much contrast and makes other colors appear faded. Small accents of black are often effective. Black carpets are sometimes satisfactory with Modern or Oriental furnishings, but they require constant care as they show all marks and dust. Black furniture, particularly Oriental pieces, is sometimes used in rather luxurious settings.

White is a recurring favorite between periods of colorful decoration because of its serenity and coolness. White and off-white are generally approved for both exteriors and interiors of houses. Some unusual interior color schemes expressing luxury, delicacy, and femininity are based on white floors and carpets. An inexperienced person might well use white walls throughout an entire house. White is valuable for the opportunity it gives to display other colors. Pure white is best with cool colors whereas cream and off-white are usually more harmonious in warm schemes.

Gray, which is produced by mixing black and white, has no particular character of its own, although in light tints it seems gentle and serene, and in dark shades dignified and restrained. Grays may be warm or cool. A pale, warm gray containing either yellow or violet makes a pleasing wall color. A dark gray wall can serve as an advantageous background for etchings or drawings. Gray stain on woodwork and furniture is more unusual than brown and is agreeable where a cool effect is desired. Gray is a valuable color in Modern decoration as it permits emphasis to be placed on the form of objects by minimizing their color. Gray should be accompanied by some brilliant color to counteract its neutrality. A dominance of gray in a home may indicate a lack of imagination on the part of the owner. Pale gray is a pleasing color for exterior walls of houses; white houses look well with roofs and shutters of slate gray.

COLOR NAMES

The list of colors that is given here is a reminder of the great variety that is available. They are mostly color names of convenience and may change with fashion.

Blues
aquamarine
cobalt
cornflower
delft
hydrangea
indigo
navy
periwinkle
sky blue
slate blue
turquoise
ultramarine

Browns
auburn
bronze
chocolate
hazel
mahogany
rust
sienna
walnut

Greens
apple
chartreuse
emerald
lettuce
jade
Kelly
lime
olive
sage

Neutrals
beige
bisque
black
eggshell
gray
gunmetal
mouse
natural
pewter
puce
putty
sand
silver
smoke
tan

Oranges
burnt orange
carrot
cedar
coral
persimmon
salmon

Purples
amethyst
burgundy
eggplant
heather
orchid
raisin
thistle
wine

Reds
beet
cerise
cherry
flame
magenta
rose
ruby
scarlet
tomato
vermilion

Whites
off-white
ivory
opal
oyster
pearl
shell

Yellows
amber
brass
canary
chamois
corn
daffodil
gamboge
gold
honey
khaki
saffron
sapphire
straw

THE USE OF COLOR

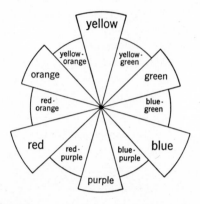

The three longest segments represent the *primary hues*, red, yellow, and blue.

The three medium segments represent the *secondary hues*, orange, green, and purple.

The six short segments represent the *tertiary hues*, red-orange, yellow-orange, yellow-green, blue-green, blue-purple, and red-purple.

Color Schemes

It would be highly desirable if everyone interested in color could develop her own color sense by experimenting and by observing beautiful examples in museums and elsewhere without studying definite ways of making color schemes. Since that would be a long process, however, this material is offered as a substitute.

Although formulas cannot insure the creation of harmonious color schemes, they are a definite help to the untrained person. In this study of color harmony four types of schemes are considered.

A Monochromatic Color Scheme. This is a scheme in which only one color is used, but it may be varied both in value and intensity. This kind of scheme is likely to be monotonous, although safe, and is sometimes highly successful. Many values of one hue like red-brown, dusty pink, slate-blue, or lime are attractive.

An Adjacent (Analogous) Color Scheme. This scheme is made by combining adjoining colors as illustrated in the pigment color circle above. Adjacent colors are harmonious because they contain a portion of the same colors; however, they are likely to be too hot or too cold unless carefully planned. It is entirely safe to combine the colors within one-fourth of the circle. Only one primary should be included. It is better not to use three colors which are equally far apart; therefore in the following sample lists of adjoining colors the first and last colors and one of the two between them should be combined.

Yellow-green, yellow, yellow-orange, orange.

Red-purple, purple, blue-purple, blue.

A Triad Color Scheme. This type of scheme combines the three equidistant colors, which occur at the points of an equilateral triangle placed anywhere on the color circle opposite. Turning the paper triangle will point out different combinations. A triad scheme is a well-balanced one, but the colors must be subdued to attain harmony. Some of the triads are:

1. Yellow, blue, red.
2. Yellow-green, blue-purple, red-orange.
3. Green, purple, orange.
4. Blue-green, red-purple, yellow-orange.

A Complementary Color Scheme. Colors that are opposite on the color circle are used in this scheme. It is a stimulating type of color plan and is well balanced. The colors must be subdued, and one should dominate. A double complementary scheme involves two or more pairs of complementary colors. In the pigment color theory some of the complements are:

1. Yellow, purple.
2. Yellow-green, red-purple.
3. Green, red.
4. Blue-green, red-orange.
5. Blue, orange.
6. Blue-purple, yellow-orange.

A Split Complementary Color Scheme. In a split complementary color scheme one color is used with the two colors that adjoin its complement on a color circle. This plan produces some subtle combinations when the colors employed are properly subdued. Some examples of split complementary schemes are:

1. Yellow, blue-purple, red-purple.
2. Yellow-green, purple, red.
3. Green, red-purple, red-orange.
4. Blue-green, red, orange.

Dominating Color. In any type of color scheme for any purpose one color should dominate in quantity, usually another color should be secondary in quantity, and if a third color is used it should be least in quantity. The smaller the area of a color the brighter it may be. See picture opposite page 46.

Color Dissonances. In modern color study, as in music, attention must be paid to dissonances as well as to harmonies. Such color schemes may be too difficult for students to create, but they are stimulating to see. The paintings of Henri Matisse of France usually contain color discords which astonish the layman.

THE PIGMENT THEORY COLOR CIRCLE

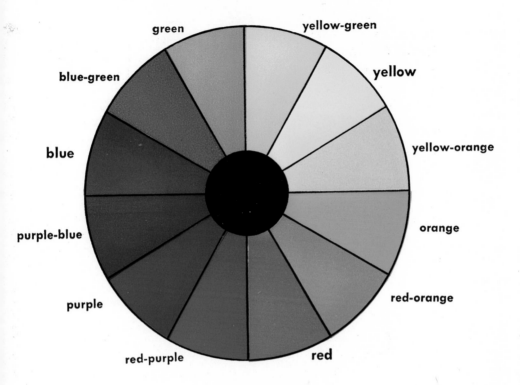

The colors of the *spectrum* are here arranged in a circle for convenience.

The *warm* colors are on the right-hand side of the circle.

The *cool* colors are on the left-hand side of the circle.

Complementary colors are exactly opposite one another on the circle. Six pairs of complementary colors are shown here.

Analogous colors are neighbors on the circle, as green, yellow-green, yellow, and yellow-orange.

Triad colors come at the three points of an equilateral triangle placed anywhere on the circle, as yellow-orange, blue-green, and red-purple.

COLOR PLANS FOR INTERIORS

An experimental attitude is conducive to success in the use of color in the home. It is much better to make mistakes than to stick to dull stereotyped color schemes, for through courageous use of color a person develops color sensitivity.

The color arrangement of the interior of an entire home is sometimes planned as a complete unit. A small house or apartment seems more spacious if the same background color is used in all the rooms. A Modern house, where the idea of continuous space is stressed, often has all the walls and ceilings in the house the same color and all the floors carpeted alike. When a unified multiple color scheme for a complete interior is made, the living room is planned first.

A color plan for the entire house in which each room is independent of the others has less unity than a related plan, but it affords more excitement and variety and permits more consideration of the exposure of a room.

FACTORS IN COLOR SCHEMES FOR ROOMS

1. The room: size, shape, exposure.
2. The mood.
3. The style.
4. The current fashion.
5. Personal preference.
6. Furnishings on hand.
7. Use of the room.

The Room. An analysis of a room is the first factor in making a color scheme for it. Every room has its own peculiarities which affect the solution of its color problem. A room that is too small gains spaciousness if the same cool, light color is used on all background parts and even on the furniture itself. On the other hand, warm reds and purples seem to reduce the size of a room. A long, narrow room can be made to appear in better proportion if only the end walls are decorated with warm, advancing colors, possibly brightly patterned. A square room seems elongated if two opposite walls are painted a dark color and the other two light.

Cold north rooms are much improved by the introduction of reds and yellows. South rooms need colors to oppose sunshine; therefore, blues, cool browns, cool beiges, and grays are suitable unless the room is dark. Rooms with too much light need dark, subdued colors and little variety in pattern.

Mood. The mood of a room can be expressed in its colors. A dignified room may be done in muted eggplant, gray blues, rose, and grays; a delicate feminine room in light dusty pink, pale jade, and white; a masculine room in wine red, gray-brown, navy blue, and beige; a gay room in cerise, white, electric blue, and lemon.

Style. The style of a room limits the choice of color therein, for each period in decoration had its own color character. Early American colors are generally subdued; Colonial colors are rich and of medium value; Federal colors are clear and light; Victorian colors are strong and pompous; Empire colors are bright and powerful; peasant colors are clear and gay; French provincial colors are earthy; Modern colors are often neutral with brilliant accents.

Fashion. Color schemes for our homes are definitely affected by fashion. Certain cycles or definite trends in taste produce types of color schemes which are used in nearly all the different fields of visual arts, for a limited period of time. The current fashion in color influences the decoration of any rooms, even period rooms which have traditional color schemes. Non-period rooms lend themselves well to change and should be kept up-to-date in color. One pleasing fashion is to employ off-white with umbers, beiges, browns, grays, or metallic colors, and to combine with them one striking, vivid, exciting color for contrast. Every home maker should keep up with color fashions by reading periodicals and visiting shops.

Personality. Personal preference rightly influences a woman to use her favorite colors, particularly in her own room. Some colorists advise blondes and gray-haired persons to adhere to cool colors and brunettes to warm colors for backgrounds as well as for clothing. It is said that children prefer light colors, youth prefers vivid colors, and others prefer soft medium colors.

Possessions. One's possessions limit the choice of colors. A novice who has to use her old furnishings might do well to add or subtract whatever articles are necessary to make the final scheme one of a definite type, such as adjacent, triad, or complementary. Among one's old possessions rugs are usually the most restricting factor in the choice of a color scheme. Troublesome Oriental rugs can be bleached, however, and almost any rug can be dyed. Slip covers for seating furniture are useful in transforming a color scheme.

Use. The use of a room influences its color scheme to a great extent. Color can help to emphasize the purpose of a room in addition to actually contributing to its efficiency. The time of day when a room is occupied most should be a factor in its color scheme; naturally a room should look its best at that time.

The *entrance hall* often has much the same type of coloring as the living room, although in larger houses it is frequently more impersonal and dignified in color than the living room. In an apartment or small house where an entrance hall is only a passage-way it should be decidedly decorative and colorful. Since a hall has very little furniture, interest should be provided by colorful treatment of floors or walls. In a two-story house the hall is the transition point between the first and second floors and so may well contain color ideas of both floors. An interior hall should be gay and novel in color and pattern, as it is usually dark and also un-furnished.

A *living room* should express cheer and hospitality along with restfulness and relaxation. Therefore its color scheme needs to be cheerful but not overstimulating, and characterful but not obtru-sive; fairly light, warm colors are usually the most desirable for living rooms except in a summer home or in a tropical home, where a simple cool scheme such as white walls and a blue ceiling and floors is refreshing. For a temperate climate white, brown, and coral with walls of pale grayed lime make a cheerful color arrange-ment, which could be varied for summer use by substituting natu-ral colored matting for the brown rug, using striped green and white slip covers to conceal the coral, and substituting thin white curtains for the draperies. In a living room it is desirable to keep the color interest and contrast on the general level of the occupants and furnishings, and not on the floor, walls, or ceiling.

An *outdoor living room* opening directly off the indoor living room should employ some of the interior colors, or others express-ing the same mood as the interior. At the same time the color of the exterior of the house and the green of growing plants must be considered when outdoor furnishings are chosen. An additional factor is the idea that outdoor colors should be few, simple, direct, positive, and cool. White is generally satisfactory for all porch furniture, but it should usually be accompanied by one color, such as chartreuse, leaf green, or the hue of the shutters or roof.

The *dining room* in a formal home is naturally in the same character as the house so its color scheme is conservative and dignified. Since most dining rooms are informal however they provide opportunities for pleasant surprises in color and decoration. The unexpected causes a lift in spirits and incites a light merry mood that is conducive to a happy time and a good appetite. A novel, colorful decorative scheme does not become tiresome in the dining room because the occupants do not remain there long.

Colors such as lettuce green, shrimp pink, butter yellow, lemon yellow, watermelon rose, or tomato red have refreshing and delicious implications. The addition of white is desirable, particularly if white is used on the table. Trite old color schemes like blue backgrounds for mahogany furniture should be avoided. Unusual experimental schemes, such as natural light wood or plastic chairs with a jade table, and pale pink backgrounds, are much more stimulating. Some successful dining rooms feature the garden idea, with sky-blue ceilings and white walls, gay colors being supplied by house plants, tropical fish, and birds.

A *kitchen* color scheme should be cheerful, light, and bright. Cool colors are thought to counteract the heat of cooking. The color of the sink, range, and refrigerator, which should all be alike, must be the basis for the color scheme. When these three basic articles are white or pale gray they are most easily fitted into a room design. Colored utilities are likely to become tiresome; therefore it is well to depend on less permanent articles to supply color.

White or light walls are usually best for visibility. Natural wood is also desirable. One vital color, such as a pure primary or secondary color, may be used in interiors of cupboards, for furniture, in curtains, and possibly on the floor, ceiling, one wall, or on the wood trim. Other colors should be supplied by dishes, pots, and plants. The colors used in the kitchen should be stimulating enough to make the cook feel creative.

The cottage or farm house type kitchen takes gay decoration well. Painted ornamentation in peasant fashion may be copied in bright colors such as the Swedish yellow and bright blue. See page 105. Colorful painted cartoons of family or local significance and favorite recipes painted on cupboard doors are personal and appropriate. There is no excuse for an ugly kitchen, for almost everything in it can be painted.

A *bedroom* color scheme is usually more personal than any other; its dominating color might well be the favorite color of the occupant. In deciding upon this color the exposure and the amount of light in the room should not be overlooked. For example, a brunette who is fond of soft chartreuse might use it in a north bedroom on walls and ceiling, in combination with white woodwork, full white net curtains, and a cherry-red bedspread.

A master bedroom used by both husband and wife should contain colors expressive of both. A man's room or a boy's room should be masculine, with rich characterful colors, possibly combined with natural wood. A woman's room or a girl's room should be bright and feminine and harmonious with her own coloring. A pretty, colorful room helps to develop a girl's personality. A guest room should be decorated in rather impersonal colors since it needs to please occupants of either sex or any age. Children's rooms are often finished with playful colorful decorations placed at the children's eye level. When bedrooms are treated as sitting rooms the colors should be darker and less personal than are customary for bedrooms in general.

Closet color schemes should be cheery. The colors may be the same as the color of the bedroom ceiling or walls or in pleasing contrast to them. Natural wood walls are not only attractive but also very convenient for attaching hooks and shelves.

Bathroom walls and fixtures should usually be white, for hygienic as well as esthetic reasons. In general, colored fixtures have proved to be tiresome. However, one bright clear positive color is needed in a bathroom; it should be used on the floor or on the upper walls and ceiling and in towels, mats, curtains, and shower curtains. Bathrooms are often decorated in colors that suggest water, like green, blue, violet, or gray. One common mistake found in bathrooms is the use of wall tiles that almost but not quite match the floor tiles.

Game-room color schemes should be bold and vigorous. The whole effect should be amusing, with colorful backgrounds supplying interest, since furniture is scarce. The walls might be painted in a warm, bright, solid color such as coral or lemon yellow, or two walls might be painted in stripes, checks, or plaids. Mural paintings and decorations suggesting a circus, a ship, or a garden might be effective.

GENERAL SUGGESTIONS FOR MAKING COLOR SCHEMES

1. Definite schemes, such as complementary, adjacent, or triad, are recommended.
2. A safe scheme consists of tints and shades of one color.
3. An easy scheme consists of white or off-white plus one or two clear colors.
4. Three colors and their variations in value are sufficient for any scheme.
5. A scheme should be definitely dark or light.
6. Either warm or cool colors should predominate.
7. A color scheme is often begun with a tertiary color.
8. A basic neutral color is generally best for large areas.
9. A more definite color is suitable for medium areas.
10. One or two brighter colors sometimes complementary to the dominant color are often used in small areas for accents.
11. If a scheme lacks sparkle a brilliant contrasting color note or white may be added.
12. Equal areas of different colors are monotonous.
13. Every color scheme should have a dominating color and a secondary color.

PROCEDURE FOR MAKING A COLOR SCHEME
FOR A ROOM

1. Review the seven factors named on page 41.
2. Review the suggestions above.
3. Consider the color schemes of the adjoining rooms.
4. Decide on the background colors.
5. Procure samples of fabrics, wall papers, and paints.
6. Select a color scheme from a fabric, wall paper, or picture.
7. Plan the color proportions. (Large, medium, or small areas.)
8. Plan the values of the chosen hues. (Lights and darks.)
9. Plan the variations in intensity of the chosen hues. (Bright or grayed.)
10. Draw floor plans locating the furniture as areas to be colored.
11. Draw wall plans locating areas for draperies and furniture.
12. On the plans write color names or paint the colors.
13. Assemble the completed color scheme, making water-color samples of colors not otherwise supplied.

Courtesy Newcastle Products and Armstrong Cork Company

The cheerful room pictured above has a color scheme of cool and warm colors with the cool definitely predominant. The pale blue walls, blue folding doors, and blue linoleum are relieved by lemon yellow and the natural color of the bamboo and reed furniture. Small accents of red complete the triad color scheme. In a small house or apartment the kitchen alcove and the sleeping alcove may be closed off with Modernfold doors as in the picture above.

COLOR SCHEMES FOR ROOMS

Walls	Ceiling	Carpet	Drapery	Upholstery
oyster-white	oyster-white	dark rose-red	pink	navy blue and white
slate-blue	white	slate-blue	lemon-yellow	cinnamon and yellow
brown	light yellow	mustard-yellow	yellow and red	lacquer-red
gray	gray	eggplant	turquoise and pink	gray and mauve
yellow-beige	yellow-beige	dark brown	canary-yellow	dark blue-green
green	white	brown	white and gold	beige and green
light pink	light pink	white	emerald-green	green and white
peach	beige	beige	turquoise and beige	cedar and turquoise
natural pine	dark green	brown	green and white	pumpkin-yellow
grayed lime	grayed lime	grayed blue-green	lime and blue-green	tomato-red
cream	cream	soft green	cocoa-brown	salmon-pink
honey-beige	honey-beige	mustard-yellow	rust	copper and mustard

PROBLEMS

A sufficient number of problems are listed so that choices may be made.

1. Make a color wheel showing red, orange, yellow, green, blue, and purple, using poster paint, crayon, or colored paper.
2. Paint a value scale from light to dark, using your favorite color.
3. Paint an intensity scale, of five sections, using one pair of complementary colors, with one of them at each end of the scale and a mixture of half of each in the middle sector.
4. Make an adjacent scheme, using paint or paper.
5. Make a complementary scheme, using paint or paper.
6. Plan a three-color scheme for a bedroom, from a fabric sample, using paint or paper.
7. Make a flower arrangement in an adjacent color scheme.
8. Tack on the bulletin board four different adjacent color schemes made from overlapping sheets of colored paper.
9. Select a color scheme for a living room, specifying the color of the wall paper, rug, draperies, upholstery, and accents.

READING REFERENCES

BIRREN, FABER. *Color Dimensions.* The Crimson Press, 1934.

BURRIS-MEYER, ELIZABETH. *Color and Design in the Decorative Arts.* Prentice-Hall, 1935.

GRAVES, MAITLAND. *The Art of Color and Design.* McGraw-Hill, 1941.

JACOBS, MICHEL. *The Art of Color.* Doubleday, Doran, 1926.

MCDONALD, STERLING B. *Color—How to Use It.* Follett, 1940.

MUNSELL, ALBERT H. *A Color Notation.* Munsell Color Co., 1936.

PATMORE, DEREK. *Color Schemes for the Modern Home.* Studio Publication, 1936.

SARGENT, WALTER. *The Enjoyment and Use of Color.* Scribner's, 1923.

CHAPTER 4

PRINCIPLES OF DESIGN

Certain clearly defined principles of design or arrangement are common to the space arts of painting, sculpture, architecture, handicrafts, industrial arts, commercial arts, and related arts. These principles of design are not formulas for creating beauty, but they do help in determining why an object is artistically good or poor. One of the most significant tenets maintained in this book is that almost anyone can acquire dependable standards of taste through experience with the principles of design and can become more and more sensitive to beauty.

Since the same classification of the fundamental principles of esthetics is not accepted by all authorities, one should study different opinions. The following list of principles agrees with the report of the Committee on Terminology of the Federated Council on Art Education. Proportion, balance, emphasis, rhythm, and repetition are called the five major principles because they are the most distinct and most important. Alternation, sequence, radiation, parallelism, transition, symmetry, and contrast are known as the minor principles. These sometimes overlap each other and also the major principles.

The outline below has been given in slightly different form in the chapter on the elements of art, but it is repeated here for convenience in reference. A person should apply the art principles to the art elements when trying to attain these objectives.

Principles	Elements	Objectives
Proportion	Line	Beauty
Balance	Form	Expressiveness
Emphasis	Texture	Functionalism
Rhythm	Color	
Repetition	Pattern	
	Light	
	Space	

49

PROPORTION

The principle of proportion underlies all other principles. It states that the relations between parts of the same thing or between different things of the same group should be satisfying. It deals with relationships in size, shape, color, light, texture, and pattern. Its most prominent application in home planning and home furnishing, however, is to the relationships of areas.

The appearance of the exterior of a house is due primarily to its proportions, first the total mass, which depends on the height in relation to the length, then the proportions of roof, walls, and foundation, and finally the relationship of doors, windows, and other elements that must be organized into a unified whole. The shapes of rooms and of every article of home furnishing should be judged by their proportions. The heights of flower arrangements and the shapes of flower beds are also problems in proportion. The ability to recognize fine proportion is an invaluable asset to the home maker.

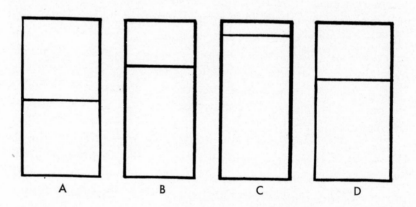

The figures above show the effect of dividing an area so as to produce interesting and uninteresting proportions. In *A* and *B* the divisions are too simple to form interesting areas, although *B* is much better than *A*. In *C* the spaces are too unlike to be related by the mind. In *D* the dividing line is placed somewhere between one-half and one-third of the length of the rectangle, thereby determining areas that are pleasantly related because they are enough alike to be compared easily yet different enough to arouse interest.

Greek Proportion. Any study of proportion must begin with the achievements of the ancients, because they set standards that are followed to this day. The Greeks, through long study, became very sensitive to fine relations in space. They formulated rules based on the proportions of the human body.

The three orders or designs in Greek architecture illustrate some of the cultural attributes of proportion. The *Doric* column, the first, about six diameters in height, expresses the vigor and austerity of the race during the period of its development. The *Ionic* column, which is the next type, has a height between eight and nine diameters and is characteristic of its period, being more graceful and delicate, in agreement with the advancing refinement of the race. The *Corinthian column*, with its height of ten diameters or more, and rich, elaborate ornament, typifies the greater pretentiousness of the people of that final period. Proportions employed changed from the sturdy and useful to the attenuated and sophisticated.

The *golden section* used by the Greeks is considered to be a model of good proportion. This proportion is found in any rectangular oblong which can be divided into two unequal areas, one of which is a square, so that the smaller one is to the larger as the larger is to the whole. In the same way, any line can be divided at a point so that the shorter line will be to the longer as the longer is to the whole line. This division of a line is pleasing.

Geometric Divisions. To the layman it may be somewhat shocking to find that artists often use mechanical means of obtaining fine divisions of space. Two great art periods, the Greek and the Renaissance, exhibit the use of geometric divisions. J. Hambidge's books on dynamic symmetry deal with the geometric divisions used in Greek proportion.

The trained person as a rule creates good proportion without conscious effort, but the untrained person generally finds some system of geometric division very helpful. After practice with mechanical divisions of spaces, a person becomes sensitive to space relations and may be able to depend entirely upon his judgment. It has been observed that space divisions freely chosen by highly trained artists very often agree exactly with the space divisions obtained by applying some mechanical scheme.

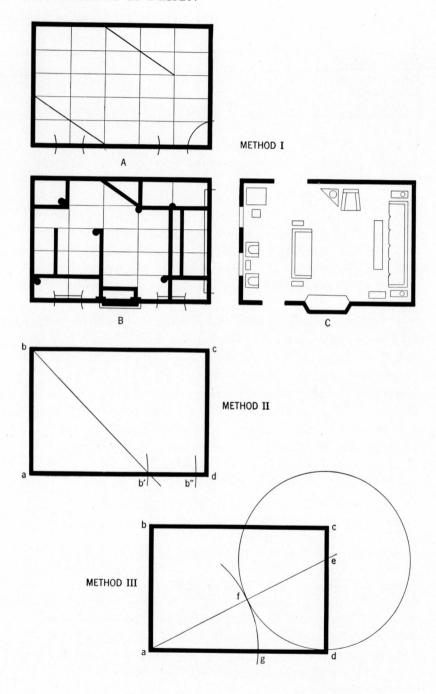

METHOD I

A

B

C

METHOD II

METHOD III

In architecture and interior decoration, the most helpful way to use mechanical divisions is to find a definite length or area that can be employed over and over again, in order to give unity to a façade or a room. Of course this length or area, which we will call a unit of measurement, must have some relation to the dimensions of the house or the room. Simple arithmetical guides are often as effective as more complicated ones. For example, units of measure depending upon related numbers such as 2, 4, 6; or 2, 4, 8, 16; or 2, 3, 5, 8, 13, might be used. Only a few other methods for selecting a unit of measurement for a room are described here. They apply also to exteriors of houses.

Method I. It is supposed that a room under consideration is rectangular. The simplest and perhaps the most effective method is to draw a rectangle having the same proportions as the floor. Divide its short side and also its long side into the same number of equal lengths, five or seven or any suitable number, as in diagram A on page 52. Then draw connecting lines so that the rectangle is divided into small oblongs that have exactly the same proportions as the room. Draw the diagonal through one or more rectangles, or mark off the length of the vertical side on the horizontal, to get additional points and lengths if they are desired. Any length or area appearing in the figure may be taken as a unit upon which to base the decoration and furnishing of the room.

Diagram B shows one way of dividing the same plan into interesting spaces, with some important points indicated. Many other divisions are possible.

Diagram C is a furniture arrangement plan based on the spacing indicated in diagram B.

Method II. By means of ordinary geometric constructions based on the dimensions of a room, it is possible to obtain in various ways significant lengths that may serve as units of measurement for articles and spaces within the room. Let the rectangle $abcd$ represent the floor of a room. Let $ab' = ab$. Lay off the length of the diagonal b to b' on the line ad to locate the point b''. The lines $b'b''$, $b'd$, or $b''d$ may be used as a unit of measurement anywhere in the room. The point b' is an important one to be considered in placing the furniture, but its value depends somewhat on the shape of the room, as well as on the location of the doors and windows.

Method III. The line *ad* has a most pleasing point of division represented in the diagram by *g*. To find this point, with the length of the line *ad* as the diameter draw a circle tangent to the line *ad* at the point *d*. Suppose that the point *e* is the center of the circle. Now draw a line connecting *a* and *e*, establishing the point *f* where the line *ae* crosses the circle. With *af* as radius draw a circle with *a* as center, intersecting *ad* at *g*. The point *g* is the mean division point of the line *ad*. This point is sometimes called the harmonic division and should be considered an important point in decorating and furnishing. The unit of measurement might be the line *gd* or the difference between *gd* and *ag*. The chosen unit may be used in many ways; for example, it may be laid off on all sides, or from the corners, or from the point *g*, and may serve as a guide for the selection and arrangement of the furniture.

SCALE

Under the general heading of proportion, scale is the proper term when considering relative sizes without regard for shapes. Correct scale, or, in other words, consistency in size, is indispensable in garden design, exterior house design, interior design, and furniture design.

In garden design it is necessary to choose plants and trees that are in scale with the grounds and the house. In exterior house design the scale of the openings and features such as columns and eaves in relation to the house are very important factors in appearance.

In home furnishings the requirements of scale apply in four different ways. Each article must be in scale with the room containing it and also with the other articles in the room. The various structural parts of each article must be in scale with one another and with the whole. The decoration of each article must be in scale with it.

The most common mistakes in scale are made in combining articles of inconsistent sizes such as large lamps on small tables, large bouquets in small vases, small pictures hung on walls, and tiny art objects on large tables. Examples of violation of scale are so general that the reader can probably see several by looking about her. Things that are not related in size should not be a part of the same group, for the mind refuses to consider them together.

BALANCE

Balance is as fundamental in the visual arts as it is in life itself. Moreover it is so simple that almost anyone can understand that a feeling of steadiness, repose, and balance is the result of the equalization of attractions on either side of a central point. Balance must be attained in color, texture, pattern, and light as well as in weight.

Formal balance results when objects of equal weight are placed on each side and at equal distances from the center; when they are identical the balance is symmetrical.

Informal, occult, or asymmetrical balance results when objects are arranged so that a large one near the center balances a small one farther away from the center, like a large boy and a small boy on a teeter totter.

Formal balance is a matter of the intellect; informal balance, of the feelings. Informal balance is felt, and is much more creative than the formal, because there are no rules to guide one in producing it. Formal balance is less difficult and less subtle, and also more passive, than informal balance. The fireplaces in the pictures on page 210 illustrate formal balance and informal balance.

The *exterior design* of certain types of houses, such as the English Georgian, the Colonial, and other descendants of the Italian Renaissance, expresses dignity and reserve through the use of formal balance. Early English, Norman French, some Mediterranean types of houses, and rambling ranch houses express friendliness and hospitality through informal balance. See page 190 for illustrations of these qualities.

The type of balance present in the *interiors* of houses helps to determine the emotional effects created. Formal balance in a room naturally creates an air of formality. Therefore it is not the effect usually desired in a simple or small room or home, or in any place that should have a gay, young, or casual air. Formal interior architecture usually requires some formality in furniture arrangement.

Balance is by far the most important principle employed in *furniture arrangement*. The halves of each single wall should be equally weighted with furniture. Opposite walls should also be equal in weight.

EMPHASIS

Emphasis is the principle that directs us to have a center of interest in any arrangement, and a dominating idea, form, or color in any scheme. In order to place emphasis on any special feature, others must be subordinated or simplified. Emphasis on a dominating idea is considered on page 3, dominating color on page 40, and dominating shape on page 12.

The Center of Interest. If possible every room should have a center of interest, which is the most important point in the room and should be worthy of the attention given to it. It may be an architectural feature, as a hearth or a bay window, or it may be some interesting furnishings. It is not always desirable to emphasize the same feature in summer and winter or even by day and by night. A large room may well have secondary points of interest also.

How to Emphasize. Emphasis can be created at any desired point in the room by using the art components in a dramatic way, as by means of:

1. Large or unusual forms.
2. Positive surface pattern.
3. More light than elsewhere.
4. Unusual texture.
5. The brightest or the most contrasting colors.

When emphasizing a particular part of a room, the other parts should be subordinated. Some decorators distribute the emphasis so that the observer will give attention to the accessories, the furniture, the floor, and the walls, in this order. Sometimes, however, this order is deliberately reversed in order to withdraw attention from things that should be minimized. For example, nondescript furniture should be eclipsed by especially attractive wall paper. Although the floor is not the place to focus attention, some floor coverings, especially Oriental rugs, are so conspicuous that they cannot be obscured. If such a rug must be used the only solution is to subordinate everything else in the room.

A warning should be given to the amateur decorator; it is very much better to underemphasize than to overemphasize in interior design. It is pleasant to feel that the decorator has plenty of reserve power.

RHYTHM

Rhythm is organized movement in continuity. It occurs in regular, repeated movement and also in variable transitional movement. It is important in art and in nature.

Regular measured rhythm is the simplest and oldest way of producing harmony and order. It is the basic element in music, the dance, and poetry, and it is important in architecture and interior design. It is a system of regular accenting such as is found in a row of duplicate columns or in striped fabrics.

Variable rhythm is found in the irregular intervals of dissimilar parts. This rhythm may carry the eye along smoothly flowing lines or it may force the attention abruptly here and there in order to convey the desired emotional effect. This type of rhythm is employed to attract the eye throughout a painting until it is seen as a whole. Such rhythm unites all the articles in a group of furniture and also connects each group with adjoining groups. Variable rhythm dominates in natural landscaping and in flower arrangements of the curvilinear or diagonal types.

REPETITION

Repetition is closely related to rhythm, for its use may result in rhythm. Repetition is generally necessary in producing beauty; it is the simplest way to achieve order. The theme is repeated in almost any form of art for the purpose of making a composition. In home decoration, colors, lines, and shapes used in a room should be repeated for the sake of unity. Repetition is also the outstanding principle employed in the creation of surface patterns. This principle is fundamental in nature as well as in man-made beauty; it is the basis of design in flowers, leaves, shells, and other natural objects.

THE MINOR PRINCIPLES

Alternation means repeating two lines or forms alternately.
Sequence refers to regular progression in a series.
Radiation refers to lines radiating from one center.
Parallelism refers to the use of parallel lines and forms.
Transition means gradual change.
Symmetry results from two similar vertical halves.
Contrast means opposition of things or qualities.

PROBLEMS

A sufficient number of problems are listed so that choices may be made.

1. Draw a floor plan for an oblong room and find a unit of measurement for it by any method given in the text. Locate pleasing points and lines.
2. Design the front view of a cabinet, using a geometric unit of measurement.
3. Analyze a room for proportion.
4. Analyze your classroom for balance.
5. Bring to class examples of plant material showing regular, irregular, and radiating rhythm (pine cone, vine, leaf, etc.).
6. Analyze reproductions of paintings to find the center of interest (emphasis).
7. Point out articles with informal or formal balance (hat, dress, book cover, package label, pattern in fabric, etc.).

READING REFERENCES

AMERICAN INSTITUTE OF ARCHITECTS. *The Significance of the Fine Arts.* Marshall Jones, 1926.

GOLDSTEIN, H. and V. *Art in Everyday Life.* Macmillan, 1940.

HAMBIDGE, JAY. *The Elements of Dynamic Symmetry.* Brentano, 1926.

WHISTLER, J. A. M. *Ten O'Clock.* Mosher, 1916.

The principle of rhythm is well demonstrated in the room pictured above. Connecting lines carry the eyes all around the room. This gay ensemble expresses youth and informality.

Emphasis is well concentrated in the room below. The fireplace is easily the center of interest. The bare floor, the pine wall, and the provincial furniture are particularly appropriate in farm homes as well as in town cottages. *Courtesy Walter Johnson, Inc.*

Formal balance is well illustrated above. A very tall Modern flower arrangement would have been suitable against this background space. *Courtesy Pittsburgh Plate Glass Company.*

Informal balance is a feature of the breakfast room in the home of Robert Young. The corner shelves with one long and one short side constitute a delightful variation. The curves of curtains, plates, tables, and scallops in the rug provide pleasant repetition and rhythm.

Rhythm is the outstanding design principle apparent in the odd chair at the left in the picture above. It is thoroughly functional, for it fits the lines of the human body. Curved laminated wood is good looking and durable. The table legs are out of scale with the chairs.

Pleasing proportions are used in this overstuffed furniture. The arms and cushions are not too bulky, yet the pieces are architectural in size and appear comfortable. This is a type of furniture that can be used with most styles. The pictures are well chosen and well hung; the mirror frames are interesting. The room is somewhat sedate because of lack of pattern; however, it is restful. *Courtesy Montgomery Ward.*

Good proportion is the basis for this well-designed furniture. Note that the upper portion of the wall cabinet is about two-thirds as high as the lower part. The door below the bookshelf is about the height of the upper section of the cabinet; it is also the same width as the section above it. Unity results from these repetitions. *Courtesy Herman Miller Company.*

Fine proportion is a feature of this house. The relation of length to height, the proportion of roof to wall, and the shapes of the windows and chimney are pleasing. Informal landscaping and the picket fence produce a friendly effect. *Courtesy H. Roy Kelley, architect.*

PART TWO

STYLES IN HOUSES AND FURNISHINGS

CHAPTER 5

TRADITIONAL STYLES IN HOUSES

Since the present American houses and furnishings are usually classified as period (traditional), or cottage, or Modern in style, these three different types will be explained in this book. Another type known as Non-period will have to be recognized when it becomes more generally used.

The following survey of the traditional styles in domestic architecture features those which have contributed most to American homes, the English, Spanish, French, Italian, and Greek.

Home makers should be able to identify houses built in the Colonial, English, French, or Spanish manner as a matter of appreciation and also for the ability which it will give them to visualize houses they are planning. Although a period house is not now copied literally, the elements of a traditional style, such as the roof, doors, windows, and moldings, are freely used. Retaining some characteristics of the period styles gives a traditional character to many houses of today. Period exteriors can be adapted to fit floor plans of today, even though they are entirely different from those of the past. This subject is developed in Chapter 11.

When considering traditional styles in houses it is well to realize that some of their peculiarities and characteristics developed because of the position of the rooms, which were located to suit the manner of life of the occupants. Other characteristics developed because of the few available materials and limited facilities. Now when the manner of living is different and materials and processes are adequate it is absurd to copy any of the inconveniences or limitations of old houses. On the other hand, the features that have brought esthetic satisfaction to home owners for centuries provide a valuable precedent for those who are planning to build a home.

63

OLD HOUSE MUSEUMS

The most interesting and vital way to study traditional styles, both period and cottage types, is to visit original old houses that have been preserved as museums. Massachusetts has about one hundred such houses; some states have none. Motorists should inquire about the old house museums located on their routes. These houses are owned by the nation, states, counties, cities, universities, museums, organizations, or private individuals.

Among the most famous of our house museums are the homes of George Washington and Franklin D. Roosevelt. John D. Rockefeller's restoration of the entire city of Williamsburg, Virginia, converted every building in the town into a house museum of esthetic and historic interest. At Natchez, Mississippi, many beautiful old homes are open to the public.

Henry Ford's Edison Institute at Dearborn, Michigan, is preserving many buildings that are of great educational value in the study of Americana. The Wayside Inn of Longfellow's poem is one of Henry Ford's preservations in its original location. See page 101. A group of Norwegian pioneer log cabins is now located on the campus of Luther College, at Decorah, Iowa. Old house museums are usually self-supporting through admission fees.

Every county in the United States should have as a local museum at least one typical early dwelling in which the original furnishings of the locality and other historical material can be preserved. Future Americans can best understand and appreciate the manner of life of their ancestors through the observation of their houses and furnishing. The sacrifices and hardships of the brave pioneers who created the new nation are evident in their homes. This evidence should be preserved, especially that which illustrates the two great American dramas which can never be repeated here, the immigration of European settlers founding a new nation and the westward drive of the pioneers on the frontiers.

Those interested in the preservation of old historic or typical houses and their furnishings should study the great outdoor museums, Miahaugen in Norway and Skansen in Sweden. Here even the caretakers are in the garb appropriate to the houses they show. French provincial house museums are among those which are of great benefit and interest to citizens and tourists.

THE ENGLISH CONTRIBUTION

England has influenced our residence architecture more than any other country. During the American Colonial period, England underwent one of the few great European-wide style changes, the transition from Gothic to Renaissance. English Gothic type houses are now known as English Medieval, and the Renaissance houses as Georgian. Both these types were in turn employed by the American colonists, who faithfully copied English fashions.

English Medieval. The classification English Medieval covers also such terms as Gothic, Tudor, Elizabethan, Jacobean, Cotswold, or English cottage. Some of the houses were built of stone, but most of them were made of heavy timber frames filled in with brick, stone, or wattle, which was often plastered with clay or stucco and then whitewashed. The thatched or tiled roofs were steep in order to shed rain and snow. The small windows of tiny diamond-shaped panes were irregularly spaced. The entire composition was usually picturesque as illustrated on page 73.

The old English style has been freely copied in the United States, but it has now lost its popularity. Imitations of half-timbered construction and thatched roofs are now understood to be insincere and illogical, as well as unreasonably costly. Only free adaptations of the style with plain stucco walls and larger windows are at all feasible.

Early American. The seventeenth-century homes of the English-American colonists had the small casement windows of the medieval style but the symmetrical plan of the Georgian style, with a single room on each side of the central chimney, upstairs and down, and a plain gable roof extending lower in the rear to cover lean-to rooms. The second floor often projected over the first floor so that occupants could shoot down at Indian enemies. As the half-timbered walls suitable to England were too cold for New England, a covering of weather boarding was applied over the exterior walls. The low foundations were often made of boulders. Many of the buildings were humble and crude, but they had the dignity and restraint that come from plain, strong masses and structural honesty. See page 74. A few contemporary American houses are based on the Early American type; the chief characteristic employed is the overhanging second floor.

English Georgian. The English Georgian style developed early in the eighteenth century. Its beginnings, however, were a century earlier, when England's greatest architect, Inigo Jones, returned from Italy, where he had studied the Classic designs of the Italian Renaissance. Sir Christopher Wren, the worthy successor of Inigo Jones, continued to develop the Georgian style. The Georgian house had as characteristic features a central hall and staircase with symmetrical rooms on each side, both upstairs and down, hipped roofs, tall chimneys on the end walls, projecting cornices, brick walls sometimes parapet, with corners of stone, delicate moldings, large regularly spaced windows, central doorways with pediments, and Roman Doric, Ionic, or Corinthian columns. Georgian houses had restraint, dignity, and beauty, and also were comfortable. See page 73 for an illustration.

American Colonial. Georgian-type houses appeared in America soon after the style developed in England. These Colonial houses were built by amateur architects and skilled carpenters, who often made changes in the style although they studied the English books of Classical designs. Samuel McIntyre was one of the best American master builders of the period. Impressive Colonial houses were constructed for prosperous ship owners, merchants, and plantation owners from Massachusetts to Virginia. Distinct characteristics developed in the architecture of various sections because of climatic conditions, materials available, and social and economic factors. The three most definite types of houses were the New England Colonial, the Middle Colonial, and the Southern Colonial. See page 73 for good examples.

New England Colonial houses were usually built of wood although stone and brick were sometimes used. The houses were rectangular and symmetrical like their Georgian models. At the edge of the low gable or hip roof was a Classic molding or a balustrade. One central chimney or two end chimneys were used. The front doorways, which dominated the façades, were of the Classic temple front pattern, with slender columns, pilasters, and pediments. The large double-hung windows on the front were evenly spaced in relation to the door, which was in the exact center. The ornamentation, copied from Renaissance design books, was more delicate in wood than the originals, which were in stone.

Cape Cod houses are simplified, reduced, and varied versions of New England's Georgian Colonial houses, which nevertheless have retained dignity and beauty. The original Cape Cod cottage was either one story or a story and a half, with a plain gable roof and no dormers. The outside walls were usually of white clapboard or gray shingles. See page 74. Double-hung windows with small panes and wooden shutters were typical; one or two windows were located on either side of the central door. Cape Cod cottages, which are now being copied extensively, are among the most desirable traditional small houses in this country.

Middle Colonial is the usual classification for the dignified Colonial houses of brick and stone that were built in the middle colonies, especially in the eastern part of Pennsylvania. This was a more robust style than that of New England, with heavier cornices and plainer details.

The *Dutch Colonial* houses which developed in New York, New Jersey, and eastern Pennsylvania have doors and windows like the other colonial houses, but the roofs are decidedly different. Gambrel roofs, of two slants, extend outward to cover porches on the fronts and backs of the houses. See page 74. Originally the houses had no dormer windows, but the contemporary interpretations usually have single dormers or the less desirable shed dormers. The original one-and-a-half-story cottages were made of stone or brick, or both; modern interpretations are frame houses with white siding, accented by green shutters. This style is comfortable, and it is attractive if the general shape of the house is long and low and the dormers are not too large.

The *Southern Colonial* houses which were built in Maryland and Virginia, and in near-by sections, were much different from those in New England, as they were made of brick and were more truly Georgian. Many of the large houses had a central unit flanked on either side by a smaller building with which it was connected.

Colonial Revival. The twentieth century has seen a revival of the Colonial house, which is now the most popular traditional style in the United States. This style is recommended because of its adaptability to modern construction methods and materials, and also because of its honesty, dignity, and beauty. Colonial houses make pleasing settings for one of America's favorite types of furniture, the eighteenth-century English, Colonial, and Federal.

THE SPANISH CONTRIBUTION

Spain has developed a type of domestic architecture designed to make living pleasant in a warm, dry climate. The houses are usually built with arcaded porches around three sides of the open patios, which serve as living rooms and work rooms. Low tiled roofs with broad overhang protect the tinted stucco walls. Beautiful ironwork and colorful tiles are characteristic features of decoration. All the floors, including the patio, are paved with brick or tile.

The Spanish type of house was brought by Cortez and his followers to Mexico, including what is now the southwestern part of the United States. These *Spanish Colonial* houses were simple, however, owing to unskilled Indian labor and crude materials such as large sun-dried adobe bricks for walls, and poles and hand-made tiles for roofs. The patio floors were usually just swept earth. The missions, which were of the same style and materials as the houses, also enclosed patios with beautiful gardens.

A great revival of the Spanish Colonial style occurred in the semi-tropical parts of the United States in the present century. See page 75 for examples. Unfortunately an excessive number of both small and large houses of Spanish derivation have been built here, because the style has seemed so appropriate in certain sections. A reaction against the style has arisen since many inadequate interpretations of the original houses have appeared. It is recognized, however, that, when designed with taste, Spanish Colonial houses have special charm. Some of the most important and most beautiful dwellings of this type are to be found on the hills of Santa Barbara, California. Among the more modest examples of this style are the delightful, informal, rambling ranch houses built around the inevitable courtyards and surrounded by olive, fig, lemon, or orange trees. These ranch houses were usually inspired by the unpretentious farm homes of Spain, Mexico, New Mexico, Texas, and California.

The *Monterey style* is a special type built by carpenters who had come from New England to California. See page 194. They combined Atlantic coast styles with Pacific coast materials and ideas. This interesting type of Spanish Colonial architecture is having some influence in semi-tropical sections of the country.

THE AMERICAN INDIAN CONTRIBUTION

In Arizona and New Mexico the Spanish colonists built houses inspired by the homes of the Pueblo Indians, of which an excellent example is the Taos Indian pueblo in New Mexico. The Indian houses are made of adobe and have flat roofs and parapet walls. The roofs are supported on heavy poles over which peeled saplings laid close together form unique, characterful ceilings and support the layers of the roof, the top one of which is turf. The poles and wooden spouts for rain water sometimes extend out from the roof. Pole ladders on the exterior take the place of stairs.

The Indian-Spanish type of architecture is appropriate in New Mexico and Arizona, where it is indigenous. This tradition is followed in the buildings of the University of New Mexico in Albuquerque, and in dwellings and other structures in Santa Fe and many other places. Small adobe houses are easy to build and are remarkably cool in summer and warm in winter. See page 75 for illustrations of the original houses and also a modern adaptation.

THE ITALIAN CONTRIBUTION

Architecture is greatly indebted to the Romans for practical building methods as well as for beauty. Domestic architecture owes much to Palladio, a famous architect of the Renaissance period. His buildings and designs were the inspiration for the work of the English architect Inigo Jones, who developed the Georgian house, which in turn inspired the Colonial house of America. Today's familiar portico with columns, the doorway which consists of a large central arched section flanked by small rectangular openings on either side, and the four-sided pitch roof are true adaptations of Palladio's design.

The typical Palladian Florentine villa was Classical and formal, standing on a marble balustraded platform overlooking an equally formal garden, which contained fountains and sculpture. These villas have been the models for some large, dignified houses in the United States. The simple Italian house or low, rambling farm dwelling has been the inspiration for some delightful informal houses here. Such a house has a flexible plan which usually included a courtyard. The walls of stucco are unbroken except for a few windows and doors.

THE FRENCH CONTRIBUTION

French Colonial houses were built by early French settlers in Louisiana, some of whom were Acadians from Canada. Old original French houses are still in use in Louisiana cities, on plantations, and on small farms, particularly throughout the bayou region, which is occupied by trappers and fishermen of French descent.

A typical Louisiana French Colonial house of some importance has a high raised basement to protect it from dampness and floods. See page 76. It has a high, steep hip roof of slate, two dormers, one tall decorative chimney at each end of the house, a formal façade with French windows and shutters, and a porch (gallery) with one-story columns across the front and back.

In other parts of the United States, also, a symmetrical type of the French house has been copied. In fact, its use is at present increasing, because the formal, high-roofed design is considered appropriate for a city house. Its delicate refinement, its studied proportions, and its materials express dignity and restraint.

On the other hand, the picturesque French Norman cottage, which is asymmetrical in design, is no longer popular in the United States. Its open timbers and its varied materials are illogical here. The American adaptations have lost the quality of sincerity which is inherent in the original cottages.

Another distinct example of French architectural influence is found in the Vieux Carré style in New Orleans. Here the Creoles, descendants of French and Spanish immigrants, built houses which combined French and Spanish architectural ideas, dominated, however, by the Spanish. Because space was extremely limited in the Vieux Carré (Old Square), the buildings, which consisted of stores on the street floor and living quarters above, were built in juxtaposition. A paved courtyard and garden behind the house, with a building for slaves at the rear and high walls at the sides, completed the plan. Characteristic and pleasing features of the house were colorful stucco, arches, balconies, and lacy ironwork. Most of these picturesque houses are in good condition and in constant use. The beauty of the Vieux Carré is being protected by the supervision of a board which prevents the construction of discordant buildings.

THE GREEK CONTRIBUTION

Our architecture and that of Europe have been largely developed from the Classic architecture of Greece. Interpretations by Italians, English, French, and Spanish modified the forms brought to us, but the original style was created by the Greeks in a period of artistic achievement that has never been equaled.

The first half of the nineteenth century witnessed in Europe and America a return to the source of Classic architecture, which was known as the Greek Revival. In the United States it was promoted by the architect and statesman Thomas Jefferson.

At first the Greek Revival was confined to public buildings, but in the eighteen twenties Greek porches and porticos with columns were added to Georgian houses. Finally entire dwellings were built in the Greek temple pattern even though this plan was an inflexible one that could not ordinarily be adapted to comfortable living. Conforming to temple architecture, these houses were usually turned so that a gable end of the house became the front façade. The gable roof of the house often extended unbroken over the front porch, where it was supported by two-story columns made of brick and covered with stucco.

On the exteriors of dwellings Greek cornices were copied faithfully and decorative door and window treatments were kept true to style. Cast ironwork in Greek designs was freely used for fences and window grilles. On the interiors the mantels, woodwork, cornices, and plaster rosettes on the ceiling were Grecian.

Greek Revival houses of different kinds were numerous as far west as Illinois and south to the Gulf of Mexico. In the deep South, the large old plantation homes, which were adaptations of the Greek Revival style, proved very satisfactory. The enormous high porches (galleries), central halls, large rooms, high ceilings, and French windows were conducive to good ventilation and comfort in a hot climate. In addition, these magnificent houses, often entirely surrounded by porches with pillars, were truly expressive of the scale and luxury of the lives of the wealthy slave-owning planters. See page 76 for a typical example.

Contemporary use of the Greek Revival style includes interpretations of the Regency houses of England of the same period; however some of them are quite Modern in character.

PROBLEMS

A sufficient number of problems are listed so that choices may be made.

1. Classify pictures of houses according to their styles.
2. Identify the types of houses in a specific block in your city.
3. Name the architectural style of your college buildings, church, post office, home.
4. Trace a page of traditional houses suitable for your locality.

READING REFERENCES

Architectural Record, December, 1935; November, 1936. Restoration of Colonial Williamsburg.

CESCINSKY, HERBERT. *The Old World House.* Macmillan, 1924.

CHAMBERLAIN, SAMUEL. *Cape Cod in the Sun.* Hastings House, 1937.

GILPIN, LAURA. *The Pueblos.* Hastings House, 1942.

HANNAFORD, D. R., and EDWARD, R. *Spanish Colonial or Adobe Architecture of California.* Architectural Book Publishing Co., 1931.

KIMBALL, FISK. *Domestic Architecture of the American Colonies.* Scribner, 1922.

SCOTT, GEOFFREY. *Architecture of Humanism.* Scribner, 1924.

TALLMADGE, THOMAS E. *The Story of Architecture in America.* Norton, 1936.

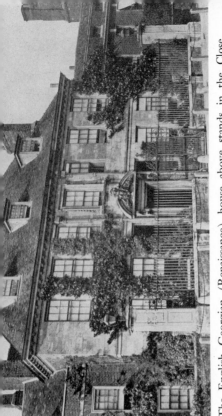

The English Georgian (Renaissance) house above stands in the Close, Salisbury. It has fine symmetry and proportion. *Courtesy Library of Congress.*

The Southern Colonial type is exemplified by Westover, a famous plantation house in Virginia. The two wings are omitted here. The Southern Colonial style below is much like the English Georgian pictured above.

The English Medieval (Gothic) style is illustrated by the old Cotswold cottage above which was imported and rebuilt at Dearborn, Michigan. *Courtesy Edison Institute.*

The old New England Colonial house below is derived from the English Georgian. Notice that it has a gable roof and is built of wood. The façade has a fine symmetrical design with an interesting doorway. *Courtesy Richard Koch.*

A typical Cape Cod cottage is shown above. It is the Kendrick house at South Orleans, Massachusetts. Note the pleasing symmetrical façade and the weathered shingles. *Courtesy Library of Congress.*

The Dutch Colonial house pictured below is preserved as a museum by the City of New York. The old Dyckman house has typical variety in building materials. Note the roof line.

The famous Early American house above is the Old Copen House at Topsfield, Massachusetts. The second-story overhang made it possible to shoot at Indian assailants below. *Courtesy Massachusetts Development Commission.*

The old pioneer cabin of hewn logs pictured below expresses strength and simplicity. The compactness and lack of adornment are desirable qualities in all architecture. *Courtesy Edison Institute.*

This section of the main old pueblo near Taos, New Mexico, is a typical example of American Indian construction. The poles which support the roofs extend out between the adobe blocks of the walls. *Courtesy Norman E. Rutt.*

The new house below is one of many, built in Santa Fe and other parts of New Mexico, modeled after Indian architecture. This style and this material are logical choices for the treeless desert sections of the Southwest. *Courtesy Norman E. Rutt.*

Most of the original Spanish Colonial houses of California were made of adobe covered with stucco and had low sloping roofs of hand-made tiles. *Courtesy Los Angeles Chamber of Commerce.*

A four-room stucco house of Spanish derivation, built about 1930, is shown below. The style is suitable for southern California. The larger windows of the present time improve livability but impair the design. *Courtesy Virgil D. Westbrook, architect.*

The typical Colonial cottage pictured above left is the Old Bracken House in Williamsburg, Virginia. Modern copies of this should retain the pleasing scale of the doors and windows but reduce the size of the chimney and lower the foundation. *Courtesy Williamsburg Restoration.*

The kitchen building pictured above right at Mount Vernon has excellent proportions and would be a desirable model to copy for a cottage. Double windows would be more functional. *Courtesy Mount Vernon Ladies Association.*

The typical old French house pictured below left called Madam John's Legacy is said to be the oldest house in New Orleans. Note the high basement, the roof extending over the porch, the columns, the long French windows, and the symmetrical façade. *Courtesy Richard Koch.*

Greek Revival architecture at its height is illustrated below right by Greenwood, a beautiful old plantation home located near St. Francisville, Louisiana. The style was desirable in a hot climate, for the great porches, central halls, and enormous rooms helped to reduce the heat. *Courtesy Anne Plettinger, photographer.*

CHAPTER 6

TRADITIONAL OR PERIOD STYLES
IN FURNISHINGS

A period in art is a span of time during which the ideals and necessities of people cause them to create certain characteristic forms which we call *period styles*. The last section of this book consists of detailed information about the period styles. If time permits, it should be studied at this point. However, since many courses will omit this section, a brief résumé of period furniture is offered here as a substitute. Style refers to major modes of expression and should not be confused with fashion, which refers to brief prevailing taste.

Advantages of Period Furnishings. Well-chosen traditional articles probably will not become passé with changes of fashion. The owner of good period furniture has the satisfaction of knowing that she has something that has been judged beautiful and has stood the test of time. Reproductions of superior period articles copied from museum pieces made by the world's most famous designers are usually available. Period furniture is fashionable; therefore stocks are large, and variety in price and style is obtainable in normal times. Since many dwellings are traditional in architecture, furniture of the same tradition is certain to be harmonious. Period furniture will be enjoyed and admired by the majority of those who see it, particularly the elderly.

Disadvantages of Period Furnishings. They are not harmonious with modern bathrooms and kitchens. They do not suit Modern architecture. They were designed to be handmade, not machine-made. They require more care than modern women should give them. They are not always comfortable. They were expressive of the times when they were made; they cannot be expressive of the twentieth century. They discourage the original designers of today. They prevent their owners from taking a part in the great revolution in style that is in progress.

77

SELECTING PERIOD FURNISHINGS

No one should buy furniture merely because it is antique or looks antique. Period furnishings should be regarded as having two distinctly different values, *historic* and *esthetic*. Furnishings, as well as architecture, sculpture, painting, clothing, and writing, are historical records of the ideals and practices of the people who produced them. Especially through their furniture are we able to picture their more intimate, daily lives. The things they created to supply their needs portray the character of the people and the state of civilization of their time. All authentic furnishings have *historic value*.

On the other hand, the *esthetic value* of period furnishings depends upon fine relation of parts, well-designed and suitable ornament, beautiful materials, good workmanship, and appropriate finish. There are many persons whose esthetic sense is so confused that they regard all old styles as beautiful and all new ones as ugly. The home maker should realize that mere authenticity is not nearly so important as beauty, except perhaps in a museum. Discrimination is as necessary in selecting period furniture as in selecting any other type. Veneration for the traditional styles sometimes prevents the proper critical analysis of their appearance.

It is usually advisable to buy correct reproductions of period furniture in preference to the so-called adaptations, as the original designs are usually the better. The furniture designer of today is not likely to feel the inspiration which prompted the designer of the original period, and his alterations may not be in sympathy with the original idea, for he is influenced by the possibilities of modern manufacturing and is aware of the great variety of design that is usable in an eclectic era.

However, period furniture must be revised enough to be comfortable if it is to be enjoyed. Although the traditional styles fulfilled perfectly the requirements of their own time, the seating furniture in particular must be upholstered to meet our standards of comfort. The most difficult esthetic problem for the user of traditional furniture is to select those pieces that have been modified to fit our present-day needs and yet have lost none of their beauty or character.

COMBINING PERIOD STYLES

Where traditional furnishing is used in a home several period styles are usually combined. Complete restriction to one style may lack individuality and seem stilted and monotonous. Furthermore, when any style was first created, it was probably used with pieces of the transitional period preceding it and also with imported pieces. The present interpretation need not be more pure than the original style was. See page 89 for illustrations.

Variety within unity is the goal to be set in combining styles, as in other art problems. Enough variety should be sought to give interest, but not enough to disrupt the unity. A lack of unity and a museum-like feeling result from furnishing different rooms in one house in widely varying styles.

The *art components* are excellent guides in combining period styles. Styles which agree in expressiveness, texture, scale, form, and color can be used together.

The *expressiveness* of combined styles should be in accord. For example, the playful Rococo cannot be combined with the stern Cromwellian. The popular eighteenth-century group consists of a variety of styles that all express the same feeling.

The *texture* of furnishings is involved in their assembling, for fine and coarse effects should not be combined. The kind of wood and the kind of upholstery material are important. For example, the elegance of a Sheraton mahogany chair is incompatible with the crudeness of a Tudor chair of oak.

Proper *scale* precludes the use of heavy and light styles together. Both size and weight are factors. For example, Renaissance and Neo-Classic forms have the same source, but their bulk is so different that they are not compatible.

Related *forms* are the most harmonious. Important differences in form indicate important differences in spirit.

Color is a guide of significance. The dark stains and rich colors of heavy furniture cannot be combined with the pale colors and gilt of delicate furniture.

The *international decorative movements* form a broad basis for combining furniture of different periods. In general, all Renaissance furniture is harmonious, all Baroque furniture is harmonious, and all Neo-Classic furniture is harmonious, regardless of nationality.

PERIOD FURNITURE

Distinct period styles evolved during each of the three great international decorative movements which developed in Italy and spread over Europe and to America. *The Renaissance movement* occurred in the fifteenth and sixteenth centuries; *the Baroque movement,* in the seventeenth and eighteenth; and *the Neo-Classic movement,* in the late eighteenth century. For descriptive and historical charts of period furniture, see pages 428 and 429.

An easy although not entirely accurate way to identify period furniture is as follows:

1. Large straight-legged = Renaissance (Ital., Span., Eng.).
2. Large curved-legged = Baroque (Italian, Louis XIV, Queen Anne, Chippendale).
3. Small curved-legged = Rococo (Louis XV, Chippendale).
4. Small straight-legged = Neo-Classic Pompeian (Louis XVI, Adam, Sheraton, Hepplewhite).
5. Splay or flare-legged = Neo-Classic Empire (Duncan Phyfe, Directoire, English Regency, some Empire).
6. Mixtures of all types = Victorian. Nineteenth century.

MODERN USE OF RENAISSANCE STYLES

Spanish Renaissance furniture is available for the Spanish type dwellings built in semi-tropical sections of the United States. Elaborate forms of Renaissance and Baroque furniture are sometimes combined in large, impressive dwellings and public buildings. A simple primitive type of Spanish colonial furniture is made for small houses or for those with a farm atmosphere. See page 106.

English Renaissance furniture is used in some large buildings, such as clubs and college buildings, especially those of Gothic architecture. See page 85. The English furniture should be supplemented by continental Renaissance items and also by more comfortable seating furniture. Both Tudor and Jacobean furniture are also suitable for early English houses but not for the Georgian. Cottage furniture of this type in oak may be used in simple homes. Good reproductions, as well as poor adaptations, of the furniture of this period are usually on the market. Early American furniture consists mostly of the simplified transplanted English Jacobean and Renaissance styles.

MODERN USE OF BAROQUE STYLES

The Baroque furnishings of Italy, Spain, and France may be combined in large Renaissance houses. The simpler English manifestations of Baroque are suitable in either large or small houses or apartments. Chinese lacquered pieces and wall paper are appropriate with this furniture, as they were used with the original.

Italian Baroque, an ornate but handsome style, can usually be combined with late Italian Renaissance, with which it agrees in scale and elegance, for use in impressive buildings.

Spanish Baroque is also combined with Renaissance in important Spanish buildings. Spanish pieces serve to add colorful notes to the furnishings of other lands along with fabrics, leather work, ceramics, and ironwork.

French Baroque is little used today except in palaces and hotels where the grand manner of Louis XIV is desired.

English Baroque furnishings are suitable in early Georgian and Colonial buildings. They are more homelike than the Continental. Chippendale furniture, suggesting elegance and cultivated taste, is well liked in America, and is used extensively in apartments as well as houses. The larger pieces of Chippendale are used with Queen Anne or Colonial furnishings. See pages 59 and 460. The more delicate examples are often combined with Neo-Classic Sheraton and Hepplewhite furniture, as at Mount Vernon. See page 477.

American Baroque or Colonial, which is about the same as the English Baroque, is a favorite style in the United States because of its historic interest and because of the comfortable, sturdy furniture it produced. It is the natural choice of furnishing for the modern Colonial houses of the Pre-Revolutionary type. The Williamsburg, Virginia, restoration provides an outstanding example of this style. See page 86.

Rococo. The furniture of the period of Louis XV in France is reproduced and used in some American women's clubs and similar places. It is also used in drawing rooms and bedrooms in Federal types of houses. The simple pieces finished in natural walnut go well with Chippendale's Rococo furniture. Americans usually want only a few French Rococo pieces to add interest and beauty to other furnishings of a sturdier character. See page 86.

MODERN USE OF NEO-CLASSIC STYLES

All the Neo-Classic styles can be combined successfully if they are properly scaled. They provide the logical furnishings for modern Post-Revolutionary (Adam) houses. They are also generally appropriate for houses and apartments of various degrees of impressiveness. They are the most popular of the period styles used in the United States, where they are usually known as *Federal.*

The Neo-Classic style comprises two types, the Pompeian furniture with straight legs, and the Empire furniture often with flaring legs. See pages 87, 88, and 90 for illustrations.

The Pompeian Neo-Classic. Derivations of the *Louis XVI* style are favorites with decorators because the small scale of such pieces as tables, commodes, and secretaries makes them adaptable to limited living space. Louis XVI is the logical style of furnishing for French houses in America.

Hepplewhite furniture fits very well into American homes of semi-formal or formal character. It can be combined with Chippendale furniture or with Sheraton. A variety of Hepplewhite furniture is available in the shops.

Sheraton furniture should be used in late Georgian or Federal homes with other eighteenth-century furnishings. It combines well with all light, graceful furniture that is mainly rectangular in form. This furniture is generally procurable at various prices.

The Empire Neo-Classic. The *Directoire* style is admired for its pure Classic lines, which sometimes flare outward even on case furniture. It is now usually possible to obtain this furniture in natural light wood or in painted versions. See page 88.

Empire furniture is not generally reproduced in its original form. Simplified pieces, reduced in size, are procurable, however. American Empire antiques are sometimes available; they are suitable for large rooms and large houses.

The *English Regency* is the latest favorite in this group. The furniture selected for reproduction is much like the Directoire and Empire but darker; in fact, some of it is black, touched with gilt.

Duncan Phyfe's designs have produced very popular furniture. His chairs, sofas, and tables are especially well liked and are suitable in many types of houses and apartments.

MODERN USE OF VICTORIAN STYLE

A detailed account of the way Victorian furniture is used today is given here, because little is known about it, and because it is very poor unless carefully chosen. An adventure into Victorian decoration is for the person who already owns some pieces of this furniture that can be redeemed from the attic and smartly re-upholstered. A person with considerable means might, however, be encouraged to experiment with the Victorian idea, if she finds it interesting, but the average woman who is gradually acquiring her permanent furniture cannot afford to indulge in a fashion which may be temporary.

It may seem strange that decorators are able to create some beauty through use of the Victorian style, which was itself usually lacking in merit. This result is possible because the decorators carefully select only certain items and place them in a setting of plain colorful walls and plain-colored carpets, instead of in the elaborate backgrounds of the original period. They usually try to retain the naïveté of the Age of Innocence. See page 88.

A few well-designed American Victorian furniture pieces are being used with only slight modification. Most common of these are oval-backed chairs and sofas with curved legs in the style of Louis XV. Their exposed wood frames are sometimes plain but often have restrained carving at the top of the oval. Smooth-textured modern fabrics have replaced horsehair. The deep biscuit tufting of the overstuffed hassocks and even their heavy cord fringe are copied, with restraint, however.

Numerous other Victorian pieces have been completely discarded in the interests of design and service. The modern home has no place for the bric-a-brac cabinets (whatnots), heavy marble-topped tables, melodions, and massive black walnut bedroom pieces. The lavish display of crimson and heavy gold and of monstrous floral patterns is seldom copied in the modern interpretations of the period.

Victorian windows were muffled in fringed and tasseled lace curtains and layers of draperies and overdraperies of heavy damasks, velvets, satins, or brocatelles. Modern designers omit all these, but they do imitate the old valances, side draperies, and the looped-back, crisscrossed glass curtains of sheer materials.

PROBLEMS

A sufficient number of problems are listed so that choices may be made.

1. Use tracings or clippings to show pieces of period furniture that would look well together.
2. Visit a furniture store, and make selections of furniture which could be used in the same room.
3. Analyze a dormitory living room to see if some pieces of furniture are incompatible with the others in scale, texture, or line.

READING REFERENCES

See also lists on pages 440, 458, and 474.

ARONSON, JOSEPH. *The Book of Furniture and Decoration.* Crown, 1936.

CLIFFORD, CHANDLER R. *Period Furnishings.* Clifford and Lawton, 1927.

GOULD, MR. and MRS. GEORGE G. *The Period Furniture Handbook.* Dodd, Mead, 1928.

MAAS, CARL. *Common Sense in Home Decoration.* Greenberg, 1939.

MILLER, GLADYS. *Decoratively Speaking.* Doubleday, Doran, 1939.

MORSE, FRANCES C. *Furniture of the Olden Times.* Macmillan, 1940.

SCHMITZ, HERMANN. *The Encyclopedia of Furniture.* McBride, 1926.

WENHAM, EDWARD. *Old Furniture for Modern Homes.* Studio, 1940.

WHITON, SHERRILL. *Elements of Interior Decoration.* Lippincott, 1937.

Spanish Renaissance furniture of the transition period probably inspired the furniture in the room at the left above. This oak furniture is suitable in houses of Spanish derivation. The wall paper is inconsistent in design.

Baroque furniture of the Chippendale style is shown above at the right. The cabriole or knee curve appears on all the legs. This elegant mahogany furniture should be accompanied by luxurious carpets. Note the wall shelf containing Oriental porcelains, which look well with original Chippendale furniture.

English Renaissance furniture is used in the living room of the men's dormitory pictured below. The heavy oak furniture is consistent with the texture of the rough bricks in the chimney and the beams in the ceiling. The leather upholstery agrees with the masculine character of the room. The crewel pattern in the curtains is correct in style. A Carolean chair stands under the picture. *Courtesy Northwestern University.*

The style of Louis XV in upper left inspired this simplified provincial example of Rococo furniture, which expresses femininity. The taffeta bedspread and the pastoral wall paper are appropriate. *Courtesy Drexels.*

The parlor in upper right of Professor George Wythe's restored home shows the use of straight-legged and curved-legged Chippendale furniture. *Courtesy Colonial Williamsburg, Inc.*

The French styles have been used successfully in this room, which is expressive of refinement and luxury. The straight-legged sofa is Louis XVI, and the curvilinear pieces are Louis XV. They combine well because they agree in scale and expressiveness. *Courtesy Arthur S. Vernay.*

Modified English Neo-Classic furniture of Sheraton influence has been used in the room above left. The secretary-desk is important enough to balance a fireplace or a group of windows. This is an effective formally balanced wall group. The framed pictures show that large mats are necessary for small pictures. *Courtesy George Moritz.*

Neo-Classic furniture has been successfully combined in the display above right. The shield-back Hepplewhite chairs, the two-pedestal Duncan Phyfe table, Sheraton sideboard, and fine Adam-type mirror provide variety within unity. *Courtesy Montgomery Ward.*

The Empire style inspired the room below. The impressive wall cabinet with its architectural pillars is the focus of interest. The pedestal center table is typical. The chair, coffee table, and sofa are attractive pieces. The two sculptured busts on the cabinet contribute a Classical Greek note. *Courtesy B. Altman Company.*

The Empire style furnished the inspiration for the room above left with its Modern Regency type dining-room furniture in black, yellow, and gold. The cupboard is well designed and is a convenient size for small apartments. The wall paper is gray with a green and yellow branch design on one wall only. The carpet is gray shag. *Courtesy Marshall Field.*

The picture above right shows the successful use of Directoire furniture in a Modern setting. The upholstery is pink-and-white-striped rayon; the dressing-table cover is white celanese voile over American Beauty moiré; the curtains are white celanese voile, and the walls are lime-green. The effect is youthful and feminine. *Courtesy Eaton's.*

Some Victorian furnishings have been used in the room below left. The tufted satin-covered sofa (a Louis XV revival) is pleasing in line. The tall chair (Empire revival) is unusual. The wall paper is consistent in style but deplorable in design. The small rug calls attention to the chief conversation center in this room.

Modernized period furniture is used in the room below right. The legs of the mirror-top coffee table are a stylized adaptation of Baroque. The handsome sofa is slip-covered, not upholstered, in blue rep bordered with loop fringe. Notice the careful location of the flower motifs in the curtain and valance. *Courtesy Bloomingdale's.*

A pleasing combination of period styles of the eighteenth century are used in the living room pictured above. The Sheraton table by the fireplace, the Baroque sofa, the Martha Washington armchair, and the Duncan Phyfe side chair agree in scale and texture. The cabinet behind the sofa that encloses the radiator is well balanced by the piano. The fabrics are attractive and harmonious, a successful contrast with the desirable plain carpet. The room expresses dignity and conservatism. *Courtesy Louisiana State University.*

An unsatisfactory combination of too many different styles occurs in the room below. In the first place the Modern mirrored fireplace invites only Modern furniture. The two angular Modern chairs do not agree in line or feeling with the other pieces. The oval Hepplewhite end table, the Empire (Greek) side chair, and the Louis XV chair with its back to the camera are smaller in scale and too delicate for the other pieces. The curved sofa is Modern, and the large chair with the wide upholstery stripes which do not suit the curves of the wooden frame is a bergère of the Louis XIV style. The drum table is English Baroque; the pedestals which precariously hold the lamps are Empire.

Baroque. Queen Anne fiddle-back chair, turned stretchers, ball and claw front feet. *Courtesy Edison Institute.*

Baroque. Chippendale. Cabriole curved knee, ball and claw feet on front legs. *Courtesy Edison Institute.*

American Baroque. Queen Anne upholstered wing chair. Cabriole curved legs.

Martha Washington armchair. Simplified version of Chippendale's Chinese style.

Neo-Classic. Early Hepplewhite. Modified heart-shaped back. Straight tapering legs with unusual stretchers.

American Empire. Duncan Phyfe. Flaring fluted front legs. Double horn-of-plenty motif on back.

CHAPTER 7

COTTAGE OR PROVINCIAL TYPES

Terminology. The term cottage types as applied to homes and home furnishings usually means all the small or unpretentious types except those that are Modern in style. These cottage types could also be classified as traditional; however, it is more convenient to consider them as a separate group. Provincial or rural types are those that developed away from the large cities; they are the opposite of urban. Peasant types are those used by the poor European farmers. Pioneer types are those made by early settlers on the frontiers of newly developed country. Provincial, rural, peasant, pioneer, or other cottage types are generally simplified versions of larger and more elaborate houses and furnishings found in the cities.

An important reason for the difference between urban and rural styles was that tools, materials, and funds were scarce in the country, and amateur carpenters were unskilled.

COTTAGE TYPES USED IN AMERICA

Various parts of the United States have developed distinct provincial types of houses. The outstanding reason for the development of dissimilar types was that immigrants reproduced the houses of their mother countries, especially where they were segregated in large communities. English, Dutch, French, Spanish, and Mexican immigrants all produced homes with native characteristics. Early American and Cape Cod cottages are English derivations built in New England; cottages of French design are common in southern Louisiana; small houses of the Spanish type are plentiful in the Southwest.

In Chapter 5 nearly all of these small houses are fully described along with their larger prototypes in order that their origins be easily understood. Cottage types that are in use in America today are listed in this chapter for review.

Early English (Tudor) cottages, described on page 65, are not recommended for use today. They are inconvenient in plan and poorly lighted. They are also costly and illogical for the materials and building methods of the present.

Early American houses, described on page 65, are being copied frequently. More windows are now added, and the overhanging second floor is featured.

Cape Cod cottages, described on page 67, are the most popular of the cottage types. They are recommended, for they have good adaptable basic design and are economical to build. See page 74.

Williamsburg type cottages are desirable. They are symmetrical and similar to Cape Cod houses. See page 76.

Dutch Colonial cottages, described on page 67, are used to some extent. They are generally well designed, featuring a two-slant gambrel roof extending over the porch, dormer windows, and conveniently low foundations. See page 74.

French Norman cottages, described on page 70, are not recommended. They are the picturesque type that is illogical, costly, and unsuitable for modern construction.

French Colonial cottages, described on page 70, have unfortunately not been copied very much. Whether the cottages are located along the Mississippi or the St. Lawrence Rivers, the design of the symmetrical façades, French windows, and setback porches is distinctive. The style is dignified and desirable especially for town houses. See page 76.

Mediterranean houses, described on page 68, are suitable for the Southwest. They are usually built around patios in the Spanish and Mexican traditions. See page 75.

American Indian houses provide suitable models only for the Southwest, where they are indigenous. They are built of large handmade adobe mud bricks which provide excellent insulation but cannot withstand rain. See pages 69 and 75.

An untrained person who has to select a design for a house without the help of an architect should consider one of the traditional cottage styles which are recommended, in order to avoid adding to the millions of ugly small houses already in existence. In addition to the traditional cottage styles listed above, however, small Modern and Non-Period houses, prefabricated or otherwise, should be seriously considered by prospective home owners.

AMERICAN PROVINCIAL FURNISHINGS

The provincial or cottage furniture of the United States is worthy of study and of reproduction. The country types are especially significant because they express the forthright character, the strength, and the usefulness of the lives of the country people themselves. In rural sections which had some contact with large cities, furniture makers often followed city fashions but simplified their products. However, in sections far from cities, furniture makers developed styles unrelated to those in general use; sometimes they were based on much earlier styles. These divergent developments result from various causes, such as the limitations of materials and tools, or the lack of skill of amateur craftsmen who also had to make their farm equipment and do their own blacksmithing. Wintertime, when there were no crops to care for, was devoted to crafts work. Women did their spinning, weaving, knitting, and sewing while the men did their furniture making.

Religious scruples against luxury or display affected some sections, resulting in severely simple, uncomfortable, unpadded, straight-line furniture. The chief reason for the development of dissimilar furniture styles, however, was the same as that which produced variety in houses—national tastes. English, Scotch, Dutch, German, Scandinavian, French, Spanish, and Mexican immigrants all made furniture with native characteristics, which has greatly enriched the complete picture of American provincial types of furnishings.

Unfortunately much of the original home-furnishing material of rural America has not been preserved, although some efforts have been made in this direction. The United States Government's Works Progress Administration was responsible for the Federal Art Project's Index of American Design which explored and recorded native American designs in home furnishings and other fields in twenty-eight states. Whereas some of the original articles are in museums and in protected old historical houses, many of the privately owned articles will be permanently lost unless they are put in museums or at least are photographed or copied.

The most important of the American provincial styles are described here. It is to be expected that designers and manufacturers may later promote different types which are now obscure.

Early American. This furniture is also called Pilgrim or seventeenth century. It was practically the same as early English cottage furniture, but the American-made articles were plainer and cruder. English and American pieces were equally uncomfortable; their owners considered comfort and luxury sinful. The American Wing of the Metropolitan Museum in New York City shows this furniture in original interiors. For further information about this primitive American furniture see page 439. This type has been reproduced in oak, pine, and fruit wood, and is generally available. See pages 209 and 240. It is well used in farm houses, Cape Cod cottages, and other unpretentious houses or apartments.

Dutch Colonial. The Dutch influence was strong around New York, on Long Island, and in New Jersey. There people made their domestic furniture like that of Holland. This simple curved-line furniture was rather heavy and was usually cottage or provincial in character. It was often made from the native wood which was left natural or was painted with naïve effects. Sometimes low-relief carving decorated these pieces, and either the pattern or the background was painted in bright colors. The kas or linen cupboard was a favorite article, as was also the high-back settle. See page 101. Rush-bottom chairs were painted black and were sometimes decorated with floral patterns. The more prosperous Dutch settlers imported imposing inlaid or lacquered pieces from Holland. The Brooklyn Museum has many interesting Dutch Colonial articles.

Provincial Colonial. This furniture style succeeded the Early American in most of the plainer city homes and in the country homes of the colonists of the Atlantic coast. It was a provincial version of the elegant mahogany furniture which featured Queen Anne and Chippendale designs. See page 102. The furniture was copied in inexpensive wood, such as maple, oak, and fruit woods, without ornamentation. Original pieces of this type are in the American Wing of the Metropolitan Museum. The many curved-leg maple pieces which we see in the shops today are reproductions of this provincial colonial furniture. They combine well with other cottage furniture, especially Early American, and are used extensively in Colonial cottages, in apartments, and in some dormitories. Since this style conveys a cottage atmosphere it is inappropriate for large pretentious homes or for formal hotels.

Spanish Colonial. Spanish colonists preceded the English, locating in what is now California, Arizona, New Mexico, Texas, and Florida. Their architecture and furnishings were patterned after those of Spain and Mexico, but were modified by Indian design, unskilled Indian labor, and crude materials. See pages 9, 75, and 106.

Spanish influences resulted in sparse use of furniture, with emphasis on textural variety and bold contrasts. The furniture in the missions was large, crude, and rectangular, but entirely appropriate. In the homes it was more varied, colorful, and light. Chairs upholstered in leather or painted in brilliant colors enlivened the shadowy interiors. The chests and vargueno cabinets were the most characteristic items. Original Colonial Spanish articles can be seen in many missions and museums.

The home furnishing of the Spanish colonists has had in this century an enthusiastic revival, followed by a reaction against it. Manufacturers made reproductions and adaptations, sometimes unfortunately stressing its more superficial features. Monterey furniture is one kind of Spanish Colonial. In Santa Fe and the vicinity Spanish Colonial furniture is well used with Indian and Mexican rugs, pottery, basketry, tinware, straw inlay work, and religious symbols. A worthy development of Spanish Colonial was the severe temporary Mission style.

Shaker. In the nineteenth century, the Shakers, an English religious sect, established colonies in the Atlantic states, particularly in Pennsylvania, New York, and Massachusetts, where some still live. They are exponents of healthful communal life and teach their members farming, carpentry, furniture making, weaving, and the other simple crafts necessary to make themselves self-sustaining. Their simple strong houses as well as their furniture, are plain, unadorned, and well constructed, designed solely for utility and suitability. It is made entirely of local woods—fruit, nut, pine, and maple. See page 263.

Shaker furniture is a truly American rural type which might well be used today where strong plain furniture is desired, as in farm houses, rustic houses, studios, cottages, or in men's dormitories. For use in a home it must be accompanied by a sufficient amount of overstuffed furniture, possibly in a straight line, nonperiod style, like a Lawson sofa.

Pennsylvania German. The German settlers in Pennsylvania naturally created homes as much as possible like those they had left in Germany and Switzerland. By 1750 they were well established and had built substantial houses, the main feature of which was a great hall or living room-kitchen. The fireplace crowned by an enormous log mantel was used for cooking, but heat was provided also by iron stoves, which were often decorated with biblical scenes cast in the iron.

The chief distinction of Pennsylvania German furniture was its colorful, painted decoration. It was generally made of walnut, but oak and pine were used occasionally. The furniture was like the German but had an American freedom in its decorative details. It was strong but not too bulky. Its ornamentation often consisted of turning and molding.

In the living rooms were large dressers which were open above to hold pewter and pottery, and closed below to form cupboards. Tables were of various kinds, including saw-buck tables, long oak refectory tables, tables with low stretchers, and round-topped, splay-legged tables. The chairs also had considerable variety, including solid panel-back, vase splat-back, and banister-back chairs, in addition to a well-known European peasant chair with raked legs and a solid, shaped back. See page 103.

Among the most interesting textiles of the Pennsylvania Germans was the hand-woven coverlet made by the traveling weaver, who carried his own book of designs. He lived with a family while he wove for them. Embroidered samplers and long homespun towels decorated with cross-stitching were hung on the walls as decorations. Fraktur work was illuminated handwriting used on birth, marriage, and death certificates, hymn books, and cards. Birds and tulips were favorite motifs for this work, as the bird represented the spirit and the tulip was the symbol of love.

One of the most famous Pennsylvania Germans, Henry William Stiegel, established the first flint or lead glass factory in this country in 1763 and sold his fine glass in all the Colonies.

The Pennsylvania Museum of Philadelphia has installed excellent original rooms and furnishings of the Pennsylvania Germans. Most of the information given here comes from the publications of the Pennsylvania Museum and the Pennsylvania German Folklore Society of Allentown, Pennsylvania.

Scandinavian Colonial. In the nineteenth century many Norwegian, Swedish, and Danish immigrants settled in Wisconsin, Minnesota, Iowa, the Dakotas, and Washington. Their first farm homes were usually dugouts or log cabins, which were soon replaced by frame houses. The pioneers made most of their plain, strong furniture, except the chests that had contained their clothing and food on the sea voyage. Log chairs, plain benches and stools, plain beds and sofas with slats, on which were placed ticks filled with straw, corn husks, or feathers, cradles with solid half-moon rockers, trestle tables, and cupboards with nail-pierced tin panels were typical pieces. Some of the furniture was stained or painted black, and sometimes it was decorated with painted rococo scrolls and flower motifs like those in Scandinavia.

Scandinavian Colonial furnishings can be studied in various museums. The Norwegian-American Historical Museum at Decorah, Iowa, contains extensive pioneer material. Swedish collections are located at the American Institute of Swedish Art, Literature, and Science in Minneapolis and in the Art Institute of Chicago. Scandinavian influence is illustrated in rooms on pages 104 and 105.

Southern Highlands. This term has been applied to the mountain region of eastern Tennessee and western North Carolina, overlapping the adjacent borders of Kentucky, Virginia, South Carolina, and Georgia. The inhabitants, who are mostly of Scottish descent, have retained their primitive pioneer culture to a remarkable degree, because of their geographical isolation and their limited resources and educational opportunities. Their log cabins were furnished with spool beds, turned-leg tables, cupboards of the dresser or hutch types, corner cupboards, high chests of drawers, blanket chests, wine cabinets, straight chairs, and mammy benches on rockers. The furniture was made of black walnut, maple, pine, cherry, or holly wood and was sometimes decorated slightly with grooves, moldings, or paint. Star, rope, barber-pole, bell-flower, diamond, and scroll motifs were employed.

Berea College in Kentucky, Berry College near Rome, Georgia, Pi Beta Phi Settlement School in Gatlinburg, Tennessee, Campbell Folk School, Brasstown, North Carolina, and many guilds, as well as shops, have promoted the revival of the beautiful old textiles, pottery, and basketry of this region. Such products are pleasing additions to any of the cottage types of furnishings.

FRENCH PROVINCIAL

During the Renaissance the furniture in the provinces of France was affected by this Italian influence. Later the court style of Louis XV also spread to all the provinces, but the Louis XVI style was less influential, and the Empire style had no effect outside urban centers. Isolated provinces retained older styles, but others followed the changing fashions of the court. When the court ceased to exist, the provinces continued with the styles then in vogue. The Renaissance style remained dominant in the provinces of Alsace, Brittany, Burgundy, Lyonnais, and Savoie; the Louis XIII style in Guienne and Gascony; the Louis XV style in Lorraine, Auvergne, and Limousin; the Dutch style in Flanders; and the typical French Rococo style in all the other provinces. However, there was a general national relationship in the furniture styles of all the provinces in spite of the diversification.

Provincial cabinet makers greatly simplified the court furniture, thereby often improving it. The limited furniture in most provincial homes usually consisted of chests, wardrobes, and cupboards made by the Joiners' Guild, and four-post beds, trestle tables, and straw-bottom chairs made by the Turners' Guild. Some pieces, such as armoires, rush-bottom chairs, and tables, were much alike throughout all the provinces. Others, such as cupboards, were affected by local needs and climatic conditions.

The brief résumé has not suggested the romance of French Provincial furniture. The gaily decorated bread holders hung on the wall in Provence, the rack suspended over the table to hold the spoons in Brittany, the master's chair in the Basque country, the table chests in Poitou, the gaily painted German furniture in Alsace, the cupboard beds in Brittany, the half-closed beds in Burgundy, the built-in furniture in Lorraine, the open-dresser shelves filled with Quimper pottery in Brittany, and the rose copper and brass kettles in the Dutch kitchens in Flanders are but a few of the fascinating things to read about or, better still, to see. Since provincial house museums are numerous in France, a person who is interested can find much material to study and enjoy.

Reproductions of French Provincial furniture are bourgeois in type rather than peasant. They are generally available in the United States but are expensive. See pages 106 and 300.

USE OF COTTAGE FURNISHINGS

Most Americans like informality and unpretentiousness; therefore they enjoy these qualities in home furnishings. Cottage furnishings are usually familiar in style and are regarded as a safe investment, not as a passing fashion. Furthermore they are obtainable in a wide range of prices, including some quite low.

Farm houses or ranch houses of the usual type are suitable backgrounds for cottage furniture. The simplicity and strength of this type of furniture are in accord with the purpose and character of a farm home. Cottage furniture is consistent, too, with sturdy homemade articles often necessary in a farm house. Weekend houses, mountain lodges, or other rustic houses usually require cottage furniture or carpenter-made furniture in keeping with the architecture.

Small houses, in town or country, normally call for cottage furniture. An unpretentious house implies the use of unpretentious furnishings. A Cape Cod house naturally indicates Early American furniture with additions in similar character if desired. Small apartments too are often furnished with cottage-type furniture. Some walls, such as knotty pine, suggest cottage furniture just as apartments with a dignified period background call for elegant period furniture.

A successful cottage interior requires the clearcut organization of all the *art elements*. It needs particularly a strong *central color* to unify it. *Textures* may be rough and bold, but textural unity must be secured. Variety in *form* is desirable, such as Windsor chairs with a trestle table. Adherence to consistent *scale* is necessary too. *Pattern* interest is provided by flowery peasant motifs. See page 59. The total result in a cottage room should be a positive statement, for uncertainty or scattered effort undermine it. Simplicity is the keynote of cottage furnishings.

Amateurs can go far astray in the use of peasant or primitive furnishings since they are likely to be most interested in the quaint elements that are involved. Placing a spinning wheel, a cobbler's bench, or an old kitchen kettle in a present-day living room makes the place seem like a stage setting or a museum instead of a home. Plain common sense is an excellent guide in the selection of cottage or primitive furnishings.

PROBLEMS

A sufficient number of problems are listed so that choices may be made.

1. Trace a picture of a piece of Early American cottage furniture.
2. Trace a picture of a piece of French Provincial furniture.
3. Trace a simple painted decoration of Pennsylvania German origin.
4. Design a cottage-type floral decoration in a playful spirit for your kitchen cabinet doors or for bathroom or closet doors.
5. Make a design for a pieced quilt.

READING REFERENCES

ANDREWS, E. D. and FAITH. *Shaker Furniture.* Yale University Press, 1937.

BOSSERT, HELMUTH T. *Peasant Art in Europe.* Weyhe, 1924.

CAHILL, HOGER. *American Folk Art.* Museum of Modern Art, 1932.

COLEMAN, LAURENCE V. *Historic House Museums.* American Association of Museums, 1933.

CORNELIUS, CHARLES O. *Early American Furniture.* Appleton-Century, 1926.

DOWNS, JOSEPH. *Hand Book of the Pennsylvania German Galleries in the American Wing, Metropolitan Museum of Art.*

EATON, ALLEN H. *Handicrafts of the Southern Highlands.* Russell Sage Foundation, 1939.

EATON, ALLEN H. *Immigrant Gifts to American Life.* Russell Sage Foundation, 1932.

HOLME, CHARLES. *Peasant Art in Sweden, Lapland, and Iceland.* The Studio, 1910.

KETTEL, RUSSELL H. *Pine Furniture of Early New England.* Doubleday, Doran, 1929.

LONGNON, H. A., and HUARD, F. W. *French Provincial Furniture.* J. B. Lippincott, 1927.

ROABACKER, EARL F. *Pennsylvania Dutch Stuff.* University of Pennsylvania Press, 1944.

WILLIAMSON, S. G. *The American Craftsman.* Crown, 1940.

Early American furniture is used in this kitchen in Longfellow's Wayside Inn, which was purchased and restored by the late Henry Ford. The slat-back, rush-seated chairs and the trestle table are typical pieces. The high fireside settle is Dutch Colonial. The open-top cupboard is a Welsh dresser. *Courtesy Edison Institute.*

The Longfellow parlor of the Wayside Inn pictured below has furniture of several types. The gate-leg table is Early American (English); the sturdy chairs are provincial Colonial—simplified versions of Chippendale. Hand-made hooked rugs are suitable with the cottage-type furniture and wide floor boards.

Provincial Colonial furniture is used in the comfortable cottage living room shown above. Plain maple is substituted for the originals of Queen Anne and Chippendale. The low windows, short curtains, and one wall of wood suit the cottage atmosphere. Note the attractive wall paper on one wall. *Courtesy Amsterdam Textiles.*

This room illustrates the present use of Early American furniture. Each piece is well designed. The flower pictures are hung in relation to the sideboard. The whole room is unified by the bold use of red-and-white-checked gingham. *Courtesy Rich's, Atlanta.*

Pennsylvania German furniture is used in this room, which was taken from the house of the miller at Millbach. The furniture is strong and pleasing in design. The fabrics are consistent. The framed sampler and Fraktur paintings have naïveté and beauty.
Courtesy the Pennsylvania Museum of Art.

This modern interpretation of Pennsylvania German has charm and sincerity. The furniture was copied from original pieces. Especially interesting are the bread-mixing trough, the hanging cupboard, the spoon rack, and the chairs. *Courtesy Cedric Gibbons.*

The cottage interior above at the left is suitably furnished with sturdy cottage furniture. The table setting is appropriate; the textures of the wooden bowl, pewter plates, and coarse mats agree with one another and with the room. *Courtesy Carson, Pirie, Scott.*

The dark Scandinavian chest was the inspiration for the room above at the right. Students in the author's classes decorated the muslin wall panels with wax crayons and also painted the furniture. The table and benches are home made.

In the picture below Early American furniture of maple looks well with knotty pine walls. The curtains, upholstery fabrics, and rag rug harmonize with one another and with the furniture. *Courtesy Heywood-Wakefield.*

Entertaining adaptations of Scandinavian elements in home furnishing are introduced in the room above. Typical floral and scroll motifs are painted on the long trestle table and on the exaggerated frame around the shadow box. Bird and feather motifs are used on the curtains and centerpiece. *Courtesy Lord and Taylor.*

The vexing question of how to make the modern kitchen take on a cottage atmosphere is solved below. The painted wall, window frame, and chest, the board surfacing, and the huge drawer pulls are gay and young. When the baby's pen is no longer needed, the alcove will be used for dining. *Courtesy Hans Van Nes.*

Distinctive Spanish Colonial furniture and decorative tin light fixtures from Mexico lo
their best in a house of harmonious style. The adobe walls, beamed ceiling, and tile floor
the room above are Spanish Colonial features indigenous to the Southwest.
Courtesy William Y. Peters.

French provincial furnishings and background are shown below. Note the practical ch
arms with wooden uprights to protect the upholstery. The extension table and the op
cupboard are strong, well-designed pieces. The attractive carpet has a hooked-rug patte
which is suitable with provincial furniture. The curves in the furniture are repeated in t
interior architecture. *Courtesy Eaton's, Toronto, Canada.*

CHAPTER 8

THE MODERN STYLE

The twentieth century is seeing the development of a new type of architecture, home furnishings, and other products, which are as unadorned and effective as the machines that inspired and produced them. This style is sometimes called Contemporary, International, Functional, or Twentieth Century; however, the term Modern is the one most generally used. The related term Modernism is in good standing, whereas Modernistic has come to refer to a superficial imitation of genuine Modern productions.

Those who maintain that Modernism is only another fad or fashion do not realize that it is a part of that basic change, the great industrial revolution brought on by the machine. The present generation can observe the beginning of a broad new culture, an experience that comes very seldom to the human race. No intelligent person can afford to be unaware of the constant evolution of this great change in which everyone can participate at least as a consumer and spectator.

This new expression is based on that creation of man which is now the dominant one in his life—the machine. Skilful engineering, while striving for perfect functioning, incidentally created a type of beauty peculiar to its products. Esthetics has correspondingly expanded to include appreciation of new proportions, functionalism, simplicity, and honesty in materials.

The speed and directness of the spirit of this century are expressed in the lines of airplanes, automobiles, skyscrapers, dwellings, home furnishings, and many other products. The same spirit is expressed in the new forms in the arts of sculpture, painting, music, and literature. It would be strange indeed if the tremendous changes of this century did not result in a revolution in taste, when there has been a revolution in our manner of living, in our ethical standards, and in our social attitudes.

MODERN USE OF MATERIALS

Modern architects and designers employ the marvelous new materials and also make more dramatic use of old ones. Each material seems to have its own special expressiveness; each one responds in its own way to machine processes. The textures of materials are important to Modern designers.

Wood is a favorite material for Modern walls and furniture. Naturalness, pleasing color, interesting texture, quietness, warmth, lightness, and malleability are some good qualities of wood. Modern designers feature the woods with beautiful grain and color. Bentwood and laminated wood are used in making distinctive new forms in Modern furniture. Modern methods of impregnating wood with resins make the wood much stronger than before.

Metal is now second to wood in Modern interiors but will probably supersede it eventually. It is stronger than wood and can be equally light in weight. It will withstand the heat and dryness of our homes. It can be molded into any form and can be as beautiful as wood if properly designed. Aluminum is one of the metals that serves in many new ways. Chromium is valued for its extreme hardness and also because it will not rust, stain, or corrode; its alloy, stainless steel, has become indispensable. Monel metal, an alloy of nickel and copper, valuable for its durability and resistance to corrosion and chemicals, is used on sinks, drainboards, and tables. Metal fireplaces are logical and are often handsome. Greater use of metals would be a desirable development in interior design.

Plastics of various kinds, the products of synthetic chemistry, are the most exciting materials of our time. Among the plastics are the cellulose compounds, ureas, caseins, acetates, and many others. Various synthetic materials are used for window screens, wall coverings, flooring, furniture, sinks, refrigerators, fabrics, lamps, dishes, and many other articles.

Glass is peculiarly characteristic of the Modern house, where it is used for exterior walls, partitions, mirror walls, sliding doors, windows, and furnishings. Repetition of the sparkle of glass in various places can bring unity and lightness to a Modern interior. The precise planes of glass make it combine well with metals and with other modern materials. Some designers are looking forward to a great age of glass.

MODERN ARCHITECTURE

For centuries the world has been looking backward in architecture and producing chiefly revivals of the Classic style with occasionally a Gothic or Romanesque interval. It remained for an American architect, *Louis Sullivan,* to break the spell and declare the independence of architecture. In the eighteen nineties in Chicago he practiced his theory, which was to express the life of his own time. He realized that materials and techniques of the machine age were to revolutionize building and require the union of the engineer and architect. His most famous biographer said, "Louis Sullivan gave America the skyscraper as an organic work of art."

Frank Lloyd Wright, who was Sullivan's student, carried his ideas to completion, founded the worldwide movement in Modern architecture, and became America's greatest architect. See page 122. Kuno Francke, a German exchange professor, published a book on Wright's architecture in 1910 while he was still practically unknown in America. This book inspired the development of Modern architecture in Europe by such men as Le Corbusier of France, Oud of Holland, and Gropius of Germany. Gropius and Breuer, Aalto and Saarinen of Finland, and Ruthenberg of Sweden are among those who later came to America to continue their work.

The United States leads the world in Modern architecture, which is acknowledged to be a genuine American production, free from European traditions. Modern architecture is democratic in principle. It does not imitate the palaces of rulers; on the contrary, it expresses itself in great projects like the dams of the Tennessee Valley Authority which are for the people's welfare.

Frank Lloyd Wright inspired many architects; current periodicals and books show their work. *Public buildings* in particular are built in the Modern style in every state in the union. In *multiple-housing projects* of the federal government progressive architects have found their best opportunities for experimentation. The government recognizes that adequate housing will help to solve the social, economic, and political problems of the underprivileged. *Dwellings* that are good examples of Modern architecture are built in the most progressive sections of the country. Unfortunately the American public is slow in appreciating Modern houses.

Modern architecture is expressive of life today. The architect interprets the social and economic structure of his time as a basis for his work. Through its design Modern architecture proclaims its own purpose and spirit as well as its own engineering and materials. Integration of art, science, and life is its aim.

Rightness of Modern architectural form derives from the architects' success in achieving the right space organization, right functioning, right materials, and right techniques. In making their decisions architects are guided, but not dominated, by the necessities of their problems. Their individual interpretations prevent the Modern style from becoming stereotyped.

That *function determines form* is the basic principle of Modern architecture. A bank should look like a bank, not like a Greek temple. Analysis of function is the scientific and also the commonsense approach to Modern building design.

Materials that have helped to shape Modern architecture are steel, concrete, and glass. Whereas previously walls had to be strong enough to uphold the roof and the upper floors, now a steel skeleton alone can carry the weight of the building and the walls can be merely glass, to provide shelter. This permits freedom and lightness in building. The new metals, compositions, and plastics are also important in Modern construction. Modern building utilizes materials simply and honestly in accordance with their natures, never imitating other materials.

Standardization of manufactured parts is an important element in Modern building. The National Bureau of Standards has helped to standardize sizes. Plumbing, windows, doors, pre-cut lumber, bricks, and other materials are planned to fit the same dimensions, which are known as a unit of *modular design.*

Engineering techniques have predetermined many aspects of Modern building. Frank and direct construction are guiding principles. Technologies change with new methods and new materials. Continuous progress is the essence of Modern architecture.

Standardization of building codes throughout the nation is an objective of extreme importance. Antiquated laws in many states prevent construction by Modern methods.

A new conception of space is a factor in planning Modern buildings. Spatial organization and continuity are important objectives in Modern dwellings as well as in large buildings.

MODERN DWELLINGS

Modern homes are expressive of the kind of life that goes on within them and around them. Materials, methods of building, and designs should be as up to date as the generation using them.

Climatic and geographic conditions influence Modern dwelling designs. Regional interpretations of Modern houses are being built; for example, where lumber is the traditional building material, it is used in a modern manner. The earliest Modern houses expressed chiefly functional and structural honesty and consequently were sometimes too severe. The later houses are better designed because they are lower and more horizontal in line, and show more variety and individuality. The roofs of Modern houses are usually flat, hipped, or with a single slope. Windows are large and plentiful and located in bands, on corners, or wherever needed.

An important characteristic of the Modern house is that it invites its occupants out of doors, through many doorways to the various sheltered living areas adjoining the house. Indoor and outdoor space are well integrated through the use of large windows or glass walls and projecting flat roofs or vertical wall extensions. See pages 191, 192, and 193.

A good Modern house is the result of organic planning, starting from the interior and letting a plan grow naturally out of the functional requirements of the members of a family. Elimination of partitions is a practical feature. The living room, dining room, hall, and music room are now often planned as one room, sometimes with partial partitions for various functional areas. A Modern house is uncluttered because of the ample storage space provided in special partitions and many closets.

Formerly separate enclosed rooms were necessary for heating purposes, but central heating has now obviated this problem. Two of the new methods of heating are *radiant heating* which emanates from pipes laid in subfloors, walls, or ceilings, and *solar heating* in which sunlight falling on glass walls or large windows helps to heat the house. Double glass provides the necessary insulation. Air cooling is an important modern feature in some climates.

The Modern house of today is true to its time, place, and purpose. The Modern house of tomorrow will no doubt be different from today's because of new materials and prefabrication.

MODERN INTERIOR DECORATION

European Developments. During the first century of machine fabrication the articles produced were generally copies of hand-made things. They were often highly decorated with imitations of handwork. The ugliness of nineteenth-century machine products was so pronounced that an artist, William Morris, and a group of reformers in England tried to revive medieval handicrafts to take the place of machine-made things. Naturally their project failed for handwork can play only a small part in a Machine Age.

Traditional forms and decorative patterns were in general use before 1900. At that time a Paris exposition introduced to the world the *Art Nouveau movement*, which had developed in Belgium and consisted mostly of new and elaborate surface decoration.

In 1925 *Paris* again held an international exposition of Modern decorative art. The products exhibited were Modern in form but were usually highly ornamented. The influence of this exhibition spread over Europe and to America.

Austria produced the Viennese Secession movement, a novel decorative fashion, brought to New York by Joseph Urban.

Sweden exhibited outstanding Modern work at the Paris exhibition of 1925. She not only has produced artistic, functional, and inexpensive articles, but also has taught her people to appreciate and buy them. For an account of this achievement read "Why Sweden Leads in Design" by Anna Rutt in the *American Magazine of Art*, April, 1933.

Norway, *Denmark*, and *Finland* have made contributions to the development of Modern architecture, glassware, ceramics, silver, textiles, rugs, and furniture. Some outstanding Scandinavian architects and craftsmen have now located in America.

Germany made an important contribution to the Modern movement through the Bauhaus, which was established at Weimar. The Bauhaus was a school where architecture, home furnishings, sculpture, and painting were unified in design, so that a house and its furnishings constituted a unit. This work was coldly intellectual and basically sound, for it was founded on science, art, and life. Hitler disapproved of the Bauhaus; therefore in 1933 it was transferred from Germany to the United States. Among its leaders was Walter Gropius, a teacher of architecture at Harvard University.

American Development. In 1925 the United States had no examples of products which were Modern in design to send to the Paris Exposition. American manufacturers, however, exhibited Modern home furnishings in the Modern buildings of the Chicago Exposition in 1933.

Manufacturers finally realized that the public was dissatisfied with the appearance of manufactured commodities, and so the industries began to employ artists to design articles for mass production. Automobiles, plumbing fixtures, stoves, refrigerators, furniture, and hundreds of smaller articles were among those that were redesigned. The artists were known as industrial designers, and the new profession industrial designing arose in the third decade of the twentieth century. Norman Bel Geddes, an artist with vision and ability, opened the first studio and research laboratory of industrial design in New York City. Another outstanding designer, Walter Teague, has had remarkable success.

Some artists have specialized in designing home furnishings; among them, Donald Deskey was one of the first to distinguish himself. Many other designers, including some architects, have made valuable contributions to furniture designing.

Modern designers plan articles suitable for mass production by machine, a process that Americans have perfected. The designers seek also to produce good appearance and perfect functioning, so that many thousands of people will want the products, will be able to afford them, and will find them satisfactory. This effort to incorporate art into all common everyday manufactured things makes the machine a medium for uniting art and life. This is a great achievement, because for several centuries art has not been closely related to life; it has been considered an attribute peculiar to painting, sculpture, and architecture. If art could be produced in common things for the common people standards of taste might eventually be raised so that only things of beauty would be made.

Unfortunately too many American manufacturers do not employ designers who understand the esthetics of designing for the machine. They prefer to copy their old traditional designs, whereas they could give much better values if they used designs intended for mass production. They would then also make an important contribution to the present revolution in taste, which has been inspired by the machine itself.

The Modern interior designer has an architectonic rather than a decorative point of view concerning interiors and furnishings. The most important tenet is absolute *unity*, or totality of impression, with close relationship of all the parts employed. Modern rooms are often unified by continuous horizontal *lines*, which are kept as low as possible so as not to detract from the architectural effect of the walls. Repetition of *forms* as well as lines help to establish unity. Unity of *idea* is achieved if every item portrays the present Machine Age. See page 121 for an illustration.

Structural integrity requires the perfect relationship of functionalism and mechanization. The form of a Modern article of furnishing is first of all functional. It must also be suitable to machine production, gaining as much beauty and utility as possible from the machine tooling. The design must, moreover, permit honest and appropriate use of materials.

In addition to observing these fundamentals the Modern interior designer makes creative use of texture and color. *Texture* is the surface element, which is stressed in Modern interior design. Rich, subtle effects are obtained by means of texture contrasts in materials. The gleam of glass, the dull softness of cork, the cold hardness of metal, the unevenness of textured carpets and fabrics, the warm plasticity of leather, and the smoothness of bleached waxed wood are elements that can be utilized to give variety within unity. Texture now takes the place formerly filled by surface ornamentation.

Color is usually subservient to form in Modern interiors. Monochromatic neutral colored rooms, sometimes with the addition of one brilliant color, are favored by some decorators. Others prefer low-valued, simple colors. Those who consider Modern interiors cold and bare can counteract this effect by means of fresh warm colors. Modern designers make good application of the advancing and recessive qualities of color.

Surface decoration is not desirable in Modern furnishings, for the machine does not produce it easily or appropriately. One important credo of the Machine Age is that design is not applied to an object but is brought out of it. In Modern interiors very little pattern is used, although fabrics sometimes have geometric or abstract patterns. Modern designers consider that surface decoration may prevent full realization of the form of a beautiful object.

In the architectural approach a room is considered a potential composition in space. Positive volumes of furnishings and negative vacant spaces are balanced. Accents are made by close, compact groups of functional furniture, either built in or movable, with ample distance between groups, an arrangement that adds spaciousness as well as comfort. These groups are located for efficiency first and then are given due consideration for appearance. Open floor spaces are regarded as assets in Modern designing.

In small quarters certain Modern furnishings are particularly serviceable. A row of contiguous sectional pieces, such as cabinets, desks, or chairs, can occupy one entire wall. They can even be stacked several units high in places. They are so designed that no matter how they are grouped the total effect is one of well-organized relationship. See page 260. Convertible tables, beds, and cabinets, which serve dual purposes, are space-savers.

Modern furniture is clear-cut in line and is based on fundamental geometric forms: cubes, pyramids, and spheres. Increase in the use of curves is predicted because relaxed lines are gaining favor. Modern furniture is low. Probably automobile seats first made us aware of the comfort of low chairs and sofas. Furniture is also fairly large, especially those anchored chairs and sofas which count architecturally. Built-in furniture is deservedly popular in Modern houses (page 10) because it can be designed to fit a given place. Modern interiors are shown on pages 26, 61, 120, and 279.

Modern furniture is now available in such adaptations as Chinese, Swedish, or Tropical Modern. See page 261. These modified types are preferred by those who want softer effects than are obtainable with the purely functional Modern style. Since the entire Modern movement is a dynamic evolving style, changes in it must be expected. Modern furnishings should always be fresh, original, and stimulating, evoking an emotional response in the beholder.

Modern furnishings are growing in popularity, particularly among young people who want the sleekness and efficiency of the motor car repeated in their homes. They realize that a simple functional background requires a minimum of attention and saves valuable time for essential work or recreation. Modern furnishings are expressive of the self-confidence and directness of youth. The uncluttered effect of Modern interiors may be of special benefit as an antidote to the confusion in a complicated world.

PROBLEMS

A sufficient number of problems are listed so that choices may be made.

1. Visit a Modern house or apartment, and write a report about it.
2. Design the front view of a Modern house.
3. With blocks of wood build a solid miniature Modern house.
4. From a large bar of soap carve a miniature Modern house.

1. Visit a furniture store and study Modern furnishings.
2. Study catalogs of Modern furnishings.
3. Design a row of contiguous pieces of Modern furniture.
4. Bring to class some small Modern article and analyze it.

READING REFERENCES

BEHRENDT, WALTER C. *Modern Building*. Harcourt, Brace, 1937.

FORD, J., and FORD, K. M. *The Modern House in America*. Architectural Publishing Co., 1940.

GIEDION, SIGFRIED. *Space, Time, and Architecture*. Harvard University Press, 1941.

HITCHCOCK, H. R., and JOHNSON, P. *The International Style*. Norton, 1932.

NELSON, GEORGE, and WRIGHT, HENRY. *Tomorrow's House*. Simon and Schuster, 1945.

SULLIVAN, LOUIS HENRY. *The Autobiography of an Idea*. American Institute of Architects, 1924.

WRIGHT, FRANK LLOYD. *Modern Architecture*. Princeton University Press, 1931.

BAYER, H., and GROPIOUS, W. A. and I. *Bauhaus, 1919-1928*. Museum of Modern Art, 1938.

CHENEY, SHELDON and MARTHA. *Art and the Machine*. Whittlesey, 1936.

DREYFUSS, HENRY. *Ten Years of Industrial Design. 1929-1939*. Pynson, 1939.

GENAUER, EMILY. *Modern Interiors: Today and Tomorrow*. Illustrated Editions, 1939.

JOHNSON, PHILIP. *Machine Art*. Museum of Modern Art, 1934.

READ, HERBERT E. *Art and Industry*. Harcourt, Brace, 1935.

ROBSJOHN-GIDDINGS, TERENCE H. *Goodbye, Mr. Chippendale*. Knopf, 1944.

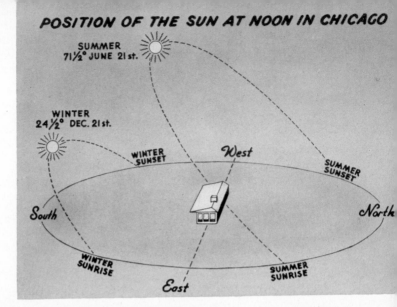

POSITION OF THE SUN AT NOON IN CHICAGO

SUMMER
71½° JUNE 21st.

WINTER
24½° DEC. 21st.

WINTER SUNSET

West

SUMMER SUNSET

South

North

WINTER SUNRISE

SUMMER SUNRISE

East

The diagram above illustrates the principle of solar heating for houses. The extending eaves (overhang) which will shade a south wall in summer will not shade it in winter, because the position of the sun is different then. Double glass walls provide effective insulation. *Courtesy Libbey Owens Ford.*

The model below shows a small house designed for modern living. The use of identical flooring indoors and out, the abundance of glass, and the many openings help to integrate the house with its surroundings. *Courtesy Cranbrook Academy of Art.*

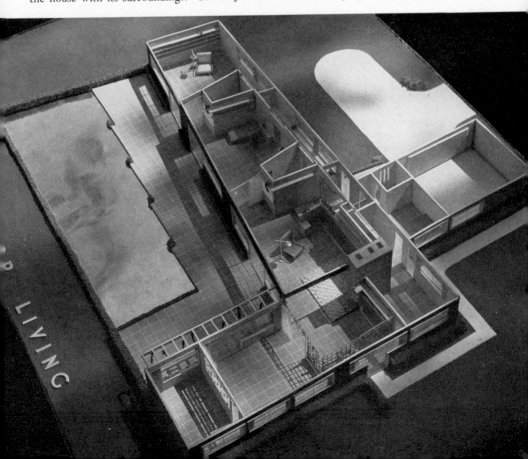

LIVING

For his home in Massachusetts Walter Gropius designed this Modern house which was somewhat influenced by the fact that his neighbors have white Colonial houses. Note the pleasing proportions. Horizontality is emphasized in the flat roof and windows. Walter Gropius was the leader of the Bauhaus (Modern) school and now teaches architecture at Harvard University. He has made valuable contributions in the field of prefabrication of houses.
Courtesy Walter Gropius, architect and owner.

The prefabricated demountable low-cost house below is well designed and will be attractive when properly landscaped. Such houses should be made by hundreds of thousands for low-income families. Electric wires should be in tubes underground, not on ugly poles.
Courtesy Federal Housing Authority.

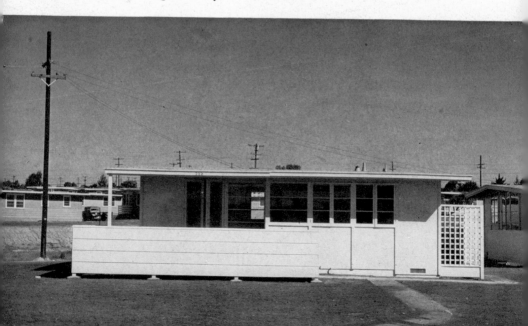

Both these houses, designed by Richard J. Neutra, show glass walls and extending roofs to shade them in summer. The house above illustrates a type of Modern which employs natural wood exterior surfacing. This adds texture and color interest and fits well into the landscape. Notice the contrast of large unbroken vertical areas against the horizontal bands. The view below reveals the multiple-purpose recreation room as seen from the patio of Mr. Neutra's home in Los Angeles. The glass wall between them is movable.

Modern open planning has eliminated walls between living and dining areas in small homes; well-designed unit furniture is here arranged to separate the two areas. Bookshelves are placed back to back with dish shelves of equal height. *Courtesy Montgomery Ward.*

This Modern bedroom furniture is effective and functional. The pictures over the beds are well hung and repeat the floral motif of the bedspreads. *Courtesy Marshall Field.*

This Modern low-cost furniture is used for dining and for study in a studio living room. The chair seats are made of the same rose-red webbing that supports the photographs along the wall. Rose-red light brightens the inside of the bookcases. The owner's hobby, which is photography, has been well utilized.

A masculine interpretation of Modern furnishings which are beautiful in form and texture is shown in the room below. The painting by Braque dominates the room and provides the color scheme, which is largely in gold. The treatment of the fireplace wall shows excellent use of natural variations in the material. The architectural chairs, the stylized skull-and-horn wall lights of Lucite, and the Chinese sculpture are unusual. *Courtesy Samuel Marx, architect.*

Frank Lloyd Wright designed this beautiful dramatic Modern house over a waterfall near Bear Run, Pennsylvania. It fits well into its setting, partly because the heavy horizontal masses in the rocks are repeated in the house. Note the beauty of the photographic composition.

PART THREE

PRACTICAL HOME PLANNING

CHAPTER 9

HOME LANDSCAPING

A brief section on selecting a lot and landscaping the grounds is necessary in a book about homes, because the home does not stop at the walls of the house but includes the entire grounds.

SELECTING THE SITE

The *objectives* that are sought in all phases of home planning should serve as a guide in the selection of a site for the house. The site must *function* as regards convenience for the family. It should be *expressive* of the same character as the house that has been planned. It should in addition have some claim to *beauty* or distinction which will lift it out of the ordinary. Finding a site with these requirements naturally takes a long time. With a definite goal in mind the search is more likely to be successful.

The choice of a site is influenced by the *character of the house* to be built. Exposed city lots are suitable for conventional, impersonal, formal houses and planting. Suburban settings fit semiformal personal houses. Country acres are best for friendly, picturesque, rambling, rustic houses. In other words, a city site demands restraint, a suburban lot less restraint, and a country site very little restraint. Dramatic settings, where both glass walls and privacy would be possibilities, and where traditional houses would not crowd them, are needed for very Modern houses. Sites that agree with them in character should be found for traditional houses.

Topography suggests definite ideas. A flat lot implies conventionality and formality; a hillside lot suggests irregularity and originality; a small sloping lot bespeaks intimacy; a hilltop with a view connotes spaciousness and strength. A valley site is usually considered to be less desirable than one that is higher.

The *neighborhood* of a home site is of great importance. A house should be located among others of its size, age, and cost. Neighbors with the same standards of living usually are harmonious and sociable. In any neighborhood restrictions and zoning are necessary. It is not well to buy in an undeveloped tract, for it may develop badly. It is unwise to buy in an old section that has passed its prime, for depreciation will set in and values fall. It is advisable to buy in a very large residence tract so that business sections will not enclose it, but stores, schools, transportation, churches, and parks should be within convenient reach.

Spaciousness is so valuable that some conveniences should be sacrificed to obtain it, particularly for children. A large lot helps to provide quiet and privacy as well as space for activities. Sometimes a highly desirable half-acre or more on the outskirts of a town costs no more than a small single lot closer in.

Exposure and outlook require careful consideration. A lot facing south is required for a living room on the front of the house, whereas a lot facing north requires the living room to be on the rear or at one side. Naturally a view of a park, lake, stream, ravine, or mountain is of great value. Full-grown trees on the lot are assets for beauty as well as for comfort.

Good drainage is essential, as a damp swampy location is bad for the health and is otherwise also generally undesirable. A slight slope is sometimes advantageous for drainage and for appearance; however, a slope often adds to the cost and difficulty of building and landscaping. A south and west slope is better than a north and east slope. A site sloping up from the street is better than one sloping down from the street or sideways. Solid, well-settled earth under the foundation of the house is so essential that this feature requires expert investigation.

When a satisfactory lot has been located thorough investigation must be made of the *title, assessments, taxes, restrictions, easements, survey,* and the *public utilities.* The lot should be appraised by a bank, mortgage company, building and loan association, or government agency, in order to determine whether the price is reasonable. The site should ordinarily be worth about 20 to 25 per cent of the total value of the house, but only 5 or 10 per cent if the utilities are not yet installed.

LANDSCAPING THE GROUNDS

The purpose of landscaping is to make the grounds around a house *usable* for outdoor living and to create an appropriate *setting for the house*. Successful landscaping provides the maximum of livability and beauty the year round for the minimum of care.

Landscape design of today is expressive of the *philosophy of the present*. We believe in living outdoors as much as possible for reasons of health, also for the spiritual refreshment of close contact with nature, and for the esthetic satisfaction obtained from spaciousness and natural beauty. Therefore our landscaping is designed to draw us outdoors and to keep us there, providing play space and exercise space for different age levels.

The same elements and principles of art and the objectives that are the basis for planning houses and interior design apply also to landscape design. Simple and direct use of mass, color, and texture produces the best gardens of today, whereas formerly they were dependent on a complex plan for their beauty. Like the other arts, landscape design has discarded elaborate details for functional and logical simplicity. Exhibition-type gardens are out of date.

If the owner can afford it, *a landscape architect* should be employed to design the landscaping of a home. The trained person can organize the space properly, recommend the most suitable plants, and see possibilities not evident to the layman. The landscape architect should be engaged at the same time as the architect, for the two should work together from the beginning, in order that the house plans and garden plans be well integrated. The cost of good landscaping is repaid not only by increased functional and esthetic value but also by the increased monetary value of the property itself and of the neighborhood.

The layman who is planning to landscape his own property would be helped immensely by a few hours of on-the-ground advisory service by a landscape architect. It should be noted that a horticulturist or a nursery man is not a landscape designer although either can usually provide invaluable information about plants. The amateur designer should read several good books on landscape design, should attend garden tours, and should observe photographs in the garden periodicals. Some elementary information about landscape designing for homes is offered here.

PLANNING

Landscaping begins with careful consideration of the *characteristics of a site*. If the site has any unusual features they should be incorporated into the landscape design. Even a ditch can be made an asset when naturally sloped and planted and appropriately bridged. Limitations are sometimes helpful in avoiding trite solutions of the landscape problem. Unusual shape, topography, or growth can often be featured to good advantage.

The site indicates the *type of landscaping* needed. For example, the usual flat city or suburban lot requires some straight lines to conform to its shape and to produce a tranquil effect. A sloping lot has more picturesque potentialities; it could be developed as terraces, each one of which could be treated differently. Only a sloping lot with natural rocks suggests the development of a rock garden. A rural acre with a winding stream and shrubs and trees should not employ any straight lines or other formal ideas but should be entirely natural. Foreign plants should be omitted in favor of native materials. The owner of a hilltop with a view should protect that view and keep all planting subordinated.

In planning the development of the landscaping the first and most important step is to *locate the house* on the site. The location is determined by drainage, exposure, space, shape of the plot, and the position of trees. The house should be placed so as to dominate the grounds. On the average city lot it is not usually advisable to align the house with those on adjoining lots. If legally permissible it would be best to place it well forward so as to provide extra space in the rear. The area between the house and the street may be one-half as deep as it is wide. However, dramatic quality can be created by placing the house very far back, with the private garden in front hidden behind a wall or hedge. A long impressive driveway expresses formality.

A house should not usually be located in the middle of the lot, but to one side, in order to allow one larger side area for landscaping. The location of the narrow side depends on the room arrangement. If the garage is at the rear, the driveway usually passes the narrower side of the yard beside the kitchen wall. The broader side might comprise a patio, loggia, or terrace, possibly with a small formal flower garden.

The first objective in developing the grounds around a house is *functional*. All the land should be organized for human use. The owners should decide what features are needed in the grounds; then the available space should be allocated in the best possible way, much as a house plan is developed.

The second objective is *esthetic* since the setting for the house should be as beautiful as possible. The artist designer uses shrubs, trees, and flowers to create pictures, selecting them for form, size, color, texture, and also for adaptability to the particular conditions.

Successful landscaping requires a detailed preliminary plan. The orderly thinking required in designing it defines the purposes and clarifies the picture that is the ultimate goal. Adherence to a detailed plan saves time and money, reducing to a minimum the necessity of moving plants or of eliminating those which should not have been included in the original planting.

A scale drawing should first be made of the house and lot. Experimental sketches can then be made on tracings of the scale drawing. A great many arrangements should be tried, until the most functional and beautiful organization possible is secured. Since landscaping is a three-dimensional art, *elevations* as well as *ground plans* should be made, showing the height of the planting in relation to the house.

In making a plan for the average plot it is usually best to divide it into three separate sections: *the private area, the foreground area, and the service area.* The structural outlines of these three areas should be indicated on the plan, the details being added later. In much of the United States the landscaping possibilities are heightened if the foreground area is on the east or north, if the service area is on the northwest, north, or northeast, and if the private area, consisting chiefly of the outdoor living room and lawn, is on the south or southeast, with possibly a small formal flower garden on the southeast or south.

In working out a plan for the entire property the *driveway and walks* must be located before any further development. They should be as direct and simple as possible. A practical circulatory system is very important in any property. If the size of the property permits, parking space for cars of visitors should be provided close to the door that they are expected to use.

HORIZONTAL AND VERTICAL

FORMAL COMPOSITION

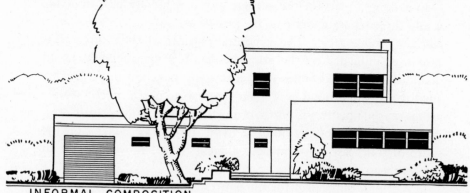

INFORMAL COMPOSITION

COMPOSITIONS IN FOUNDATION PLANTING

Foundation planting is used as a transition between the horizontal ground and the vertical building. It should be in sympathy with the mass and character of the house. *Reproduced by permission from SHELTER FOR LIVING by E. Pickering, published by John Wiley & Sons, Inc.*

THE FOREGROUND AREA

The foreground area lies between the house and the street. In the United States this area is generously left open to the gaze of the passersby, thereby improving the appearance of the whole neighborhood. A home owner should take into consideration the foreground landscaping of his neighbors when planning his own. He should not plant anything in the parking strip unless the entire street has done so. Indeed, if neighbors would cooperate in designing the foregrounds of their properties, or if the front yards of an entire street could be treated as a unit, without divisions between them, the advantage to all would be enormous.

The foreground landscaping is primarily for the purpose of enhancing the appearance of the house. A simple, open foreground that does not hide or detract from the beauty of the house is desirable. The lawn, which usually comprises most of this area, should be unbroken. Shrubs, combined with a few medium-height trees and possibly some flowers, should ordinarily frame the lawn at both sides near the house, directing the attention to the house. A restrained, dignified effect in design and color is advisable.

The planting around the foundation of the house should not be one continuous mass; empty spaces should occur. Larger masses and higher forms are usually placed at corners, because transition and strength are particularly necessary where architectural angles are the most pronounced. Between the high plants and the lawn, lower shrubs should provide a natural intermediate step. Little or no planting is needed at the base of a house which does not have a definite and visible foundation. Planting should never be allowed to obscure the views from windows.

The focal point of the front-yard planting is usually at the front entrance door. Emphasis is often achieved there by means of a pair of distinctive shrubs or trees which suit the house. They must not crowd the entrance walk or they will appear forbidding instead of welcoming.

An inviting approach is important. A straight entrance walk located at one side of the lawn, so that it can be decoratively treated as part of the border, is most desirable. If it passes through the lawn it must be without planting. Walks of bricks or darkened concrete are functional and inconspicuous.

THE PRIVATE AREA

The private area usually consists of all the space not occupied by foreground and service areas. For the sake of privacy, convenience, and quiet it is located at the rear of the house adjoining the living room and dining room, if possible.

In the past the usual treatment of the private area of the grounds was to convert it to lawn, surround it with a border of shrubs and hardy perennials, give it a center of interest, enclose it with a high wall, fence, or hedge, and supply shade trees where they are needed. A more modern and functional treatment of the private area is to organize it for outdoor living to meet the needs of every member of the family. All families need an outdoor living and dining room and places for games and exercise; some require in addition a special playground for children, a barbecue, a recreation court, or a wading pool.

The indispensable outdoor living room may be a porch, terrace, or patio. See page 176. It should have at least partial shade and a weatherproof floor. It should have some suggestion of enclosure, for man does not relax completely without at least the semblance of a wall to protect him. Climate and exposure usually determine the most effective protection from sun, wind, and insects. For example, a seacoast house might need a free-standing glass wall to exclude the wind but not the view. If possible, outdoor areas of some type should be provided on three sides of the house to meet different weather conditions in different seasons and supply shade at various times of day.

Delightful features possible in connection with a terrace are a simple raised pool or a children's wading pool. The water cools the air, reflects sky and flowers, contains colorful fish and flowers, and attracts birds. The pool should not usually be irregular in form but round, kidney-shaped, or oblong. A plentiful supply of plants in pots and tubs should be used in outdoor living areas.

The private area should be well furnished with comfortable weatherproof furniture, of a type in keeping with the house and its furnishing. Suitable combinations are unpainted wooden slat furniture for a plain cottage, metal furniture for a Modern house, and Mexican or Island furniture for a simple Mediterranean home Where contrast is desired white furniture is effective.

THE SERVICE AREA

The service portion of a lot is the part around the garage and drive, the drying yard, kitchen garden, dog run, ashpit, and tradesmen's entrance. This area should be made as compact and complete as possible and should be entirely screened from the private area, from the street, and from the neighbors.

If the garage is located in the yard back of the house it should be concealed by planting of sufficient height. If the location of the garage makes a driveway necessary it should follow the edge of the lot and should be included in the border landscaping, which might well have a hedge or vines on a link fence next to the neighboring property. Sometimes the driveway and a surfaced motor court or turning area can be used also for games. A turning area is necessary on a property located on a busy street where it is dangerous to back a car out. Other service features such as a drying yard are usually located in the area adjoining the garage. If there is no suitable place for a permanent drying yard, an umbrellalike reel that can be folded and put away when not in use is a dubious substitute, because probably it would seldom be taken down. The garbage and refuse cans may be concealed by shrubs near the kitchen door, or placed in a small lattice enclosure covered with vines, or in a box seat on the rear porch.

The service area might also contain a well-designed vegetable garden, which can be decorative as well as useful. The red beet foliage, fernlike carrot leaves, red tomatoes, purple cabbages, enormous rhubarb leaves, decorative artichokes, and prim borders of parsley are only a few of the esthetic joys of a vegetable garden. The cutting-flower garden and the rose garden, which looks ragged much of the time, and also a digging space for the children are often placed in the service area near the vegetable garden.

If the kitchen is located at the front of the house, usually a service yard adjoining the kitchen entrance should be enclosed and entirely hidden by a wall or a high hedge at the front or side of the house.

A garage that is incorporated into the house design should be well landscaped since it is ordinarily the most-used point of entrance and departure.

FORMAL LANDSCAPING

Formal landscape developments are those laid out on a geometric symmetrical plan, the two halves being practically alike. Such developments are precise, orderly, and conventional, with each separate part and the framework clearly indicated. Such architectural effects in landscape are generally created for the purpose of making an area of transition between an angular man-made house and the natural landscape. Therefore a formal development is usually located in conjunction with a house. A section of the grounds may be developed formally, or the entire grounds may be treated as one formal unit. See page 146.

The outlines and the main axis of a formal development are generally planned as extensions of lines or points of a house. The central axis of the main section usually starts from the center of the living-room window, door, or terrace. This imaginary line terminates at the far end of the lawn area in a focal point, such as a sun dial, statue, bird bath, bird house, fountain, pool, seat, tree, garden house, tea house, pergola, or arbor. See pages 143 and 145. Such a center of interest adds character to the grounds just as a fireplace does to a living room. Formal landscape design also employs secondary axes across the plot from side to side, making well-proportioned divisions. Color accents and form accents come at the termini of these axes.

If the entire private area of the grounds is developed formally, flowers are usually confined to the borders. However, where space permits, a small supplementary formal flower garden is often added. Because it is a complete unit in itself such a garden is usually enclosed by a hedge, wall, or fence. A small garden has special charm, for it can be comprehended at a glance.

The more simple the basic plan of a formal area is, the better. Most of its lines are straight, but curved lines often occur at the ends of oblongs and within squares. A formal development should not be made on sloping ground.

Walks are essential in a formal plan. They give a reason for divisions and borders that repeat the lines of the area and of the lot and house. They call attention to attractive vistas at the end of the walks. All walks should be wide enough for two.

INFORMAL LANDSCAPING

Informal landscaping appears like natural growth although it has a basic plan related to the lines of the house and lot. No straight lines or severe, geometric curves are used; the edges of the planting are irregular; the balance is asymmetrical.

Informal grounds should be designed with the utmost simplicity. Two or three main views from the terrace, living room, or dining room should first be located. A feature of interest such as a gate or seat should be placed at the end of some important views, but the development should not reveal all these features except to those who explore it. A hidden winding path which adds charm and mystery is a possibility even in a fairly small lot. Flowers should usually be located at the edges of the higher planting in a natural effect. See page 144 for examples.

Most properties should have somewhat informal landscaping, unless they are very small or very close to the heart of a city. The casual effect of informal landscaping is expressive of the attitude of today. A blending of informal design with functional design is probably the most suitable landscaping for this age, as the most important objective is to make the grounds usable.

One type of informal landscaping, which is entirely naturalistic, is copied from the woods and fields. The edge of a pasture shows nature's way of raising the eyes gradually from grass to flowers, then to low bushes, high bushes, low trees, and last to high trees. Flowers occur in casual drifts, repeated in different quantities here and there, with a great show of one particular kind of blossom at one time, but with little variety.

Wild garden areas are sometimes suitable in suburban grounds. Their purpose is educational as well as esthetic. A wild area looks particularly well in a depression, with grass paths winding through it. The arrangement of a wild section should, of course, be as natural as can be achieved. Native plant material should be freely used not only in such segregated sections but in any landscaping.

Rock gardens must also be entirely natural in appearance. They look right only where there are banks, streams, or natural outcroppings of rocks. Low alpine plants and sedums are used in such gardens, for they suit the contours of rocks and conceal the meeting of rocks and earth.

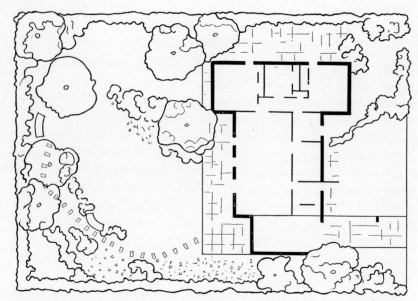

The plan above employs curved lines in an informal design, in which naturalness and usability have been stressed. Several curved benches are located beside the path of stepping stones which passes through sunshine and shadow. The many terraces and porches invite outdoor living.

The plan below is a geometric design for the formal development of a small lot. The design is knit together by the walks, one of which provides a vista from the dining-room window. A bird bath is located opposite the end of the living room.

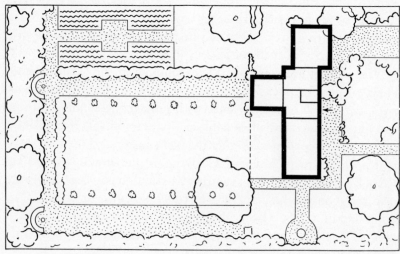

THE PLANTING

Through good planting the landscape designer can relate the house and grounds so that they become an organic unit. Since the effect of the lot and house from any point should be thought of as a picture, it is well to enclose most of it with a frame of hedges and shrubs. Trees higher than the house form a sky line which graciously eases the angular roof line of the house into the landscape. Open lawn areas permit proper views of the house and increase unity by repeating horizontally the flat planes of the building.

A careful study must be made of any house before landscaping plans for it are made. Each house is an individual problem, and no ready-made formula can be applied to its requirements. Any house limits the planting to definite *expressiveness, forms, lines, textures,* and *colors.*

A formal house needs formal grounds with clipped hedges and conventional vistas; a quaint vine-covered cottage should have a profusion of old-fashioned flowers and possibly winding walks and an arbor.

The *mass* or form of the planting should usually be designed to repeat the general lines and proportions of the house in order to unify the two. Sometimes high points in the planting are used to repeat some fine roof line or to provide contrast where it is needed.

The type of *balance* found in the architecture, too, should usually be repeated in the planting. Plant masses can also be used to improve architectural balance. If a front entrance door is located toward one end of the façade with a large expanse of wall on one side of it and a narrow expanse on the other, trees might well be planted beyond the narrow side as far as necessary to make the front door the center of the total final mass of house and trees.

Plant masses can also be used to improve the appearance of houses which are badly *proportioned.* A house that is too tall and narrow needs a high, solid foundation planting with tall, spreading, extended corner planting and tall trees near it. A house that is too flat should have some tall, slender plants in front of it to cut the horizontal lines, corner planting in front of the ends of the house, and rounded trees behind it.

Proper relativity in *scale* is essential among plant materials and also between them and the house and grounds. Only by the use of plant material of small scale can an effect of spaciousness be achieved in a small property. Mountain ash and dogwood trees, in a small foreground area, will not overpower a small house. Oaks, maples, or elms may be too large for a city lot. In any section of the country shade trees of suitable scale can be found.

Constancy of scale is an additional problem, for some plants grow much faster than others and upset the established relationship. The eventual size of the plant should be one basis on which it is chosen. Severe pruning or mutilation of a plant in order to keep it in scale usually indicates poor selection, although some plants may be pruned satisfactorily. Dwarf plants such as certain azaleas, cotoneasters, junipers, and yews are useful in retaining scale. Temporary plants can be used to fill in while the permanent plants are developing, but owners seldom remove the surplus plants.

Texture in plants usually refers to two effects: surface qualities that we can feel by touching, and the pattern of light and dark which we can see. Visual texture depends upon the size, shape, and spacing of leaves, twigs, and flowers, and the surface of the leaves. In general, large leaves, thickly spaced, produce a coarse texture, whereas small leaves create a fine texture.

Texture harmony is partly the result of repeating like textures. Variety is needed, however, to hold the interest; yet too much variety or strong contrast is unpleasant, particularly in a small property. In the planting around a house the coarsest textures and most solid masses should be at the corners; the sides should have finer textures and more openness. Projecting points anywhere in a landscape plan need coarse textures, and recessions need finer textures for depth effect. Low, fine-textured plants are often used as transition elements between the lawn and tall, coarse-textured plants. Very coarse textures are not generally suitable to small properties unless they are needed to express an exotic or Modern idea.

The entire landscape plan should be interpreted in terms of texture before any plants are chosen. The art principles—balance, proportion, emphasis, rhythm, and transition—are valuable guides for the distribution of texture.

The selection of plants begins after all ground plans and elevations are satisfactory. Any plant that will thrive and that fits the
design requirements is usually suitable. The rarity of a plant is
irrelevant; only its pictorial aspect is pertinent in landscape composition. It is well to study nursery catalogs and plant lists to
learn what plants will fit the specifications. The actual selection
of the plants usually requires some local guidance, because the
ecological factors of climate, soil, and drainage limit the choice.

The amateur designer should be warned against the confusing
wealth of plant material procurable. Most grounds have far too
many varieties of plants. Profuse mixtures not only lack coherence
but also detract from the house, which should be the center of
interest. American women have definitely eliminated the clutter
of miscellaneous objects from their houses but not as yet from
their yards. Souvenir plants and ornamental plants of all types
are unfortunately too often assembled without a definite objective.
The proper place for most gifts and miscellaneous plants is in an
experimental section.

Unity in the landscape is greatly promoted by featuring one particular kind of shrub and one kind of tree. Other plants should
be added only where variety or accent is necessary to arouse interest. Naturally the featured shrub and tree are carefully chosen.

In some properties success is attained by restricting the planting
to one type, such as tropical plants, native materials, desert plants,
or those that contribute to an effect such as Modernism or quaintness. A garden of such positive character follows the theme established by the house.

One of the most important points to ascertain in the selection
of shrubs and trees is whether they are evergreen. In cold climates a fair proportion of coniferous evergreens adds color and
contrast, but a disproportionate quantity of them creates an impression of gloom and darkness. However, the effect of evergreens on the winter landscape of the North is well worth their
additional cost. In warmer climates where many broad-leaved
evergreens thrive, it is possible to have almost the same general
landscape effect all the year round, although most gardeners prefer
the contrast of some leafless material. Bare branches reveal the
rhythmic beauty of the plant structure and also convey a message
of rest from the sleeping tree or shrub.

Trees. Sixty per cent of the planting fund for a home should usually be expended for trees. Trees do more than anything else to make a garden livable, as they are invaluable for shade as well as for beauty. Large trees are such an asset on a building site that it is usually advisable to locate the house so as to spare the trees. See page 144 for a good example.

Large trees to *shade* the south and west sides of the house should be deciduous, for in winter they do not block the sunlight. Evergreen trees may be used near the house only on the north side. Shade trees are also needed at various points in the grounds to provide shady play ground and rest areas for any time of the day.

Trees are necessary for *appearance* too. Every house needs them for a setting. Low-branched trees are desirable only in places where there is ample space for them; in small properties low branches should usually be removed in order to allow use of the space under the trees. A shrub border may include occasional coniferous evergreen trees to give an interesting silhouette. The final size of the full-grown trees must be considered because they must all be in proper scale with the house.

It is generally advisable to choose native trees, because they are most likely to thrive and also to suit the landscape. Trees and shrubs that are neighbors in their natural state usually combine well. Fruit- and nut-bearing trees should be more popular. Care must be exercised in order to obtain varieties that are not hosts to blights and other prevalent ravages. Dwarf fruit trees, pruned and trained flat against walls or fences, occupy little space and provide an interesting design element particularly when bearing blossoms or fruit. Since the dramatic element is helpful in achieving beauty, the dormant tree that suddenly bursts into bloom is an important factor in landscape composition.

A landscape designer, even an amateur, should think of trees first as *conventionalized forms:* columns, cylinders, cones, spheres, or umbrellas. Each tree has a directing line of growth, horizontal or vertical, upward or downward slanting, upward or downward curving, or flaring. The characteristics of a tree depend largely upon its architecture; a solid structure has a very different quality from an airy one. Trees will be correctly used if their basic lines and forms are considered and if an awareness of their individuality is developed.

Hedges. Clipped or unclipped hedges are often used to give privacy and protection to the small property. They also provide the framework of the grounds, defining the different areas. The boxlike forms of clipped hedges serve to ease the disparity between the unrelated forms of man-made architecture and the natural shapes of trees and plants. See page 146.

Leafy evergreen hedges are particularly satisfactory, and certain plants, such as barberry, Japanese quince, or osage orange, may be grown as hedges that dogs cannot penetrate. Where the cost of maintenance is an important factor hedges that must be clipped should not be employed. Unclipped hedges, such as dwarf privet or box, maintain a fairly satisfactory height and suit informal surroundings where clipped hedges are not appropriate. Hedges should be in scale with the surroundings.

Shrubs. A mixed planting of shrubs may be placed on the edges of a lot to give privacy. They are also good where transition masses are needed to soften the angular lines of houses or garden areas. Broad-leaf evergreen shrubs and those that bear flowers are particularly desirable near houses. The most beautiful ones should be used for accents. Some shrubs attract butterflies and humming birds, and those with berries are not only handsome for long periods but also provide food for birds in winter. Prickly shrubs should not be placed where they are likely to tear clothing or flesh. Amateur gardeners often make the mistake of having too many shrubs or too many varieties.

Vines. The angular forms of man-made houses are eased into the landscape by means of vines; ugly houses can be almost concealed by them. They can be utilized to subdue glare and provide shade in summer. A pergola, arbor, or trellis covered with flowering vines can be a beautiful sight.

Lawns. Grass is the most common lawn covering, different kinds being favored in different localities, certain kinds growing well even in the shade. Unusual types of lawn covering, some of which need to be cut only once or twice during the summer, are proving successful. In some climates, Korean bunch grass, which has beautiful texture, is very satisfactory for front yards that are not used much. English ivy, honeysuckle, yellow jasmine, or strawberry plants are effective ground covers for unused front yards in mild climates.

Flowers. In a landscape composition flowers provide the color accents. Their selection and placing constitute a problem in esthetics. A mere collection of miscellaneous flowers is not a work of art any more than a box of paints is. Flowers comprise a medium from which garden pictures can be made against suitable backgrounds. Certain flowers are selected from the enormous number of possibilities, but many beautiful ones must be excluded.

Expressiveness, texture, form, scale, and color are important factors in the selection and use of flowers. All the art principles also apply to this problem. Flowers should be well distributed and well balanced in the landscaping. Emphasis is established at those places where the flowers are concentrated.

The location of flowers in the landscape pattern is carefully designed. Flower beds are no longer scattered here and there over a property. Flowers are arranged in borders that follow the lines of the lot or house or they are placed in definite flower gardens. The term flower garden usually refers to a formal or informal area devoted entirely to flowers. It should be enclosed by a fence, hedge, or foliage wall which unifies it and gives the flowers a background. Formal flower gardens usually have a center of interest and a symmetrical arrangement of walks. Informal flower gardens have irregularities and surprises that excite interest. Some flower gardens are successfully restricted to a definite idea or theme, such as a spring bulb garden, a cactus and succulent garden, a white garden, or a gray foliage garden.

The plants in flower borders and beds should be carefully selected for height. A low perennial plant is usually desirable at the front edge of a flower border. In general, the tallest plants are at the back, but in some places they may extend to the front of the bed, suggesting alcoves. Other points to observe in planting are that diagonal drifts or somewhat triangular clumps of flowers are much more interesting than straight rows parallel to the edges. Bulbs should be planted in groups, not singly.

Some flowers should be located very near to the house so that they can be enjoyed from the interior. If a paved terrace adjoins the wall of the house, space may be left for flowers between them. Potted flowers should be freely used near the house; they can be kept out of sight except when in bloom. See the potted petunias on page 147.

The *expressiveness* of flowers should be utilized to help produce the effect that is desired in a landscape. Cacti, roses, calla lilies, and pansies excite very different emotional reactions. Every kind of flowering plant has personality and character. Whereas a rich profusion of simple old-fashioned flowers suits a cottage, a stately house requires studied planting of elegant, conventional flowers, and a Modern house suggests flowers having large, definite, and unusual forms, such as the bird of paradise or succulents and cacti.

Color is the most noticeable element of flowers. Adjacent color harmonies are more pleasing than complementary colors in flower borders as well as in bouquets. In large grounds a definite section might be reserved for flowers of adjacent colors such as blue, violet, and pink, while another part of the grounds might admit only scarlet, orange, and yellow flowers. White fits in anywhere. It is more effective to have a large quantity of one color in blossom at the same time than a mixture of colors. Long-lasting red berries affect color choices too, for example, an ardisia border precludes some iris neighbors but welcomes red amaryllis or white yucca. Ample white and light colors make a garden effective at night.

An owner who is interested in featuring the flowers in his garden should paint his house some pale neutral color. However, if the house is natural red brick or some other colored material, the color scheme of the flowers should be planned to harmonize with the house. For example, coral-colored azaleas are preferable to magenta beside a tan stucco house with a red roof.

Texture harmony makes it highly desirable to plant together those same flowers that would look well if picked and placed in a bowl together. A desirable combination is white sage, rose pinks, and forget-me-nots, which agree in texture yet have variety.

Fragrance is such an important quality that definite effort should be made to use some sweetly scented flowers such as tuberoses, Nicotiana, lilacs, and butterfly lilies.

Timing is also an element in flower gardening since one aim is continuity of bloom. Plantings should be made so that some part of the garden is always at its best, and so that the periods of decline strike the various garden areas at different times.

Economy of labor is achieved by choosing perennials and flowering shrubs rather than annuals, and by selecting plants that bloom for a long time, like verbenas, and those that are hardy.

PROBLEMS

A sufficient number of problems are listed so that choices may be made.

1. Visit gardens and write reports about them.
2. Report on the planting in your block. Does the foreground landscaping detract from, or enhance, or hide the houses?
3. Draw your own or some other plot to scale, and locate the house, trees, and plants. Plan improvements in the planting design.
4. Make an analysis of the landscaping of some section of your campus.
5. Make an individual miniature plot plan on a board or tray, using a block for the house and possibly cedar foliage, moss, or green sponge for the planting.
6. For a class or group project, landscape a small house and lot on a sand table, using grass and branches.

READING REFERENCES

BOTTOMLEY, MYRL E. *The Design of Small Properties.* Macmillan, 1934.

CARHART, ARTHUR H. *How to Plan the Home Landscape.* Doubleday, Doran, 1936.

CAUTLEY, MARJORIE. *Garden Design.* Dodd, Mead, 1935.

GOLDSMITH, MARGARET O. *Designs for Outdoor Living.* Stewart, 1941.

ORTLOFF, H. S., and RAYMORE, H. B. *Garden Planning and Building.* McGraw-Hill, 1939.

ROBINSON, FLORENCE BELL. *Planting Design.* McGraw-Hill, 1940.

TAYLOR, G. C. *The Modern Garden.* Scribner, 1936.

TUNNARD, CHRISTOPHER. *Gardens in the Modern Landscape.* Architectural Press, 1938.

U. S. DEPARTMENT OF INTERIOR. *Bulletin 189. Landscaping the Farmstead.*

VAN DE BOE, LOUIS. *Planning and Planting Your Own Place.* Macmillan, 1938.

WILDER, LOUISE B. *Pleasures and Problems of a Rock Garden.* Doubleday, Doran, 1928.

A sedum plant which withstands drought and does not require cutting is used as a ground cover on the bank and front yard of the house above. Notice the two tall, rounded shrubs that accent the picture window of the living room. Small potted plants fill the shelf below the short kitchen windows. The private garden with shade trees is in the rear. This is a non-period house planned for outdoor living. *Courtesy Norman E. Rutt.*

A hillside lot below left is being terraced to hold moisture and soil. The fence is a living wall of cacti which suits a Modern studio home in a dry climate. *Courtesy Helen O'Gorman.*

The wall fountain below right is the focal point in the walled garden of a house inspired by American Indian pueblos. The beautiful lines of the fountain repeat those of the house. *Courtesy Sternberg-Davis, photographers.*

The slope above has informal landscaping. The trees and shrubs seem as free as those in the wild woods; the flowers are in drifts and patches. This makes a beautiful and appropriate setting for a cottage. *Courtesy Richard A. Smith, photographer.*

Outdoor living areas like this one at the side of a house add greatly to comfort and pleasure. The house was purposely located where the large trees would shade the terrace.
Courtesy Santa Barbara Chamber of Commerce.

The bird bath above left is the focal point of the view from a dining-room window. Its strong plain curves are repeated in the curved niche in the shrubbery border. *Courtesy Lucille Arne.*

The decorative little old schoolhouse above right is the focal point at the end of several walks in the famous gardens of Mount Vernon. A tea house or an arbor could serve a similar purpose. *Courtesy Norman E. Rutt.*

This lily pool is the focal point in a small semi-formal garden enclosed by flowering shrubs, backed by ligustrum. The shape of the pool is pleasing. The child, rabbit, goldfish, and mockingbirds add life and charm to the garden. The seat invites one to sit and enjoy the surroundings. *Courtesy Louisiana State University.*

This formal flower garden was photographed in tulip time. The flower border around the oblong area of lawn has a background of lilacs on one side and a trimmed hedge on the opposite side. The walks of turf are good looking. The seats are appropriate and inconspicuous. *Courtesy Richard Averill Smith.*

Flower beds continue the lines of the rear porch shown below, making a pleasing, colorful outlook. The thick hedge at the property line gives privacy. The flower box makes an attractive edge for the porch. *Courtesy Katherine Bashford.*

Landscape designing is truly an art when compositions like the one above left are created.
Courtesy Paul Frankl, designer and owner.

In the picture above right, the round pool is the center of interest in a delightful outdoor living area. Either shade or sunshine is available. *Courtesy H. R. Kelley, architect.*

A walled living terrace in partial sunshine is pleasant even on windy days.
Courtesy Katherine Bashford.

The trees make a beautiful setting for the hill top farm house above. The few shrubs planted at the corners to soften the angles do not interfere with the view. Note that the three roof levels follow the slope of the hill. *Courtesy Anne Plettinger.*

The simplest farm house should be landscaped intelligently. The county demonstration agent and an energetic farm wife transformed the place pictured below, and it has proved to be an inspiration to other women. Notice that the planting conceals the barnyard buildings. *Courtesy U. S. Department of Agriculture, Texas A. & M. College.*

CHAPTER 10

HOUSE PLANNING

A family intending to build a house should be willing to do considerable preliminary study in order that the members will have a basis for the decisions that they must make. The ability to recognize excellence in appearance, function, materials, and workmanship is an invaluable asset to those who are building.

Many new books and periodicals dealing with home building are available for study. The Superintendent of Documents in Washington, D. C., has for distribution booklets containing valuable information on house building. Advertising circulars issued by building-material establishments are plentiful and useful. It is sometimes possible to find enough interested persons to petition the local high school or college extension department for an adults' course in home planning or home architecture. Correspondence courses should also be considered.

Members of a family planning to build should observe and photograph new houses, including model houses and those built by architects in the good new subdivisions in the larger cities in a progressive part of the country. It is also helpful to study historic old houses to learn how materials and living conditions produced certain styles, and also to realize that, when materials and living conditions are no longer the same, the old style is probably illogical.

This chapter presents a brief introduction to the fascinating subject of house planning, including the following aspects of the problem:

Cost	Orientation
Expressiveness	Circulation
Function	Floor plan, room by room
Beauty	Interior wall elevations

COST

In planning a house one factor that is usually fixed is the amount that can be expended for it. Experienced budget makers say that not more than one-fourth of one's income should be used for shelter, that is, for rent or for carrying charges on an owned house. Two or three years' income is usually expended for the house and lot. As a minimum, before starting to build a house, a family should have the site paid for or should have twenty per cent of the cost of the house and lot in cash. Usually a house costs about four times as much as the lot. A house should not cost more than one hundred twenty times the monthly rental it would bring.

The available funds generally settle the first question in planning a house, that of its size. A rough *estimate of the cost* of a proposed house can be obtained by multiplying the number of cubic feet in the house by established approximate costs. The cubic contents of a house are determined by multiplying the number of square feet in the floor plan by the height from the bottom of the basement to a point halfway between the floor of the attic and its ceiling.

The established approximate cost per cubic foot in any locality is known by the various firms or agencies connected with building houses. Naturally these figures are not alike in all localities or at all times, owing to the differences in prices of materials and labor. The following figures provide a basis for comparison of costs of houses of different standards: minimum standard house forty cents per cubic foot, inexpensive house fifty cents per cubic foot, medium-priced house sixty cents per cubic foot, expensive house seventy cents per cubic foot.

To the cost of the house must be added the *cost of financing,* unless the house is paid for when built. A twenty-year payment plan adds about twenty per cent to the cost. Among the organizations that are in the business of financing houses are building and loan associations, savings banks, insurance companies, trust companies, and lumber companies, some of which give better terms than others. An organization that has been endorsed by federal housing authorities is certain to be reliable. The federal government insures some organizations against loss, thus permitting builders to borrow money at very low rates.

EXPRESSIVENESS

The personality desired in a prospective house should be determined in family councils before designing of the house is begun. The *family characteristics* constitute the logical basis for the fundamental idea or mood that should be expressed in the home. Since a variety of personalities, tastes, and activities occurs in one family, however, it is not easy to formulate a definite statement of the composite personality of the group.

One method of procedure in establishing the personality is for the members of the family first to analyze themselves as individuals and each one make a list of adjectives describing his or her own characteristics. The family group should then concentrate on the words that occur most frequently in these lists. After discussion and elimination of disputed terms an idea of the group personality might evolve sufficiently to be stated in a few words, such as:

1. Sturdy, matter-of-fact, practical, realistic, independent.
2. Ingenious, communicative, imaginative, vivacious, friendly.
3. Formal, reserved, dignified, conservative, religious.
4. Methodical, quiet, self-sufficient, unsocial, studious.

After self-analysis, each member of a family group should analyze his or her ideal house, making a short list of adjectives describing it. The members should then combine their lists of adjectives, eliminating through discussion the less important terms and the contradictory ideas. The two lists, describing the family and the house, should be the basis for a fairly clear definition of the characteristics of the desired house. This should ultimately crystallize into an *idea or theme* which could be stated in a few descriptive words. The chosen theme should then be followed as a guide in making decisions in regard to the house and lot as well as the furnishings.

To illustrate, a family guided by the theme—unpretentious, honest, friendly, and rustic—might produce a farm-house type of dwelling in the country or on a hillside lot in town. Another family's theme—smart, gay, youthful, efficient, and positive—might result in a sleek Modern city house planned for entertaining. The theme—formal, elegant, distinguished, and conventional—could inspire a large colonial house in a restricted residential section.

ANALYSIS OF HOUSE REQUIREMENTS

The function of a house is to provide for the *basic needs* of a family, which are shelter, food, health, cleanliness, privacy, and service. The *necessary activities*, which are cooking, eating, sleeping, bathing, dressing, cleaning, laundering, and storing, form the basis for the house plan. The *cultural activities*, such as conversing, reading, writing, playing, entertaining, listening to music, pursuing hobbies, and working, are also important factors in making a house plan.

The *social and economic status of a family* determines many of its housing requirements. The occupation of the wage earner is an indication of family needs. For example, the families of a physician, grocer, minister, author, carpenter, teacher, mechanic, actor, or farmer require different accommodations. Their customs in dining, entertaining, reading, or pursuing hobbies would be very different. Some need larger rooms than others. Some need additional rooms, for instance, a bookroom, study, or office may be needed by a minister, teacher, or author.

The *size of the household* influences the housing needs greatly. Children of various ages or adult dependents create special problems. A resident servant changes planning requirements. Lack of servants, small families, and outdoor recreation have tended to decrease the size of houses.

The needs of *individual members* of the family should be listed and used as a guide. If space is limited, a feature which is wanted by only one member should be omitted in favor of another which is desired by several.

Changes in requirements must be taken into account in house planning, because births, deaths, and departures, as well as growth of children, change family needs. Interests and activities change with physical and cultural growth. The standard of living is no more static than the social and economic status of the family. Since farm families are usually permanent residents their houses should be planned so that convenient rooms can be added later.

Compromises must be made by the average family when formulating a final statement of requirements in a house. Compromises among financial restrictions, space restrictions, and family needs are a difficult part of house planning.

FUNCTIONAL PLANNING

Functional planning refers here to the designing of house plans which are based on function and not on some traditional style. The floor plan is designed around the needs and activities of the family. When the plan is completed and integrated functionally a suitable exterior design is found or preferably created to suit it. This method of planning from the interior to the exterior is far more logical than designing from the exterior to the interior, which unfortunately is quite common practice. Obviously it is not sensible to select a period exterior first and then try to make a floor plan which will fit the exterior and also fit the activities of a twentieth-century family. Functional planning requires many preliminary sketches. The usual method of procedure for students or home makers is suggested below.

I. Draw to scale the plot plan and analyze, showing:

Points of compass.   Location of slopes.
Direction of summer breeze.   Advantages of site.
Direction of winter winds.   Disadvantages of site.
Direction of view.   Proximity of houses.
Location of trees.   Legal restrictions.

II. Draw to scale a functional floor plan for a house on the above lot, noting:

Relationship of rooms.   Zoning areas.
Continuity of space.   Economy of space.
Circulation.   Space for furniture.
Flexibility of room.   Appearance.

III. Draw to scale interior elevations of important walls, noting

Agreement with exterior.   Proportion.
Architectural features.   Balance.
Built-in furniture.   Emphasis.
Space for wall furniture.   Repetition.

IV. Draw to scale exterior elevations of the house, noting:

Family personality.   Proportion.
Possible styles.   Balance.
Styles of neighborhood.   Emphasis.
Type of lot.   Rhythm.

Every woman should know how to read architectural plans. This ability will help her to visualize a house when looking at plans. It may save her unnecessary fatigue and inconvenience throughout the years when she occupies a house that has been built for her. It may in fact be an important factor in orderly, congenial home life. The best way to understand house plans is to draw them to scale. A brief course in house design would be of great value to a prospective builder.

Architects often use the word *plan* to mean the horizontal representation of an area, or what is commonly known as the floor plan. Such plans usually show walls as thick lines, windows as thin lines, and doors as blank spaces. Complete plans should show the direction in which doors swing and also the location of electric outlets. Actual working drawings are further developments of preliminary plans.

Elevations are representations of vertical areas, such as walls. A *façade* is the face of a building, usually the front.

Scale drawings are easily made on squared graph paper. Sheets of paper can be pasted together for large drawings. A drawing of convenient size results from letting ¼ inch on the paper represent 1 foot in the actual house. When drawing the lot to scale, ¼ inch may represent 4 feet.

When experimenting with plans it saves time to work on firm, transparent paper placed over the drawing on the squared graph paper. When making changes in plans it is well to trace that portion of the plan which is not to be changed. A drawing board, T square, and triangle are helpful in drawing plans. Special pen points and inks are useful too.

Approximate sizes of rooms of a fairly small house are given below. These may be changed freely.

Living room—14 x 22 ft.	Halls—4 ft. wide.
Dining room—12 x 14 ft.	Stairs—3½ x 12 ft.
Dining alcove—7 x 9 ft.	Bathroom—6 x 7 ft.
Kitchen—8 x 12 ft.	Lavatory—4 x 5 ft.
Bedroom—12 x 14 ft.	Sunroom—10 x 15 ft.
Bedroom—9 x 12 ft.	Utility—8 x 12 ft.
Study—10 x 12 ft.	Garage—11 x 20 ft.
Closets—2 x 4 ft.	Garage—18 x 20 ft.

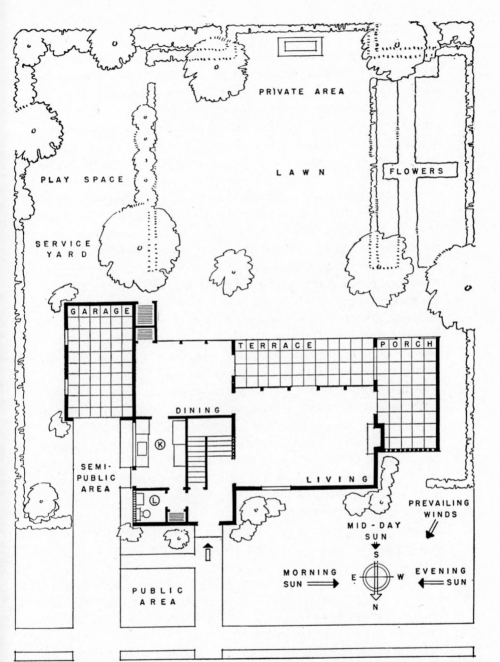

A LANDSCAPE AND ORIENTATION PLAN

A plot plan showing the relationship between the house, lot, and outdoor features. The major units of the plan have southern exposure, commonly accepted as desirable. *Reproduced by permission from SHELTER FOR LIVING by E. Pickering, published by John Wiley & Sons, Inc.*

Planning the *orientation* of a prospective house in relation to the sun and wind precedes the making of floor plans. The southern exposure is usually the most desirable one because in winter it has sunshine, and in summer in much of the country it has the prevailing breeze. However, the southern exposure usually requires shade on summer afternoons; therefore tall deciduous shade trees on the south, southwest, and west are highly desirable. Shade for the southern exposure can also be provided by modern extended roofs or louvered canopies, which are so designed that they keep out the sunshine in summer but admit it in winter. See page 117. Since modern living rooms should face the sun and also face the garden at the rear of the house, lots on the south side of the street are particularly satisfactory.

Eastern exposures are desirable in spring, fall, and winter but sometimes require shade in summer. North rooms are the least pleasant, except in hot climates, because they get no sunshine. Northwest and west rooms are likely to be hot on summer afternoons. Compromises and flexibility in the use of rooms at different seasons is therefore usually necessary.

In a one-story house the living room, which should have the best exposure, is usually located on the south or east, the outdoor living room, too, on the south or east, the dining room on the north or northeast, the kitchen on the north or northeast, the utility room on the north, the study on the northwest, the bedrooms on the south, east, or west, and the motor room on the north. Long narrow houses, only one room through, get more sunshine, air, and garden exposure than more compact houses. Difficult problems in orientation are often solved by having an irregular house plan. Sometimes turning a house only 20 degrees makes the difference between success and failure in its orientation.

In addition to the sun and breeze other factors affect room exposures. Where winter winds are bitter few openings should appear on the north. Where the view is outstanding, naturally the living room faces in that direction.

Privacy and interest are gained by locating a house out of line with the neighboring houses. The type and size of a lawn and garden areas desired and the presence of large trees also influence the placing of the house. Legal restrictions, too, sometimes affect the location of a house.

The *relation of rooms* to each other has been fairly well established by tradition, based on function. Naturally bedrooms and bathrooms are adjacent, as are kitchens and dining rooms. All customary arrangements, however, should be questioned in the light of present-day activities, facilities, and knowledge.

Continuity of space, an element which is now appreciated more than formerly, has a definite effect on the relationship of rooms. So-called *open planning* has taken the place of the small separate rooms of olden times. Continuity of space is gained by the elimination of partitions wherever possible. Thus an effect of spaciousness can be obtained even though houses are small. First-floor interior walls should be minimized. Three-foot partitions dividing functional areas are often desirable. Stairways may be entirely open. Only kitchens, bathrooms, and bedrooms require complete partitions.

Indoor space is apparently increased by the addition of outdoor space through the use of more and larger glass doors and windows. An exterior glass wall with a mirror on the opposite wall admits the space of the garden and beyond. Well-correlated outdoor living areas such as porches, decks, terraces, and patios make a house seem more spacious.

Ease of circulation, one of the most important requirements in a house, depends largely on the location of rooms. It should be possible to go directly to any place in the house from any point without unnecessary steps. The frequency of passage between rooms should be the basis for determining which part of the circulatory system must receive first consideration. Traffic is heaviest between the kitchen and dining room, next between dining room and living room, and third between bedrooms and bath. A small inside hall in a one-story house simplifies the circulation problem.

Circulation also depends on the location of doors. On the first floor of a two-story house all interior doors should be located close to the center of the house and at inside corners if possible in order to save steps and wall space. A door should swing out of the way in the direction opposite to that in which a person usually turns when passing through the doorway. Furniture should not be located near doors or in the way of passage lanes, which should be clearly indicated.

Flexibility of use should be considered in making room plans. Multiple-purpose rooms are necessary in the compact houses of today. The present generation uses houses differently from those of the past. For example, dining may now take place in the kitchen, study, living room, or out-of-doors. If there is a dining room, it may become part of the recreation or entertainment area, when so desired, or may serve as a sewing room or a study.

The traditional styles of architecture do not lend themselves to flexible planning as well as the Modern, because the regularly spaced doors and windows, high foundations and other features, impose restrictions. The basis for the arrangement of the flexible house is function.

Zoning a house so that noisy activities are separated from quiet ones is an important factor in room arrangement. A family with members of various ages and tastes requires a diversity of recreation areas. If a game room cannot be provided in the basement or elsewhere, the main living room might be given over to recreation and an adjoining quiet room be provided for those who wish to read, study, or converse. Ordinarily, however, the living room is for the relaxation of the average group while those who wish to be very noisy or very quiet are accommodated elsewhere. Closets, bathrooms, and storerooms are effective sound-insulation areas between rooms.

Economy of space is an important aim in floor planning, for the modern house does not contain useless space or idle rooms. Scrupulous attention is now paid to saving footage and using all available room to the best advantage. For example, only 6 feet of free space is needed over a bathtub; above that cupboards may be built.

Space for furniture is a factor that influences floor planning. Dimensions of average articles of furniture must be considered. Space must also be allowed for the use of a piece of furniture; a 2-foot space is required in front of a chair.

Appearance should be considered even while a floor plan is being developed. Since the floor plan cannot be final, however, until the exterior has been planned, visual beauty is considered more fully in later developments of the plan. Even in making the preliminary plans, however, it is well to group windows together and to create well-proportioned rooms, avoiding squares as well as long, narrow rooms.

TYPES OF PLANS

Plans of houses usually conform to one of the basic shapes, *square*, *oblong*, *L-shaped*, *T-shaped*, *U-shaped*, *H-shaped*, or their variations. Of these the T-shaped and L-shaped plans and their adaptations are asymmetrical, the others are symmetrical.

These types are the basis for plans of all houses, regardless of whether they are one, one and a half, two, or three stories high. The number of floors in a house depends upon the needs of the household, and also upon the lot, the climate, and the neighboring houses, with which it is best to conform. *One-story houses* are more popular than two because they make better-looking small houses. They are also more convenient, particularly for a family that includes small children, invalids, or aged members.

The *story-and-a-half house* can be attractive and economical. It utilizes the attic space that is usually wasted in a one-story house. Successful insulating material has now made rooms close to the roof usable in hot or cold weather. English and French cottages have steeper roofs and consequently more attic space than American colonial cottages. Dormer windows, which are often added for light, should be made subordinate to the house design.

Because a *two-story house* covers less ground than a one-story house containing the same floor space, it is sometimes more desirable on a small lot. A house of two stories is more economical to build than a one-story house because the roof and the foundation costs are about the same for two stories or one. It is also easier to heat than a one-story house. In a damp climate the second floor is drier than the first and therefore affords a better location for books, storage, and closets.

Whether to have a *basement* depends on the budget, personal taste, and drainage conditions. It is usually more costly to excavate, drain, and build walls underground than above ground. Laundry and furnace rooms can, of course, be placed on the first floor, although in many localities they are usually put in the basement. In very warm climates, naturally cool underground rooms could be made to serve as retreats on hot days, provided that drainage is perfect. Farm families make good use of cool basement storage space. A recreation room in the basement helps to keep the rest of the house quiet.

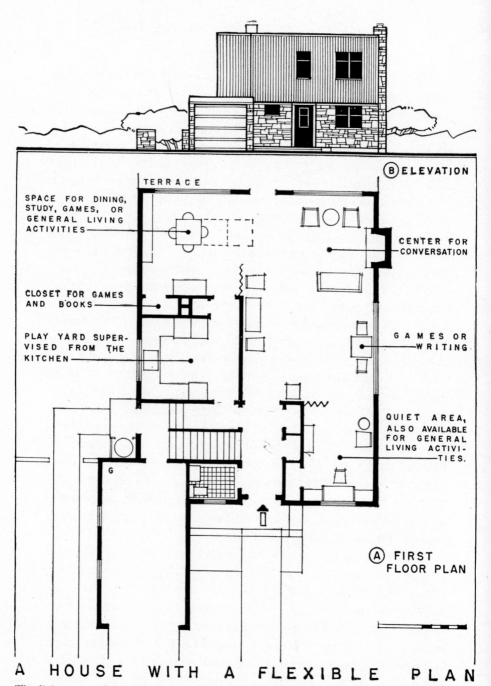

B ELEVATION

TERRACE

SPACE FOR DINING,
STUDY, GAMES, OR
GENERAL LIVING
ACTIVITIES

CENTER FOR
CONVERSATION

CLOSET FOR GAMES
AND BOOKS

PLAY YARD SUPER-
VISED FROM THE
KITCHEN

GAMES OR
WRITING

QUIET AREA,
ALSO AVAILABLE
FOR GENERAL
LIVING ACTIVI-
TIES.

G

A FIRST
FLOOR PLAN

A HOUSE WITH A FLEXIBLE PLAN

The living area of this house may be used as a single unit or divided into three spaces for divergent types of activities, either quiet or active—dining, conversation, games. *Reproduced by permission from SHELTER FOR LIVING by E. Pickering, published by John Wiley & Sons, Inc.*

LIVING ROOMS

The living room should provide for all the more quiet recreational activities of the family, such as reading, conversation, quiet games, and low music. Secondary living areas are usually needed, however, if a family consists of more than two persons. A room that can be shut off when necessary, such as a book room, hobby room, work room, study, den, or modified dining room, would take care of varied activities of some members which might interfere with relaxation or order in the living room proper. Such a room could accommodate younger groups which enjoy themselves and their friends more when away from their elders. If music is a special family interest space may be needed for a piano, for a phonograph and records, and possibly for special architectural installations to improve the rendering of recorded music.

The *appearance* of the living room, as well as its functioning, must be pleasing if the house is to be satisfactory. Other rooms should be slighted, if necessary, to give the living room advantages. It should have the best view and a southern exposure if both are possible. The living room should be large, as spaciousness there makes up for small areas elsewhere. In a small five-room house it might be about 14 feet by 20 feet. If a dining area is included it might be considerably larger.

The living room should be well proportioned, not square, but possibly two-thirds as wide as it is long. It must not be a passageway; therefore it is well to make it a dead-end room with doors concentrated at one end. At least two exterior walls with plenty of large windows are necessary. It takes careful planning to meet these requirements while also allowing wall space for furniture.

A real fireplace is highly desirable; nothing can equal it for radiating cheer and charm. It should usually be located in a long wall of the living room, with near-by windows but not near-by doors. See page 104. Exactly opposite the fireplace, space should usually be allowed to accommodate a long sofa with lamp tables at each end. Bookshelves and other built-in furnishings should be located in the earliest plans. They fit into the design of a room better than movable furnishings and are cleaner and more space-conserving. All the interior architecture of the living room should be carefully unified in line.

DINING AREAS

Before a house plan can proceed far, a family should decide whether it can dispense with a dining room proper and eat in an alcove or end of the living room. The average family finds this desirable in order to create spaciousness by combining these two rooms. The dining area in the living room might when necessary be isolated by a sliding curtain wall on tracks, by a screen that rolls up vertically, by a low bookshelf partition, or by some other device. See pages 239 and 425. Sometimes the dining and working area is differentiated by a lower ceiling.

A separate dining room is needed in a home where a considerable degree of formality is observed. A large family, too, usually finds it a necessity, especially for small children. If a separate dining room is planned, a very large opening between the living room and dining room is desirable for spaciousness and for convenience in entertaining large groups. French doors opening onto a dining terrace off the garden add to comfort and beauty. A swinging kitchen door, which should be located near a corner, might be concealed behind an anchored screen or a short fin wall.

A dining room should have some conspicuous architectural feature such as a bay window, picture window, glass wall, French doors, or corner cupboards. In an average house the dimensions of the room should be planned to accommodate some of these ready-made architectural features, in stock sizes.

In a dining room built-in features are particularly desirable for convenience and also in order that conventional furniture may be omitted. See page 60. Built-in corner cupboards in one or two or all corners are good looking and less costly than separate cupboards. They make use of space which would otherwise be wasted. One entire wall from floor to ceiling might consist of dish storage cupboards. Shelves and drawers built into the wall between the kitchen and dining area, opening into both rooms, are a step-saving device.

A spacious dining room might have two eating places: a permanent oversize table for occasions when there is a large group, and a small table for one or two, for extras, or for children. The small table might fold up into a wall depression.

KITCHENS

The kitchen should be located so that the morning sun makes it cheery at the time when it is used most. The kitchen must, of course, be adjacent to the dining room, and if possible it should be easily reached from an outdoor dining area, from the garage or driveway, and from the service yard. A corner is desirable for good ventilation.

Kitchen planning has been made very simple and sensible. The three work centers are placed according to the sequence in which they are used in preparing a meal, the refrigerator, the sink, the range. The *refrigerator* should adjoin a work counter over which dry staples are stored, and under which are cupboards for utensils needed in mixing and baking. The *sink*, with windows above it, should be next to the other end of this work counter. Dish-washing materials, vegetable-preparation equipment, and dishes should be stored near the sink. Beyond the sink, the *range* and serving counter form another unit. Pots and pans, serving dishes, trays, coffee, tea, and salt should be within reach. This center should be close to the dining unit or the dining-room door.

The *U-shaped kitchen* is the most efficient type because it is the most compact and traffic does not pass through the working area. See page 175. The work counters, cabinets, and equipment form one unbroken line around three sides of the room. The sink is in the middle of the end wall with windows over it. The *L-shaped kitchen* has equipment along two adjoining walls, usually with a dining unit located in the opposite corner. The *corridor type of kitchen* is very convenient if there is little traffic through the room. The window side contains the sink with counters and cupboards; the opposite side contains the refrigerator and range with a table between them and possibly shelves above it.

An attractive place to eat in the kitchen is desirable if a woman does her own work. Two fixed benches beside a table, or a wide table shelf under windows looking out over the garden, or a bar with stools are some possibilities.

Some women have abandoned the sleek hospital-type kitchen for a sitting-room-farm type, with comfortable furniture, gay decorations, and walls of wood. See page 105. Guests are entertained in these cozy kitchens.

HALLS

The entrance hall is a transition between the exterior and interior of the house. An entrance hall is not a necessity in a small house where space is at a premium, but it is desirable in order to promote privacy, to exclude outside functions from the living room, and to keep heat from escaping in winter.

When planning a front hall, interesting proportions, pleasing decoration, and convenience should be sought. At least one coat closet and possibly a powder room may be located off the entrance hall. Closets can be fitted under a stairway; bookshelves and cupboards can line the walls. See page 349. Halls may be plain or lively. Decorative and durable floors of linoleum or tiles are suitable in the halls of some homes.

The back hall in the average home should be as small as convenience permits, extending only exactly far enough to include the necessary doors. In a one-story house a passage connecting the kitchen with a bathroom is desirable.

BEDROOMS

Sleeping rooms should be located so that they are private and are protected from noise and morning sun. On a noisy street they should be placed at the back of the house. They should have cross ventilation and if possible should be exposed to the breeze so that they cool off quickly when the sun goes down.

To add interest to the house plan, bedrooms should be of different shapes, with one larger than the others. Bedrooms in general are smaller now than formerly. Small individual bedrooms for children are preferable to double rooms.

Bedroom doors and windows must be carefully located in order to allow convenient furniture arrangement; corner windows are especially advantageous in this respect. All large rooms should be designed to accommodate twin beds. Beds should be placed so that occupants do not have to face windows. A boy's room or a girl's room sometimes has double-decker beds for the use of juvenile guests. See page 171. Where space is limited a disappearing bed of some type may be desirable. When two single beds are needed in a small room, it is sometimes advisable to buy a pair, one of which is made to fit underneath the other one when not in use.

BATHROOMS

Americans require plenty of bathrooms. For resale purposes alone, two bathrooms should be built even in a two-bedroom house. The ideal arrangement is for each bedroom to have its own bathroom or a concealed wash bowl. Every house should have at least one shower bath either in a stall by itself or in connection with a built-in tub with a high tiled wall. For convenience the toilet is sometimes located in a separate room. A two-story house having bathrooms only on the second floor needs a lavatory and toilet on the first floor. Locating bathrooms over or near the kitchen or laundry is economical of plumbing.

Bathrooms need not be large; in fact, 5 feet by 6 feet are adequate dimensions. A bathroom that is nearly square may be more comfortable, more space-saving, and better looking than a long one. The bathtub, which need not be long, may be placed across one short end of the room if the location of the door permits. New offerings in bathtubs should be investigated before building plans are made. Square tubs and sunken tubs have some advantages but are awkward to clean. The hand hold, taps, and soap dish should be placed at the middle of the side of the tub. A flat over-size brim on the wash bowl is a great convenience. See the built-in bowl on page 174. The bathroom window should be as large as the inside conditions and the exterior design permit.

All bathroom plans should locate the furnishings and conveniences. Space should be allowed for a small chair, scales, and an instantaneous air heater in the wall. One or two large medicine cabinets and towel cupboards are necessary.

A woman's bathroom might well be combined with her dressing room, particularly if her bedroom is also a sitting room. This combination bath-dressing room should have a large built-in unit extending across one wall consisting of drawers and a central dressing table with a mirror above it flanked by windows. Drawers of different sizes for toilet articles, lingerie, and supplies are necessary. Decorative, shallow, open shelves might surround the mirror, holding a collection of attractive bottles and jars.

Complete prefabricated bathrooms planned by outstanding designers are on the market and should be investigated by prospective home builders.

CLOSETS

Order, which is the basis of beauty, is possible only where there are plenty of closets. Many small closets are more useful than a few large ones; even a small house needs at least ten closets.

Clothes closets of the wardrobe type, slightly deeper than clothes hangers, are convenient and space-saving, their chief drawback being that their sliding or swinging doors occupy considerable wall space. Partitions between rooms may consist of shallow closets. Closets are often combined with dressing rooms, so as to eliminate chests of drawers from bedrooms which serve also as sitting rooms. Prefabricated units of shelves, sliding trays, and drawers are desirable for such closets. Women's closets should have high poles for long dresses, medium space for day dresses, and short spaces for blouses and jackets. Men's closets should be planned in the same manner. The spaces above and below the clothes are useful for shelves or drawers, to hold hats, shoes, or whatever is necessary.

A coat closet near the front door is required for family wraps. Unless a near-by bedroom can be used for visitors' wraps, a second coat closet is advisable. It should have shelves for hats and an umbrella rack in addition to a rod for coat hangers.

A clothes storage closet which can be mothproofed and locked should hold blankets and winter clothes in summer, and summer clothes in winter. Two dustproof linen closets or cupboards are needed, one for table linens and one for bedroom linens. A cleaning closet is required for broom, floor mop, and vacuum cleaner.

UTILITY ROOMS

A house with a basement may require only a storage closet on the first floor, but one without a basement needs a utility room for storage cupboards, heaters, laundry equipment, freezing unit, work table, garbage can, and miscellaneous articles. A farm-house utility room is also a dirt-catching room where work clothes and dirty shoes are kept and washing facilities are provided. A storage room may be an inside room without windows. A utility room can be made attractive now that laundry machines, tubs, and dryers are designed in good-looking block forms which are built in. See page 175. A combination utility-laundry-breakfast area may be built as an alcove off the kitchen and decorated exactly like it.

PLAYROOMS

A play room of some kind is indispensable in a home where the members of the family are of various ages and tastes, so that noisy activities and games can be relegated to this room. Even the man of average means, under normal conditions, now has leisure time in which to relax, play games, and dance. Daughters should have a place away from the family group for their dates. Small children, too, need indoor play space in unpleasant weather. All these wants can be met by one well-planned recreation room. It may be located in the attic, first floor, or basement. See page 211.

GARAGES OR MOTOR ROOMS

It is not logical to place the garage at the rear of a lot where it definitely spoils the landscape, necessitating an ugly long driveway. Its position there is a holdover from the days when stables were placed far off because of their stench. For reasons of safety, convenience, and appearance, the motor room should be made a part of the house proper. There it can be heated from the central system and can be reached in comfort. The best solutions to this problem incorporate the garage into the total house design so successfully that it does not appear as an unrelated unit. A corner lot permitting the motor room to open on the side street is especially suitable for this arrangement. A lot that slopes to one side across the front permits the garage to be located on the low side under the house. The motor room that faces the front street may be minimized by placing it about 6 feet farther back than the front line of the house. See page 192. Carefully detailed or paneled doors add interest to the house design. Automatic door-closing devices help to prevent the possibility of garage doors being left ajar. If possible, the less desirable northern exposure should be assigned to the motor room, which would then help to protect the house from the north wind.

The disadvantages of an attached garage are that often it is not well designed, that it decreases first-floor window space, that it adds to the cost of the house in localities where fireproof walls are required, and that it sometimes increases the cost of insurance. Car ports may replace garages in mild climates. See page 193.

OUTDOOR LIVING AREAS

Outdoor living is fortunately becoming an important part of American life. Homes should provide convenient furnished outdoor areas. Space around houses should be organized for porches, sun pockets, sleeping porches, verandas, decks, patios, or terraces. It is essential that such areas should have surfaced floors. See pages 147, 176, and 190.

New-home builders who wish to feature outdoor living areas are advised to select the twentieth-century Modern style because it lends itself better than any other to the integration of exterior and interior space. The sliding glass walls permit ready access to the outdoors. The flat roofs can be used as sun decks and can also be extended as overhangs to protect the first floor from sun and rain. Traditional types of houses with formal balanced plans, high foundations, or few and small openings cannot easily be integrated with outdoor living areas.

The special needs of a family determine what outdoor areas are necessary, but one well-furnished outdoor living room, preferably on the east, is essential in every home. If possible, comfortable outdoor places for lounging and for eating at any time of day, in any reasonable weather, should be provided. Some architects maintain that the minimum requirement is a summer terrace or porch and a winter terrace or porch. Porches or terraces that are only partly roofed are most accommodating. No porch roof should be allowed to shut out the winter sunshine from the living room. If a porch is built on the south it should have a roof of glass, screen, or louvered slats slanted so as to admit the winter sun and exclude the higher summer sun. In certain sections of the country the first requisite for comfort is to have the outdoor living area well screened. Low surrounding walls or planting will make roofless areas private and sheltered. A high single wall extending from the house serves as a wind break.

For those who like to cook outdoors a comfortable high fireplace should be built near the house, possibly back to back with the living-room fireplace. Outdoor sleeping areas should be planned for those members who wish them; protection from wind and rain is necessary; access to two bedrooms from one porch is desirable. A place for sun bathing should be provided.

DESIGNING INTERIOR WALLS

In designing a house, tentative interior elevations are developed along with the floor plans. These cannot be made definite, however, until the exterior elevations of the house have been designed. *Function* directs much of the designing of interior walls, for space must be devised to suit the furniture, and good circulation determines the location of doors. Moldings, which are dust-catchers, are minimized for the sake of function. *Beauty* can be attained along with good functioning by proper designing. The five principles of design, proportion, balance, emphasis, rhythm, and repetition, are excellent guides to pleasing appearance.

Proportion applies to the walls and to all the shapes that occur in them. Height is an important factor in the proportion of walls and in their expressiveness. High walls are necessary in large rooms; low walls are desirable in small rooms, especially those of cottage type.

Proportioning the other architectural features that give character and interest to rooms requires study. Fireplaces, built-in bookshelves, corner cupboards, and seats may be ugly or beautiful. A fireplace must be in scale with the room and have good proportion. See page 476. A large fireplace is suitable only in a large room or a rough-textured room; a small fireplace is necessary in a small room or a room of refined type. It scarcely need be said that gas- or electric-heated logs or coals do not require built-in fireplaces and chimneys; such imitations are insincere and should be avoided.

Balance of openings desired in an interior wall may conflict with the location desired on the exterior of the house. In a compromise between them usually the exterior balance is considered more necessary for interiors can be balanced by the location of furniture.

Emphasis on some part of a room may be obtained by means of an important architectural feature. Emphasis on one direction of line often creates a desired effect.

Rhythm occurs in the relation of doors, windows, and other architectural features.

Repetition is a factor conducive to unity. For example, built-in bookshelves, cupboards, and seats should continue the lines of the doors and windows. The upper line of doors and windows should be at the same level if possible.

PROBLEMS

A sufficient number of problems are listed so that choices may be made.

1. Copy a floor plan drawn by an architect in order to learn technique.
2. Visit some unfinished houses and write reports.
3. Draw a floor plan for a kitchen with a dining nook, locating the utilities.
4. Draw an original floor plan for a small, one-story house.
5. Draw a living room wall showing built-in shelves and seats.
6. Design a floor plan with the kitchen on the street front.

READING REFERENCES

ERICKSON, E. E., and SOULES, R. L. *Planning Your Home.* Manual Arts Press, 1938.

FIELD, DOROTHY J. *The Human House.* Houghton Mifflin, 1939.

GORDON, ELIZABETH, and DUCAS, DOROTHY. *More House for Your Money.* Morrow, 1937.

GRAY, GRETA. *House and Home.* Lippincott, 1935.

PICKERING, ERNEST. *Shelter for Living.* Wiley, 1941.

ROGERS, TYLER STUART. *Plan Your House to Suit Yourself.* Scribner, 1937.

WAUGH, ALICE. *Planning the Little House.* McGraw-Hill, 1939

PERIODICALS

American Architect	*Better Homes and Gardens*
American Home	*California Arts and Architecture*
Architectural Forum	*House and Garden*
Architectural Record	*House Beautiful*

This functional prefabricated house interior illustrates the omission of partitions to give space. The sink and refrigerator harmonize with the walls of plywood. The total achievement is as new and American as the great T.V.A. itself. Such houses should be built by tens of thousands in this country. *Courtesy Tennessee Valley Authority.*

The room below shows a convenient arrangement of bunks for two boys. Knotty pine is a decorative and practical permanent wall surface. A boy's personality is expressed in the nautical idea that is carried out in the fishing-net curtains with cork floats, the portholes, ship's lantern, ladder, and bedspread. *Courtesy Western Pines Association.*

The two pictures above show the sleeping bay and the kitchen bay in a one-room house. Spaciousness is gained by the omission of walls between these areas. Note the built-in bed and the bamboo screen that can be unrolled as needed. Interesting textures make patterned materials unnecessary. *Courtesy Richard J. Neutra.*

In the pleasing room below, the square columns suggest a wall but do not block the continuity of space. The floor-to-ceiling windows and the brick wall around the fireplace are noteworthy. *Courtesy L. M. Yost, architect and owner.*

In this home, meals are served in the dining alcove or on the terrace. A pleasant outdoor feeling has been produced by the large openings, bamboo chairs, and rush matting. Beauty is the result of fine proportions and uncluttered space. *Courtesy Harwell Hamilton Harris.*

The end of the living room pictured below is well designed, the bookshelves and the windows making one pleasing unit. The floral pattern arranged in vertical stripes in the draperies is effective. Conventional period furniture is used. The tea service is removed after serving. *Courtesy Tamley, Inc.*

Above at the left the built-in wash basin and the lighting panels in the ceiling are pleasing architectural features. The lower end of the ladder of tubing can be lifted to the shower spigot and attached there, providing a place to hang clothes to dry. A permanent fixture above the tub would be even more practical.

Above at the right a cupboard for each member of the family is a convenient arrangement. Wall paper patterned with stripes to match the floor would have been desirable in this room. *Courtesy Armstrong Cork Company.*

A practical play room is pictured below. It can be used as a study room when necessary. Note the screen and projector. A Modern tubing chair would be more consistent here. *Courtesy Congoleum-Nairn Company.*

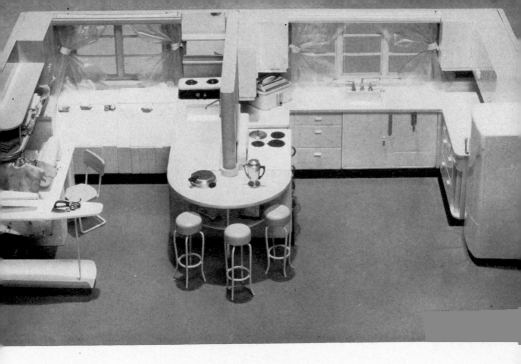

The model room above shows how a kitchen and utility room can be combined. When the ironing equipment is put away the laundry room can be used as a dinette. The washing and drying machines under the window look well because of their architectural lines.
Courtesy Westinghouse.

The kitchen below was built to fit this well-designed, prefabricated, L-shaped equipment. Notice the stainless steel counter which is well lighted from tubes concealed under the cupboards.

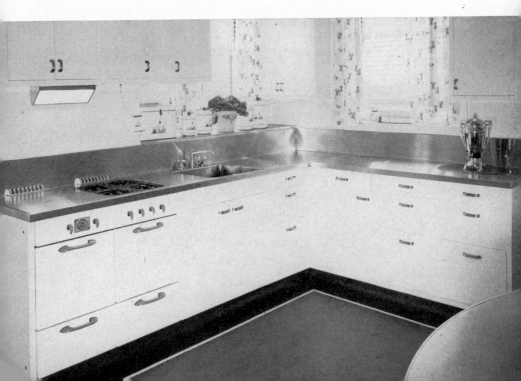

Above is a dramatic night view of the outdoor living room and the indoor living room of the delightful Neutra home in Los Angeles. Notice the circular table around a tree and the end of the stone seat with the waterproof cushions. *Courtesy Richard J. Neutra.*

The house below was designed to make indoor-outdoor living pleasant and easy. Every house should have at least one convenient living terrace.
Courtesy Wurster, Bernardi, and Emmons, architects.

CHAPTER 11

EXTERIOR HOUSE DESIGN

After the interior floor plans of a house have been tentatively designed to fit the needs and activities of a family an exterior must be found or preferably created to suit the interior. It is sometimes possible to find a ready-made plan so nearly like the one evolved by the family that its ready-made exterior design can be used. Generally, however, the family that cannot afford complete architectural service should engage an architect to design at least the exterior and to revise its tentative interior plan where necessary for convenience, economy, and appearance. The architect's experience and taste should enable him to crystallize the ideas of the family into exterior and interior plans for a practical and beautiful house.

The choice of the exterior design often depends on whether a sloping roof or a flat roof is desired. Sloping roofs are more familiar for they are used on most traditional houses. Flat roofs, however, cost less, weigh less, do not waste space, and can easily be extended. Compare the roof lines on page 191.

Some interior floor plans indicate clearly what the exteriors should be like. If a floor plan is symmetrical with a central entrance hall and a room on each side, the house may have one of several different types of balanced exteriors. It may be based on a Cape Cod, Colonial, Dutch Colonial, Georgian, Regency, or French house. All these houses with their passive, symmetrical façades should stand on flat ground.

If a floor plan is irregular, the exterior may be designed as Non-Period, Modern, Jamaican, rural Mediterranean, or a ranch-house type. Asymmetrical houses like these are suitable for either flat ground or hillsides. Irregular houses must be more restrained in the city than is necessary in the country.

177

One way to judge the exterior appearance of a house intelligently is to test the color, texture, form, and lines of the house by the *art principles:* proportion, scale, balance, emphasis, rhythm, repetition, transition, and variation.

The *color* of a house should be neither too conspicuous nor so drab that it is not noticed. One that harmonizes with the colors of neighboring houses is advisable. White and off-white are the most popular colors for houses; grays, tans, and beiges are also good. Brighter colors are suitable in semi-tropical sections.

Painting the trim around doors and windows and on corners and edges to match the walls adds to apparent size and solidity of a house; it also makes the faults of a poorly designed house less conspicuous. Brighter colors are often used on shutters and occasionally on doors. Shutters painted to match the roof usually look well.

Roofs are usually slate gray, grayish brown, or the modified natural red of tiles, depending somewhat on the style of the house. Deliberate spotting or other color variation in shingles, calling attention to the roof, is objectionable.

The *texture* of exterior materials should have more affinity than contrast. For example, wood and brick combine well, both expressing friendliness. Sleek glass, steel, and plastics are harmonious, all expressing Modernism. Deliberate texture effects are likely to be unpleasant, such as exaggerated trowel marks on stucco walls. Textural variety should be avoided on small houses; therefore they should be surfaced in one material only.

The *form,* or mass, which is by far the most important of all the elements of house design, should be as simple as possible. Complex so-called picturesque massing of several boxlike units is undesirable. Fairy-tale shapes and deliberately quaint houses quickly become tiresome. A good simple floor plan is likely to result in a house having strong, plain masses.

Line can scarcely be considered separately from form on the exterior of a house, but a roof line is too conspicuous to overlook. Hipped roofs have more smoothly flowing lines than gable roofs. The angles of various gables must be alike for the sake of unity. Flat roofs look well on horizontal masses. Chimneys should be plain, pleasing in line, and in harmony with the house. See page 62.

Proportion is a basic principle that refers to pleasing relationship in line and spaces. In judging the exterior of a house the proportion of the whole composition as well as every detail is a matter of concern. Low, broad houses like those on page 190 are more pleasing in proportion than tall houses. One important consideration is the relative heights of the foundation, walls, and roof. Only a small amount of exposed foundation is desirable, particularly in a small house. The wall and the roof must not be equal in area as observed from the front walk. Each wall should have pleasing dimensions, like one-third more length than height.

Windows and doors suggest definite ideas by their proportions: low, broad windows and doors are informal; high windows and doors are stately. Although traditional double-hung windows are most common, where ventilation is of first importance the most serviceable windows are either the casement type or the modern type with horizontal panels, opening outward to exclude rain. Large floor-to-ceiling windows and bay windows provide more light and more interest than ordinary types. Good proportions can be obtained in all these types. Small windows above fireside bookcases or above a buffet are awkward in proportion; furthermore, they do not provide a view and are difficult to curtain.

In all moderate-priced houses ready-made windows and doors should be purchased complete with frames and weather stripping for the sake of economy and also for smooth functioning.

Scale refers usually to the size of details in relation to the size of the entire house. For example, a small house must have narrow cornices and moldings, small windows, and fine proportions in doors. Windows, especially dormer windows, are often too large for the places where they are used. Small-paned windows are usually in better scale with a small house than large panes, and they often add charm and give a feeling of privacy. Unfortunately doorways are sometimes too large or too small for the scale of façades of houses.

Porch columns may appear too large for the small weight above them. On the other hand, modern columns may appear too small, for we have not yet become accustomed to the fact that slender columns when made of steel can support great weight. One unbroken line from floor to ceiling is desirable, therefore porch columns should not be placed on high bases. See page 191.

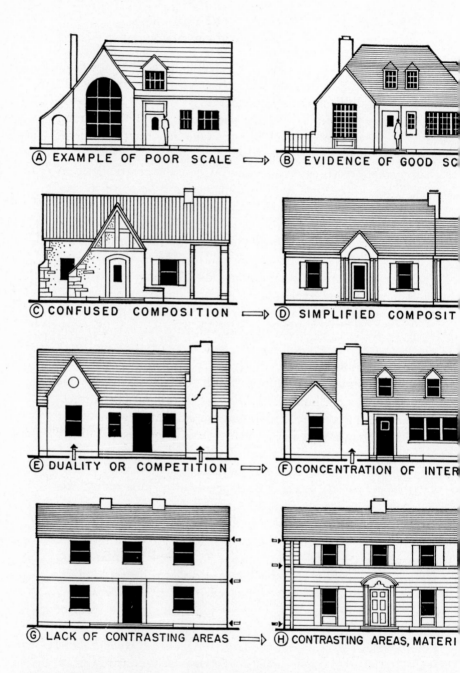

ILLUSTRATING THE PRINCIPLES OF DESI

Sketches showing poor exterior design in traditional types of houses and methods of im
ing the appearance of these homes by the application of the principles of design. R
duced by permission from SHELTER FOR LIVING by E. Pickering, published by
Wiley & Sons, Inc.

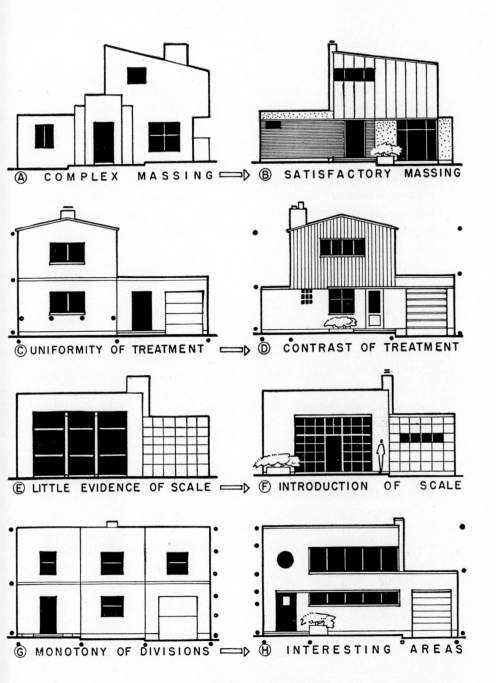

Ⓐ COMPLEX MASSING ⟹ Ⓑ SATISFACTORY MASSING

Ⓒ UNIFORMITY OF TREATMENT ⟹ Ⓓ CONTRAST OF TREATMENT

Ⓔ LITTLE EVIDENCE OF SCALE ⟹ Ⓕ INTRODUCTION OF SCALE

Ⓖ MONOTONY OF DIVISIONS ⟹ Ⓗ INTERESTING AREAS

UNSATISFACTORY AND IMPROVED EXTERIORS

In the exteriors on the left there is evidence of unsatisfactory massing, monotony of treatment, and lack of scale. These faults are corrected in the drawings on the right. *Reproduced by permission from SHELTER FOR LIVING by E. Pickering, published by John Wiley & Sons, Inc.*

Balance in relation to exteriors of houses may be formal or informal. Formal or symmetrical houses are alike on both sides of a central vertical axis. Usually a formal front façade has a central doorway with identical windows on the two sides of it and second-floor windows located directly above first-floor openings. However, side or rear walls are not necessarily symmetrical. Symmetrical houses are expressive of dignity and restraint. Formal balance should not be secured at the expense of a functional floor plan, as, unfortunately, it often is. Houses with formal balance are less difficult to design than the informal, and desirable models that may be copied are numerous.

Informal or asymmetric balance is usually found in Modern, Non-period, ranch, or hillside houses. The front view of an asymmetrical house often shows the kind of balance that is demonstrated when a big boy and a little boy sit on a seesaw. A large part, the entrance, near the center on one side is balanced by a smaller part, windows, farther away on the other side. It is not easy to create or to judge informal balance, as there are no definite guides, but a house that does not appear one-sided is likely to balance. Informal balance is highly desirable. It is active, not passive; it is subtle and friendly and often has charm and beauty. Most important of all it is consistent with functional floor plans of any shape. An architect is more capable of judging balance than others are. On page 194 the two houses above have informal balance and the two houses below have formal.

Emphasis applies in several ways to the exterior of a house. There should be one large block or mass of the house that dominates the entire composition; wings should be considerably smaller and possibly lower than the main body. One surface material should dominate but should not be conspicuous.

The entrance on the front façade should have dignity and style. The entrance door should be definitely the center of interest. It may be emphasized by purely decorative architectural embellishment or by a useful element such as a small hood or roof, possibly with columns. See page 73. It may also be accented by a pair of tall distinctive shrubs or other features in the landscaping. Restraint in emphasis is as important as emphasis. The sensitive observer rejoices at evidence that a designer has not employed emphasis to its fullest extent but has held his power in reserve.

Rhythm does not occur in a perfectly plain wall but where openings, details, or changes appear. The eye is attracted to such features, and they may be so designed that they lead the attention about in a rhythmic connected path.

In an orderly arrangement the lines of doors and windows are related to the lines of the house. The upper line of windows and doors on one floor should usually be on the same level. Arched openings are sometimes inharmonious with rectangular openings. Uniformity in the size and shape of windows and window panes is desirable. The angle, as well as the size of dormer windows and gables, is an important factor in rhythm.

Repetition usually occurs in any form of architectural ornamentation. The exterior surface material is often full of the rhythm of repetition. Shadows cast by clapboards or shingles sometimes make a strong repeat pattern. Bricks and the mortar between them create repetition, but conspicuous difference in color between brick and mortar is objectionable. Other types of rhythm are radiation, which occurs in the spokes of a fanlight, and transition, which occurs in arches or other rounded forms.

Variation in line, size, texture, and color adds interest to exterior house design if used discreetly. An example of variety in direction occurs where boards on the first story of a house are horizontal and boards on the second story are vertical. Variety in form and size occurs where wings project from the main mass of the house. Variation in surface texture and color is undesirable in small houses. Since variety is not unlike seasoning it must be used with restraint. Variety within unity is the goal to seek.

Objectives to be sought in the appearance of the exterior of a house are simplicity, unity, and finally beauty. Simplicity and modesty are essential in the design of small houses; no pretentious details are appropriate for them.

Unity results when the house design consists of harmonious parts combined in a well-integrated whole. Dominance of the main mass of the house and dominance of one material, one color, and one idea insure unity.

Beauty is elusive; it can best be recognized or produced by those who understand how to analyze the elements of art according to the principles of design; understanding is attained by practise in analysis.

HOUSE BUILDING MATERIALS

Wood is a popular material because workmen understand it; it is relatively cheap, looks well, and gives good insulation. It is possible to buy chemically treated wood, which is practically termite-proof and much more durable than ordinary wood. Good-looking, durable plywood panels are now used for exterior walls, as well as interior. They are particularly valuable in prefabrication and in other rapid construction.

Brick provides good insulation, has a pleasing variety of color, does not require painting, and is fire-resistant and vermin-proof. A brick house is worth the extra cost, if the budget permits.

Stucco is an exterior surfacing made of Portland cement, sand, water, and sometimes lime and mineral coloring matter. Stucco is weatherproof, rot-proof, and fire-resistant. However, ordinary stucco may crack and termites may infest the wood underneath.

Concrete is a weight-bearing material made from proper proportions of cement, sand, gravel or crushed rock, and water. It can be poured between forms, making solid walls on the job, or can be bought as blocks containing large hollow spaces which are valuable for insulation. These blocks should be used more than they are, for they are relatively cheap and are available anywhere. Concrete is fireproof and termite-proof, and its surface can be painted or stuccoed. It should not be used in damp locations.

Hollow clay tiles are a valuable weight-bearing material which also should be used more for houses. The tiles are harder than bricks and can be stuccoed or painted with special paints.

Glass sheets are used for walls in Modern homes where the elements of light and space are stressed. Glass blocks admit light and sunshine while excluding sight, sound, heat, and cold.

Composition panels of many types for exteriors are now on the market. Some of the best, which are fireproof and waterproof, are made of cement and asbestos. Various vegetable fibers, plaster, and plastics, among other materials, are also used. The panels, which are often one story high and of different widths, lend themselves to rapid construction and mass production.

Steel framing is more desirable but more costly than wood framing. Steel panels are practical and are particularly good in prefabricated houses.

SELECTING A BUILDER

An architect, a contractor, or a carpenter is usually engaged to direct the actual construction of a house. The ideal way to build is to have an *architect* plan a house to order and supervise its construction, for both esthetic and practical reasons. His knowledge of design and effective use of materials should insure a well-arranged, soundly constructed, and good-looking house. As an investment a house deserves the expert protection which only an architect can give it.

Architects' fees ordinarily range from 6 to 10 per cent of the total cost of a house. When only plans and specifications are desired the fee is about 3 per cent. In the largest cities it is possible to get less costly expert service on houses which cost less than $8,000 from a cooperative architectural agency.

The best way to select an architect is to find a house which is pleasing, learn the architect's name, visit his office, and see other houses he has built, at the same time ascertaining his business methods and his ability to direct construction. Almost all reliable architects belong to the American Institute of Architects.

The architect's work is to act as a professional adviser and an arbitrator between the owner and the contractor. He makes preliminary studies, prepares working drawings, writes specifications, makes necessary scale and detail drawings, receives bids and lets contracts, supervises construction, checks contractor's requisitions for payment of labor and materials and the receipts for them, orders changes desired by the owner, and examines public records on account of liens.

The architect's preliminary work includes consultations with the client and the making of sketches and tentative cost estimates. The client should not hurry through this stage, for here he can change his mind without cost. He should have a small model made of the house before he accepts the design.

When design and estimated cost are satisfactory, the architect has working drawings made and specifications listed. The specifications are a condensed record of everything that will be used in building the house. The owner should study the specifications with the architect.

The *contractor* should be selected with the utmost care whether one has an architect or not. The wisdom and honesty of the contractor often determine the success of a house. The contractor must be a very able man to know the ability of his men, to obtain proper sequence, to purchase wisely, to direct a staff of competent workmen, to maintain harmonious relations with the labor unions and the inspectors, and to finish a building within established limits of price and time. For inexpensive houses it is well to have a single contractor responsible for the entire house under a standard general contract. His legitimate profit is about 10 per cent of the cost of the house.

Carpenters working by the day build some houses, especially in small towns and in the country, without the services of contractors. A prospective builder who chooses this method must realize that he will have to take over an enormous amount of work and responsibility in a field where he most likely is inexperienced. He will have to direct plumbers, electricians, and painters as well as carpenters. He will have to make decisions on problems of drainage, foundations, termite proofing, and insulation, which may have local solutions. The success of the house will depend largely on the head carpenter, who should be a reliable permanent resident of the community as well as an able builder. The head carpenter directs his helpers. Day labor is usually more costly than contracted labor. Carpenters' labor should cost about twenty per cent of the total expenditure for a house.

Contractors and carpenters working without an architect usually require *stock plans* to guide them. Among the various agencies supplying stock plans is the Architects' Small House Service Bureau, sponsored by the American Institute of Architects, which has a large number of stock designs made by competent architects, obtainable with complete plans and excellent specifications for about forty dollars. Plans are procurable from some periodicals, lumber companies, manufacturers' associations, and contractors. Some agricultural colleges and government departments also furnish plans, particularly for farm houses. Builders must conform to the local building codes and planning commission regulations. The National Bureau of Standards of the United States Department of Commerce has established standardized building codes which have been adopted by the most progressive states.

PREFABRICATED HOUSES

England, Australia, Sweden, Russia, and the United States have made the most progress in prefabrication of houses. Emergency housing necessitated by the world wars and the reconstruction periods brought about tremendous developments in this field.

The purpose of applying mass-production methods to making houses is to save time, material, and labor, thereby reducing the price of houses. In a machine age it is not economical to continue making small houses by hand. Assembly-line methods are as good for small houses as for bombers. When prefabricated houses become generally available to the two-fifths of the United States population which has an annual income of $1,000 or less they will fill a vital need. Machine-made houses should also be made suitable for all incomes up to $5,000. Custom-built houses fit only the purses of the wealthy.

Different manufacturers offer various degrees and kinds of prefabrication of houses. The catalog of one firm describes a movable $3,000 one-piece house that is like a three-room apartment with a gas range, ice refrigerator, heater, and hot-water heater, all ready to connect with plumbing and utilities. Certain prefabricated houses are made in three-dimensional sections that are brought in trucks to the site.

Most prefabricators offer a packaged house made up of separate standardized panels for walls and for floors which are fastened together when the house is erected. Such panel construction promotes flexibility, because the dimensions of rooms and the location and the number of doors and windows can be made to suit the owner. Rooms can be easily added to suit changing family needs. The best prefabricated houses are entirely complete; they are fireproof, termite-proof, soundproof, and air conditioned. See pages 118 and 171.

Well-designed simple prefabricated houses in both Modern and traditional styles are obtainable. Some houses are ugly, however; imitation materials or processes and quaint effects should be avoided. Certain gifted American architects are devoting their time to prefabrication, and some famous institutions of learning promote extensive research in it.

PROBLEMS

A sufficient number of problems are listed so that choices may be made.

1. Visit a new residence section. Write descriptions of several small houses that are simple in design.
2. Make quick drawings of houses with attached garages.
3. Identify the building materials in the houses in a specific block.
4. Trace the façade of a symmetrical house from a periodical.
5. Trace the façade of an asymmetrical house.
6. Draw the ground plan of a house, showing a winter terrace and a summer porch.
7. Visit a demonstration house or some other new house to observe new features.

READING REFERENCES

ARCHITECTURAL FORUM. *The 1940 Book of Small Homes.* Simon and Schuster, 1941.

GLASER, SAMUEL. *Designs for Sixty Small Houses.* Coward-McCann, 1939.

MEAD, MARCIA, and HIGGINS, D. P. *Homes of Character.* Dodd, Mead, 1926.

NEWCOMB, R., and FOSTER, W. *Home Architecture.* Wiley, 1941.

NATIONAL BUREAU OF STANDARDS. *Recommended Minimum Requirements for Small Dwelling Construction.*

Reports of Committees. President's Conference on Home Building and Home Ownership, 1932.

The house above is an American ranch type with its long low lines and its timber construction. *Courtesy U. S. Farm Security Administration.*

The house below was made of rammed earth, which is satisfactory in some climates. This house is purely functional in design. *Courtesy Federal Public Housing Authority.*

The stone house below has good lines. Some foundation landscaping would improve its appearance. *Courtesy University of Texas.*

The house above has beauty in its roof line and in its proportions. It fits into the landscape because it is built low and also because of the quiet color of the redwood exterior. Naturally, the house faces the mountain view. *Courtesy Harold J. Bissner, architect.*

The low-roofed house below has pleasing variety; painted brick contrasts with redwood. *Courtesy California Redwood Association.*

The Modern house above reveals its design for living outdoors. The landscaping is suitable for the desert conditions at Palm Springs, California. *Courtesy Richard Neutra.*

The charm of the house below is due partly to the exterior surface, pecky cypress board and batten contrasting with horizontal weather boarding. The numerous windows and the roomy porch suggest enjoyment of the outdoors. *Courtesy R. C. Murrell, architect and owner.*

The modified Modern house above is attractive and livable. Asymmetric balance indicates an irregular floor plan. Note the horizontal slab shading the picture window and door. The large potted plants help to emphasize the entrance. *Courtesy Robert Ainsworth, architect.*

The pleasing traditional cottage below has a satisfactory location for the garage. The floor plan is evidently irregular, as is also the design of the façade.
Courtesy Weyerhaeuser Sales Company.

A. Lawrence Kocher has designed this very livable and attractive prefabricated house, which, if produced in mass, should sell for about three thousand dollars. The location of the rooms and the wall design can be varied; therefore houses need not be alike. The room arrangement shown here permits access to terraces on all sides. Fin walls provide shelter for the terraces. *Courtesy Revere Copper and Brass, Inc.*

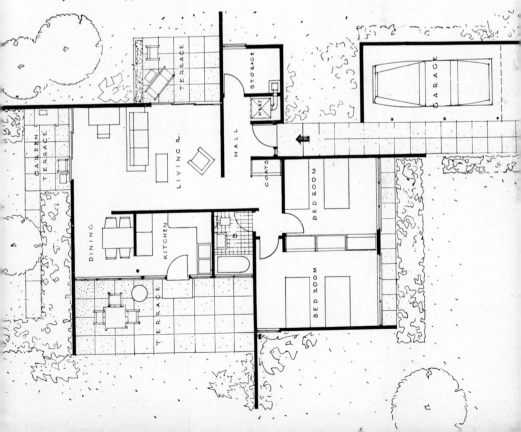

The Monterey-type house above combines California and New England characteristics. The vertical siding adds interest. An informal floor plan is apparent here. *Courtesy California Redwood Association.*

The English Colonial house below has formal balance, dignity, and restraint. The hipped roof, double chimneys, and decorated cornices are typical features.

The pleasing non-period house above is the home of the designer and author, Paul Frankl. It has an irregular, informal floor plan. The walls are light gray stucco; the door and window frames and roof are black. The wall at the right encloses a garden on a higher level.

The French Colonial style is followed in the new Louisiana home pictured below. Note the hipped roof, tall chimneys, and low foundation. Its formal balance gives it dignity, while its many openings give it a friendly quality and provide for necessary ventilation. *Courtesy Richard Koch, architect.*

CHAPTER 12

INTERIOR FINISHING

The most-used finishes are presented here. Plaster, composition panels, plywood, wood, metal, and miscellaneous materials for walls, ceilings, and floors are considered, and paint, wall paper, and fabric-covered interior surfaces are discussed briefly. However, much more information about them should be acquired, possibly from the pamphlets of manufacturers of materials.

Plaster. Plaster is the most common interior wall finish. It may be left in its natural color, it may have color mixed throughout, or it may be painted. Mixing the color with the plaster is desirable because then it cannot accidentally be rubbed off. Whitewashed plaster is excellent for cottages, particularly of the Spanish colonial type.

Unsmoothed plaster showing the natural trowel marks slightly is permissible in some types of homes, such as primitive, Spanish, or early English. Smooth plaster is necessary background for fine furniture, such as that of the eighteenth century. In fact, smooth plaster is quite generally used, because it is more pleasant to touch than rough plaster and is a good base for paint or wall paper.

One of the disadvantages of plaster is that it cracks. Plastering also is a slow process and requires expert workmanship. It must be applied wet; the moisture affects all the wood in the building, and, when swelling subsides, cracks are often left. Wet plaster also freezes and may fall off in very cold weather.

Composition Wall Boards. Asbestos, wood fibers, sugar-cane fibers, cement, and other materials are made into interior wall boards, which can usually be procured in room heights and to fit different areas, so that their joinings can be made a part of the architectural design. Wall boards are now extensively used, particularly in housing projects where rapid construction is necessary. See page 211.

Metal. Copper, aluminum, Monel metal, and gun metal are sometimes employed in Modern interiors as partial or entire wall covering. It is expected that metal walls will be common in pre-fabricated houses.

Glass. Blocks of glass make walls that admit light yet provide privacy. Panels or sheets of colorful opaque glass are perfect walls for bathrooms. An outside wall of clear, double, insulated glass is almost a requirement in a Modern living room.

Mirror. Mirror walls of glass or gun metal are important in producing an illusion of additional space.

Ceramic Tile. These clean and durable tiles are confined mostly to bathrooms and kitchens, except in Mediterranean houses.

Linoleum. Light-weight linoleum is suitable for walls in modern rooms in which durability is stressed, such as nurseries, game rooms, and bathrooms.

Cork. Panels of cork make walls of interesting texture, which unfortunately require considerable care.

Wood. Walls and ceilings of wood have a special kind of beauty due to the variations of the grain and the pleasing natural color which gives them a warm and friendly quality. Gum or redwood can be treated to suit either plain or elaborate rooms. Pine, which is usually informal, is often chosen for plainer rooms. Knotty pine and pecky cypress have especially interesting textures. Dark walnut paneling is rich. See pages 9 and 26.

Different forms of wood are available. *Plywood panels,* one story in height, are easily installed and provide a good substitute for plaster. *Flexwood,* a very thin wood surface which is successfully handled in rolls like wall paper, is particularly useful for curved surfaces. See page 210. *Squares of wood,* with the grain at right angles in adjoining squares, are effective in Modern rooms.

The average small home might well have some rooms sheathed entirely or partially in wood; even in kitchens and bathrooms it is satisfactory. Naturally, the same kind of wood should be used for walls, ceiling, interior window casings, bookshelves, and if possible for interior doors. Wax or water-white lacquer will protect wood and will not change its color much. Walls of wood require very little work or expense for maintenance. However, grooved edges on boards used for wall sheathing are not functional for they harbor the webs of small spiders.

DECORATING

Color. A brief survey of colors suitable for backgrounds (walls, ceilings, and floors) is presented here. In the distribution of color values in backgrounds, the out-of-doors is a good model. Just as the earth is darkest, trees are medium, and the sky is light, so the floors might well be darkest, walls medium, and ceilings light. Interesting modern variations of this are dark ceilings and floors with light walls, or light ceilings and floors with dark walls. Medium values are usually better than light or dark for wall colors in rooms where the wood trim is permanently dark, or where ungainly furniture must be used.

One color idea throughout all the background is usually desirable. For example, beige walls, ceiling, wood trim, doors, floors, and rugs, with some areas darker than others, are pleasing. Various tints and shades of gray-green, with the darkest shade in the rug, make cool, delightful backgrounds if relieved by considerable gray, white, and black in fabrics and furnishings. However, two colors are often effective in backgrounds. For example, grayed lime walls with emerald-green doors and carpet would be stimulating.

Although the ceiling is now considered a part of the room, not a separate item, and is usually treated exactly like the walls, many different solutions are possible where a more novel effect is desired. The color of the ceiling may be like the background or foreground of the wall paper, contrasted with the walls, like some color in the drapery, like the rug or floor, or like the painted woodwork or doors.

All the walls of a room need not be treated alike; some may be painted a different color or covered with wall paper or fabric for the sake of variety or emphasis. See page 104. The fireplace wall is often featured in color. A wall with a view window can be stressed by painting it light and the other walls dark. Sometimes proportions are apparently improved by differences in the color of walls. A room too long for its width needs warm, dark colors on the two end walls only; a square room would be improved by having light colors on two opposite walls and medium or dark colors on the others. An alcove in any room may be painted in a bright color if the room needs it, even though the other walls are neutral.

Background colors can be utilized to remedy some undesirable conditions. Where walls are imperfect, light blue, light green, flesh color, or ivory is recommended; white or lemon-yellow exaggerates irregularities. In dark rooms, white, flesh, peach, or yellow is most desirable for the reflecting qualities. A room too large for the furnishings should usually have walls of warm, advancing colors. Unless it is dark, a small room should have cool-colored walls, with ceiling and wood trim to match. A room that is too high would be improved by a contrasting dado, a contrasting ceiling, or a drop ceiling. Wide horizontal stripes can be painted on walls that are too high; vertical stripes, on walls that are too low or too long. The use of painters' tape insures straight lines. An old room with unrelated textures and cut-up walls can be unified by covering the wall paper, wood trim, dadoes, cornices, and fireplace brick with flat washable paint in one subdued but definite color, such as French blue.

Neutral colors such as white, off-white, gray, beige, brown, and natural color are good safe colors for backgrounds. Brown or dark gray should be accompanied by a generous quantity of white for contrast. Cream and tan are rather commonplace.

Positive, clear, fresh colors that have been neutralized somewhat without loss of clarity or character are highly desirable for backgrounds. Grayed lime, grayed pink, grayed peach, light slate-blue, light turquoise-blue, sky-blue, sage-green, pale lemon-yellow, and golden yellow are excellent wall colors, combining easily with other colors. If every article in a room is exactly right in color, dark blue-green, clear medium blue, cherry-red, or chartreuse walls are beautiful. A person who can paint her own walls or can have them done every year should certainly make use of some positive colors.

When a color arrangement is planned for a definite room, the backgrounds and furnishings should be considered together. Usually the entire scheme is based on the color of a fabric, carpet, or wall paper which unifies the total effect. This subject is developed toward the end of Chapter 3. Clear colors should not be chosen as backgrounds for dingy, shabby furniture. Patterned wall paper in medium soft tones is most kindly to old possessions as it attracts attention away from them, even while it blends with them. Such a background is also kindly to middle-aged figures.

In this dining room the clear cool green of the walls predominates. It provides an effective contrast for the off-white furniture. Yellow-green linens, dishes, and plants would complete the analogous scheme with the yellow ceiling and orange-yellow upholstery.

In the children's bedroom three values of green are employed on the walls. The lightest green should have been used on the ceiling also in order to make green dominant in quantity. The green and the dark magenta (raspberry-red) are both fresh, clear colors suitable for a child's room.

The kitchen reveals the pleasing use of red-violet for the floor and a pale tint of the same color for the ceiling; it is definitely the dominant color in the room. The dark blue-violet on the counters gives sparkle to the scheme.

The color schemes of all three of the Modern rooms on this page consist of combinations of warm and cool colors. The top picture has an *analogous scheme* of green, yellow, and orange-yellow; the middle picture has a *complementary scheme* of green and red; the bottom picture has a *split-complementary scheme* of pale orange-yellow with its opposites red-violet and blue-violet. *Courtesy Newcastle Products.*

Paints. In the last decade the paint manufacturers have developed many new types of paints through the introduction of new pigments and solvents, synthetic resins, and synthetic oils. The home owner should become acquainted with the offerings in this field. Some of these paints are made for special purposes; therefore information on labels must be followed carefully.

Oil Paints. Oil paints consist of four components: the pigment, which is a bulky opaque substance; the vehicle, which is an oil, usually linseed, soybean, perilla, or tung; the thinner, which is turpentine; and the dryer, a compound that absorbs oxygen quickly.

Glossy paints are more durable than flat paints and consequently are better in kitchens and bathrooms and on doors and other places which become soiled. Dark-painted walls are usually made glossy so that they will reflect light to brighten them.

Semi-gloss paint is better looking than glossy paint. It is more resistant to soil and wear than flat paint; therefore it is a better finish for doors and wood trim.

Flat paint, which is either dull or satiny in finish, is most desirable for walls, provided that it is washable. Flat paint on doors, window sills, and lower walls usually requires a light coat of liquid wax or varnish for protection.

One of the chief advantages of oil paint is that any desired color can be obtained in it. This paint can be easily applied, and even an amateur job looks well if carefully done. Important practical considerations are that it is durable and washable. Sometimes a thin coat of starch is put on a newly painted wall, then, when the starch is soiled, it is washed off and replaced by a coat of clean starch.

Oil paint can be applied to plaster, composition panels, wood, fabric, metal, and other surfaces that are not waxed. If the plaster is imperfect, a fine canvas covering should be put over it before it is painted. Oil paint can be used over other oil paint or varnish, although it does not wear so well over varnish. A thin glaze of one color may be applied over a closely related color, often producing a rich effect. A coat of sealer paint is necessary over absorbent surfaces before oil paint is used. A finely stippled finish is usually desirable. A small quantity of oil paint of each color which is used should be saved for making repairs.

Water-Soluble Paints. These popular interior finishes come in powder form and are mixed with hot or cold water before they are used. Their advantages are that they are cheap, easy to apply, and quick-drying. Their chief disadvantage is that they are not usually washable.

Calcimine. This common water-soluble paint is made from whiting and coloring matter with glue as a binder. Calcimine colors are usually light; however, additional dark-colored pigment can be added.

Casein Paints. Casein, which is made from milk curds, is a common binder for pigments mixed with water. The casein paints dry quickly, conceal a surface with one coat, and are washable. They can be applied to plaster, wall board, stucco, and cement.

Resin Emulsion Paint. Paints for both exteriors and interiors are made from pigments combined with emulsions of synthetic resins and thinned with water. They are quickly applied, cover well, dry rapidly, and are washable. They can be used on fresh plaster, wall board, wall paper, cement, stucco, concrete, and brick.

Cement-Based Paints. Portland cement mixed with pigments and water makes durable water-insoluble finishes for masonry.

Rubber-Based Paints. Chlorinated rubber has been combined with pigments to make paints that are remarkably durable.

Aluminum Paints. Paints are made of aluminum flakes and special thinners and binders. They are valuable as priming coats for wood surfaces and as finishing coats on structural steel.

Enamels. Made from pigments and special varnishes enamels are employed for many purposes. They are easily applied, do not fade or become dull, and are usable indoors or outdoors. A porous surface should have a priming coat before enamel is applied.

Varnishes. Clear varnishes without pigment are used as protective coats or as ingredients of paints and enamels. They are made by cooking natural resins or fossil gums with alcohol or a drying oil and volatile thinners and driers. Spar varnishes are the best quality.

Shellac. This may be a sealer or a finish for floors, wood trim, and furniture. It is made from a resinous substance called lac deposited on trees in India and the far East.

Lacquer. A quick-drying finish containing cellulose, resins, solvents, and sometimes dye or pigment is called lacquer.

Wall Paper. Wall paper was first made to take the place of high-priced tapestry and textiles. At the outset Italian booklining papers in small sheets were used; later they were followed by Domino papers, which were small marbleized squares. Subsequently France produced the present type of wall paper of continuous design but printed by hand, and also picture papers and scenic wall papers. Machine-printed wall papers such as we have today were the next development.

Wall paper has some important advantages. It can be applied to walls by amateurs, especially now that the pasting medium is already on the paper. Although acceptable wall paper is obtainable at a low price, the better-quality paper is more durable and offers more choice in patterns.

Wall paper is very useful in covering imperfect surfaces. It can supply texture or pattern, which are necessary at times. It can improve poor proportions, vertical stripes adding height and horizontal stripes adding breadth.

Patterned wall paper effectively contributes to the theme of a room. Polka dots or gingham plaids suggests intimate cottages (page 104); broad, five-inch stripes or stylized motifs (page 209) add to Modern effects; Greek motifs contribute to the formality of an Empire room; western, military, or nautical motifs usually suit a boy's room. On page 86 Rococo wall paper and furniture are harmonius and expressive of femininity.

Sometimes patterned wall paper is put on one wall or perhaps two, the other walls being left plain. Page 223 shows patterned wall paper used on the ceiling only.

Although ordinary wall-paper borders at the ceiling line only are usually not desirable, a very high room may possibly be improved by one width of patterned paper as a border. Paper borders may also be put around the doors and windows and above the baseboard on plain walls.

It is difficult to select wall paper, because so few good patterns are available, and because those that appear satisfactory as samples may become overpowering on large areas. Desirable wall papers are pictured on pages 209, 240, and 279. A roll of each of the papers under consideration should be hung in the room for several days before selection is made. Many wall papers are now waterproof and washable.

Some wall papers to consider are those with:

1. Grass cloth surfaces.
2. Thin wood surfaces.
3. Solid colors.
4. Marbled patterns.
5. Stripes.
6. Plaids and checks.
7. Polka dots.
8. Diamonds or stars.
9. Leaf forms.
10. Copies of botany prints.
11. Copies of period prints.
12. French toile flower patterns

Some wall papers to avoid are those with:

1. Weak, trailing or scattered flowers or leaves.
2. Pressed or embossed surfaces.
3. A spotty effect with motifs too dark.
4. Figures that are out of scale with the rooms.
5. Mixed motifs combining delicate and bold figures.
6. Strong diagonals (opposed to architectural unity).
7. Papers that have three-dimensional effects.
8. Contrasting color schemes.
9. Brocade and satin stripes and medallions.
10. Restless busy patterns suggesting movement.
11. Silver or gilt.
12. Pictorial patterns, like hunting scenes.
13. Imitations of draped or puffed materials.
14. Imitation plaster effects.

Scenic wall paper is probably the most difficult kind to select and use, but it is sometimes hung as a background for period furniture where it is historically authentic. Halls and dining rooms, where people do not remain long, seem to be favorite places for it. See page 10. The person who has scenic paper should treat it with proper respect. There should be no high furniture to cut the figures in the wrong places. An effort should be made to fit the motif to the wall spaces. Landscape panels are generally better designed than the usual continuous scenic wall paper. Some Chinese landscape papers are particularly desirable; some bird and floral papers are attractive. See page 278. Since there is little restraint in the pictorial aspect of scenic paper, it is usually advisable to select a one-color effect, preferably brown or gray. The woodwork and doors in the same room should usually repeat the chief light color in the scenic paper.

Fabric-Covered Walls. Fabrics are now being used frequently to cover one, two, three, or four walls in a room. They may be attached to the walls, hung loosely, or stretched on frames so that they can be removed for cleaning. Fabrics from either the dress goods or the drapery departments can be used if they are sunfast and suitable. The purchaser should realize that usually only solid colors or unobtrusive patterns should be considered when such a large quantity of material is employed.

Unattached fabrics can be hung to cover entire walls by nailing them to a molding at the ceiling line. They can be pleated, gathered, or just eased on, depending partly on the stiffness of the fabric. Gingham, toile, corduroy, raw silk, chintz, brocade, canvas, denim, or, in fact, almost any firm material is usable. This method is ideal for persons who live in rented places and wish to take their improvements with them when they move. See pages 302 and 314.

Fabrics to be attached to a wall should be firmly woven, such as canvas, linen, or burlap. Where texture is to be emphasized, grass cloth, which comes in many varieties, is the best material. Where pattern is desired, ginghams and percales in checks, plaids, and small floral patterns are attractive. Leatherette makes an appropriate finish in a book room, a den, or a man's room. Dull-finished oilcloth for walls comes in excellent designs and is practical, for it cleans well and wears well.

It is sometimes desirable to cover only a part of each wall with a fabric. The upper two-thirds can be a fabric, with a molding and a dado below. Fabric-covered panels can be placed on the wall behind a sofa or a bed; generally the same material should appear elsewhere, possibly all over the opposite wall, or as a bedspread, or draperies. Panels are easily made by tacking a narrow wooden lath around a space and stretching or pleating the fabric over this, using small tacks. Sometimes the edge is covered with a narrow wood molding.

A family with an artist member, even an amateur, should provide some canvas-covered walls for personal mural paintings. Children's rooms, recreation rooms, and bathrooms might well be settings for bold amateur experiments in murals. See page 212. When the family is tired of the painting it can be expunged with paint remover; then a coat of paint or another decoration can be applied.

WOOD TRIM

In old-fashioned houses the wood trim was considered important, but today it is subordinated, or even omitted in certain types of houses such as the Mediterranean and some Modern. Formerly woodwork and doors were stained dark, the idea being that they were then pleasantly harmonious with the dark furniture, whereas in reality they broke up the light walls in a very disturbing way. Today the wood trim is usually treated as part of the walls and painted as nearly like the wall as possible. A natural wood finish is often preferred to paint because it requires less expenditure for cleaning and refinishing.

Some Modern decorators deliberately make the wood trim a color that contrasts with the walls, especially in a dull room. For example, a green wood trim would look well with soft yellow-green or pale yellow walls. In a room with wall paper the wood trim may be painted to match the background or foreground of the paper, preferably the one that is most like the floor covering. Picture molding should be inconspicuous; therefore it should be painted like the wall, not like the wood trim.

DOORS

Doors are commonly painted to match the walls, or finished so that the natural grain of the wood shows. If doors are properly spaced and are not too numerous they may well be decorated in an interesting manner. They may be painted a solid color to match the rug or draperies, or painted with appropriate designs. The panels of doors may be decorated with patterned wall paper in a room with plain walls.

Doors can also be constructed in unusual ways. For example, doors into closets can be made of slats forming designs, with many openings for ventilation. Dutch doors with the upper halves opening separately from the lower halves are often desirable. So-called tropical interior doors for summer use are short, leaving a foot of open space at top and bottom for ventilation. Louvered doors with slanted slat panels also provide good ventilation. Doors that fold vertically in the center are sometimes used where the wall space against which the door opens is very narrow.

FLOORS

Qualities sought in floors are *resilience, silence, ease of cleaning, durability, warmth, resistance to fire, reasonable cost, and beauty.* Floors that are to be covered with linoleum or carpet to the wall need not be made of expensive materials.

Wooden floors are more common than any others, particularly in small houses. Red or white oak, which is obtainable in several grades, is probably best, but maple, birch, and beech also make very hard floors. Pine is the most popular soft wood; cedar, fir, hemlock, larch, redwood, tamarack, and spruce are also satisfactory. The character of the house determines the type of wooden floor to choose. Narrow hardwood boards suggest refinement, whereas wide boards or even planks are better suited to less pretentious types of furnishing. Interesting block floors are not uncommon.

Several procedures for finishing wood floors are used. One is to scrape, sand, fill, stain, shellac or varnish, and wax. Floors are often stained somewhat dark with walnut or a similar stain. Light-colored floors are best with light-colored rugs and are useful in dusty sections. Floors are sometimes painted rich dark colors, such as dark green, dull blue, black, or Indian-red. Slippery floors are a menace anywhere but particularly where there are children or elderly persons.

Linoleum is resilient, durable, and easily cleaned. Pages 59 and 223. It is made of a mixture of cork flour, linseed oil, gums, coloring matter, and sometimes wood flour pressed while hot into burlap backing. It is made plain, streaked (jaspé), or patterned. The plain is most desirable, the jaspé next, and the patterned last. Patterns may be attractive in bathrooms and kitchens; plain or jaspé linoleums are best for dining rooms, bedrooms, or halls. Linoleum makes a good surfacing for concrete floors.

Wood fiber blocks make effective floors. *Cork tiles* are resilient, quiet, and good looking. *Ceramic tiles,* which wear well and clean well, make excellent bathroom floors but are too cold and hard for kitchens. *Rubber tiles* are resilient, quiet, and colorful, but easily damaged by grease or oil. Among floor materials to be investigated are *terrazzo, Zenutherm, asphalt tile* (page 422), *Linoflor,* and other new products.

DECORATING AN APARTMENT

Before starting the decoration of an old apartment or flat a person should consider the possibility of making a few necessary architectural changes. A desirable tenant who will sign a three-year lease can usually accomplish some reforms in this respect. The most common need is for the removal of ceiling and wall lighting fixtures. It is really a very small matter for the janitor to remove these before decorating. The holes in the walls can be covered with a metal cap which is painted like the surrounding area. Radiators can be moved by a janitor without too much trouble or expense. A radiator which occupies a bay window in winter can be stowed in a closet or on a rear porch in summer.

Paneled walls are undesirable as they interfere with furniture arrangement and picture hanging. Sometimes the wood strips of the panels can be removed and the walls papered. Built-in features, such as an imitation fireplace, sideboards, or bookshelves, which are ugly or too large, can ruin the appearance of a room. They should be remodeled or removed; but if that cannot be done, they can sometimes be concealed by building removable bookshelves or cabinets over them. They can be made less important by painting them to match the walls.

Sometimes removing a partition or cutting a large opening through a wall makes an apartment much more livable. Persuasiveness coupled with good pictures of the results desired may gain the landlord's permission to make even such changes.

If an apartment is to be decorated by a contractor supplied by the owner of the building, it is necessary to have a complete understanding beforehand of the work to be done. Every item should be written in detail on the blank provided for that purpose. For example, it is not enough to write under closets "paint everything." Specify, instead, "baseboards, walls, ceiling, door, door casing, window casing, both sides of shelves, poles, hooks, light fixture, and electric cord."

A tenant should be given an opportunity to work out her color schemes without haste. She should see the decorator's wall-paper catalogs a week before the decorating is to be done, so that there will be time to find other papers if there are no suitable ones in the catalogs.

Sometimes landlords will grant a concession or a lower rent to the renter who is willing to take care of her own decorating.   In that event the tenant may wish to do the work herself.   Before making her decision, however, she should obtain a painter's bid for doing the job and should also ascertain the cost of materials if she does it herself.   She can then decide intelligently whether it is worth while to do the work herself.   As has been stated before, amateurs are able to paper or paint ordinary rooms satisfactorily. Furthermore, most city people need the opportunity this work offers to do creative work with their hands.

It often happens that an otherwise pleasant apartment has dark stained woodwork that detracts from its appearance.   This can be entirely concealed by applying one coat of oil paint of medium value, to harmonize with the rugs.   However, if a room is very light, and a Modern effect is desired, the walls may be painted dark with glossy oil paint to match the woodwork.   Light rugs, light furniture, and some brilliant colors are needed in such a color scheme.

It is often possible to economize by putting a coat of a thick, special water paint over walls and woodwork too, as it is quite satisfactory for a year or so in a family of adults.   Picture moldings should be painted like the wall or ceiling.   Radiators and electric outlets should be painted like the walls.   The very light-colored, high-varnished, hardwood floors which unfortunately are common in apartments should be somewhat darkened if possible, unless the rugs are light.

PROBLEMS

A sufficient number of problems are listed so that choices may be made.

1. Collect paint samples, wall-paper samples, patterned envelope lining papers, colored papers, and fabrics.
2. Make decorative schemes with small samples. Show wall color, floor color, drapery color, upholstery colors, and possibly others.
3. Design one wall containing unusual windows and draperies.
4. Group project. Paint or otherwise finish a floor, doors, woodwork, or walls.

READING REFERENCES

BURRIS-MEYER, ELIZABETH. *Decorating Livable Homes.* Prentice-Hall, 1937.

DRAPER, DOROTHY. *Decorating Is Fun.* Doubleday, Doran, 1940.

GILLIES, MARY D. *Popular Home Decoration.* Wise, 1940.

KOUES, HELEN. *How to be Your Own Decorator.* Tudor, 1940.

MAAS, CARL. *Common Sense in Home Decoration.* Greenberg, 1938.

McCLELLAND, NANCY V. *The Practical Book of Decorative Wall Treatments.* Lippincott, 1926.

PATMORE, DEREK. *Decoration for the Small Home.* Putnam, 1939.

STOREY, W. R. and H. E. A. *A Handbook of Home Decoration.* Bridgman, 1941.

The wall-paper pattern above has unusual beauty, but it is too formal to use as a background for this Early American furniture.

Wall paper with pleasing stylized foliage motifs arranged in stripes is consistent with the Modern furniture in the room below. Plain living-room walls contrast well with patterned dining-room walls. Note the convenient collapsible door curtains, the indirect light torchères, and the beautiful empty flower container on the table. *Courtesy Newcastle Products.*

This period room shows a dignified paneled wood wall, which has beauty and delicacy of detail. The fluted effect appears on both wall and fireplace. The cornice unifies the room, giving it dignity and style. Three walls are papered. A plain-textured rug of a medium tone, such as this one, is satisfactory for general purposes. Note the beautiful candelabrum on the mantel shelf. *Courtesy H. Roy Kelley.*

The Weldtex plywood wall surface in the picture below has pleasing texture due to uneven striations. The brick fireplace is novel and interesting in design. Note the outlet for heat at the upper corner. *Courtesy United States Plywood Corporation.*

Dark painted or papered walls require the contrast of a light-colored ceiling, wood trim, furniture, draperies, and usually light floor covering. Note the smart Modern furniture which is slightly traditional in line. The picture is the right size and is well chosen and well hung. *Courtesy W. and J. Sloane*

Walls, ceiling, bar, and sofa in this attractive basement recreation room are made of composition boards. *American Home* designed this room, which expresses functionalism, informality, cheer, and youth. *Courtesy Celotex.*

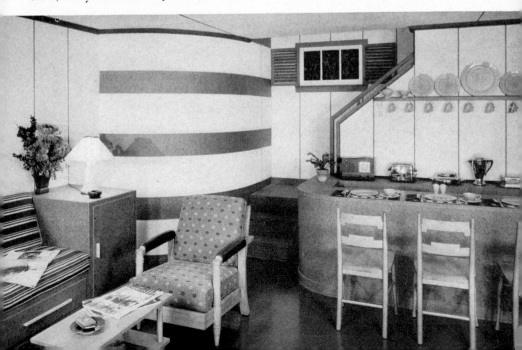

This Smith College dormitory loggia is decorated on one wall with enlarged photo murals of early Northampton scenes. The color scheme is in black, gray, and yellow. Note the uncluttered, functional effect relieved by the large plants in carefully planned locations.

A map or some other subject which has personal or family interest may be painted on one wall of a playroom, study, dining room, or bedroom. When it is no longer entertaining it can be easily covered with a coat of paint.

PART FOUR

PRACTICAL HOME FURNISHING

CHAPTER 13

FURNISHING COSTS AND BUDGETS

Women as spenders of family incomes are faced with problems as serious as those of the men producing those incomes. Women should give serious constructive thought to the possibilities of consumers' organizations and cooperative buying societies. Furniture, in particular, is unnecessarily costly; therefore investigation of mass production and profit control should be encouraged. Two billion dollars are paid out for furniture annually in the United States in ordinary times.

Buying furniture is a very important investment for most families. In many cases it not only exhausts the family savings, but, if the furniture is bought on the deferred-payment plan, it also mortgages future income. If wisely used the installment plan can be a service, but it is dangerous for the unwary. A family should expend only half of one year's income for furnishings, or about one-fourth of the value of a house.

The needs, activities, objectives, and social status of families, as well as their financial situations, modify the amounts to be invested in home furnishings. The ownership of a house justifies a larger investment than tenancy. The family that is likely to move far or often would naturally buy inexpensive things that can be disposed of readily. A family with small children may not care to buy permanent furniture until later.

Any plan of procedure should take into account the fact that discrimination develops, and the untrained person is likely to buy things she will not want later. Neither should one disregard the fact that decoration is far from static, and that inventions of materials, like plastics, may produce furniture more desirable than any the world has known.

A Plan. A three-year buying plan which provides for the purchase of a few important pieces each year is usually recommended for newly wed couples on a low income. This not only fits the purse but also insures more satisfactory results as it allows time to acquire knowledge about furnishings.

The *first-year* purchases for the living room should include a sofa or studio couch, an overstuffed chair, four straight chairs, a painted kitchen table, painted bookshelves, three end tables, two lamps, three scatter rugs, and simple thin white curtains. For the bedroom a good permanent spring and mattress can be used without a regular frame. A painted stool and chest of drawers could be added. A shelf under a mirror may be draped for a dressing table.

The *second-year* purchases should include a living-room rug and a good permanent table. The scatter rugs should then be put in the bedroom. A coffee table can be improvised from a large tray placed on a folding luggage rack.

The *third year* should see the purchase of another upholstered chair, an easy chair, draperies, and another lamp or two for the living room. The bedroom might gain an easy chair, night tables, and lamps.

Plans of this kind provide for the necessities only, at the beginning. One should realize that vacant space is not unpleasant but restful. The permanent pieces should usually be of the best quality in the class of furnishings within one's means. Temporary pieces such as lamps and dishes should be very inexpensive.

Any plan should be elastic so that it can be adjusted to meet new conditions. Five-year plans are sometimes more practical than three.

A young couple with imagination might well consider their low budget a challenge and make a game of creating something useful and beautiful out of ordinary things, possibly from second-hand stores. They should be frankly poor and cherish most those things which were their greatest bargains, or which they themselves had made. See pages 225, 257, and 417.

It is usually well for newly weds to postpone investing in any furniture until a careful study has been made of well-designed interiors and furniture in books and periodicals as well as in the shops.

A brief survey of the various types of furniture procurable at low cost, at low-medium cost, and at high-medium cost is presented here. New types of furniture may also appear in these price ranges. Costly furniture is not treated in this section because it is usually purchased under the guidance of decorators.

LOW-COST FURNITURE

The amount of usable furniture available to the person with an extremely low-cost budget is limited. In this price range attractiveness depends on good lines, smart colors, and unusual textures, which can often compensate for the lack of costly materials and processes.

Unfinished wood furniture, the most commonly used low-cost type, can be found in most of the large department stores, which usually carry a fairly varied selection of chests, tables, chairs, bookcases, and hanging wall shelves, in Non-Period, Modern, and Early American styles. Tables, cupboards, and chairs intended for the kitchen can often be finished in a fashion suitable for the living room. For information about finishing see page 257.

Sometimes inexpensive *porch furniture* is available which can be used successfully indoors to supplement other types. See page 25. For example, a good wicker chair adds textural interest.

Second-hand furniture stores, junk shops, and antique shops provide a possible source of supply for a person with little money but time to spare. Diligent search may bring as reward basically good tables, chairs, or even sofas and love seats that can be satisfactorily reworked. These are particularly suitable in old-fashioned rooms.

Homemade furniture of rectangular Non-period or Modern types can sometimes be made by the owners. An amateur can build tables, benches, bookshelves, cabinets, or anything that does not have drawers or upholstery. See page 104. A carpenter or woodworker can usually duplicate simple pieces from photographs. Prospective home makers should collect pictures of articles which they might like to have copied.

Mail-order catalogs should also be consulted by those working with a low budget. Reputable mail-order companies sometimes sell the products of the best manufacturers without identifying the brands; the volume sold enables them to reduce the prices.

LOW-MEDIUM COST FURNITURE

Considerable variety is possible in the low-medium cost furniture class, as both cottage and Modern styles are available at this price. Oak, pine, pecan, hickory, maple, gum, and wicker furniture is manufactured in large enough quantities to make it reasonable in price. The most important requisite of low-medium cost furniture is that it should not pretend to be expensive furniture by imitating either the costly woods or the costly processes such as carving. The following paragraphs name some types of furniture procurable in the low-medium price range.

Early American, also known as Pilgrim Colonial, is the most desirable traditional furniture to use in the greater part of the United States. See page 104. Adaptations and reproductions of the original designs, usually made of maple, are generally available.

English Provincial style furniture, often in gray oak, is usually available in the department stores. Some pieces may be combined with Early American. This English furniture suggests boys' rooms or breakfast rooms.

Pennsylvania German reproductions are sometimes available for cottages or apartments in which simplicity is the keynote. However, it is well to combine this furniture with other cottage types. See page 103. Sometimes genuine original pieces are procurable.

Spanish Colonial furniture is the natural choice for a home of the Spanish derivation in the Southwest. Care should be taken to find good, simple articles, for some are exaggerated in style. American and Mexican Indian pieces are appropriate with this oak furniture. See page 106.

Bamboo and *wicker* furniture of good design are usually procurable, and they add interest to groups of wood furniture. See pages 173, 226, 240, and 262.

Modern furniture of good design is available in this price range. It can be manufactured economically because of its simple lines and planes. For this reason the United States Resettlement Administration used Modern furniture in many of the houses which it built for families in the twelve-hundred-dollar to two-thousand-dollar annual income class.

Non-period furniture includes simple, straight-line sofas and easy chairs usable with nearly all types of furnishings.

HIGH-MEDIUM COST FURNITURE

High-medium cost furniture is naturally finer in finish, stronger in construction, and made of more valuable wood than less expensive furniture. Mahogany and walnut are often used, although gum and birch are freely substituted. Period, cottage, and Modern styles are usually procurable in high-medium cost furniture. In this price range one can expect to find some accurate reproductions of museum pieces of period furniture.

Colonial furniture, made of walnut or mahogany after Queen Anne and Chippendale designs, is ordinarily plentiful.

Federal furniture, which includes American Sheraton, American Hepplewhite, and Duncan Phyfe designs, made of walnut or mahogany, is also plentiful.

Nineteenth-century furniture, particularly Empire and Victorian, is sometimes procurable in antique or second-hand shops. New reproductions are usually simplified in design and reduced in scale.

English Regency furniture, of graceful Classical forms, finished in black and gold or dark wood, is usually procurable.

French Directoire furniture, similar to English Regency, but lighter in color, is not yet generally procurable.

French Provincial furniture of this and costlier types is often procurable.

Biedermeier furniture, a Modernized German version of the Empire style with peasant ornamentation, has been manufactured here and is sometimes available.

Modern furniture, made of wood, plastics, or metal, is plentiful in progressive sections of the country. Furniture designed by the best living designers is procurable and should be sought.

Scandinavian Modern furniture, made in the United States, is available in several price ranges. The wood is usually light and the fabrics colorful. Swedish Modern is a favorite style which successfully combines native, Classical, Empire, and Modern ideas. Finnish, Norwegian, and Danish Modern employ laminated wood and bentwood effectively.

Chinese Modern furniture consists of Modern forms to which have been added Chinese lines such as curved, upturned edges. See page 261.

HOME-FURNISHING BUDGETS

The money to be used for furnishing must be carefully apportioned to the various rooms. Budgets are given here, but they are merely suggestions because the size and needs of the family and all the features of the home affect the budget. It is difficult to consider kitchens in making theoretical budgets because in many rented houses and apartments the refrigerator, stove, and cabinets are provided, whereas in others they are not. Kitchen furniture and utensils comprise about 15 per cent of the total cost of furnishing a new house. No figures are given here for a radio, dishes, silver, or linen because such requirements vary greatly in different families. The following budgets should be treated as elastic, but they might well serve as guides, particularly to the inexperienced. During periods of inflated prices considerable adjustment of these lists may be necessary.

PROPORTIONAL ROOM PERCENTAGES

	2-room home	3-room home	4-room home	5-room home	6-room home
Living room...............	67%	45%	40%	32%	30%
Master bedroom............	33	25	20	21	17
Dining room.........................		22	20	19	17
Hall...............................		8	6	6	6
Guest room (or)..............			14	14	{11
Child's room................					{10
Sun porch or nursery...				8	9
Total..................	100%	100%	100%	100%	100%

FURNISHING BUDGETS FOR 5-ROOM HOMES

	Budget of $450	Budget of $1,000	Budget of $1,800	Budget of $3,000
Living room.................	$180	$400	$720	$1,200
Master bedroom	90	200	360	600
Dining room............... ...	90	200	360	600
Child's or guest room..........	63	140	252	420
Hall or sun porch..............	27	60	108	180

LIVING-ROOM BUDGETS

	Budget of $180	Budget of $400	Budget of $720	Budget of $1,200
Furniture (65 to 70%)				
Sofa, davenport, or settee.......	$ 55.00	$110.00	$125.00	$220.00
Easy chair....................	20.00	40.00	60.00	80.00
Table........................	10.00	20.00	30.00	60.00
End tables...................	5.00	7.50	18.00	30.00
Small easy chair.	15.00	25.00	50.00	65.00
Occasional chair..............	4.50	7.50	32.00	35.00
Mirror.......................			20.00	37.50
Floor lamp and shade.........	7.50	15.00	25.00	40.00
Table lamp and shade.........		10.00	20.00	37.50
Desk or secretary.............		27.50	50.00	115.00
Desk chair...................		7.50	10.00	30.00
Additional chair..............				20.00
Hanging bookshelf............			17.00	
Magazine rack................			5.00	
Bookcase.....................				25.00
Total for furniture...........	$117.00	$270.00	$462.00	$795.00
Floor covering................	36.00	75.00	150.00	225.00
Curtains.....................	14.40	32.00	57.60	96.00
Accessories (pictures, flower bowls, ashtrays, etc.)..............	12.60	23.00	50.40	84.00
Total......................	$180.00	$400.00	$720.00	$1,200.00

DINING-ROOM BUDGETS

	Budget of $90	Budget of $200	Budget of $360	Budget of $600
Furniture (65 to 70%)				
Table........................	$18.50	$ 35.00	$ 65.00	$100.00
Chairs.......................	20.00	40.00	80.00	150.00
Sideboard or equivalent.........	20.00	40.00	65.00	100.00
Serving table or tea wagon......		15.00	24.00	40.00
Floor covering................	18.00	40.00	72.00	120.00
Curtains.....................	7.20	16.00	28.80	48.00
Accessories (pictures, etc.)......	6.30	14.00	25.20	42.00
Total......................	$90.00	$200.00	$360.00	$600.00

BEDROOM BUDGETS

	Budget of $90	Budget of $200	Budget of $360	Budget of $600
Furniture (65 to 70%)				
Bed.	$10.00	$ 22.50	$ 40.00	$ 70.00
Bed spring.	8.50	10.00	17.50	40.00
Mattress.	12.50	20.00	25.00	40.00
Chest or dresser.	15.00	35.00	55.00	90.00
Dressing table.	12.50	30.00	55.00	90.00
Chair.	5.00	12.50	17.50	27.50
Additional chair or desk.		5.00	10.00	12.50
Bedside table.			8.00	15.00
Lamp.			6.00	10.00
Total	$63.50	$135.00	$234.00	$395.00
Floor covering.	15.20	35.00	72.00	115.00
Curtains.	6.00	16.00	28.80	48.00
Accessories.	5.30	14.00	25.20	42.00
Total.	$90.00	$200.00	$360.00	$600.00
Total with twin beds.	$116.00	$245.00	$435.00	$725.00

Note. In addition to those named above, the following pieces would add to the usefulness, beauty, and comfort of some bedrooms: cedar chest, mirrors, sewing table, chaise longue, and extra tables, lamps, and chairs.

These budgets are copied, with slight changes, from the United States Department of Commerce pamphlet "Furniture."

PROBLEMS

1. Make a budget for furnishing a young woman's combination study and bedroom, using new unpainted furniture.
2. Make a budget for furnishing a two-room apartment on a salary of $2,500 a year.
3. Make a budget for furnishing a house with a living room, dining alcove, one bedroom, bath, and kitchen.

These two pictures show interiors of a house in the permanent housing project at Greenbelt, Maryland. They prove that furniture can be well designed and also inexpensive. Manufacturers should be encouraged to produce such furniture.
Courtesy the U. S. Resettlement Administration.

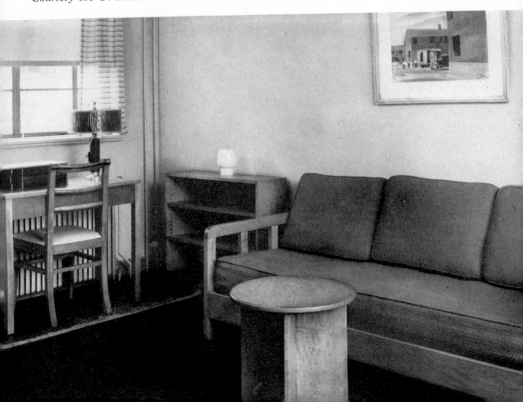

Early American furniture, such as this, is often procurable unpainted. It deserves its popularity, for it is well designed and unpretentious.

Second-hand stores often have usable pieces that can be refinished or slip-covered. The cottage theme is well expressed in the room below; the hooked rugs are appropriate. Nothing should be hung on the fireplace unless it is actually used there.

These two pictures show opposite corners in one room. The furnishings and interior finishing of this room cost one thousand dollars. Cottage-type furniture predominates. Strong dark and light contrasts make the room sparkle. *Courtesy Altman's.*

Before and after transformation. These two pictures show the same room and the same furniture. The most ingenious change was putting the two pieces of wall furniture together to make one. The legs of both and the mirror were removed, new knobs added, and the piece painted, so that it gained a contemporary appearance. The fringed slip covers and swag curtains are effective. The beflowered tablecloth and wall paper add a Victorian touch which is sometimes fashionable. The composition dado and floor surface are important contributions to the transformation of this room. The original room had Mission furniture, and an impossible rug of the imitation Oriental type, which unfortunately is still available in some stores. *Courtesy Armstrong Cork Company.*

The room above shows good-looking home-made furniture, cupboards, and bookshelves. The unpainted wood is pleasing. The effect is masculine. *Courtesy Sternberg-Davis.*

The head-board unit below, including the end tables, could be copied at home. The bedside lamps are not functional because they are not adjustable.

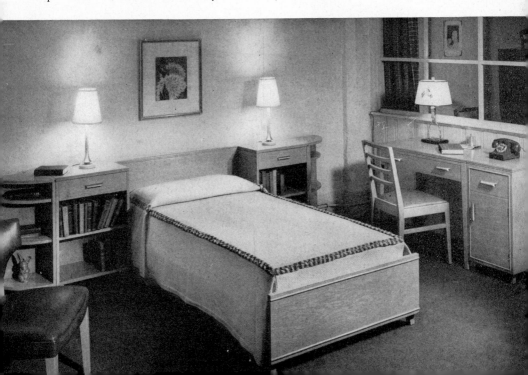

Kitchen chairs and tables of good, simple lines may be used in dining rooms or living rooms. The accompanying wall paper should, however, have cottage character.

Bamboo furniture of good design is procurable in different price ranges. It is often used to supplement living-room or dining-room furniture in the early years of home making.
Courtesy Louisiana State University.

Modified Modern furniture is available in several price ranges. This roomy chest is particularly useful in an apartment or small house where space is at a premium. *Courtesy Montgomery Ward.*

Traditional furniture, like these Duncan Phyfe copies in the picture below, is procurable in the medium price range. The lines of the chairs and tables are pleasingly related without the monotony found in a matched suite of furniture.

CHAPTER 14

FURNITURE ARRANGEMENT

When the tentative budget for furnishings has been made, and the type of furnishing has been decided upon, the interesting problem of planning the furniture and its arrangement, room by room, is next. Careful preliminary plans of orderly arrangement are necessary for the creation of beautiful, comfortable rooms. Just as the artist works with paints to compose a picture and the landscape designer uses plants, so the interior designer constructs with furniture and accessories.

Balance is the basis of good furniture arrangement. Each of the four sides of the room should seem about equally heavy to produce a feeling of equilibrium; opposite walls in particular should balance well. Each wall, too, should be balanced with equal weight on each half; the highest part should usually be at the center.

Either formal or informal balance may predominate in a room. *Formal balance* is appropriate with formal types of architecture like the Georgian colonial. With formal balance centers of interest such as fireplaces, sofas, or secretaries are often flanked by a pair of chairs. Too many pairs of articles, however, are likely to make a room appear stilted; a pair of sofas before the fireplace and a pair of end tables holding a pair of lamps are sufficient. Even a formal room seldom makes use of formal balance exclusively, because some irregularity is necessary for relief and charm. See page 240.

Informal balance is desirable in most houses and is a requirement in unsymmetrical types of houses such as the early English, the farm-house types, and the Modern. See page 104. A room with irregular openings is more difficult to arrange than a symmetrical room. It requires ingenuity to distribute the masses in such a way that the room feels steady and balanced. When successful, however, informal (occult) balance is likely to have more charm than formal (symmetrical) balance.

227

Clearly defined and sufficient space for *passageways* and activities must be allowed when making furniture arrangement plans. Major traffic lanes should be about 6 feet wide, and minor lanes about 4 feet wide. Between the groups of furniture facing each other in front of the fireplace 5 to 6 feet are needed. Passageways must be located so as not to interfere with the function of the furniture groups. Approaches to doorways should be kept clear. Easy access to radio, fireplace, and bookshelves is important.

Furniture should be arranged to conform to the *architecture* of a room. Large pieces are always placed parallel to the walls; otherwise they violate steady basic lines. Upholstered chairs are placed at angles successfully because they have variety of line in themselves. Straight chairs look well against walls.

Furniture should be combined *in groups*, for service, for conservation of space, and for beauty. These groups are focal centers that make arrangements logical and useful. They are based on activities—conversation, writing, reading, and enjoying music.

Unity in line, texture, scale, and color is necessary within the groups. At the same time variety is needed to stimulate interest; differences in bulk and height are desirable. Texture and color variation provides relief, as illustrated by an unholstered chair in a group of wooden pieces. Interesting groups may be composed around important articles of furniture like secretaries, chests, high desks, bookcases, large tables, or pianos, by adding chairs, lamps, pictures, and other transition pieces of furniture. Tall pieces should seldom stand in or near corners.

Large empty spaces between groups help to achieve a desirable uncluttered effect in a room. Spaces between the parts of a group should be less than spaces between separate groups. Even a picture that functions as part of a group composition should be hung so low that there is little empty space between it and the furniture below it.

Functional considerations are even more important than esthetic considerations when furniture is being arranged. The first requisite for all rooms is comfort, but additional needs must also be met; for example, living-room arrangements must not handicap sociability. The special requirements of various rooms are considered here.

PLANS MADE TO SCALE

Furniture arrangement should first be planned on paper, since paper patterns are much more easily moved around than the real furniture. Plans must be made in actual scale if they are to be useful. First the floor plans of each room are drawn on squared graph paper, where ¼-inch squares represent 1-foot squares in actuality. The measurements of doors, windows, fireplace, and built-in features should be taken and indicated correctly on the floor plan. Electric outlets should be located also.

Small cut-out patterns of colored paper should be made to represent every piece of furniture. They should be in correct scale, the actual measurements of the floor area covered by each piece of furniture being transposed so that 1 foot becomes ¼ inch. Patterns of standard measurements can be traced from page 230.

APPROXIMATE FURNITURE SIZES

Living Room

Sofa	3' x 6'
Love seat	3' x 4'
Overstuffed chair	2' 6" x 3' 6"
Wing chair	2' 6" x 2' 9"
Bridge chair	1' 6" x 1' 6"
Flat-top desk	2' 6" x 4' 6"
Winthrop desk	2' 3" x 3' 9"
Secretary	2' x 3' 6"
Highboy	2' x 3'
End table	1' x 1' 8"
Coffee table	3' x 5'
Bridge table	2' 6" x 2' 6"
Console table	1' 6" x 3'
Round lamp table	2' dia.
Round coffee table	4' dia.
Round drum table	3' dia.
Round table	3' dia.
Grand piano	5' x 7'
Upright piano	2' x 5'

Bathroom

Bathtub	2' 6" x 5'
Lavatory	1' 6" x 2'
Toilet	2' x 2'
Shower	2' 6" x 2' 6"

Dining Room

Rectangular table	3' 6" x 5'
Refectory table	2' 6" x 5' 6"
Round table	5' dia.
Side chair	1' 6" x 1' 6"
Arm chair	2' x 2'
Buffet	2' x 6'
China cupboard	1' 6" x 4'
Serving table	1' 6" x 3'
Chest	1' 6" x 4'

Kitchen

Sink	2' x 4'
Range	26" x 44"
Refrigerator	2' x 3'

Bedroom

Twin bed	3' 3" x 6' 6"
Three-quarter bed	4' x 6' 6"
Double bed	4' 6" x 6' 6"
Bed table	2' x 2'
Dresser	1' 6" x 3' 6"
Chest	1' 6" x 4'
Dressing table	1' 6" x 3'
Bench	1' 6" x 2'
Easy chair	2' 6" x 2' 6"
Side chair	1' 6" x 1' 6"

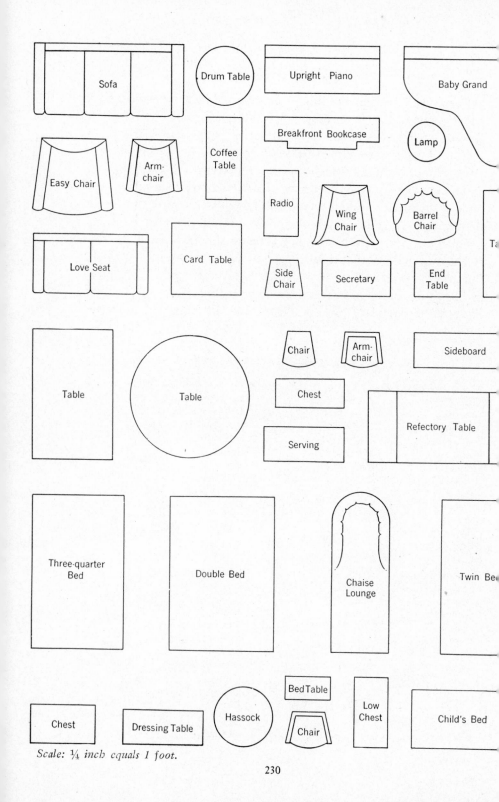

Sofa

Drum Table

Upright Piano

Baby Grand

Easy Chair

Arm-chair

Coffee Table

Breakfront Bookcase

Lamp

Radio

Wing Chair

Barrel Chair

Love Seat

Card Table

Side Chair

Secretary

End Table

Ta

Table

Table

Chair

Arm-chair

Sideboard

Chest

Refectory Table

Serving

Three-quarter Bed

Double Bed

Chaise Lounge

Twin Be

Chest

Dressing Table

Hassock

Bed Table

Chair

Low Chest

Child's Bed

Scale: ¼ inch equals 1 foot.

ENTRANCE HALL

The entrance hall is important because it gives the first and the last impression of the home to the person who is arriving or leaving. The hall should not be slighted, and it should indicate fairly clearly the character of the furnishings in the rest of the house. It should be treated in a somewhat impersonal way, even to the extent of formality.

Since empty space is desirable in a hall, the pieces of furniture should be few. A small hall needs only a chair or bench and a mirror, although a small table is useful. In a large hall such pieces as a table, console, chest of drawers, low chest, bench, or sofa with end tables are suitable. Pairs of things are sometimes used to give a formal effect. See page 60. As a hall should not invite one to linger, pictures and very comfortable chairs are usually out of place in it. Needless to say the hat rack is out of date, as visitors' wraps are for short periods placed on a seat or for longer ones left in a hall closet.

LIVING ROOM

The living room should be the kind of room that its name indicates, for every member of the family should live in it. It should express the spirit of home to the family, and of welcome to the friends of the family. The ideal living room should have gay curtains and flowers, a comfortable sofa, a radio, a table to work on, a desk, a rug that can be rolled back for dancing, and a hearth with a fire on it whenever it is cold, comfortable chairs drawn up near it, and plenty of lamps, books, and magazines close by. A place for each member of the family to follow his or her occupation with a well-lighted, comfortable chair for each is a necessity in the home of average size.

Furnishings should be arranged so that the living room has a *center of interest*. This feature should be emphasized so that, upon entering the room, one looks there. A secondary center of interest, too, is often desirable particularly in a large room. See page 314. A fireplace, a sofa or another distinctive piece of furniture, a hobby collection, or a group of pictures may be the center of interest. See page 59. A picture window, which is the center of interest during the day, loses its importance at night.

Two points of emphasis in the living room, the center of interest and the principal group of seating furniture, can sometimes be combined, thus securing a unified effect.

The *major conversation group* of furniture is the most important furnishing in the living room. It should be so well placed and so comfortable that it is conducive to conversation. This group should seat about eight persons, without the necessity of dragging up chairs. Wherever possible, part of this seating furniture should be built-in; it should all be considered as anchored. In a Modern living room a conversation corner is usually arranged with an L-shaped sofa, with built-in seats, or with sectional seating units that turn a corner satisfactorily, accommodating several persons on each side of the corner.

In a living room with a fireplace, the main conversation group may consist of two sofas or two love seats, one on either side in front of the fireplace, possibly with chairs at the ends toward the room. Instead of two sofas, one only need be used, opposite a pair of identical chairs. In a small room the sofa usually stands against the wall across the room from the fireplace.

Where a window is the nucleus of the main conversation group, a sofa or love seat may well be placed so that it faces the window with two comfortable chairs of different types at right angles at the ends, or the sofa may be at right angles to the window wall with two identical chairs opposite. The featured window should frame a view, or hold glass shelves with plants, or be curtained very well, or have distinction in some other way. Page 240 shows a summer arrangement.

Sometimes a rug that is just large enough for the main group of furniture serves to unify it as on pages 59 and 240. Necessary adjuncts in a group of seating furniture are a large, low coffee table in front of the sofa and large lamp tables at the ends of the sofas and between the pair of chairs. The comfort which a room offers depends partly upon how well it is supplied with these conveniences.

Furniture that is arranged for comfort usually looks well, too. If the living-room chairs are "all out of place" after guests have departed, it may indicate that the usual arrangement was less interesting as well as less convenient, and it may be well to let them remain as the guests left them.

A reading or study group consisting of a table and a chair or two is a convenience in a living room. Good lighting for day and night is essential, and so this group should be located near a window.

A special writing group needs a large desk and a chair that is comfortable for writing. It should have a good lamp and be near a window and bookshelves. Reading and writing groups should be as far away from the conversation group as possible.

A music enjoyment group may consist merely of a radio, flanked by two easy chairs, and a low stool. A radio, phonograph, and records are often placed close to a sofa. The person who likes to lie on a sofa and listen to the radio should have a low end table radio that can be reached comfortably.

The piano is a difficult article to locate properly, as it is large enough to upset the balance of even a fair-sized room. A group of windows, a sofa with pictures above, high bookshelves, a secretary, or a fireplace provide enough balance for a piano placed against the opposite wall. A grand piano should stand with its keyboard parallel to a wall. See page 172. It is permissible to place a chair or a table in the curve of a grand piano.

An upright piano is usually backed against a wall, but where there is space enough it may be placed to make an interesting division in the room by standing with an end to the wall and possibly its back to the room. It may thus serve to give privacy where the entrance door opens directly into the living room. A sofa and a piano should not usually be placed at the same end of a room.

A tall, important article like a bookcase, secretary, or cabinet is sometimes needed across the room to balance the fireplace or the center of interest. See page 262. In place of furniture a large mirror can also balance the fireplace effectively, partly by reflecting it.

A woman should rearrange her furniture occasionally in spite of the objections of the men of the family. A reasonable amount of change keeps the atmosphere of the home interesting and alive. Unusual arrangements should be tried, such as placing the end of a table or a flat desk against a wall. Audacity is an excellent quality to exercise when arranging furniture.

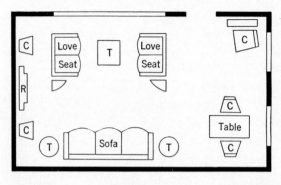

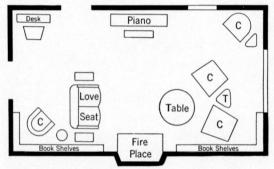

1. A window as a center of interest.

The pair of love seats and the sofa focus attention on the window and view. The table is out of the way and may be used for cards, study, or food.

2. A fireplace on the side of the room.

An upright piano balances the fireplace. One quiet corner is for a desk and one is for a chair and a lamp beside the book shelves.

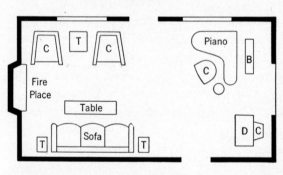

3. A fireplace on the end of the room.

A baby grand piano balances the fireplace and sofa. The two straight sides of the piano are parallel to the walls. The desk has a secluded corner near a window.

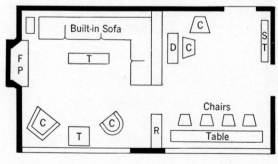

4. A combination living and dining room.

A low partition divides the areas. The built-in sofa provides a conversation center. The diners may face the window. The serving table fits the allotted space.

DINING AREAS

Dining-room arrangements of furniture are likely to be rather obvious since it is usually most convenient to place the table in the middle of the room. If space allows, however, other positions may prove more entertaining. See page 62. In some rooms the table can be placed against the windows with the diners facing the garden, which can be lighted to make it attractive at night.

Although plenty of wall space is more important than wall furniture in a small dining room, it is sometimes well to put one tall, interesting piece of furniture across the room from the windows for balance and also to create a center of interest.

A serving table near the door into the kitchen is a convenience; if drawer space is needed, a chest of drawers may be substituted. Two identical serving tables designed for use also as extension sections of the dining table are practical.

Where the dining room serves two or three purposes, being also a study, sitting room, music room, or sewing room, it should be furnished as an extension of the living room. Comfortable furniture should be arranged in groups. A center of interest could be established with a secretary, not a buffet or sideboard. If the living room adjoins the dining room the floors of both rooms should be treated exactly alike to unify the rooms.

A dining alcove or area in the living room is sometimes located behind a low shelf partition or in a bay window; between meals there need be no evidence that the place is used for dining. See page 120. A drop-leaf table standing against a wall can be pulled out for meals. Instead of having the usual single dining table, a pair of identical rather long narrow tables could be used, one in the dining area and one in the living area. For a buffet supper, they could be placed end to end.

Breakfast rooms are usually very convenient for eating as well as for several other purposes. A mother of small children finds that this sunny room is the ideal place for baby's play pen while she is doing her kitchen work.

A small family need not be confined to any particular spot for meals but can eat before the fireplace, beside a sunny window, on the porch, or wherever it is most interesting or convenient.

BEDROOMS

The location of doors and windows usually restricts bedroom-furniture arrangement. The furniture should be arranged for convenience first of all; however, if feasible, a center of interest should be created and the furniture grouped attractively.

A very flexible arrangement is necessary for comfort in a bedroom, as the furniture should be readily movable to suit changing conditions. For example, a person confined to bed by illness should not have to face a window. Builders' provisions notwithstanding, the heads of beds should be located against a wall with windows. See pages 172, 241 and 422.

Good ventilation usually requires a different location of beds in summer from that in winter. Fresh air without a draft over the bed is always desirable.

The usual arrangement of one or two beds is to extend them into the middle of the room from the center of a wall. Whereas this is sometimes necessary, it is often possible to place the beds parallel to the wall in corners, leaving the middle of the room free. Two couches or Hollywood beds look well meeting in one corner.

A chaise longue should not be put in a small bedroom. In a large room it is best placed near the windows. A slightly diagonal position is more pleasing than an extreme diagonal, but a position parallel to the wall promotes architectural unity.

A well-lighted place near or in front of a window is the best location for a dressing table. In a combination sitting-bedroom a desk can be placed under a mirror and used as a dressing table, with all the equipment concealed in its drawers.

The remaining furniture is located for convenience. A bench or a chest for blankets at the foot of the bed is useful. An easy chair with a reading lamp, end table, and sewing stand belongs near a window. A straight chair is convenient beside a desk or table. An end table beside the head of the chaise longue should be the height of its arm. A bedside table should be large with a drawer that can be opened by a person in bed.

Two identical chests of drawers sometimes look well side by side, particularly if they are low. See page 421. In Modern interiors drawer space is usually provided in closets and dressing rooms, however, so that chests are not needed in bedrooms.

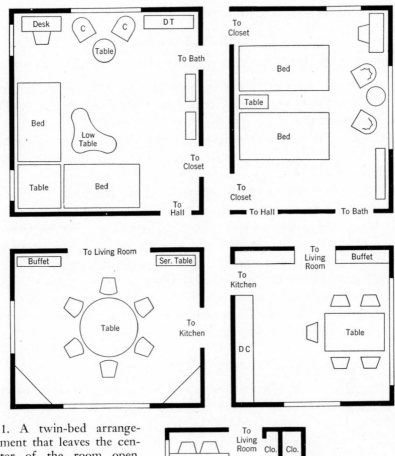

1. A twin-bed arrangement that leaves the center of the room open. The square corner table may be a container for blankets. The curved triangular table is bed height and has no corners to injure shins.

2. A conventional twin-bed arrangement. Beds arranged in this manner are convenient to make.

3. A formal arrangement in a symmetrical room.

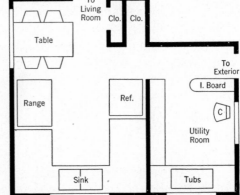

The corner cupboards occupy space that would otherwise be wasted.

4. An informal dining-room arrangement. Opposite the table is a built-in dish cupboard covering the wall.

5. A U-shaped kitchen with a place to eat beside a window. A utility room containing a cupboard, laundry tubs, washing machine, drying machine, chair, and ironing board.

PROBLEMS

A sufficient number of problems are listed so that choices may be made.

1. Draw a rough sketch of a floor plan of a one-story house. Locate the circulatory system, where the residents will walk the most.
2. Design the furniture arrangement for the floor plan in problem 1 (above), using loose paper shapes for furniture. See page 230.
3. Draw furniture arrangement plans on squared paper for your rooms at home. See pages 234 and 237.
4. Using three-dimensional miniature furniture make furniture arrangements for families of various sizes. This furniture is usually procurable among school supplies. See page 242.
5. Make plans for children's doll houses.
6. Report on famous miniature rooms and their furnishings.
7. If possible obtain some practice in furniture arrangement in homes, dormitory rooms, or in lounge rooms.

READING REFERENCES

DRAPER, DOROTHY. *Decorating Is Fun.* Doubleday, Doran, 1940.

MAAS, CARL. *Common Sense in Home Decoration.* Greenberg, 1938.

SOOY, L., and WOODBRIDGE, V. *Plan Your Own Home.* Stanford University Press, 1940.

WHITON, SHERRILL. *Elements of Interior Decoration.* Lippincott, 1937.

A living room without a fireplace might well feature a conversation corner. The one shown above is made of a sectional sofa, which can be changed in size if the owner moves to a different house. This is a conservative type of Modern furniture that is highly recommended. *Courtesy Montgomery Ward.*

The arrangement of the furniture makes this a pleasant functional combination living-dining room. Notice the redwood walls and the fiber floor covering. The couch can be drawn out to become a bed. *Courtesy California Redwood Association and Harwell H. Harris, designer.*

A winter arrangement of furniture is shown in the picture above. The fireplace is naturally the center of interest. This cottage furniture is attractive and comfortable. *Courtesy Carson, Pirie, Scott.*

A summer arrangement of furniture is shown in the room pictured below. Ordinary windows, too, may be used as centers of interest in summer. Note the attractive lamps, fabrics, and porch chairs. *Courtesy Libbey, Owens, Ford.*

This corner arrangement of twin beds is highly desirable in a dormitory room or a bedroom that is also used as a sitting room, because it leaves the center of the room open. Dan Cooper designed this furniture. The coffee table fits the triangular space; the round corners prevent injured shins. Note the telephone niche and adjustable lamp. *Courtesy Hotel Friederica.*

The arrangement of the twin beds in the room below is desirable for it leaves the center of the room free. The rather primitive oak furniture and the heavy rag rug are in harmony. The room would be suitable for boys or men if the wall-paper pattern were stronger in character.

The two pictures on this page demonstrate the use of miniature furniture in the study of furniture arrangement. The pieces are carefully scaled; other styles are available. *Courtesy Paul Mac Alister, Inc., Ardmore, Pennsylvania.*

CHAPTER 15

SELECTION OF FURNITURE

After the budget has been made out, a style selected, and a furniture-arrangement plan made, shopping for specific articles begins. The minimum requirements are about the same in most homes of average size.

Living-Room Pieces. An overstuffed sofa and several overstuffed chairs are the most important furnishings in the living room. The sofa and chairs should not be alike, for suites are monotonous and do not allow individual expression and charm. However, one pair of identical chairs is sometimes desirable. A wing chair and a barrel chair may be used for variety in form. Two occasional chairs and a pair of straight side chairs are also needed in some living rooms. See page 89.

One particularly fine piece of wall furniture in a traditional room may lift the tone of the entire room to a higher level. A breakfront bookcase, secretary, cabinet, desk, or highboy can serve in this capacity.

End tables to hold lamps and other things are needed at each end of the sofa and beside each chair. The end tables should have shelves or drawers for utility and should be the exact height of the arms of the sofa.

The coffee table, which is a very important item, should preferably be large with a shelf underneath. It should be a trifle lower than the seat of the sofa. Page 241 shows an excellent low table. Other pieces for the serving of food, such as a nest of small tables, a large tier stand, or a large tea table on wheels, are also convenient. The nest of tables may remain permanently in the living room.

A piano can be obtained in a style to fit a variety of decorative schemes. A small model is desirable as far as appearance is concerned. Among other pieces of furniture required by some families are a large table, desk, large screen, radio, and ottoman.

Dining-Room Pieces. Dining rooms have usually been dull and monotonous in the past partly because the furniture for them was sold only in manufacturers' suites. Original combinations, which have replaced sets to a great extent, consist of pieces that agree in scale and in general character but have interesting differences.

Dining-room chairs need not be like the table, nor do they need to be alike. For example, a pair of peel tub armchairs or other reed, bamboo, or Mexican chairs may be combined with wooden chairs. Armchairs may be placed at the two ends of the table. All dining-room chairs should be padded or upholstered for comfort. As chairs receive hard wear, they should be selected for strength as well as appearance. The dining table is the piece to economize on if funds are low. Painting an inexpensive table a positive color is sometimes advisable. A rectangular table is thought to be better looking than a round one, which is, however, easier to serve.

An outstanding piece of wall furniture is frequently the center of interest in a dining room. The person who desires a distinctive room does not now buy the usual sideboard or china cabinet except possibly for a period room; corner cupboards, tall cupboards, hutches, dressers, cabinets, hanging shelves, or a built-in wall of cupboards are more interesting. See pages 10, 60, and 106.

A dining room also needs a serving table, which should ordinarily be an inconspicuous piece. A large screen sometimes hides the door into the kitchen. A combination dining-sitting room may have for dining chairs three different pairs of comfortable chairs.

Bedroom Pieces. Comfort and personal preference should guide the selection of bedroom furniture. Beds should be the most comfortable that one can afford. A well-made inner-spring mattress and box spring are essential. New types of mattresses such as the rubber sponge and air-cooled mattresses should be investigated before buying. Single beds are recommended, even though they cost almost as much as the double, in order that everyone can sleep alone. Bed frames are available in all styles and prices; however, they are often omitted. A four poster is shown on page 302. Dressing tables of plastic, metal, or wood are possibilities. A chest of drawers, an easy chair, a side chair, an upholstered stool, a bench, and a large bedside table are useful.

EXPRESSIVENESS

The *theme* of the home or room limits the choice of furniture. For example, a cottage expressing informality, comfort, and simplicity calls for furniture of the same characteristics. The kind of wood, the shape of the article, the style, and the color, all are elements that help to create the mood or expressiveness desired.

STYLE

Three general choices of style are possible: period, cottage, or Modern. If the choice is period or cottage, specific periods or types must be selected. Naturally the furniture on hand and the style of the house affect these decisions.

BEAUTY

Good design in furniture is somewhat scarce. Poor design is illustrated on page 247. One general rule to follow as a guide in the selection of furniture is that the plainer things are the better. The most distinctive furniture is that made by well-known designers, some of whom have their own shops in large cities. See page 264 for a good example.

UTILITY

The first test of a piece of furniture is utility. Unless an article is *useful* it should not be given space in the home, regardless of its beauty or sentimental association. In a small home a Duncan Phyfe sofa would be less desirable than a Non-period sofa that could serve as an occasional guest bed.

Sometimes *double purposes* make furniture more valuable, as the radio that is also an end table (page 422), the low bookshelves that can be used as a seat when a large group is to be accommodated for a short time, or the useful electric cabinet that is a heater in winter and a cooler in summer.

The most utilitarian furniture procurable for small quarters is the modern *unit furniture* consisting of cupboards, shelves, tables, radios, desks, and chairs designed to fit into compact, contiguous groups. See page 260. Unit furniture helps to make a room serve several purposes since it conceals miscellaneous equipment. The effect is architectural with pleasing continuity of line.

COMFORT

Comfort in furniture means more to most people than any other characteristic. The livability of a home depends largely on its comfortable furnishings. For individual comfort it is necessary that a person selects his or her own pieces of furniture, trying them out thoroughly before purchase.

Most furniture is designed to fit a person of average height, 5 feet 8 inches. Standard-size sofas, love seats, and chairs have the same measurements. A standard easy chair has a seat depth of 22 to 24 inches and is 17 inches high in front and a little lower at the back. An occasional chair is 19 inches deep and 18 inches high. Arm rests are about 7 inches above the seat. Seat backs are 17 to 19 inches high.

Furniture that does not conform to standard measurements is procurable, however, and a person who is more or less than average in height should select his or her own pieces of furniture, particularly chairs. A chair should be deep enough to reach to the back of the knees of the seated person. The chair back should have a comfortable slant and should support the shoulder blades well, or even the head if that is desired. Low Modern chairs suit the lolling posture of some but are difficult for others. Ottomans are comfortable adjuncts to lounging chairs.

An uncomfortable bed is a poor investment. Tests have shown that comfortable beds are necessary for complete rest. The individual who is to use a bed should select it, to be sure of getting a satisfactory degree of softness. The possibility of procuring air-conditioned mattresses should be investigated in hot climates.

Children's furniture should suit their measurements. Some furniture is made on which the adjustable legs can be lengthened as the child grows.

The *weight* of furniture and its *mobility* are features that also affect comfort. Some very light chairs or stools that can be moved easily are needed in living rooms. See page 89. All movable furniture should be well shod with castors or with smooth metal disks procurable at any dime store. The most mobile and useful lawn and porch chairs and tables have wheels in place of back legs or are of the wheelbarrow type.

The sofa and overstuffed chair have several faults: they are too bulbous, too heavy at the base, have two kinds of fabric, and are overdecorated.

The buffet, which is an uninteresting, coffinlike shape, has conspicuous veneered panels unrelated to the design of the article. Its Modernistic decoration is not in accord with the turned legs, which are of period character.

The ornate round table, with its writhing ornamentation, is in very bad taste. The wooden chair is an exaggerated example of a rustic style.

The dressing-table mirror is unrelated in line to the rest of the article.

The Modernistic dresser at the right is ugly in line because the oval mirror has no relation to the angular form of the article. The veneered diamond shape does not agree with the shape of the drawer and is too conspicuous.

The separate mirror has a vulgarly ornate frame and weak decoration.

CONSTRUCTION

No one should purchase a piece of furniture without making a complete examination of it and acquiring information about it. The purchaser should look at the back, the bottom, and the inside of each piece as well as at the front. Drawers should be taken out, doors opened, drop leaves examined, and surfaces, edges, and joints studied. Good workmanship is indicated by complete finish on backs and undersides and by the use of screws, not nails.

Firmness and rigidity under pressure are very important features of good construction. Firmness depends largely on how the different parts are joined. The legs and the frame (rails) should be fastened together with glue and also with dowels, screws, steel clips, corner blocks, or corner metal plates.

Joints in wood are of two types, *mortise and tenon*, or *dowel*. In the first type one piece of wood has a tenon, a projecting block left by cutting away the wood around it. This is covered with glue and inserted into the mortise or hole, which has been made in the other piece of wood. In the dowel joint a wooden peg is inserted into holes which have been bored in both pieces of wood to be joined. Double dowels have two pegs. Cylindrical dowels are best, if grooved spirally and longitudinally to take care of air bubbles. Too many dowels close together may weaken structure. The mortise-and-tenon joint is somewhat stronger than the dowel, but both types are very good. Since a customer cannot see which type of joint is used she should request that the sales slip should state what they are, and also name the kind of glue used. Medium- and high-priced furniture should have phenol-resin glue, which is very strong and is heat and water resistant. Vegetable glue and milk-products glue are less desirable and less costly.

Corner blocks should reinforce both types of joints. They are triangular blocks, cut to fit into the unseen backs of corners, and glued and screwed to the frame or rails. If nails are used they should be handled carefully to avoid splitting the wood. Corner blocks prevent dowels from breaking under heavy pressure. They are a sign of good construction, but they cannot be used in some pieces where the legs are inserted directly into the frame of the chair seat.

Legs and Posts. Legs should stand squarely and firmly on the floor. They should look large enough to support the top of the article. Rungs and stretchers connecting the legs make them stronger but are omitted in certain styles. Having the grain of the wood run the length of a leg or post increases the strength of the article. Bentwood, therefore, is particularly strong. If grain cuts diagonally across a chair leg, the leg may split with the grain. Large legs, built up of several pieces glued together, require a guarantee that the glue will not deteriorate.

Drawers. The corners of drawers should be dovetailed, locked together with triangular teeth that fit tightly. Poorly constructed drawers are often nailed and glued at the corners. The bottom of the drawer should be supported by extending into a groove in the end walls of the drawer. A drawer should slide smoothly and evenly while guide strips underneath the drawer hold it straight. All surfaces of a drawer should be shellacked or varnished rather than waxed or left unfinished. They should be tested to see that they will not snag hosiery and delicate fabrics. Partitions between drawers make them dustproof.

Hardware. The quality and appearance of the hardware are important. Well-designed strong hinges and drawer pulls are placed on good furniture. Thin stamped metal that looks and is weak should be avoided.

Castors should be so strong and so well made that even heavy pieces of furniture can be turned and rolled easily. Castors and their sockets should be examined to see if they are strong.

Mirrors. *Plate-glass mirrors* have been ground and polished so that they do not distort objects at any angle. *Window glass* or *shock mirrors* are made of glass that has not been ground or polished and therefore causes distortions at an acute angle. Plate-glass mirrors are supposed to have blue labels to identify them, and window-glass mirrors yellow labels. The National Bureau of Standards specifies three classifications of plate-glass mirrors, "A" quality, No. 1 quality, and No. 2 quality. Beveled or rounded edges are considered more beautiful and are more costly than plain edges. Some mirrors have an unpleasant color; blue mirrors are used decoratively in Modern settings. Backs of mirrors should be made moisture-proof.

Upholstery. Upholstered furniture depends largely for its real worth upon its inner construction. Two easy chairs that look exactly alike may actually be so different in the quality of inside materials and workmanship that one is worth five times as much as the other. The purchaser has to depend upon the integrity of both the manufacturer and the retailer when he buys upholstered furniture.

An article of upholstered furniture consists of five important parts: frame, seat, springs, filling, and fabric. The *frames* of upholstered furniture are usually made of ash, birch, chestnut, or hard maple. These woods are strong and take glue and finish well. Gum and pine are somewhat less desirable and are less expensive. The *base for the springs* may be of textile webbing, steel webbing, or wooden slats. All are satisfactory if they are strong and placed so that springs can be deep, to give comfort. The coiled *springs* are made of enameled high-tempered steel wire. They are fastened together, and to the webbing, and to the frame, with strong hemp twine. A layer of burlap or canvas is placed over the springs. The *stuffing* is placed over this, and it in turn is usually covered with a pad of cotton which makes a smooth surface for the *lining* and *covering material*.

Curled horsehair is one of the best stuffings because of its resiliency. Cattle hair and hog hair are somewhat less desirable. Moss is a vegetable growth closely resembling hair. Palm fiber consists of shredded palm leaves. Coir fiber is made from the husk of the coconut. Kapok is a soft, silky fiber which encloses the seeds of the bombax tree. Tow is the crushed fiber of flax straw. Cotton stuffing may consist of long fibers or of less desirable short ones. Excelsior is shredded wood and is used only in cheap furniture. Down is the soft plumage next the skin of birds and fowl; it makes excellent but costly stuffing. Feathers are often mixed with down to give it body.

Unscrupulous manufacturers use papers, dirty old clothes, carpets, and old mattresses as stuffing for new furniture, sometimes without fumigating them. Some states require a label of guarantee as to the kind of stuffing put in upholstered furniture and mattresses, but, even so, regulation is difficult.

Upholstery fabrics are considered on page 294. Rubber foam and similar compositions are being substituted for upholstery.

WOOD

Wood is used for the construction of most of our furniture. Its popularity is natural because it is generally available, has beauty in itself, is flexible, is not hot or cold to touch, and is not noisy under impact. Wood has been much abused by craftsmen who have had less regard for their materials than for their tools. They have often failed to see that the beauty in the grain and the color of the wood itself were usually superior to anything they could add to it. Modern designers, however, appreciate this organic material and feature the natural beauty of the wood without stain or adornment of any kind.

Nearly all woods can be roughly grouped in two main divisions, hardwoods and softwoods. *Hardwood trees* are those that shed their leaves in the fall, like the oak, maple, gum, and walnut; *softwood trees* are those with needlelike leaves which they retain during the winter, like the pine and spruce.

American Hardwoods. Close to 90 per cent of the wood made into furniture is native hardwood. The following figures give the United States Department of Commerce report of hardwood used for furniture in units of 100,000 board feet in one year.

Gum	500	Chestnut	78
Oak	170	Tupelo	60
Poplar	150	Walnut	50
Birch	115	Beech	40
Maple	100	Others	83

Walnut. Walnut, called *Juglans* by botanists, is almost perfect for furniture making, as it is workable, durable, and beautiful. Walnut furniture passed through an ugly period when it was highly ornamented and stained dark; but now it is handled more simply and with lighter finishes.

Much of the present-day furniture is made of walnut or walnut veneers. In this country the term walnut ordinarily refers to American black walnut, but the butternut is a member of the same family and is called white walnut; there are also European and Oriental walnuts, some of which are not genuine walnuts. Circassian walnut comes from the Caucasus and is prized for the pattern produced by its gnarled fibers.

Oak. There are two general groups of oak woods, the red and the white. This wood is rather heavy, hard, and tough, but it is easily worked with tools; the grain is interesting though rather coarse. Quarter-sawed oaks are popular because of their grain. Quarter-sawing is cutting a log into quarters and then into boards by cutting alternately from each face of the quarter—a more costly process producing more beautiful grain than ordinary cutting. There was also an ugly period in oak, the recent golden oak era, that made oak disliked by people of taste. At the present time, oak is returning to favor as it is used in the modern and also in early English, Spanish, and French provincial styles. Most oak pieces are rather large, solid, and masculine in effect.

Maple. There are two principal varieties, hard and soft maple, with the Oregon maple about halfway between the two. Hard maple is best for furniture because of its great strength, its hard, smooth surface, and fine, light reddish brown color. The grain is usually straight, although veneers of curly and bird's-eye maple are prized. Maple is one of our choicest furniture woods, suitable for dining rooms, bedrooms, and living rooms. It is commonly used for reproduction of early colonial furniture. In addition Maple is sometimes utilized for commonplace furniture and also for frames, drawers, and stretchers of other furniture where strength is very important.

Gum. Red gum is the name of the tree and also of the heart-wood of the tree, which varies from rich reddish brown to dark chocolate-brown in color. Sap gum is the name of the sapwood of the same tree; it is light pinkish. Boards showing both heart-wood and sapwood are striking in color and value variations. Gum is a recent addition to the furniture woods, as its use has been made possible by modern methods of seasoning wood. Formerly it became twisted while drying. Now it is one of our most important hardwoods although it splits and becomes dented rather easily. It has a pleasing grain and color and takes finish so well that it is often stained to imitate other woods. It is used for the less important parts of mahogany pieces, posts and rails being made of red gum and the veneered panels of mahogany. Furniture manufacturers consider that this substitution is perfectly legitimate provided the piece is not sold as all mahogany.

Tupelo and black gum are also called gums but are not botanically related to the gum. They are harder and heavier than red gum and in color range from white to grayish brown. They are almost identical, but the tupelo is considered superior. Black gum has a ribbon stripe when quartered. These gums are used for kitchen furniture and for hidden parts of furniture.

Birch. Birch is considered one of the strongest furniture woods. It takes and retains finish well over its fine grain, and it can be made to imitate costlier woods. It is combined with other woods for strength in plywood and is also used in the construction of early provincial pieces and bentwood.

Ash. White, green, and black ash all have white sapwood. The heartwood of white and green ash is light grayish brown; that of black ash is darker. Ash is desirable furniture wood as it has a nice grain, is fairly strong and hard, is easily worked, bends well, and does not warp.

Other American Hardwoods. Beech is a plain, strong wood. Chestnut resembles oak and is used for outdoor and simple indoor furniture. Cherry is strong and beautiful in grain and color but is very scarce. Elm is a durable plain wood. Holly is a hard white wood used for inlays. Hickory is remarkably strong, tough, and elastic. However, hickory shrinks and is attacked by boring insects; pecan is the most popular of the hickory group. Sycamore is used for concealed parts of furniture mostly, although it has grain. Cottonwood is soft and uniform in texture.

American Softwoods. Softwoods comprise less than 10 per cent of the furniture woods in the United States. They are especially valuable because of their flexibility. Western fir, spruce, hemlock, red cedar, pine, white pine, and redwood are employed. Southern yellow pine is used for common furniture. Eastern red cedar is used largely for chests, because of its fragrance and its resistance to moth larvae.

Imported Hardwoods. True mahogany is the best known of the imported woods. It comes from the West Indies and Central and South America. Other imported hard woods are primavera, tanguile, lauan, rosewood, satinwood, and ebony. However, they amount to less than 3 per cent of the wood used for furniture in the United States.

Seasoning of Wood. Lumber from the sawmill must be seasoned or dried until its moisture content is from 5 to 8 per cent before it is suitable for furniture making. Natural air drying usually reduces the moisture content to 15 per cent, after which kiln drying completes the seasoning. Improper or inadequate drying is not evident when furniture is purchased, but warping and shrinkage presently show. A reliable manufacturer will guarantee the proper seasoning of his wood; merchants should give their customers the same guarantees.

Plywood or Laminated Wood. In plywood construction several layers of wood are glued over one another with adjacent layers at right angles and are placed under heavy pressure. Plywood is particularly useful for large surfaces and for curved planes. Laminated wooden chairs of unusual and interesting form are sometimes available. See page 61.

Most of the furniture of today is made partly of plywood and veneer, as it is more beautiful, more serviceable, and more economical than solid wood; it also offers much better resistance to changes caused by dry air. A properly made plywood panel is said to be 80 per cent stronger than solid wood. Plywood construction may, however, be very unsatisfactory through inferior workmanship, poor glue, or unseasoned wood.

Veneer. Freak logs and stumps having eccentric figure and grain are cut up as thin as possible, so that the interesting figure will not be wasted, and are used as veneering. A small amount of veneer wood is produced by sawing and slicing, but nearly all is made by rotary cutting. In this process the logs are first steamed or boiled and then turned against a knife, a continuous sheet of very thin wood being produced which is dried by air or heat. This interesting wood is generally used for outside layers of plywood; the inner layers are plain.

Solid Wood. Solid-wood construction has certain advantages as well as disadvantages. Solid wood can be carved, and it can be chipped or worn or planed down without showing other wood underneath. It does not peel or blister, and there is no danger from poor workmanship. Solid woods, however, may check or split from the lack of humidity in our heated homes. This danger is minimized by making a part like a table top of three adjoining strips and sealing all the surfaces of the wood.

Carving. The present trend is away from carving as a means of decoration. It is not adapted to machine production. Furthermore, it is difficult to clean and not very pleasant to touch. Most carving is done by machinery, but in the very finest furniture the carving is only started by machinery and is finished by hand. Inferior imitations of carving are made by pressing imprints into softened wood or by molding composition in the form of carving and then gluing it on.

Inlay and Marquetry. Inlay is a form of decoration in which contrasting segments of wood, bone, ivory, or metal are set into grooves made to receive them. Marquetry refers to an elaborate type of inlay having colored wood, ivory, and shells over an entire surface. This is often put together in a sheet of thin veneer and then glued on the article to be decorated. When the design is sunk into solid wood it is called intarsia. Overlay or onlay refers to decoration produced by gluing segments of wood to the surface of a panel. Imitation inlay can be made by painting, but this much inferior type of decoration should be recognized by the purchaser of furniture.

Finish. The reasons for finishing wood are to seal the pores so that changes in humidity will not affect the wood, also to protect it from vermin, dirt, and wear, to facilitate cleaning, to add a pleasing luster, and to bleach or darken it or otherwise change its color.

Finishes differ greatly in quality. The ideal finish has luster and depth obtained by many coats of finish which have been very well rubbed and sanded. This treatment brings out the natural beauty of wood. Some coffee- and card-table tops are finished with a new phenol-resin lacquer that is resistant to heat, alcohol, and acid. Paint or enamel finishes should be as smooth and lustrous as lacquer or varnish. A good finish on furniture is an indication of good quality in general.

Finishes should be carefully examined in bright light and tested. A poor finish is often very shiny and hard, making the wood appear almost metallic. Defects or rough spots in the finish can be seen. A poor finish would probably show a white scratch if a finger nail were rubbed across some under edge. Sometimes the surface of a poor finish will become powdery or sticky if a spot is rubbed with a finger until it is warm.

Willow, Rattan, Reed, and Fiber. Technically only willow furniture should be called wicker, but often the term is meant to include rattan, reed, and fiber furniture also. Willow is the only native wood that can be woven. Rattan is an Asiatic vine. It does not take color, so it is sometimes scorched by a blow torch for decoration, although this type of embellishment is usually poor. Reed is the heart of the rattan left when the hard outer covering is taken off. It is woven into durable, good-looking furniture. Whole or split bamboo is made into screens and furniture. Fiber is a wood pulp or paper product consisting of strands wound around wire, which is then woven into chairs and sofas. All these materials are used in the construction of furniture for informal rooms and porches. Good plain designs are procurable but much of this furniture is too cirvilinear and confused in design. See pages 25, 173, 226, 240, and 262.

Metals. Metal furniture is satisfactory in many respects. It is highly utilitarian, for it is fireproof, durable, and light in weight; dry artificial heat does not affect it; humidity does not cause drawers to stick and to acquire a musty odor. Various metals and their combinations (alloys) are suitable for furniture. Chromium plating, baked enamel, painted steel, and painted iron are procurable.

The designer of metal furniture can produce beauty if he respects his medium and does not imitate wood in design or finish. The strength of metal permits special constructions such as a chair with flat or tubular front supports for a cantilevered seat without back legs. At present the chief use of metal furniture is for offices, waiting rooms, and porches, and also for Modern homes. See page 176.

Plastics. The most interesting innovation in furniture material in centuries is plastics. Functionally, plastic furniture is almost perfect, as it is practically unbreakable, dent-proof, and scratch-proof. It is easily cleaned and light to handle. Plastics are also ideal from the designer's point of view because they can be molded, cast, or cut into any desired shape. There is no limitation in color, either; however, the crystal-clear plastics have a special radiance from the way that they reflect light. Beautiful furniture is already being made from plastics. Some designers say that period styles should not be portrayed in such Modern materials as plastics. See the pictures on page 261.

REMODELED FURNITURE

A person who has to use old furniture can do much to improve its appearance. Oversize pieces of reasonably good structural lines can often be secured at a very low price and can usually be cut down to the right scale. Very tall cabinets can be cut in two horizontally, making two chests. Cabinets that are too deep, extending too far out into the room, can be cut in two vertically from side to side.

The top part of ornate sideboards can be removed entirely. Legs can be lowered or entirely removed from chests and cabinets. Dressers are easily converted into chests of drawers with the mirrors hung separately. Drawer pulls can be replaced or replated. The glass in cupboard doors can be replaced by diagonal wire mesh. Two bedside tables can be made from a vanity dresser.

Tables can be lowered to the height of coffee tables or end tables. A round table can be cut in two, making a pair of consoles. A new top covering of leather, black glass, or mirror improves a table or flat desk.

Easy chairs can often be modernized by cutting down high old-fashioned legs, making the back legs a trifle shorter than the front ones. Straight legs can be substituted for curved. Slip covers can transform old chairs. See page 224.

All ornamentation should be removed from remodeled furniture if possible. Glued-on ornaments can sometimes be pried off, and other protuberances sawed off.

Finish. Either old or new furniture usually requires bleach, paint, stain, wax, or varnish as a finish. New unfinished furniture may be treated as follows: sandpaper carefully with the grain, fill nail holes with putty, apply clear shellac, rub with fine sandpaper, and apply three coats of white wax, polishing each one thoroughly An old piece of furniture usually requires removal of the old finish, which can be done with paint remover or household ammonia and a putty knife and steel wool. Even golden oak furniture bleaches successfully. However, the old finish can sometimes be covered with paint or enamel. Off-white or black are safe colors; yellow, green, vermilion, and blue are sometimes desirable. Large dark pieces, such as pianos, poster beds, dressers, chests, or cupboards, can be minimized by painting them light.

PROBLEMS

A sufficient number of problems are listed so that choices may be made.

1. Examine the classroom furniture for design, material, construction, and finish.
2. Visit furniture stores. Learn the differences between weak and strong furniture.
3. Visit a furniture factory, if possible, and report.
4. Design a Modern garden chair.
5. Design a plain sofa of the Lawson type.
6. Refinish a piece of old furniture, possibly painting an old dark Victorian piece with a light color to match the wall.
7. Make and finish a small piece of furniture that you need.
8. Make a dressing table and stool from waste materials, such as an orange crate and a nail keg. Use a gathered fabric skirt for the sides.

READING REFERENCES

HARMES, EARL. *Furniture for the Amateur Craftsman.* Bruce, 1940.

HJORTH, HERMAN. *Forty Pieces of Fine Furniture.* Bruce, 1939.

HOUSEHOLD FINANCE CORPORATION. *Better Buymanship—Furniture.*

JUDSON, JEANNE. *What Every Woman Should Know About Furniture.* Stokes, 1940.

KELSEY, C. B. *Furniture, Its Selection and Use.* U. S. Department of Commerce, 1931.

KOEHLER, ARTHUR. "Identification of Furniture Woods." *U. S. Department of Agriculture Bulletin* 66, 1926.

SHERWOOD, MALCOLM H. *From Forest to Furniture.* Norton, 1936.

SLOAN, LOUISE. *Revive Your Old Furniture.* Studio Publications, 1943.

WARING, R. G. *Wood Finishing and Painting Made Easy.* Bruce, 1940.

Cottage-type furniture that is attractive and comfortable is generally available. Notice how the curved-line element has been repeated in the sofa, tables, shelves, and fireplace. The arrangement of plates over the mantel is effective. The pictures are hung at the right height. The walls of wood are friendly and also functional. *Courtesy Montgomery Ward.*

This is Martha Washington's sitting room. The Hepplewhite chair at the left, the all-curved tilt-top table against the wall, the Baroque wing chair, and the Neo-Classic center table are beautiful models that are copied by manufacturers. The person who is buying period styles should try to get pieces like the originals provided that they are comfortable. *Courtesy Mount Vernon Ladies Association.*

An interior of a resettlement house at Greenbelt, Maryland, shows the type of furniture that was made to fill government housing needs. Manufacturers should supply consumers with inexpensive, good-looking furniture. *Courtesy U. S. Resettlement Administration.*

Unit or sectional furniture designed by Gilbert Rohde is shown in the picture below. Different combinations and groupings of these units are possible. This furniture is well designed and space-saving. *Courtesy Herman Miller Company.*

Plastic furniture made from colorless Lucite methyl methacrylate cannot be marred or broken and is light in weight. The non-period design at the left is more suitable for the new material than the period design at the right. Grace and lightness can be stressed in plastic furniture. Both tables have glass tops and shelves. The marmalade jar and food cover are plastic. The dishes are good looking but somewhat conservative for the surroundings.
Courtesy du Pont Company.

An analysis of this good-looking sofa reveals that one of its best design features appears in the ends or arms which taper from the base towards the top. Another attractive feature is the continuous line at the top of the back and arms. A Chinese feeling appears in the black lacquer furniture, in the painted fret on the wall, and in the fabric pattern. The room-high silver screen is handsome and functional; it can be moved wherever needed.
Courtesy Bloomingdale's.

In the upper left picture Gilbert Rohde designed this handsome four-purpose piece of furniture which he calls a compact. The top is a bookcase and china cupboard. The writing shelf slides back into the case when not in use. The lower compartment contains a drop-leaf folding table, which need not be removed for only two diners, as one leaf can be raised where it stands.

Above at the right unusual experimental forms and textures are features of the Swedish Modern furnishings. Note the cord seat of this comfortable chair.

The loggia below contains some reed furniture and some metal furniture of good design. The chair in the rear is a Mexican type upholstered in leather, which is popular in southwestern homes. Notice the bas-relief panel over the fireplace and the niches for flower arrangements. *Courtesy Smith College.*

 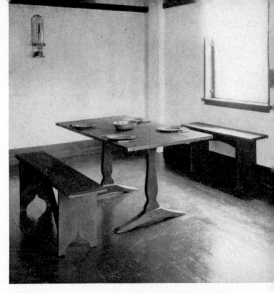

These typical examples of Shaker furniture, which were made by hand, were displayed at the Berkshire Museum. Sincere, unpretentious furniture of this type should be adapted for contemporary use. *Courtesy E. D. Andrews.*

Early American furniture is used in this historic old house, which has been acquired, restored, and furnished by Smith College. Other colleges should follow this good example. *Courtesy Smith College.*

This Modern porch furniture was designed by Dan Cooper. It is made of laminated wood bent into graceful functional lines. The woven seats are good looking and comfortable; the table top is damage proof. The beauty of this photograph is noteworthy.
Courtesy Hotel Friederica.

CHAPTER 16

RUGS AND CARPETS

This brief survey of floor coverings deals with the character and suitability of rugs and carpets, their color, texture, pattern, cost, durability, and the kinds available.

A floor covering makes a room comfortable and gives it a finished appearance. In winter it is usually well to have a carpet or a large rug in all the rooms in the house except the kitchen and bathroom. However, in the summertime, or at any time in the tropics, bare floors appear clean and cool.

One of the first problems to settle in the selection of floor covering is whether to have a large rug or a wall-to-wall carpet. Some advantages of a rug are that it can be reversed to prevent wearing in spots and it is more easily handled and cleaned. However, rugs and carpets can now be dry cleaned without removal. Rugs are adaptable for use in different rooms and also in different houses; those who move often should have rugs of standard sizes. Broadloom carpeting can, of course, be bought in any desired length and treated as a rug.

Carpeting from wall to wall makes a room seem larger than a rug does; it can be made to fit irregularities such as bay windows so that they will not appear to be separated from the room. Considerable expenditure to fit specific places is justified only in an owned house, however. Wall-to-wall carpeting permits having inexpensive floors in a new house, and in an old one serves to conceal worn floors. See page 302.

The ideal floor covering for the house or apartment of average size is the same wall-to-wall carpeting in all the rooms on one floor, except, of course, the bath and kitchen. This sameness produces remarkable architectural unity and spaciousness and conveys feelings of quiet, warmth, and luxury. It also suggests a pleasing slightly formal effect which is just the opposite of that produced by scatter rugs.

265

CHARACTER

A rug or carpet must agree in *expressiveness* with the room where it is to be used. It cannot be expected to set the mood of a room, but it must not be in conflict with it. For example, grass or rush rugs carry on the idea of a tropical room or a sun room; rag rugs have a cottage flavor; deep pile suggests luxury; Mexican Indian rugs seem primitive or masculine.

STYLE

Carpets must conform also to the style of furnishings in a room. A plain carpet is a desirable background for any style. There are, however, special designs meant to accompany particular periods.

The *Early American* rugs and carpets are excellent in design and color and have textural effects which make them appear homespun. Faithful reproductions of the original hand-hooked patterns of New England are available in rugs and carpets. See pages 106, 277, and 350.

The *eighteenth-century style*, known as Georgian in England and Colonial in America before the Revolution, calls for no specific floor coverings. However, plain colors are very desirable. Genuine Oriental rugs are usable but Oriental reproductions are not recommended.

The French styles of *Louis XV and XVI* suggest the use of reproductions of the French Aubusson and Savonnerie rugs with their scrolls and floral motifs and subtle colors. Solid pastel colors in broadloom are most desirable for French furnishings; bleached Oriental rugs are also appropriate.

Directoire, Empire, and English Regency need solid-colored broadloom, light or dark, with or without borders. Reproductions of rugs with a Classic feeling are appropriate.

Victorian rooms require carpeting from wall to wall with plain dark-colored broadloom, usually red, or with subdued reproductions or adaptations of the large floral and scroll patterns of the original period.

The *Modern or twentieth-century style* usually requires plain solid colors in carpets reaching from wall to wall. Light colors are emphasized. Texture interest and texture patterns are employed if variety is needed. See pages 121, 240, and 282.

COLOR

The color of the floor covering depends on the colors of the wall, draperies, and upholstery. If the wall is about the same color as the rug, even if much lighter or darker, harmony is assured. If the color of the rug is to be in contrast with the wall, it is much more difficult to select and must be tried in the room before it is purchased.

The present fashion suggests lighter colors for carpets and rugs. Beige, gray, off-white, wood tones, rust, grayed green, grayed blue, and grayed rose are favorites. The lighter colors do not show dust and footprints as darker colors do, but they do require more frequent dry cleaning. Darker floor coverings, however, are usually advisable where a firm foundation is required for dark walnut and mahogany furniture in traditional styles. Since a floor area is large, a brightly colored rug is not usually desirable. A grayed rug permits a change of color scheme in the room more frequently. The exposure of a room also affects the color choice.

PATTERN

The most important point to make about patterned floor coverings is that they are generally undesirable and that plain carpets and rugs are nearly always much better. Rug patterns are usually poor in design, although each year brings some improvement in them. For horrible examples see pages 24 and 224. A patterned rug unfortunately draws attention to the floor. Texture patterns that are exactly the same color as the rug itself are usually good looking. See pages 240 and 278.

Occasionally patterned rugs are usable and even desirable. For example, a cottage bedroom with plain furnishings gains interest by the addition of a carpet in a hooked-rug pattern. Small patterns (page 261) or tweed effects (page 349) are serviceable in halls that are subject to hard wear or in dining rooms or bedrooms used by children.

The person who is determined to buy a patterned floor covering should consider a quiet pattern of leaves (page 241) in a two-toned effect. However, a sheared pattern in a one-tone carpet is much more desirable. Factory-made reproductions of Oriental rugs are pretentious and insincere.

TEXTURE

The recent interest in texture is nowhere more evident than in rugs and carpets. Some of the most interesting new one-tone carpets have texture variations or patterns made by the combination of *cut and uncut loops,* by combinations of *straight and twisted yarns,* or by *several heights of pile.* Shaggy rugs of string, white fur, and others with emphasis on texture are favored, particularly with Modern furnishings. See pages 278, 348, and 424. The woman who is selecting a rug should keep in mind the other textures in her room.

DURABILITY

To judge the durability of rugs and carpets it is necessary to understand how they are manufactured. Pile rugs and carpets are made like other textiles by interweaving weft threads crosswise through lengthwise warp threads, but in addition wool tufts are fastened into the rug or carpet fabric.

A shopper would be able to judge the durability of a rug if a factual label were provided with it. The necessary information should include a statement of the *kind of materials* used, particularly in the pile, the *weight* of each kind of fiber, the *ply* of the yarn, the *pitch,* the *wires,* and the *shot.*

Carpet yarns are usually wool or worsted, although worsted is seldom employed at this time. Worsted is made of the longest wool fibers and is more durable and more costly than wool. However, wool is much more durable and resilient than any other fiber. Pile yarns should consist entirely of wool fibers. Cotton is now used for pile and for backing. Rayon has been considered a weak fiber. Nylon and other synthetic fibers may prove to be valuable in weaving carpeting. Jute and hemp help to make firm backs for carpets and rugs. Jute is strong and inexpensive but will decay under continuous moisture. Paper yarns which are sometimes used as filling fall to pieces when wet. Glue is often used on the backs of rugs for sizing, but the glue is not evident on a good rug. It should be noted that stiffness is not strength.

The *weight* of each kind of fiber woven into a rug would be valuable information for the consumer. The rug with the most wool will wear the best and will crush the least.

The *ply of yarn* is determined by the number of small wool yarns that are twisted together to form larger yarn. Six-ply is a thick yarn which makes large tufts when used as pile. It is well to recognize the ply of the warp and weft yarns, for the larger ones are stronger.

The *pitch* refers to the number of tufts of pile per inch crosswise of the rug. Strength is indicated in a rug by a large pitch number and close tufts. The *wires* refer to the number of rows of tufts per inch lengthwise. In the weaving process the wool yarn is looped over wires ending in small knives which cut the loops. Loop pile rugs are woven over wires which do not cut the loops. The *shot* is the number of crosswise yarns which attach the pile to the backing material of the carpet or rug. In a two-shot rug, one strand of yarn shows between the crosswise row of tufts; in a three-shot rug two strands of yarn are visible. Three-shot rugs require more loom work and more material.

Consumers should soon be able to get definite information about the wear resistance of all carpets and rugs, for the National Bureau of Standards' *wear-testing machine* has been used for this purpose. The machine has demonstrated that the most important factor in durability is closeness of the pile, and this results from having a large number of pile tufts per square inch. The tufts can be counted on the back of the carpet by marking off a square inch, well away from the edge, and counting the tiny squares within it, each of which indicates a pile tuft.

The *height* of the pile is also a point in durability, but it is not so important as thickness. High pile is luxurious, but it crushes somewhat more easily than short pile. Thin pile crushes more than thick. In places where wear is hardest the carpet will appear lightest.

Underlays or *underpads*, according to the National Bureau of Standards, increase the wearing qualities of the carpets from about 75 to 150 per cent and also contribute to comfort. Since underlays cost much less than rugs they are a good investment and should be bought with the rugs. There are various thicknesses and textures in pads, including a special non-skid material for small rugs. Pads should be mothproof.

A consumer should require *color-fast guarantees* with carpets and rugs, to cover sunlight, shampooing, and dry cleaning.

COST

The general tendency is to expend a disproportionate amount of money on floor covering. A very costly or rare rug is often a handicap in furnishing a room, for it requires a certain standard to be sustained throughout. Ordinarily it is good decorating practice to save on floor covering in order to have more effective things nearer to the eye level. Usually it is well to buy the best quality of floor covering in whatever class the budget allows. For example, a first-class velvet rug is the type most suitable for the average home. However, ample size of rug is more important than quality in producing an effective room.

For the very low-budget home, felt, rag, hooked, string, jute, fiber, and porch rugs are good selections.

SIZE

A rug should fit the size and shape of a room, leaving a margin of 6 to 12 inches all around it. The standard sizes are 6 feet by 9 feet, 9 feet by 12 feet, and 11 feet by 15 feet, but rugs of many different sizes are now obtainable. A rug without a border looks larger than one with a border.

Small scatter rugs are sometimes desirable in halls, bedrooms, or living rooms. Those in the same room should be identical or as nearly alike as possible. If used on a plain carpet they should be like it in their background coloring.

Small rugs must be arranged thoughtfully. They should not be placed diagonally, because that would violate the architectural lines of the room. Small rugs should not stray out into the middle of the floor but should be placed before the most important pieces of furniture or be combined as bases for the various groups. Sometimes small rugs are laid so that their long lines all follow the same direction. It is better to have too few than too many small rugs because they must not suggest a store display.

On a stairway a strip of narrow carpet is sufficient, unless the lower hall is carpeted from wall to wall, in which case it is also well to cover the stairs entirely. An extra yard or two of length should be purchased in a stair runner so that its position could be changed occasionally in order that it would wear the more evenly.

TYPES OF CARPETS AND RUGS

Flat weaves, which are usually alike on both sides, are woven flat without pile from wool, linen, cotton, rags, fiber, or grass. *Loop-pile* carpets and rugs are those with uncut loops or pile, like body Brussels, tapestry, and certain texture contrast weaves. *Cut-pile* carpets and rugs are those with cut loops, like velvets, Axminsters, Wiltons, chenilles, and most Orientals.

FLAT WEAVES

Grass, fiber, and other flat rugs have been improved so much in appearance that they are now suitable indoors as well as on porches. They are most attractive without any decoration. Sometimes enormous ugly stenciled designs make them unfit for use. Stripes and plaids are usually satisfactory. For examples see pages 26, 173, 226, 239, and 279.

Fiber rugs are made from spruce-wood paper twists or yarns woven in the basket, twill, or Jacquard weave. They are durable when dry but disintegrate when wet.

Wool and fiber rugs are woven on cotton warp with alternate stands of wool and fiber. The wool adds an interesting color element and also pleasing softness.

Grass rugs are woven in the simplest over-and-under weave from continuous undyed grass strands procured only in the marshes of Minnesota, Wisconsin, and Canada.

Sisal rugs are made from a tough, heavy fiber obtained from the leaves of a plant grown in the West Indies, Yucatan, and Central America. Some strands are dyed. *Rush squares* about 1 foot in size, fastened together, make good-looking, durable rugs. *Chinese sea grass* rugs and *Hawaiian mats* made of wide fibers are excellent.

Linen rugs are medium in cost, wear very well, look well, and come in a large variety of plain or mixed colors. They are useful in dining rooms, sun rooms, porches, and halls.

Rag rugs of the manufactured variety are usually made of cotton rags, in fairly light colors. They are washable and durable but light in weight. See page 241.

Thread and thrum carpets are made of a thick cotton warp and a thin wool weft, and resemble tapestry weaves.

DOMESTIC PILE WEAVES

Velvet rugs and carpets make up 30 per cent of the total carpeting sold in this country, but the percentage will be higher as consumer taste improves. Most solid-color rugs and carpets including broadlooms are made in this weave. The rightly popular textured rugs of cut or uncut pile or combinations of both are usually of velvet weave. The velvet weave is simple and comparatively inexpensive to produce. Salesmen often deliberately call velvet carpets Wiltons for reasons of salesmanship.

Tapestry rugs and carpets are made like velvets, but the loops are not cut and therefore wear very well.

Axminsters are made on special looms that can handle very many colors. This is doubtless the reason why these rugs are usually poor in color and in design. Axminsters can be recognized for they cannot be rolled crosswise because of stiff jute ridges. Axminsters unfortunately comprise more than 50 per cent of the rug and carpet yardage of this country.

Wilton carpets and rugs make up 15 per cent of carpets sold today. They are woven with the Jacquard mechanism which controls colors by means of perforated cards. When one color appears on the surface all the other colors are underneath it. Saxony rugs are a type of Wilton with a coarser pattern owing to larger tufts. Wiltons include desirable hooked rug patterns and many poorly designed, multicolored rugs, among them the unfortunate imitations of Oriental rugs. See page 106.

Brussels carpets and rugs, which are seldom made now, are almost the same as Wiltons, except that the loops are not cut.

Chenille carpets or rugs constitute less than 1 per cent of the total amount of carpeting produced in this country. They are luxurious, costly, plain or patterned, and are usually made to order. Smyrna rugs are double-faced chenille with shorter pile.

Some related terms which are often misunderstood are: *broadloom* which refers only to the width of a carpet or rug; *lock-stitch* carpet which does not ravel when cut because the back has been coated with a heavy sizing of rubber and pyroxylin, and *frieze* carpet which is made of hard twisted yarn causing an interesting texture. These different types of carpeting are made in several kinds of weaves.

HANDMADE RUGS

European handmade rugs particularly from Scandinavia and central Europe have constituted some of the finest products available in our shops. The beauty of the Swedish rugs exhibited at American expositions has been an inspiration to American designers. Aubusson and Savonnerie rugs have been imported from France for a great many years, and attractive flat woven rugs have been imported from the Balkan countries.

American handmade rugs of original and distinctive design are woven in private establishments in various parts of this country. Some rag carpeting is still made on hand-and-foot looms, and round or oval rag rugs are braided and sewed or crocheted. See pages 104 and 277.

American and Mexican Indian rugs and blankets are probably the most interesting handmade rugs sold in this country. The design motifs are geometric; the colors are usually neutrals sometimes combined with positive colors. The more limited the colors the better the effect. The most usable patterns are those that have the design and color well broken up and distributed over the rug rather than concentrated in a few large spaces. American Indian saddle blankets are particularly good. The symbolism of the motifs used by the Indians adds interest. See page 279.

Efforts should be made to encourage the handwork of the Indians and to prevent the commercialization of this very interesting native craft. The most beautiful old rugs and blankets are in museums and private collections. Indian rugs are now used in southwestern or Modern houses or in masculine-type rooms.

American and Canadian handmade hooked rugs are usually available in our stores. Hooked rugs are often delightful, naive, individual, and expressive of the lives of thrifty, sturdy people. Hooked rugs are suitable in simple or old fashioned rooms, like pioneer or Early American rooms. In a quaint type of bedroom two or three hooked rugs look well on a painted floor; in a living room hooked rugs may be used on a wood floor or on a plain carpet. See pages 222 and 263. Hooked rugs are made of rags or yarn pulled up through burlap in loops which may be cut or left uncut. The woman who is planning to make a hooked rug should take the utmost care to get a design having artistic merit.

ORIENTAL RUGS

Antique Oriental rugs are those that are more than fifty years old. These rugs were made by the nomad tribes of southwest Asia who wandered about seeking pastures for their sheep, which provided them with food, clothing, and rug materials. The wool was washed by hand and dyed with vegetable and animal dyes, and the rugs were woven by hand. The designs were often symbolical of the history of the family or tribe. Family pride, care, and patience helped to produce rugs that were works of art. The older ones are now in museums and in private collections.

Semi-antique Oriental rugs are newer unused rugs, made by commercial methods, but not chemically bleached and glazed. Some of these rugs have pleasing design and color.

Modern Oriental rugs comprise most of those that are available for purchase. These rugs are made in the Orient by weavers who have been gathered into factory centers to work on a commercial basis. The wools are now chemically washed and dyed with aniline dyes, and much of the rug is made by machinery. The designs and colors have been adapted to suit the taste of American and European rug merchants. Importers subdue the garish aniline colors by an injurious process of bleaching with chemicals and then retouch them and add an artificial gloss by means of glycerine and hot rollers. These products are not works of art and should not be confused with beautiful old rugs.

Oriental rugs are not now fashionable. They are difficult to use because they attract too much attention to the floor, and because all other furnishings must be subordinated to them. For correct use see page 282. Some owners of Oriental rugs have had them bleached to very pale tints to accompany Modern furnishings.

Some *guides* to prospective purchasers of Oriental rugs are: the *condition* of a rug is important—damage results from age, wear, moths, and beatings; the *workmanship* and *materials* are determining factors in the price; long, even, erect pile is most desirable; the *number of knots* to the square inch is significant, 100 to 200 knots denoting good quality. Some art factors are: small compact *patterns* and many *borders* are desirable, central medallions are not; strong *color contrasts* and sharp *value contrasts* should be avoided.

Persian rugs have been the most popular of the Oriental rugs. They are outstanding for expert workmanship, subtle coloring, and fine design. Their rather small conventionalized designs are based on natural forms, such as flowers, trees, vines, birds, rivers, and clouds. The rugs are completely covered with a profusion of these graceful motifs. A beautiful example appears on page 280. Among the best-known rugs are the Bijar, Feraghan, Ispahan, Kashan, Kermanshah, Saraband, and Sarook. The names of cities and provinces where they are made are usually given to Oriental rugs.

Turkish rugs are bolder in design than Persian rugs. Patterns consist of more highly conventionalized floral and geometric forms. The lines of city architecture and Turkish symbols such as pinks, tulips, and hyacinths are favorite motifs. The color is less varied and suave than in the Persian rugs, but not so limited as the Caucasian. Among the Turkish rugs are the Anatolian, Armenian, Bergama, Ghiordes, and Yuruk. See page 281.

Caucasian rugs are made by the tribes living on the mountainous isthmus between the Black and the Caspian seas. These rugs are even bolder in design and color than the Turkish. Among the design motifs are geometric forms of animals and humans, snow crystals, stars, crosses, and latch hooks which are combined into mosaic effects. Representative rugs are the Cabistan Daghestan, Kazak, Shirman, and Soumak.

Turkoman rugs, made by tribes in central Asia, are usually a rich, dark red. The design motifs are simple geometric forms without symbolism. The outstanding rug is the Bokhara (see pages 281 and 476), others are from Afghanistan, Beluchistan, Samarkand, and Turkestan.

Chinese rugs of the seventeenth and eighteenth centuries were beautiful (page 280), but the modern rugs are often without merit in design, for in them naturalistic dragons, clouds, waves, trellises, flowers, and birds, usually blue, are scattered around over light backgrounds in confusion. A promising new development has been the production of one-tone, textured, patternless rugs.

Indian rugs, from India, have no distinction of their own. Their designs have been copied from other countries and are usually more realistic and therefore less beautiful than their models. They display great variety in color and texture.

PROBLEMS

A sufficient number of problems are listed so that choices may be made.

1. Visit a rug department in a store, and write a report of the trip.
2. Design a hooked rug or a Modern rug with poster paints or crayons.
3. Visit a local home weaver, and report on the trip.
4. If possible visit a textile or rug factory and write a report about it.

READING REFERENCES

Encyclopædia Britannica. "Rugs" and "Carpets."

HOLT, ROSA B. *Rugs: Oriental and Occidental, Antique and Modern.* McClurg, 1927.

KENT, WILLIAM W. *The Hooked Rug.* Tudor, 1937.

MUMFORD, JOHN K. *Oriental Rugs.* Scribner, 1915.

REICHARD, GLADYS A. *A Spider Woman. Navajo Weaving.* Macmillan, 1934.

U. S. Department of Agriculture Bulletin 1219. "Floors and Floor Coverings."

A hooked rug of green, yellow, brown, and white sets the color scheme for this room. Gingham in the same colors was used for ruffles. The effect is gay, entertaining, young, and possibly somewhat temporary. *Courtesy Marshall Field & Company.*

A large braided rug is an ideal floor covering to accompany Early American furniture. Its texture is suitable, and its round lines repeat those of the table and the Windsor chair backs. The swing-leg table is American Provincial Colonial.

The small rug above helps to unify the group of seating furniture in a combination room where a definite dining area exists. Excellent design and texture are features of this rug, which would suit either Modern or traditional furniture.

The textured rug below is a definite contrast to finely finished furniture. This room is built around a collection of fine old Chinese porcelains with wall paper in yellow, white, and blue. The table and buffet are of sycamore in blue-black lacquer. Side chairs are in oxblood-red lacquer, and end chairs in Chinese yellow. *Courtesy Lord and Taylor.*

An American Indian rug of geometric design is suitable with Modern furniture. This excellent furniture above was designed by Hans Knoll. *Courtesy Bloomingdale's.*

The inexpensive flat woven rug below is primarily a porch rug but is satisfactory with simple Modern furniture. The geometric lines of both agree. *Courtesy Wanamaker's.*

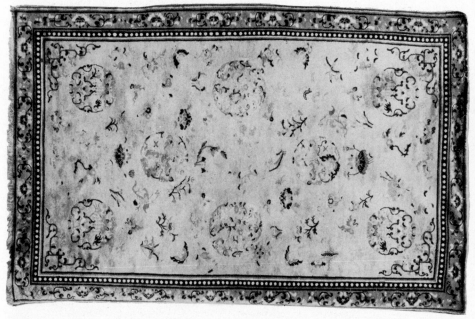

This Chinese rug of wool and cotton was made in the Ch'ien Lung period (1736–1795). It emphasizes curved lines; no straight lines are employed except in the outlines of the border. Unconnected scrolls and floral forms are scattered among the eight definite circles, which are symmetrically located. *Courtesy the Metropolitan Museum of Art.*

The Persian carpet pictured below is of the Herat type. It was made of wool in the sixteenth century. Note the delicacy and grace of the stylized floral motifs. The three borders strengthen the design. Rhythm and color are outstanding qualities of this rug. *Courtesy the Metropolitan Museum of Art.*

The Caucasian rug above is of the Cabistan type. As in all Caucasian rugs the motifs are purely geometric and borders are numerous.
Courtesy H. Michaelyou, New York City.

This small Turkish prayer rug is of the Bektashi Ghiordes type. The stylized flowers, trees, and buildings are typical. *Courtesy H. Michaelyou.*

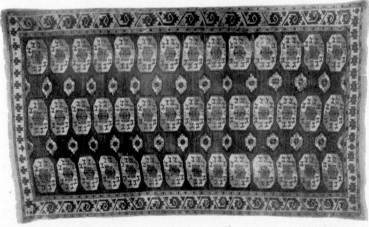

This Turkoman Turkestan rug, of the Saryk (Saruk) type, was made in Central Asia early in the nineteenth century. The design, which is not symbolic, is geometric; octagons, squares, triangles, crosses, and combinations of them appear in distinctly separated motifs. *Courtesy the Metropolitan Museum of Art.*

With an Oriental rug or any other patterned rug, walls and fabrics should be perfectly plain. Elegant fabrics, period styles, and a formal arrangement are associated with Orientals. *Courtesy L. Bamberger.*

A plain carpet is desirable in any room. Here a small Modern rug unites the window group of furniture and draws attention to the picture window. These are comfortable modified Modern chairs upholstered in an interesting fabric.

CHAPTER 17

FABRICS

Historical Background. It is probable that the earliest form of weaving was the interlacing of reeds for shelter. This was followed by basket weaving. Later, fibers were woven into cloth which could be substituted for the pelts worn by early man. Archaeologists have discovered evidences of spinning and weaving in the very oldest of the homes of prehistoric man. Among the ruins of the Swiss Lake Dwellers of the Stone Age were found fragments of fabrics of linen and wool, some of them decorated with designs of human figures. During the Bronze Age, spindles, looms, and needles almost like those used by some primitive tribes today were developed.

The earliest of ancient history reveals the great skill of the East in spinning, weaving, dyeing, and ornamenting fabrics of wool, flax, cotton, and silk. The whole process of textile making is depicted on the walls of the ruins of Thebes, Babylon, and Nineveh. Ancient Egyptian mummy cloths and Coptic textiles are among the finest in existence. The knowledge of spinning and weaving spread westward from the East. Greece and Italy taught Spain, France, and Flanders; from them Germany learned, and in turn taught England and Scandinavia.

In America ancient Peruvians wove cloth of fine conventional design and of exquisite colors, which has lasted at least a thousand years. In the homes of the Cliff Dwellers of the southwestern United States fragments of different types of textiles have been discovered. Some American Indian and some Mexican Indian tribes still work today as primitive weavers have since the craft began.

The power loom which was invented early in the nineteenth century is not fundamentally different from early hand looms, although improvements now equip it for weaving much more intricate patterns.

Fibers. Fabrics are usually made from fibers of silk, wool, cotton, linen, and rayon or other synthetic products, alone or in combinations. When selecting fabrics the purchaser should inquire about their fiber content.

Yarns. Fibers are spun into yarns which vary in size, evenness, smoothness, elasticity, strength, amount of twist, and length of fiber. A purchaser should untwist and examine separate strands of yarn or threads drawn from fabrics. A yarn that breaks easily is poor; short or coarse fibers usually indicate weakness, whereas round, hard, well-twisted yarns are strong. Sometimes durability, however, is not so important as beauty or novelty.

Construction of Fabrics. Methods of making the fabrics help to determine their durability and appearance. *Weaving* is the principal method although a few fabrics are made by other processes. Jersey is *knitted*, nets consist of *knotted* threads, and some articles are *braided*. Felt is made of *pressed* matted fibers. Fiberless fabrics are made from fluids which become *solidified* in sheets.

Weaving. Methods of weaving differ, but in all of them the warp threads, which run the length of the fabric, make a support for the weft yarns, which are interwoven through them back and forth from selvage to selvage. The three types of simple weaving that are the basis for all others are the *plain* weave, as in taffeta, the *twill* weave, always diagonal in effect as in serge or denim, and the *satin* weave. Novelty weaves with beautiful textures are made by combining coarse and fine yarns or unusual twisted yarns. Patterns are made by lifting the threads in groups.

Dyeing. Fabrics can be dyed at different stages in their manufacture. Sometimes raw fibers are dyed before the yarn is spun; sometimes the finished yarn is dyed; often the entire fabric is dyed after it is woven. Manufacturers' labels are helpful in determining color permanence.

Printing. Patterns are usually printed on fabrics by a series of copper rollers, each of which prints one color. In some fabrics the pattern is printed on the warp thread only. In discharge printing a bleach removing the color in the shape of a pattern is applied to a plain material. Resist printing is done by means of a substance which prevents the dye from acting in the places where it is applied.

ELEMENTS OF ART IN FABRICS

Beauty of fabrics depends largely on their expressiveness, texture, color, and pattern.

Expressiveness. A single outstanding idea can be portrayed in the texture, color, and pattern of a fabric. When these three elements fuse to give one impression, the effect is enhanced and dramatized and a distinctive fabric is created. For example, the utmost quaintness may be expressed in a calico with a prim little nosegay pattern in faded rose, green, and white. See page 302 for such a pattern. Dignity, delicacy, sophistication, or almost any theme can be found in fabrics.

Texture. The most significant quality of a fabric is texture, which determines its character more than any other element. Textiles are to be felt as well as seen. The modern trend is to emphasize textural variety in order to obtain interest and beauty without employing pattern. See the glass fiber spread on page 302.

Color. Since fabrics often provide most of the color interest in a room, subtle and beautiful colors should be sought in them. One or two colors are more effective than a greater number. Finely related colors in drapery, upholstery, and rugs are essential for beauty.

Pattern. Decorative pattern is usually produced by weaving, embroidery, or printing. Printed patterns should suit the textiles on which they are stamped. Woven patterns that grow out of the weaving process itself are in the main more distinctive than those that are printed on finished fabrics. Textile designers create patterns especially intended for execution in warp and weft. Some of the most beautiful modern woven patterns have come from the looms of Paul Rodier of France. Many one-tone fabrics exhibit woven patterns of the same color as the background. Patterns designed by famous designers are shown on page 299.

Stripes, checks, plaids, or dots are the safest patterns. Stylized patterns and Modern geometric patterns are often desirable. Ferns and other large foliage patterns are among the best designs. Floral patterns are difficult to select as they are more often poor than good, the naturalism and sentimentalism of Victorian times still persisting in them. Excellent period patterns, based on the original designs, are often available for period rooms.

WINDOW TREATMENTS

Draperies	Cornices
Casement curtains	Bamboo shades
Glass curtains	Reed shades
Roller shades	Interior Venetian blinds
Valances	Interior shutters
Swags	Exterior Venetian blinds
Ropes and cords	Exterior shutters

Draperies. Overdraperies may be used alone or with glass curtains, roller shades, or Venetian blinds. They should reach the floor, and ordinarily they should be made so that they can be drawn over the windows.

Casement Curtains. Sill- or apron-length draw curtains, often made of standard casement cloth or a plain medium-weight opaque material, usually function in place of shades or blinds to give privacy. They may be used alone or with draperies. See page 9.

Glass Curtains. Sheer curtains hung next to the window may be used with or without draperies. Net, organdy, dotted Swiss, voile, Celanese, scrim, marquisette, rayon gauze, madras, lace, or ninon are used for this purpose. Glass curtains give daytime privacy, soften the light, and modify the harshness of the frame and shade. They may be long or short, but the long glass curtains are more decorative and now more fashionable. They should be exactly the right length, stopping at the window sill, bottom of the window frame, or 1 inch from the floor. They should be very full, well tailored, and perfectly clean. Plain sheer material is best. Sheer curtains with wide ruffles are effective without draperies, especially in early American or colonial rooms.

Roller Shades. Roller shades are practical, as they are easily adjusted to give privacy or to exclude light. Although there is structural unity in having all the shades at the same level, a shut-in feeling results from keeping them all halfway down the windows, as many women do. It is often advisable to keep them rolled up out of sight unless utility demands otherwise. As a rule, it is well to have roller shades light in color, preferably like the walls or woodwork. Roller shades are sometimes made by tacking oilcloth, chintz, or other fabric to rollers.

Valances. As the top parts of window treatments are often unattractive in appearance, they are sometimes concealed by means of valances. A fabric valance may consist of a gathered or pleated ruffle or a shaped piece stiffened with buckram. A valance board is a narrow shelf to which the fabric curtain is attached.

Swags. A simple type of valance consists of a length of pliable material carried across the top of one or more windows, passed through festoon rings or holders of plastic, wood, or metal, possibly tied in a knot, and allowed to hang down to whatever length is desired. Swags may be used alone or with blinds, shades, curtains, or draperies. See page 300.

Ropes or Cords. Curtains or draperies are omitted where ropes or cords are hung as a substitute, particularly in summer. They are effective over Venetian blinds or to develop some period effects or nautical, western, or masculine themes.

Cornices. A window treatment may be finished at the top with a cornice, which is a wood or composition molding or frame, from 4 to 8 inches wide, painted or covered with some material. A decorative tin or wire arrangement may substitute for the usual wood cornice.

Bamboo or Reed Roller Shades. These shades in natural colors can be used indoors to induce a tropical, studio, or garden effect.

Interior Venetian Blinds. These blinds, made of adjustable slats of wood, composition, or metal, function well as they admit light and air while giving privacy. They have a trim tailored look which is generally desirable. They should usually be light, matching the walls or woodwork in color. They may be used without curtains, especially in summer. See page 24.

Interior Shutters. An effective foreign custom is to have two narrow hinged, folding wooden shutters inside each window instead of shades and curtains.

Exterior Venetian Blinds. These new adjustable metal blinds are practical, for they not only admit light and air but also prevent the sun from shining on the glass windows, which reduces indoor heat many degrees. Some are especially useful for first-floor windows because they are burglar-proof.

Exterior Shutters. Although customarily used for decorative purposes only, outdoor shutters should also be made to function.

SELECTION OF WINDOW TREATMENTS

The window treatments discussed here are suitable alone or in combinations. The present tendency is toward very little window curtaining in order to allow the window to fulfil its functions of admitting air, light, and view.

Fashion. Since changes of fashion occur frequently in window treatments women should be alert to changes as shown in periodicals, moving pictures, and shops.

Personality. The owner's taste, personality, and needs are such important factors in selecting her window treatments that she should not permit a professional to do this for her.

Theme. The mood of a room suggests the type of treatment suitable for its windows. They can be made to appear stately, dramatic, gay, informal, severe, studied, or whatever is wanted. A reed roller shade used alone creates a masculine or studio effect. Sheer ruffled criss-cross curtains suggest femininity. See page 60. Long rich draperies finished at the top with regular groups of pleats and looped back showing long glass curtains connote stateliness. Long silk draperies with an extra foot of material lying on the floor express luxury. Short full curtains with gathered valances are informal. See page 102. A bold swag of pliable fabric knotted into Lucite rings at the top of a Venetian blind appears dramatic.

Style. The style of furnishing of a room indicates the proper treatment for the windows. For example, a *period room* should have a window treatment in the mood of the original period. See page 88. The original should be only suggested, however, not copied as it was on page 87. A single pair of well-chosen draperies, in modern colors, is sufficient to accompany certain periods, such as Regency or Victorian, which were originally characterized by many layers of curtains. Curved-line Queen Anne or Colonial furniture suggests curved-line draperies as a transition between the straight lines of the window frame and the furniture. The upper right hand picture on page 85 illustrates this point.

Various window treatments are possible for *Modern rooms*. Page 314 shows an effective one, which is to hang a gathered or pleated fabric from the ceiling to the floor, not only beside the windows but also all over one or two other walls.

Line. The proportions of a room affect the lines of the window treatment. For example, short curtains are suitable for the lines of low cottage rooms, although long ones are more fashionable. Where additional height is desired in a room draperies and curtains are hung straight because looped-back draperies appear to reduce height. Rooms with extra high ceilings are improved by valances, which also appear to cut height. The lines of the curtains and draperies must be in accord; if both are looped, the tie backs of both should be at the same level. Straight draperies may be used with sheer looped-back curtains, however. Both sides of a window should be looped back at the same height, which should be either above the center of the window or, preferably, about 12 inches above the window sill.

The number of windows is an important matter, for whatever treatment is chosen must bear repetition as many times as there are windows. Naturally, a striking window treatment which would be successful for one window group forming the center of interest in the room may be too bold for repetition. In a room with many windows the drapery may be treated as part of the background and repeat the exact color of the wall.

Groups of windows may be treated as a unit in their curtaining. A single wide Venetian blind or a reed roller shade is often made to cover two or more windows. A continuous valance usually ties such a group together, even continuing around a corner to include windows on another wall. In such a treatment, all the intervening wall space is hung with the drapery fabric.

The shape of the window affects the curtain design, particularly if it is unusual or difficult. A window with a curved top line may have the draperies curved to fit but curved-top windows are often concealed behind straight-top draperies. Windows that are too narrow should have the drapery cover the entire window frame and extend over a foot or so of wall at the side, the valance or cornice concealing the top of the drapery. Too high windows should have deep valances covering the upper part of the glass. Too short windows may have a wide valance hung high enough so that its lower line barely conceals the top frame of the window. If windows are too wide their curtains can be set inside the frame at the sides and top also.

The upper drawing shows three windows treated as one unit by means of a valance ruffle and drapery placed only on the ends.

The middle drawing shows the use of drapery on the entire wall except for the net curtains hanging over the windows. The shaped wooden cornice may be a matching or a contrasting color. This treatment is a pleasing change from the usual method of curtaining.

The lower drawing shows how two windows that are different in size and shape can be made to appear alike by the use of a Venetian blind and drapery hung over the entire wall. A wooden cornice effectively conceals the mechanics of hanging.

SELECTION OF DRAPERY FABRICS

The cost of fabrics for curtains might well be low compared with expenditures for other furnishings, because draperies should be changed every five years or so. In almost any room that needs reviving, the most effect for the money expended is obtained by the acquisition of new curtains.

When shopping for samples of fabrics it is well to have along a sample of wall paper, upholstery materials, some threads from the carpet, and samples of paint used in the rooms. Departments other than the drapery and curtain departments should be visited. Sometimes a tablecloth or a bedspread can be cut and hung to advantage as curtains. See page 422. Often cotton, silk, or linen dress goods, or suitings are more original and effective than ordinary drapery material. They must, however, hang well, press well, and wear well.

Delicate rooms require such fabrics as silk, raw silk, chiffon, satin, silk gauze, velvet, velour, taffeta, or embroidered silk. *Sturdy rooms* need monk's cloth, bed ticking, sail cloth, tarletan, fish net, Osnaburg, natural cottons, oilcloth, corduroy, rough novelty cloth, or similar materials. *Informal cottage rooms* suggest dotted Swiss, net, marquisette, casement cloth, chintz, theatrical gauze, voile, calico, gingham, pongee, colored sheeting, organdy, scrim, or any thin washable fabric. *Elegant stately rooms* require crewel embroideries, raw silk, satin, velvet, velour, damask, brocade, silk rep, metallic cloth, woolens, block-printed linens, or other high-grade textiles. *Modern rooms* can use either the new sleek shiny composition fabrics or the boldly textured novelty weaves which provide contrast for Modern smoothness.

Other fabrics and weaves are craft, terry, pebble weave, waffle, mohair, jersey, cashmere, faille, cretonne, and rajah, and the cheaper denim, gingham, and cheesecloth. Rubberized silk or cellophane meant for shower curtains may also be considered for bath and kitchen windows. Imitations of costly fabrics, such as cheap satins and damasks, should be avoided.

Manufacturers will provide fadeproof, waterproof, mothproof, flameproof, dirtproof, deteriorationproof, and mildewproof fabrics if consumers demand them. In such materials light colors will be practical for draperies and for general use.

The *pattern or lack of pattern* in the drapery material should depend on the amount of pattern already in the room. See page 24. A patterned rug or patterned wall paper calls for plain draperies. If a room has uninteresting furniture or is dull for other reasons it should usually be enlivened by an attractive contrasting pattern in the drapery fabric. Since draperies hang in folds, patterns should be viewed in folds. See pages 240, 300, and 424.

The *color* of the draperies may be white, off-white, cream, beige, ecru, or any grayed tints, or the exact color of the walls in rooms where they are considered as part of the architectural background. On the other hand, where draperies are to be featured they should have beautiful clear colors. Some draperies, by containing all the different colors used in a room, help to unify it.

The *texture* of the drapery must agree with the mood and style of the room, as has been stated before. Variety in texture is necessary, but extremes of contrast are incompatible. Texture patterns instead of color patterns should be considered in selecting fabrics. See page 282.

MAKING DRAPERIES

Almost any woman can make her own draperies. They should be cut extra long so that they can be altered and also because they shrink from cleaning and from exposure to the air. An extra half yard of material can be concealed in a curtain by making double hems at the top and bottom.

Draperies and curtains of all types should be made very full, a width or more of the material being allowed for each side of the window. If the window is narrow, it is enough to have drapery on only one side. An ample quantity of a cheaper fabric is far more effective than a narrow curtain of more costly material.

A few miscellaneous observations are worth mentioning. Selvages must be cut off some materials before hemming to allow curtains to hang well. Hems intended for the insertion of curtain rods should be sufficiently wide to allow easy movement. Net curtains should be hemmed by hand, as it is almost impossible to rip machine stitching on net. Small weights are sometimes sewed along hems of draperies to make them hang well. The lower lines of lining and drapery fabrics should not be sewed together, for each one should be free to shrink or stretch independently.

Lining. It is not necessary to line draperies, particularly if they are very full, but lined draperies usually hang better. They also last longer, as the interior fabric is protected from the sun, which rots and fades it. Costly fabrics are usually lined. Linings need not be made of the usual cream or beige sateen; a turquoise fabric might well be lined with a contrasting yellow material.

Trimming. As a rule draperies do not need any trimming. Some glass curtains are improved by ruffles, however, and curtains like chintz sometimes look well with white cotton balls or thick fringe. See page 120 for novel use of fringe. In color, trimming should be either a perfect match or a desirable contrast. Too much trimming can be as cheapening to draperies as to dresses. Naturally never more than one kind of trimming should be used.

Tie backs, if used, should be placed so that they divide the drapery about in thirds, never in halves. A tie back is generally made from the drapery material, but a cord may be substituted. Sometimes a tie back is looped over a nail with a rosette of crystal or metal as its head. Wood, metal, or plastic arms are also used to hold drapery back.

HANGING DRAPERIES

The *mechanical means* by which draperies are hung should be concealed or rendered inconspicuous. Valances of various sorts are useful in concealing roller shades and rods and rings. Rods, poles, and supports that show should be painted the color of the wall or wood trim behind them. Curtain poles and their supports should be plain to avoid attention. Unfortunately some shops carry only poles with ornamental ends and highly decorated brackets. Satisfactory plain wooden poles can be found among lumber materials and plain metal rods in hardware stores. Their selection depends, of course, upon what will fit best into the decorative plan. The metal should match the other hardware in the room. In some rooms Lucite rods, rings, and tie backs are suitable.

Curtains should be hung so that they are easily adjustable to meet changing needs for air and light. Pulleys are necessary to draw draperies and to prevent handling them. Draperies finished at the top with pinch pleats and small rings sewed on the back can be pulled easily and compactly. See page 89.

UPHOLSTERY FABRICS

It is wisest to shop for upholstery, slip-cover, and drapery fabric samples all at the same time. A plain rug and a plain wall allow either the upholstery or drapery fabric to dominate. When the upholstery is featured, usually two chairs are covered with the same large patterned material, other pieces with stripes and smaller motifs, and some with plain or mixed fabrics. A room with a patterned rug or patterned wall paper usually necessitates plain upholstery fabric. Sometimes it is best to upholster all chairs in the same color but in different textures. For interesting upholstery fabrics see pages 88, 282, and 424.

Naturally the mood of the room and the lines and size and material of the chairs affect the choice of upholstery fabrics too. A Neo-Classic room might employ striped light blue and lavender satin on a Sheraton sofa. See page 476. Oak furniture suggests heavy fabrics, whereas metal chairs are in accord with sleek composition fabrics. Quaint patterns appear on pages 59 and 104, inconspicuous materials on pages 26, 240, and 260.

The common upholstery fabrics are the printed textiles like chintz, cretonne, linens, Jouy prints, and warp prints; the decoratively woven materials like damasks, brocades, brocatels, armures, reps, and denims; the pile fabrics like velvets, velveteens, corduroy, plush, and friezes; the smooth silks and satins; crewel and needlepoint embroidery; mohair and other wools; and composition fabrics. Leather is also used. The durability of the fabric is important but does not usually take precedence over color and pattern. The purchaser should realize, however, that flat-surfaced materials such as satin, damask, rep, brocatel, brocade, and tapestry show wear sooner than a material such as frieze, which is a pile weave with loops uncut. All firmly woven fabrics wear better than loosely woven ones. Fabrics that are easily cleaned are preferable. A buyer should have dyefast, mothproof, and possibly flameproof guarantees.

Various techniques of upholstery are tufting, quilting, cording, the use of buttons or nails, or trimming with welting, tape, fringes, or braid. Any of these must be employed with restraint. Only one fabric should appear on one chair; having the back different from the seat destroys unity.

SLIP COVERS

Slip covers have become an important item in home furnishing. They no longer are limited to summer but are sometimes used all the year round, with different sets for winter and for summer. Overstuffed furniture can be purchased in the muslin or sateen stage before final upholstering, and covered only with slip covers, for economy and for convenience. Slip covers are also good for covering old furniture, which may be ugly, or worn, or inharmonious with the decorative scheme. See pages 59, 222, and 224.

Slip covers can be made of almost any medium-weight material. Some of the possibilities are chintz, cretonne, calico, percale, gingham, uncrushable linen, crash, awning, bed ticking, denim, bath toweling, gabardine, rep, mohair, poplin, corduroy, taffeta, velveteen, silk, sateen, and satin. Effective slip covers are also made from fabrics which have been quilted at home or in the factory. A plain fabric sometimes requires contrasting piping to make an interesting slip cover. See page 88.

Naturally, slip-cover fabrics should harmonize with the decorative scheme of a room in *pattern, texture, and color*. For example, widely spaced restrained motifs, smooth textures, and suave colors suit formal rooms, whereas rough checks and plaids of positive colors belong in simple settings.

The fabric should also conform in pattern and texture to the *style* of the furniture it is to cover. A provincial chair should be slip-covered with a material that suggests informality and quaintness, such as gingham, calico, or chintz of a small pattern that lends itself to ruffles. A heavier or more modern piece of furniture might have a heavy, plain, striped, or plaid slip cover and be finished in a tailored fashion, possibly with knife or box pleating and welting.

If the pattern and color of the material chosen are not conspicuous, the same fabric may form slip covers on several chairs and sofas in one room. This plan would be the safest for the amateur to follow. On the other hand, two or three different materials may be used in the same room by combining a dominating one with others of less importance. Page 301 illustrates the success of such a plan; page 24 illustrates the mistake of combining several conspicuous patterns.

Making Slip Covers. Care and patience are needed in making slip covers. It is not necessary to have them as tightly fitted as some professionals advocate. They should be made large, reaching entirely to the floor, with very deep hems to allow for shrinkage. A band or a pleated ruffle can serve as a finish at the bottom, the ruffle being the more informal and also more bulky. A wide band with only one deep box pleat by each leg looks well.

To make a slip cover, lay the material over the chair and cut it into approximate lengths roughly, allowing plenty of material. Center the pattern carefully on the back, seat, arms, and sides of the chair, using many pins and fastening together the pieces of cloth so that the seams come over those of the original covering of the chair. Fit the pieces to the chair, keeping the material smooth, by pinning darts or gathers wherever needed, and leaving plenty of material around the back edges of the seat to allow for the movement of the springs. Mark and cut the opening if one is needed. Then remove the cover from the chair, baste it, fit and adjust it, and finish it by machine.

One method of finishing the slip cover is to stitch it on the right side, then trim the seams evenly about ⅜ inch from the stitching and bind with folded tape. Other methods are to sew a French seam on the outside, or to sew welting in the seams.

BEDSPREADS

Bedspreads should suit the character of the rooms where they are used. In Early American rooms there may be handmade counterpanes (page 312) such as patchwork quilts, candlewick spreads, woven coverlets (page 103), or peasant spreads from other countries. India prints, chintz, calico, plaids, or checked materials are also suitable for bed covers in such rooms. A bedroom of feminine type may have a satin, taffeta, or similarly fine bedspread. See page 477. For a room shared by a man and a woman, the bedspreads and other fabrics should not be too feminine in feeling. The bedspread in a man's room could be heavy and rather dark, such as brown corduroy. See page 25.

Some materials for bedspreads are cotton taffeta, chenille, upholsterer's sateen, plain English broadcloth, arras cloth, slip-cover cloth, cotton crepe, unbleached muslin, and curtain materials. Quilted materials are effective. See page 86.

A couch-bed, at present called a Hollywood bed, which usually consists of a regular twin-size bed without a visible frame, is easy to cover. A loosely fitted boxlike slip cover with a big box pleat at each corner, or a large sheetlike spread that reaches to the floor at the ends and sides of the bed, is desirable. See pages 241, 312, 421, 422, and 424. For a couch-bed in a combination study and bedroom, the spread should be a darker color and more restrained than for one located in a bedroom proper. Plain colors are usually best; however, mixtures, stripes, plaids, or checks are satisfactory patterns because they produce a desirable tailored effect. It is often well to have plain cushions with a figured cover, or vice versa, so that the amount of material of one kind will be less. See page 9 for a couch cover with unusual texture interest.

The fabric for a couch-bed spread should be pleasant to touch and heavy enough so that it will not wrinkle easily. Heavy velour, corduroy, monk's cloth, crash, denim, and printed mohair make good couch-bed covers in rooms where they are appropriate. For summer, a large India print (page 345) edged with a plain colored band makes a satisfactory bedspread; an identical India print may be made into window curtains or hung on a wall beside the bed.

A bedspread must be *functional*. In a small home, bedspreads or couch covers should not be too good to be used freely. If a busy woman wants to lie down for a few minutes' rest without removing her shoes, the spreads should be dark enough to permit her to do so. See page 422. There should be a folded shawl or blanket of harmonious color and pattern on the bed in cool seasons for the comfort of anyone who lies down during the day.

Making a bedspread is not difficult. A spread should be made very long to cover the pillows adequately. It is often advisable to make the main bedspread separate from the mattress flounce, dust ruffle, or valance which conceals the box spring and the space under the bed. The top counterpane and the side ruffle need not always be of the same material. When making a spread for a bed with an ugly frame it is well to consider making slip covers for the head and foot boards, too, from the same material. See page 302. Quilted fabrics are especially effective for this purpose. Separate shaped, padded headboards and sideboards, to be covered with the same material as the bedspread, are usually procurable, or can be made by an amateur. See page 421.

PROBLEMS

A sufficient number of problems are listed so that choices may be made

1. Analyze large fabric samples for expressiveness in texture, color, and pattern.
2. Visit a decorator's shop or a decorating department in a store to study fabrics. Report on the trip.
3. Make a fabric chart, using real samples and prices.
4. Design a number of simple valances.
5. Group project. Make curtains for a place where they are needed.
6. Write a report on some new quality in fabrics, as non-inflammability.
7. Cut out and paint shaped wooden valances for your own room.
8. Group project. Make a slip cover for a sofa, upholstered chair, side chair, or an ugly bed frame.

READING REFERENCES

CANDEE, HELEN C. *Weaves and Draperies, Classic and Modern.* Stokes, 1930.

CLOUZOUT, HENRI. *Painted and Printed Fabrics.* Metropolitan Museum of Art, 1927.

DANA, MARGARET. *Behind the Label.* Little, Brown, 1938.

EVANS, M., and McGOWAN, E. B. *Guide to Textiles.* Wiley, 1944.

Periodical Index. "Glass Fabrics." "Plastic Fabrics."

PICKEN, MARY BROOKS. *Sewing for the Home.* Harper, 1941.

RODIER, PAUL. *The Romance of French Weaving.* Stokes, 1931.

U. S. Department of Agriculture Bulletin 1873. "Slip Covers."

U. S. Department of Agriculture Bulletin 1633. "Window Curtaining."

WETTERGREN, E. *The Modern Decorative Arts of Sweden.* American Scandinavian Foundation, 1926.

WINGATE, ISABEL B. *Textile Fabrics and Their Selection.* Prentice-Hall, 1935.

Eero Saarinen (Finnish-American) designed the pattern for the woven wall hanging above.

Ruth Reeves (American) designed the pattern for the textile above.

Raoul Dufy (French) designed the printed pattern below, called the Jungle.

Bruno Paul (German) designed the printed pattern below, for Schumachers.

Cedric Gibbons designed this attractive room above left in Michelle Morgan's provincial house. The fabric has a Colonial quilt pattern in green and white.

The fabrics used in the picture above right are all consistent and interesting in texture. The round motif in the curtains repeats the shape of the plates and the light fixture.
Courtesy American Walnut Manufacturers Association.

In the room below left, informality and femininity are expressed in the curtains. The triple ruffles in different color values and the dainty, restrained floral motifs are pleasing.

A swag of material like the bedspread is used at the top of the windows in the room below right. The wall between the two windows is also curtained so as to make a unit of the two.
Courtesy Quaker Lace Company.

Slip covers or upholstering may be finished with a ruffle or a straight flounce as shown above. The straight flounce is preferable for large chairs. Notice that the flower motif is well centered on the back, side, front, cushion, and arms of the chair. Plain glass curtains give privacy and subdue the light but exclude sunshine and view. The box valance, painted like the wall, makes a neat finish. Fairly symmetrical formal flower arrangements taller than the containers look best in urns.

A wall covered with a gathered fabric is shown in this room designed by Dan Cooper. The decorative picture panels are unusual and are well hung. A flower arrangement with a studied design would have been preferable here. *Courtesy Rich's.*

A single uncut piece of fabric makes this effective bedspread and pillow cover. A fern-leaf motif appears in the spread and in the carpet. The furniture was designed by Dan Cooper. *Courtesy Hotel Friederica, Little Rock.*

In the room below, the same fabric is used effectively on the furniture and on the closet door panels. This cheery room was designed for a young girl; the draped swag over the mirror is a youthful superfluity. The color scheme is sharp pink, white, and acid green.

In the room above, plain fabrics have been used for the window draperies and for the canopy bed because the wall paper is strongly patterned. The room is feminine in character and period in style. *Courtesy Marshall Field.*

The desirable bedspread below has been woven in the bubble weave from glass fibers and edged with a mass fringe of the same soil-proof fibers. The spread is strong, washable, flame proof, mildew proof, shrinkproof, and stretchproof. The shelf which serves as a head board is pleasing.

CHAPTER 18

LIGHTING

Artificial light has been an important influence in the growth of civilization, and its development is an interesting study. The greatest single improvement in lighting was effected by electricity, since it reduced simultaneously the labor, dirt, heat, and the danger of fire that were connected with other means of illumination. New forms of lighting include the fluorescent tube and the mercury-vapor lamp. The fluorescent tube, which gives two and a half times as much light as the incandescent bulb or tube of equal wattage, is more like daylight and produces very little heat. Germicidal light to destroy air-borne bacteria is a desirable development. The very newest lighting methods should be installed in a new house because even these will be outmoded before the house is old. The future possibilities of lighting are enormous.

The lighting industry has specialists who will help a home owner solve his lighting problems correctly. Light meters are used to show the amount of light needed, and how it should be distributed. It is now recommended that outlets for electricity be located at the floor line every 5 feet or less for convenience.

Several methods of measuring light are practiced. In one system the standard unit is a foot-candle, which is the illumination on a surface one foot away from, and perpendicular to, the rays of a standard-size candle. Ten thousand foot-candles of light occur in sunshine; about one thousand in the shade of a tree on a sunny day. About 5 foot-candles of light fall on a book directly underneath a 40-watt lamp. From 10 to 20 foot-candles is considered suitable for occupations like kitchen work or card playing, 25 to 50 foot-candles for close work like studying, newspaper reading, or sewing, and 50 to 100 foot-candles for close work over a long period of time. However, these figures may be increased, for recent tests show that insufficient light has been customary heretofore.

Lighting of houses must be *serviceable* and also *decorative*. Lighting experts say that two types of lighting are necessary for service, namely, general and local.

General lighting should be provided in various intensities, so that pressing different buttons produces bright, medium, or subdued light, or very dim light for television. General lighting may be direct or indirect, or a combination of both. Indirect light is the reflection and diffusion of light which is first thrown upward onto a light-colored ceiling or wall. See page 314. General lighting may emanate from troughs at the top of the walls or above doors or windows, from ceiling or wall fixtures, from ground-glass panels flush with ceiling or walls, or from indirect lamps. See pages 350 and 424. Cove lighting or other architectural lighting is a great improvement over fixtures as it is inconspicuous and conforms to the lines of the architecture. See pages 176 and 312.

Direct or indirect light coming from the ceiling has some disadvantages. It is somewhat unbecoming to the occupants of a room; it calls attention to the uninteresting ceiling; and produces an even, monotonous, overall light. Nevertheless, it has great advantages.

Local lighting is produced in particular places, usually by portable floor and table lamps, but also by straight or curved lighted rods, and by lights behind ground glass that is flush with the wall. Lamps are necessary for reading, writing, working, and card games. Every easy chair should be near a lamp; a desk, piano, or table should have its own adjustable lamp.

Light is *decorative* as well as functional and must be treated as an art element, to be employed and controlled so as to enhance the beauty of a room. For example, a room having only indirect cove lighting around the entire room would be equally lighted all over and monotonous in effect; but the addition of a few lamps with direct lighting would provide pleasing accents of light to give the necessary contrast. The lamps should be placed at the centers of interest so as to focus the attention where it ought to be. Light accents at the wrong places can spoil an otherwise beautiful room. Decorative use of light on the stage and screen gives suggestions for home lighting. Colored light soon becomes tiresome; therefore it is not desirable in homes, except possibly to light a flower niche or similar focal point.

FIXTURES

Central ceiling fixtures are generally undesirable for esthetic reasons and because of distressing glare and impracticability for reading. *Wall fixtures* also are unsatisfactory because they make glaring spots at the eye level and interfere with picture hanging and furniture arrangement.

The designs of many fixtures found in the shops are over-elaborate and incredibly poor; those that resemble built-in lighting equipment are among the best. One should be satisfied with nothing but a good, plain design suitable to the style of a room. See page 313. Light tubes or bulbs should always be shaded; light globes should never be made to represent flame on imitation candles.

Adapter fixtures that are very useful are now available. They usually consist of semi-indirect bowls or drums large enough to envelop completely and conceal ugly old-fashioned lighting fixtures suspended from the ceiling.

Period light fixtures are still found in some traditional rooms even though lamps are preferable. See page 278. Such fixture lights should be dim, and supplemented by lamps.

LAMPS

Lamps are very important in a decorative scheme and should be of the best quality that can be afforded. When lighted they are the most conspicuous objects in a room, and even in daylight they are the most important of the accessories.

Function. Floor lamps are often more convenient although usually less decorative than table lamps. Adjustable lamps or swivel-type lamps are functionally superior to others. See pages 264, 335, and 422. For many purposes the purely utilitarian gooseneck lamps are excellent. See page 241. Lamps should be much larger than they generally are, both for function and appearance. They should have reflection bowls inside the shades to reduce glare.

Lamps bearing an I.E.S. tag have met the specifications of the Illuminating Engineering Society, covering fifty-four points, and insuring lighting performance, mechanical soundness, and electrical safety.

Design. Many of the lamps obtainable in the shops are poor in design, possibly because electricity is so new that it is hard for designers to think of suitable media for it. Floor lamps are particularly offensive. The conveyors of light should be quiet, since light itself is so conspicuous. The greatest need is for more simplicity in design. The poor designer decorates every possible area on a lamp, whereas a good designer employs plain areas and beautiful forms, as illustrated on pages 240 and 260.

Unity. The base of a lamp and the shade must agree in scale, line, texture, and color, so that the entire lamp will appear a unit. Good illustrations appear on page 311. It is well to test many shades with each base before making a selection. Proper *scale* is easily judged because if the shade is too large the effect is top heavy; if the shade is too small it appears base heavy. The *shape* of the base and shade should be in harmony; for example, a four-sided base suggests a four-sided shade, and a round base indicates a round shade. The shade of a table lamp should overlap the base to such an extent that they appear one unit. The *texture* of the shade and base must be consistent. Shades such as silk or pleated parchment are suitable on the finer bases; shades made of split reed, rough fabrics, or similar textures harmonize with heavier bases. The *color* of the base of a table lamp is often the same as the shade, particularly if the vogue is to have them both off-white. If the base is colored, a white shade may be decorated with a few lines of the color of the base in order to unify them. Some shades can be painted all over with oil paint to conceal poor decorations.

Lamp Bases. Beautiful table lamp bases of pottery which emphasize texture and form are made by individual potters in various parts of the country and also by several commercial manufacturers of pottery. Other plain, well-designed bases which are usually procurable are made of alabaster, plastic, metal, or wood. Lamp bases suitable for certain rooms can be improvised from glass jugs, demijohns, urns, wood cylinders, or other objects that are simple in form. Stability is attained by putting lead or shot in a container base. If a lamp base is unsatisfactory in color it may well be painted a dull white.

Lamp bases should not be made from a statue or an art object that is important enough to be used alone. Nearly all ornamental bases are poor.

Lamp Shades.   Lamp shades which are to emit light should be a pale, warm color or preferably white or near white, and they may be lined with pale pink or pale amber to cause a pleasant glow on faces.   Lamp shades in other colors, particularly cool colors, should be entirely opaque so that no light comes through them.

Lamp shades should have little or no decoration.   It ought to be evident to anyone that landscapes, portraits, or flower pictures do not belong on lamp shades but in frames hung on the wall.   Frilly lamp shades are usually undesirable; very tailored equipment is best suited for electricity.   See page 311.

Shades with open tops are needed on high lamps in order that light may be well distributed.   They may also be used on table lamps below hall mirrors although lamp shades below the eye level of a standing person should ordinarily have tops or lids to conceal the bulbs.

Among the materials appropriate for lamp shades are plastics, fabrics, metals, papers, compositions, mica, reed, and raffia.   Fashion dictates new materials and designs frequently.   At present it is desirable to have off-white imitation parchment shades in every room in the house.   All lamp shades should be discarded when they are shabby or out of date, which is about every five years.

It is not difficult to make lamp shades over ready-made wire frames.   Braid or tape can be used to cover the stitches.   Gathered chiffon, pleated white buckram, or tightly stretched taffeta are possibilities; many other materials are also suitable.   Imitation parchment and similar materials can be glued to wire frames.

Harmony.   Lamps must, of course, agree with the rooms in which they are placed.   Period, Non-period, and Modern rooms require special lamps.   See page 209.   Lamp bases of brass, copper, or silver are suitable for fine rooms, whereas pewter, aluminum, or tin belongs with sturdier things.   Glass, pottery, or wood lamp bases are procurable in different degrees of refinement.   The color of a lamp base and shade should be selected in relation to the specific room where it is to be used.   For example, a foliage-green base and shade of opaque material would be attractive in a knotty pine room by daylight and also by artificial light.   The indirect floor lamps on page 209 are suitable only in Modern surroundings.   The adjustable functional lamp on page 221 is well designed and fits its surroundings.

SUITABLE ROOM LIGHTING

Hall Lights. A hall may have a direct or an indirect ceiling light that can give brilliant, medium, or subdued light as required. A pair of table lamps or a floor lamp may constitute a part of a group of furniture in a hall. In the main hall there should be switches for upstairs and down.

Living-Room Lights. It is not necessary or desirable to have ceiling or wall fixtures in the average living room. General illumination can be provided by three-way floor lamps or by some form of concealed architectural lighting. See page 314. In addition, portable adjustable floor and table lamps are necessary. They should be located for service and also for emphasis. A large pair of lamps should stand one on each table at the ends of the sofa. Another pair, balancing the first pair, may be placed at another conversation center. See page 240. All the lamps in the room should have the same height—about 58 inches from the floor to the top of the shades. For bridge table, piano, or desk, plain utilitarian lamps are best.

Dining-Room Lights. The most becoming and most pleasing light for a dining table is that which emanates from a ground-glass section inset in the center of the top surface of the table, lighting up the faces and food but keeping the rest of the room in shadow. A similar effect comes from hollow, frosted glass sculptures and abstract forms made to contain light; these are sometimes available for the table and sideboard.

Indirect ceiling light is in general use for dining rooms. The light can come from two reflector floor lamps, from two urns on the sideboard, or from bulbs concealed in coves along the top of the wall or only above the window frames. A hidden spotlight or two can be placed to throw extra light on the table. A ground glass panel inset in the ceiling is pleasing. A ceiling fixture in the dining room usually necessitates a fixed position for the table. See page 300. Some interesting new fixtures are hung so low that they throw light on the table but not on the diners.

Candlelight is soft, friendly, and becoming, its flickering, uneven quality lending additional interest. At least four candles are needed on a small table. Tall candelabra and tall candles are necessary to keep the light above the eye level

Kitchen Lights. The kitchen should be particularly well lighted. It is better to have wall or ceiling lights over the working places than to have one central ceiling light that throws the worker's shadow over the sink or stove. Indirect lighting in a groove around the room at the top of the walls should be installed when building a new house. Recessed lights behind flat ground-glass panels are excellent for special places. Some of the new pre-fabricated units of sink, work table, cabinet, and refrigerator have concealed lights that illuminate the sink, the table, and the inside of the refrigerator. See page 175.

Bedroom Lights. Bedroom lights should usually be local lights, in the places where they are needed. Lights attached to either side of the mirror are satisfactory if they are not too close together. A light is often placed at the top of the mirror. An excellent dressing-table light is one that hangs over the table not far above the head of the seated person. The important point in placing the mirror light is to be sure that the light falls on the person rather than on the mirror.

Most women think it necessary to have a strong central ceiling light in a bedroom, preferably in connection with a ceiling fan. The lamp for reading in bed should be whatever kind one prefers; it must be adjustable so that the light will shine on the book and not on the face of the reader. A desk should have its own lamp. In at least one bedroom there should be a special master switch to light the whole house, in case of an emergency.

Bathroom Lights. Bathrooms usually have a ceiling fixture and a mirror light. Narrow rods of light enclosing the mirror are utilitarian as well as decorative. See page 313. Built-in panels of frosted glass on both sides of the mirror provide pleasing lighting. Overhead panels, as on page 174, excel in appearance and functionalism.

Outdoor Lights. Strong lights over the front and rear entrances are necessary. A light back of the house number and another near the ground beside the steps are desirable. Outlets should be provided for the Christmas tree and for some garden spotlights, which are better than an overall floodlight. The garage light should turn on as one approaches it. Page 26 illustrates a combination of indoor and outdoor lighting.

PROBLEMS

A sufficient number of problems are listed so that choices may be made.

1. Visit a lighting equipment shop or department. Notice what percentage of offerings is functional, plain, and restrained.
2. Design a torchère, sconce, or candlestick.
3. Design a large functional table lamp base and shade which are in scale; first cut experimental shapes from newspapers.
4. Bring to class pictures showing good home lighting, preferably with lamps and without fixtures.
5. Write one page on how to improve the lighting of your home, including a rough estimate of the cost.
6. If possible, visit lighting demonstrations by utility-company experts.

READING REFERENCES

Bulletins of manufacturers of lighting equipment.

GENERAL ELECTRIC CO. *Home Lighting Fundamentals.*

ILLUMINATING ENGINEERING SOCIETY. *Artificial Light and Its Application in the Home.* McGraw-Hill, 1932.

KUNERTH, WILLIAM. *Textbook of Illumination.* Wiley, 1936.

PEET, LOUISE, and SATER, LENORE. *Household Equipment.* Wiley, 1944.

Report of Committee on Fundamental Equipment, President's Conference on Homes. Washington, D. C., 1931.

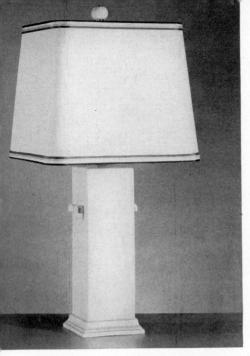

The white plastic lamp at the left above is functional, for it will not wear out and it is easily cleaned. The base and shade agree in shape. *Courtesy Modern Plastics Magazine.*

The base of the table lamp above at the right is heavy enough so that it will not upset easily. The shade is sufficiently large to conceal a diffusing bowl and a light with three strengths. In addition the lamp has beautiful simplicity. *Courtesy William Manker Studio.*

The handsome round glass base below at the left has a round shade with a pleasing geometric pattern that agrees with the pattern in the base. The style of the lamp suits either a period or a Modern room. *Courtesy Orrefors Galleries.*

The lamp below at the right is well designed and would look well in Modern surroundings, masculine settings, or in a non-period studio home which features craft work. It is particularly interesting in texture.

Above left, lamps of a cottage type are suitable with the Early American furniture in this room. These may, however, be somewhat too small to function well.

Above right, fluorescent tubes of light concealed behind the window valance combine with portable lamp light to create a pleasant lighting scheme in this eighteenth-century living room. Radiators of this type should be covered.

Architectural lighting adds to the beauty of this bedroom. The ornate lamp bases are undesirable. The attractive curtain fabric matches the bedspread. The decorative mirror screen adds spaciousness by its reflections.

Above left, a very satisfactory dining-table light in the ceiling directly above the table comes from an inconspicuous fixture. The furniture is attractive. *Courtesy Milo B. Foley.*

The hemispherical light fixture above right is pleasing in form and is also functional, for it can be hung low enough so that light does not shine in the eyes of diners. *Courtesy Wanamaker's.*

The geometric wall fixture below left is one of the few that have beauty. It would look well with Modern furnishings. *Courtesy Rena Rosenthal.*

Neat bathroom light fixtures are shown below right. The tubes of light beside the mirror are satisfactory. *Courtesy Westinghouse.*

The indirect cove lighting at the ceiling line produces pleasing general illumination. This room is large enough so that the furniture is arranged to have two important centers, the window group for summer and the fireplace group in winter. Note the curved plastic supports of the coffee table and the plastic fire screen. The window drapery covers one section of the wall, thereby uniting the windows effectively. This thoroughly Modern room shows excellent restraint in pattern.

CHAPTER 19

TABLE EQUIPMENT

Chinaware, glassware, silver, miscellaneous wares, decorative accessories, and table covers are considered in this chapter. Those principles, elements, and objectives that apply particularly to table appointments form a basis for the study of their selection and arrangement.

Expressiveness. Interesting problems arise in connection with the mood or theme that can be expressed in table appointments. A formal home in which some meals are served with dignity and formality is usually well equipped with conventional table service, including precious porcelain and beautiful crystal. For the unpretentious home, and for porch use generally, a variety of suitable and interesting things is available, such as colorful pottery, heavy glass, wood, plastics, bone-handled flatware, and fiber, string, or reed mats.

Arranging a tea table for a club, dormitory, department, or home provides an opportunity for expressing the theme or the idea of the particular occasion that is being celebrated. The present trend is away from trite arrangements; original ideas and even whimsical themes are used provided they have beauty. A tea table can be properly expressive of a definite theme only if the essential equipment is available to produce unity. For general use a complete silver service including flatware, hollow ware, candlesticks, and vases is needed. For spring and summer themes, cups, plates, and candlesticks of glass should accompany the glass punch bowl. For fall themes when yellow, orange, and brown flowers, berries, and leaves are available to decorate for harvest time, home coming, football teas, or Thanksgiving, harmonious color schemes would result from combining brass-colored flatware and hollow-ware with a brass samovar. A set of wooden articles is useful in expressing informal ideas. Appropriate dishes and napkins can be found for each type of equipment.

Functionalism. A thought that must be ever present in the selection of table appointments is that, since they are not to be hung on the wall to be observed, but are to be used for eating, they must not be chosen for their beauty alone. When selecting dishes and glassware one should imagine them full of food. Only dishes that can be handled comfortably should be considered. Some of the most common violations of functionalism are: dishes with handles too small to hold firmly, pitchers that do not pour well, top-heavy glasses that upset readily, plates with centers too small or too shallow for the food, and silverware uncomfortable to hold. In searching for table appointments the aim should be to find articles that function perfectly and also please the eye so that their use is conducive to complete satisfaction.

Structural Design. A table and all its appointments should be considered a design in three dimensions. The table itself should have fine, simple, structural, and functional design, agreeing with the dining room in shape and scale. It is usually acknowledged that individual units of a table setting look better on a square or an oblong table, but that a round one is more easily served. On a round table, all the flat silverware may be pointed toward the center of the table. Circular or semicircular mats or doilies are best on a round table; rectangular mats agree with the lines of a square or oblong table.

Ornamentation. In exhibitions of table settings in the most progressive parts of the United States the trend is away from decorated table equipment. See page 334. Most trained designers consider that any assemblage of the appointments necessary for a meal, not forgetting the flowers and food, provides sufficient line and form without the introduction of surface patterns.

Those who desire surface decoration, or those who already possess decorated appointments, should be guided by that art principle which imposes restraint in emphasis. If patterns are used on chinaware, or silverware, or glassware, or table covers, that part is necessarily featured, and all other accompanying equipment may well be entirely plain. Esthetic confusion results from combining a variety of decorative styles, such as a Victorian rose design in the damask, a Neo-Classic pattern on the silverware, a Modern motif on the glasses, and a Colonial design on the dishes.

Color Harmony. The coloring of the dining room itself affects the choice of color schemes in the table settings. Whenever possible, daring color schemes should be encouraged for the table since the assemblage is of brief duration. In selecting a color plan for a table setting all the articles on the table, even the flowers and food, must be considered. The tablecloth or mats, which may be dark or light, can be the dominating color in the scheme, with the chinaware providing the secondary color. The flowers may match the cloth or dishes or may be a note of the opposition color. Different colors may be emphasized in dishes and food in different courses of the meal. It should be noted that some colors affect certain foods. For example, yellow plates detract from the appearance of meat.

An adjacent color scheme of a lavender-blue cloth, orchid-pink glasses, and violets suggests springtime. A complementary or contrasting scheme of a brown cloth with pale yellow plates, violet-blue glasses, and an arrangement of chartreuse-colored leaves suits either an Oriental or a Modern theme.

Texture Harmony. A formal dinner served in a conventional manner may combine textures such as those of fine damask, thin china, crystal, and silver, with roses and gardenias to repeat the polished surfaces of the appointments and of the mahogany table itself. See page 336. For eating in a corner of the kitchen, checked gingham doilies, pottery plates, pewter cups, and zinnias make a delightful combination. See page 104. The table service for outdoor eating should be in harmony with the texture of the porch furniture, such as wood, pottery, or metal dishes on fiber mats or on a bare table. Complete textural harmony would be achieved with transparent plastic dishes, tumblers, flatware, and even a fiberglas table mat, on a glass table top. For a tea table it is conducive to harmony to have candlesticks, flower containers, and sandwich plates made of the same material as the teapot or the punch bowl.

Beauty. When a table setting has unity in theme, in design, in color, and in texture, and has a fine relationship of parts, the separate elements enhance each other and heighten the total effect of beauty. A table setting that has real beauty deserves to be photographed in color for a permanent record.

CHINAWARE

History. The study of ceramics of today and of the past would no doubt prove of great interest to all those who have time to read about it, visit museum exhibits, and possibly collect china. The material is condensed as much as possible here; it is hoped that the reader will not stop with these few lines.

All peoples from the time of the Neolithic age have molded and baked clay articles. Some authorities on ceramic art say that Egypt may be considered its cradle, Greece its nursery, and Rome its childhood home, after which it was neglected in Europe during the Dark Ages, to be revived during the fourteenth century in Spain. The Moors on the north coast of Africa learned the art from Persia, Arabia, and China and carried it to Spain and Sicily, whence it spread to Italy and the rest of Europe. Porcelain (china), which is the finest work of the potter, was first made in China, possibly between 100 B.C. and A.D. 100. Porcelain has been imported from China by Europeans since the sixteenth century, even after they too learned how to make it. The Florentines made soft paste porcelain as early as 1580; the Germans made hard paste porcelain after Johann Böttger of Dresden discovered its secret in 1709. The English first made bone china about 1750. Both china and earthenware were made in the American colonies.

The *terminology* of ceramics is rather confusing to laymen, because many merchants do not use the same terms as the museum curators, potters, and writers. In addition continental European authors do not agree with American and English usage, which is, however, observed in this book.

Manufacture. Pottery and porcelain objects consist of *body* and *glaze*. The body or paste is made of clay mixed with other ingredients, depending upon the type of product desired. It is then shaped on a potter's wheel, cast, or built up by hand. The degree of heat needed in firing depends upon the materials. The glaze may be glossy, mat (dull), or medium, and either transparent or opaque. Some crackle glazes are produced by suddenly cooling the article so that it contracts unevenly. Salt glaze results from putting salt in the kiln, not on the pottery, however. A glaze applied over a glaze of a different color adds interest.

China and Porcelain. The synonymous terms china and porcelain refer to all china that is in any degree translucent. An entire piece may appear opaque because of its thickness, but if the edges or a thin fragment of it are translucent it is porcelain.

We are now fully accustomed to beautiful porcelain or chinaware and take it for granted, but in the eighteenth century it was so highly prized that many of the factories had royal support, and the nobility generally made collections of it. China was the name given to this ware by the English, because it first came from China. Porcelain consists mostly of a special clay (kaolin) and feldspar. It is baked in a kiln to the fusing temperature, which means that most of the ingredients are nearly melted into each other so that they become almost one substance. A broken piece of china shows that the glaze and the body have merged completely, making a very hard material. The advantage of the hardest china is that it is most durable, and, if it becomes chipped or cracked, the exposed break will not absorb dirt but will remain clean.

There are three classes of porcelain: hard paste, soft paste, and bone paste, which is medium. Hard-paste porcelain is sometimes called true porcelain. It is very hard, impermeable to liquids, and dazzling bluish white. Bone china is medium in hardness and impermeability. Soft-paste porcelain is more translucent but less hard and more permeable than the other porcelains.

Earthenware and pottery are synonymous terms referring to all the entirely opaque wares. The usual test of an article is to hold it against very strong light; if it is so opaque that the fingers do not show through at all, it is considered to be earthenware. Earthenware includes products ranging from clay flower pots to fine tableware. Earthenware is made of potter's clay, and usually of earth containing lime and sand. It may also be classified as soft or hard, depending upon the nature of the ingredients and the degree of heat at which it is fired. A broken piece of pottery shows the glaze like a separate layer on the outside and the body more porous than porcelain. Cracks and chips in pottery soon become unclean and discolored. Some American manufacturers and retailers designate the lighter pieces as earthenware and the heavier ones as pottery. The average customer usually makes the mistake of calling all fine dishes china.

Selecting Dishes. Since dishes are the most important part of the table setting and the most difficult to select, one usually acquires them first and then looks for other things to harmonize with them. Whether one buys fine china or simple earthenware dishes, much care should be given to their selection.

Although it should not be forgotten that American manufacturers make as good china as any in the world, it is well for the sake of variety to acquire some *foreign* dishes, such as Oriental, Mexican, or European wares, when they are procurable. Oriental dishes may be combined with traditional or Modern dishes, making a transition between the old and the new.

It is sometimes possible to buy seconds or slightly imperfect dishes in the shops or at the factories where they are made. It is always advisable to buy a dozen of each kind of dish or glassware in the table setting, in order to allow for breakage.

Complete *sets of dishes* are not so popular as formerly. Even conservative china shops now approve of diversified table service of harmonious dishes. The service plates, salad plates, and dessert dishes are often different, but the dinner plates, bread-and-butter plates, and cups and saucers are usually alike. It is particularly unwise for a family in a small home to buy a hundred-piece set of dishes. With a limited budget and limited space for storing the dishes, the set would probably prevent the purchase of any other dishes. When interesting possibilities are so numerous, it is unfortunate to own only one pattern and color. Then, too, there is little chance for personal expression in buying a set. It is a dull and easy solution to a problem that a person with imagination solves differently.

Dishes should be not too varied, however. Each place at the table should look exactly like the others, as a rule. Where there are so many different articles, it is necessary to have this repetition.

The main set of dishes should be purchased from an *open-stock pattern* if possible, so that replacements can be made at any time. It is well to know how long a considered pattern has been used, as some patterns go out of fashion and the line is discontinued. The person of average means should usually buy plain undecorated china, with fine structural lines, in white, bone-white, off-white, or cream, like that in the lower picture on page 335.

Color. Color conduces to a definite effect in dishes; therefore refined colors usually belong with exquisite dishes, and vigorous colors are suitable with simple or Modern dishes.

In planning a table setting, the color of the dishes and the food should be considered together. A bluish green salad bowl is equally interesting with yellow-green lettuce, vermilion tomato, or slices of purple cabbage in it. A dish with a lime-colored lining looks inviting filled with sliced beets, sliced oranges, or persimmons. Placed on a yellow cloth, it looks as gay as a design by Dufy. Adjacent color schemes are very successful in combinations of food, dishes, and linens.

One important color decision that has to be made by nearly every home maker is whether to have cream, white, or off-white dishes. Cream color is pleasing, provided the linens too are cream, however linens are easily tinted. A very sensitive colorist may feel that the cool color of silver which must be a part of the scheme is more harmonious with white linen than with cream. As has been stated before, off-white tones in dishes and linens are good.

Texture. Texture, form, and color are just as inseparable esthetically as they are technically in dishware. Heaviness in the ware is an invitation to boldness in form and color. Texture in dishes refers chiefly to weight but it depends also upon the materials from which the dishes are made and upon the firing process. The only desirable surface texture for dishes is a very smooth one for sanitary as well as esthetic reasons.

Design. In general the best forms in dishes are based on the circle and the sphere. The simpler structural forms have the pure continuity of line that delights the trained eye. Particular notice should be taken of the relation of a handle to a dish. It should appear to grow out of a form, to be a part of it, and not look as if it were just stuck on. Handles must be large enough to be held comfortably. The weight of any dish must be well balanced. The function of a dish helps to determine its shape.

It is possible to find dishes with lines and forms that agree with the dominating forms in one's home. Geometric shapes are available for Modern homes, Classic urns for Neo-Classic or Federal surroundings, and squatty forms for cottage backgrounds.

Pattern. Decoration that grows out of the manner of making an article is usually better than that applied after the form is completed. Therefore chinaware may well depend on the plastic quality of the clay itself for its decoration, for lines or spaces can be depressed or built up in clay. See pages 23 and 334.

Design should emphasize form rather than enhance it. In other words, a pattern should usually follow the lines of the object it decorates. A band following the outer edge of a plate is absolutely correct, whereas a triangular decoration does not fit a round plate. Restraint in decoration demands that, if the border decoration is interesting, the center should be plain. An ornamented center makes it unnecessary to decorate the edge of a plate. Bits of pattern scattered here and there over a dish are quite likely to be poor. Indeed, compactness is usually a good quality in design of any kind.

All three types of decorative motifs, *naturalistic, stylized,* and *geometric,* are to be found on chinaware. Unfortunately, commonplace naturalistic designs are most numerous. Pictorial designs on chinaware are lamentable but common, ranging from hunting scenes to college buildings. Affection for one's alma mater is not most appropriately expressed by putting gravy on her dignified façades. Stylized and geometric designs are usually superior to the naturalistic, although some excellent naturalistic designs can be found. See page 333.

Traditional patterns in chinaware are reproduced for use with period furniture. Some of the authentic old designs are worthy of revival, but many should be discontinued.

Some of the best designs that ornament dishes are found in *peasant wares.* In them there is a decoration freely and joyously applied without too much mechanical measuring beforehand. The freshness of design in the ware comes from skill of the designer, however, and not from lack of skill.

Modern chinaware is usually without ornamentation although some of it is well decorated. The decorative designs often consist of a highly stylized motif, possibly a flower or fish, which appear in the center of the dish, without repetition. Although it is in reality a carefully studied design which fits into the space it occupies, it has the appearance of being freely drawn. Such designs are usually planned to suit modern mass production.

GLASSWARE

History.   However brief it may be, no history of glassware should omit the statement that small glass objects were found in the tombs of the Pharaohs.   Later, Rome became the leader in making glass.   In the thirteenth century Venice was famous for its handmade glass, and the rest of Europe soon learned from her. In the United States, glass making, the first industry, was established in Jamestown in 1608.   Wistar, Stiegel, and Sandwich glassware were the most famous in colonial days.   The Sandwich factory invented pressed glass as a substitute for blown glass.

Manufacture.   The quality of glass depends largely upon its composition and treatment.   The principal ingredients are sand, lime, and some alkali.   Lime glass or lime crystal is a dull-finish glass, which is pressed or molded.   Flint glass or crystal is heavier and more brilliant than lime glass; it is used in making cut glass. Common or bottle glass is a cheaper grade that breaks more readily than costly glass.   It has such defects as bubbles, lumps, and a pinkish color from certain chemicals.

Glass may be blown by the breath or by compressed air.   It may be blown in a mold, that is, while it is being blown it is held against forms that shape it, or it may be pressed in a mold.   In making fine glassware hand processes are still employed.   Handmade glass has the charm of variety, for no two pieces are exactly alike.

Color.   Glass can be made almost any color from palest tints to dark, rich shades.   Certain chemicals produce the coloring in glass: gold and copper oxide make reds, cadmium and uraniums make yellows, and copper or cobalt oxides make blues.   Colored glassware can be used effectively, producing color contrast for the table at a minimum cost.   Dark blue glass tumblers and salad plates are attractive with a white, yellow, or red cloth.

Texture.   Glassware has developed new textural interest by the deliberate inclusion of bubbles in the glass, and by extra weight and thickness.   Hob-nailed glassware is an older type with special texture.   See the vases on page 335.   Unusual textures should not be allowed to make a glass difficult to clean or uncomfortable to handle.   Entirely smooth undecorated glassware feels very pleasant to the touch.

Design. The basic form of glassware is round since it is shaped by blowing it as a bubble. Beautiful rounded contour lines with subtle curves are prized in articles made of glass. Interesting proportions of spaces are important, too. For example, the relation of the stem and the bowl of a glass should be noted. Long-stemmed goblets express formality and elegance in their proportions; short stems are informal and functional. For general use short-stemmed goblets with wide tops or footed tumblers are good choices. The base of a tall glass should be especially heavy to keep it from upsetting. All glasses should be well balanced so that it is easy to drink from them. The weight and size of a glass affect the impression of delicacy or strength that it gives. Especially delightful in colorless crystal are large, plain, round salad or fruit bowls accompanied by matching salad plates or fruit dishes.

Ornamentation. Glass articles of fine form and technical perfection need have no decoration, for the utmost in beauty is theirs. The lower left-hand picture on page 336 illustrates this point. When decoration is used it should be restrained and confined to a structural contour such as lines on the stem of a glass as demonstrated in the handsome ware in the lower right-hand picture on page 336.

Molded or pressed ornamentation is a part of the inexpensive molding process by which most glassware is made. Much of it is too ornamental, and the convolutions are too deep.

Etched glass can be made by a costly plate etching process or by the common inexpensive needle process. Anyone can etch initials or patterns on glass by covering all but the pattern with melted beeswax and applying hydrofluoric acid to the pattern.

Cut glass is made by holding the glass against a revolving wheel made of abrasive stone. Simple restrained designs are now procurable, replacing the elaborate allover patterns which were pormerly used to conceal defects in the glass.

Engraved glass is cut with thin electrically driven copper wheels of different sizes. Skilled artists are required for the work, and only fine hand-blown crystal articles are engraved; therefore the result is usually beautiful although costly.

Painted glass is made by applying paint and then baking the glass. Iridescence, lusters, enamels, and metal decorations also are made in this way.

SILVERWARE

History. Owing to its useful physical properties and attractive appearance silver has long been treasured by man. Lack of banks often caused people to put their wealth into silver utensils, which could be melted down when necessary. The word sterling is an abbreviation of Easterling, the name of a German family famous in the twelfth century for making articles of almost pure silver. Sterling now means silver containing 7½ per cent alloy. Silver plating was originated in Sheffield, England, in 1742 by Thomas Balsover.

Quality. An important question for the buyer is whether to choose sterling silver or plated ware. This is a very personal matter, but it seems advisable for those with a small income to buy plated silver. The plate is just as comfortable to use, it looks exactly as well, it does not seem too good to use often, it does not entail worry as to its safety, and it is less expensive. On the other hand, sterling silver is an investment of permanent value. Having cherished sterling silverware in a family helps to keep alive memories of festive occasions.

Design. The most hazardous part of buying silver is the selection of the design. The quality of ware that one buys depends upon one's means, but the design may be ugly or beautiful at the same price. Not one of the principles of art or design should be overlooked by the person who is debating the merit of a design. An excellent design is shown on page 23.

The woman who is using *traditional furnishings* will be able to find silverware in the same feeling. All the decorative movements produced their own patterns, which are now reproduced and often simplified. Certain Neo-Classic motifs are exactly right to accompany Wedgwood dishes. The rugged simplicity of the Early American silver makes it very desirable to go with Early Colonial furnishings. Paul Revere, the Revolutionary hero, was a fine silversmith.

Silverware to accompany *Modern furnishings* is also procurable. Modern flatware has been designed with attention to making smaller and sharper cutting edges of knifes. Long-handled forks and spoons are made to match the knives; however they are not as comfortable to use as those of ordinary shape.

Flatware. A set of flatware usually consists of dinner knives, dinner forks, salad or luncheon forks, butter knives, teaspoons, and soup spoons. A double supply of teaspoons is desirable. The soup spoon should be of the long-bowl type sometimes called a dessert spoon which can also be used for cereal or berries. After-dinner coffee spoons may well be different from the set.

A practical method of gradually acquiring sterling silver is not to buy six or eight of just one article at one time but to get one complete place setting, that is, one of each of the articles needed to set one place.

The bride-to-be who is selecting her flatware pattern has a difficult task because poor designs are more numerous than good ones. Knives, forks, and spoons have so little space for decoration that any design should be very simple. Decoration should follow the line of the object or should be placed only at structurally important points, such as the base or top of an article. For example, a floral motif at the narrow part of the handle of a spoon has no relation to the shape of the spoon and is therefore poor. Monograms are always appropriate on handles. Beautifully shaped flatware without surface decoration is very desirable; it is appropriate with any type of table equipment from Early American to Modern. See the assortment of flatware on page 333.

Hollow Ware. Silver hollow ware has many advantages as well as disadvantages when compared with china. It is durable, and it can be used with different sets of dishes, but it does require polishing, and it is valuable enough to need safe keeping. Silver hollow articles usually help to unify the table, as they repeat the color and texture of the silver flatware. Salt and pepper shakers, cream pitchers, sugar bowls, covered vegetable dishes, tea and coffee pots, water pitchers, carafes, and flower vases are some of the articles procurable in silver.

The design of the silver hollow ware should be chosen to conform to the general style of the dishes with which they are to be used. Elegant formal appointments suggest tall slender outlines; robust ideas call for low, broad shapes; and Modern equipment invites pure geometric forms. Distinctive handmade silver can sometimes be procured in the shops of outstanding designers like Georg Jensen. The upper left-hand picture on page 336 displays an attractive conservative serving dish.

MISCELLANEOUS WARES

Bone. Flatware with bone handles and stainless-steel blades is suitable with pottery dishes or other informal table equipment.

Yellow Metal. Flatware and hollow ware in gold color are procurable and constitute an interesting change from the silver, particularly with warm color schemes.

Pewter. Pewter hollow ware seems less hard than silver and has a handmade appearance and a texture that go with unpretentious things. Chinese pewter tumblers and plates are effective with pottery dishes. Vases, pitchers, sugar bowls, and salt and pepper shakers of pewter are favorites. See page 101.

Chromium. Chromium articles have a smart appearance because the modern material and modern forms seem in perfect accord, and ornamentation is omitted.

Aluminum. Spun aluminum dishes which are unusual and pleasing in texture are effective for the studio types of homes and for informal or outdoor use anywhere.

Copper. Copper dishes are delightful in color. Improvements are being made in the treatment of copper so that it can hold food without being lined with glass or other metal.

Plastics. Various plastic materials are used for dishes some of which are heat-proof. Lucite and Plexiglas are clear plastics resembling glass. Shellflex is a translucent plastic used especially for plates, bowls, and drinking tumblers in pastel tints. Safety ware is a satisfactory line of plastic dishes. Pyrex is an established glass-like, heat-proof material which is particularly practical because food can be baked and served in the same dish. In time plastics will partly replace porcelain and pottery. Their advantage of durability will doubtless overcome the obstacles of unfamiliarity or prejudice.

Wood. Our colonial ancestors used wooden dishes during their first century in this country. We now use them in rustic or other simple settings or outdoors, for ordinarily they express informality. However, beautiful bowls and trays which are refined in feeling are now made of wood. Handsome wooden trays simulate the shape of large stylized leaves. They are used for serving and also to hold fruit and leaf arrangements. A large fork and spoon of wood are desirable for serving a leafy salad in a wooden bowl.

TABLECLOTHS AND PLACE MATS

A good-looking table top, which has been made heat resistant, needs no cover of any kind.

Expressiveness. Informality is the theme of most meals of today; therefore tablecloths have been replaced by small mats. Fabrics, fiber, tin, wood, cork, plastics, and string are employed for mats, consequently they vary greatly in character. See pages 102 and 104. The monogrammed mats on page 336 are personal.

Large damask linen cloths are still used for *formal* occasions and sometimes for buffet service. They are, however, difficult to procure and arduous to launder. Other formal covers are made of embroidered linen, appliqué, lace, or cut work, in white, cream, or very pale tints. Some designers think that lace is an unsuitable material to place on wood; it is obviously incompatible with the textures of copper, pottery, autumn leaves, zinnias, or fruit.

Color. In the average home it is well to use brightly colored napkins and place mats or small tablecloths, especially if the glassware and dishes are colorless. Some designers feel that snowy white tablecloths and mats are unresponsive backgrounds for their appointments and food and, decoratively speaking, consider them as white elephants in most rooms. A woman who owns much white linen should dye some of it pale yellow or other tints to harmonize with the surroundings. The tablecloth sometimes acts as a link in color between the table and the rest of the room.

Pattern. Decorative design is, of course, not necessary in tablecloths or mats, but if patterns are used they should preferably be stylized or geometric. See pages 334 and 336. Naturalistic motifs are structural if they are concentrated in definite areas such as borders. Stripes, plaids, polka dots, or simple borders are the most attractive departures from plain tablecloths. Period designs of merit, for traditional homes, are sometimes procurable. Plastic mats on which pictures are reproduced are absurd.

The best tablecloth designs in lace work, drawn work, cut work, or in other types of patterned cloths are those that follow the lines of the table and are controlled and confined to small definite areas. Some of the most structural lace designs consist of small units containing solid areas. Most of the lace cloths cannot be considered background for they attract too much attention.

DECORATIVE TABLE ACCESSORIES

The central table decoration should have the same feeling esthetically as the china, glassware, and table cover. In other words, all should agree in mood, style, color, and texture.

Mood. The centerpiece expresses the *theme* of the table setting. The more personal, original, and delightful a centerpiece is the better. Holidays and special occasions provide reasons for center-pieces expressive of some definite idea as formal, merry, or casual. A table centerpiece for a children's party should be very different from that for grandmother's birthday dinner, a bridge luncheon, or a Fourth of July buffet supper. A jolly mood is expressed by a bouquet of lollypops on sticks combined with magnolia leaves. If the food is something special it naturally sets the theme for the table decoration.

Style. It is customary to have a table centerpiece agree in style with the table, table equipment, and surroundings. For example, a Victorian feeling could be produced by a lush flower mound, a three-tier epergne, or a pair of ornate vases. One of the flower arrangements on page 378 is a period type. At a Creole gumbo luncheon the old New Orleans style and spirit could be indicated by a group of colored minstrel musicians in porcelain or pottery standing on a wooden slab surrounded by a fence of paper lace in imitation of iron lace, with trimmed umbrella plants for palms.

Color. The centerpiece really sets the color scheme for a meal. Although each course may well vary somewhat in color, all should be in harmony with the centerpiece. For example, a gray linen cloth, a low compact mound of orange and yellow zinnias in a pewter bowl, yellow candles in pewter candlesticks, and amber glasses and bread-and-butter plates would determine the color scheme for the dishes and food. Different courses might offer avocado and pomegranate salad on amber glass plates, soup in sea-green bowls, fried chicken, rice, carrots, and peas on bone-white plates, chocolate dessert on vermilion plates, and coffee in bone-white cups. These would change the picture in a stimulating way without conflicting with the center decoration. If the chinaware has much pattern and varied colors, the accompanying flowers should be limited to white, or green, or colors matching the dishes. Sometimes small nosegays contain all the colors in the dishes.

Materials. *Flowers* are the most popular of all table decorations because of their loveliness. Although flowers are ordinarily placed in the center of the table they may be put elsewhere. Interesting variations are a bouquet at each of the four corners of a square table, or a nosegay, which is to be worn later, at each plate. A long narrow table may have all the flowers along one side and the covers along the other. Low arrangements are desirable as they do not obstruct the view. When vines, leaves, flowers, or berries are placed directly on the table without containers, they should be held to a definite organized composition, with the greatest mass at the center and less at subordinate places.

Many special *flower containers* for tables are now on the market. Those with curved lines look best on round tables. Some receptacles come in sections so that a small or large arrangement can be made with different aggregates of parts. The sections can be separated and placed around a central arrangement of some kind or distributed on the table.

Fruit or vegetables combined with seedpods or green leaves also make interesting table decorations, supplying rich, warm colors that are especially pleasing in autumn and winter. See page 381. Artichokes, grapes, acorns, leaves, and other plant materials covered with silver paint make attractive table decoration; they look well with the silverware. Whatever is used to decorate the table must appear immaculate and appetizing.

When flowers, potted plants, or leaves are not available, other materials should be supplied. The shops sometimes have clever centerpieces of glass or plastics. Infrequently artificial flowers made of glass, wire, or other odd materials can be found that are so well designed as to form desirable centerpieces. Flowers or fruit that could never have grown on land or sea because they are pure design are usually good looking. One offering is an orange-colored pottery pineapple decorated with diamond-shaped sections, each one bearing a small tin rosette and sprouting shiny leaves of tin at the top. Mexican pottery fruit and gourds both plain and decorated gayly with dots and dashes are cheering. Lest this mention of artificial fruit and flowers be misunderstood, it is necessary to state that nearly all artificial fruit and flowers should not be used on the table or elsewhere, because they are mere imitations of natural fruits and flowers.

Table decorations frequently include *candles*, often in combination with flowers. Beautiful candlesticks and candelabra are available in silver, pewter, chromium, iron, pottery, glass, plastics, or wood. Many styles, too, are represented from the delicate Neo-Classic to the precise Modern. Candle holders can also be improvised in several ways. For example, low glass salt cups glued to cardboard strips of interesting shapes make effective holders. Some unusual candle holders for special parties should be acquired, like a Mexican tin Christmas tree supporting many holders. For pictures of candlesticks see pages 59, 104, 210, 334, and 345.

For an informal Christmas dinner a thick wreath of fir or magnolia leaves might lie flat on the table surrounding a thicket of tall orange candles. The magnolia wreath could be natural or shellacked or painted white with sparkles added. Unless they are lighted candles should not be used for table decoration.

Sometimes amusing or beautiful little *porcelain or glass figures* of humans, birds, animals, or plants are combined with flowers for central table compositions. Children especially enjoy these figures. They must be selected with discrimination, for some, such as the common porcelain dancing nudes, are particularly poor in design and in idea. An example of good usage is a 12-inch Staffordshire dog or rooster (page 350) standing in the middle of a tightly packed low bed of blue bachelor buttons arranged in a flat tin baking pan, which has been painted white. An effective centerpriece can be made quickly by fastening a dozen small china or glass birds with clips on a well-chosen bare branch.

Paper decorations such as curls, laces, fringes, scrolls, and festoons in white, color, silver, or gold are sometimes needed to give a delightful gay touch of festivity and artificiality. For example, an effective St. Valentine's Day table employed, on the bare polished table, a central rose-colored cardboard heart edged with a flaring white lace paper frill cut from the edge of paper doilies. A similar heart was hung over the fireplace. Arrangements of rose and white camellias added life and beauty. In this centerpiece the artificial material was larger in quantity than the natural material; the reverse would have been equally satisfactory.

Between meals no cloth, doily, or runner is desirable on a dining table. A mat is sometimes needed under the centerpiece of flowers, fruit, leaves, vegetables, porcelain, or other material.

PROBLEMS

A sufficient number of problems are listed so that choices may be made.

1. Group together table-service pictures and articles which express the same idea.
2. Visit a shop to see china, and write a report.
3. Make a design for a Modern knife and fork.
4. Bring to class a 5- or 10-cent dish with good lines.
5. Bring the materials and make a complete place setting.
6. Set a breakfast or sick-room tray.
7. Make a table centerpiece of flowers or a substitute.
8. Make a clay bowl and have it fired if possible.

READING REFERENCES

BIDDLE, D., and BLOM, D. *The Book of Table Setting.* Doubleday, Doran, 1936.

EBERLEIN, H. D., and RAMSDELL, R. W. *The Practical Book of Chinaware.* Lippincott, 1925.

FORSYTH, GORDON M. *20th Century Ceramics.* Studio, 1936.

HANNOVER, EMIL. *Pottery and Porcelain.* Scribner, 1925.

HOUSEHOLD FINANCE CORPORATION. *Dinnerware.*

SPARGO, JOHN. *Early American Pottery and China.* Century, 1926.

SPRACKLING, H. *Setting Your Table.* M. Barrow and Co., 1941.

JANNEAU, GUILLAUME. *Modern Glass.* Studio, 1931.

KNITTLE, RHEA M. *Early American Glass.* Century, 1927.

MOORE, N. H. *Old Glass, European and American.* Stokes, 1924.

WAUGH, SIDNEY. *The Art of Glass Making.* Dodd, Mead, 1937.

AVERY, CLARA LOUISE. *Early American Silver.* Century, 1930.

BIGELOW, FRANCIS H. *Historic Silver of the Colonies.* Macmillan, 1925.

COTTERELL, HOWARD H. *Pewter Down the Ages.* Hutchinson, 1932.

JONES, EDWARD A. *Old Silver of Europe and America.* Lippincott, 1928.

VARNUM, WM. H. *Pewter Design and Construction.* Bruce, 1926.

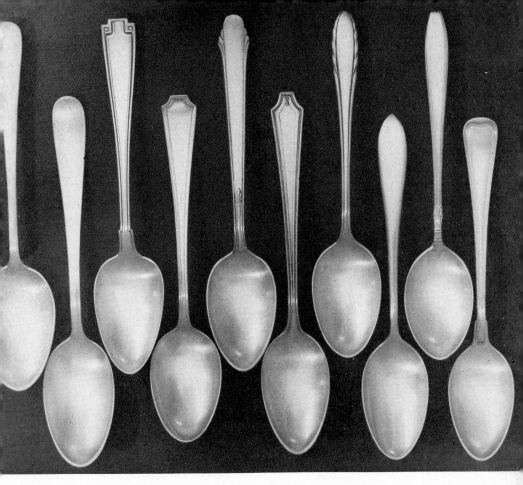

The spoons show patterns particularly desirable for their simplicity. The three perfectly plain patterns can be used with Modern, period, or cottage-type chinaware.
Courtesy the Gorham Company.

This row of Syracuse china plates shows only patterns having simplicity and beauty. Note that the last plate has a novel depressed line decoration. A range of prices is represented here.
Courtesy Onondaga Pottery Company.

The table setting above expresses beautiful simplicity. The food and flowers provide pattern and color. The dishes are well designed. The silver flatware is simple and can be used with dishes of any type. *Courtesy Gladding McBean.*

The plates below show the superiority of design which grows out of the method of construction of an article, compared to applied painted decoration. The glassware and linen also have leaf motifs. If both of them were plain the plate design would be more appreciated. *Courtesy Theodore Haviland & Company.*

This simple cottage-type table setting is based on Pennsylvania German design. The table mats and napkins designed by M. Mergentime were inspired by illuminated handwriting used on birth, marriage, and death certificates, hymn books, and cards. A bird was a symbol of the spirit; the tulip signified life. The pottery is Pfaltzgraff; the furniture is true to the period. The sturdy geraniums in old-fashioned containers are in the right spirit for this table setting. *Courtesy John Wanamaker, Philadelphia.*

The table setting below is suitable for a Modern room. Table equipment without any decorative pattern is usually the choice of artists. Note the knives with wooden handles. A Modern flower arrangement would have been desirable here. The furniture is beautiful in line. *Courtesy Gilbert Rohde.*

Conservative designs in silverware and china like these above left should usually accompany traditional furnishings. The silver pieces help to unify the table. The plates have a pleasing pattern. *Courtesy the Gorham Company.*

The modified type of table equipment above right can be freely used. The flower arrangement is a suitable height. *Courtesy Georg Jensen.*

This table setting below left has Modern flower arrangements which are in the right mood and style. Plain glass luncheon or salad plates are especially pleasing in summer. *Courtesy the Gorham Company.*

The Modern American crystal stemware below right is in the pleasing Embassy pattern. The gold braided blackamoor and the gardenia arrangement are less Modern. *Courtesy Libbey Glass Company.*

CHAPTER 20

ACCESSORIES

Accessories have a much more important role in decoration than the average person realizes. They are the elements that bring charm, individuality, and vitality to a room. The right accessories help to stress the decorative idea of a room; they can be the ultimate expression of the style of furnishing that is employed; they can portray the very essence of the theme of a home. Without accessories it might be difficult to achieve a positive effect. In the accessories a home maker has also a special opportunity to express her originality and personality.

Furnishings depend so much upon accessories for charming effects that it is possible for the very same furniture to appear uninteresting in the model apartment of a furniture store but distinctive in a home when accompanied by well-chosen accessories. Decorative accessories supply the indispensable finishing touches to a room, as dress accessories do to a costume. Like dress accessories, too, they are not chosen for their beauty alone but for what they can do to promote the appearance of the ensemble, the costume or the room as a unit.

Accessories should be placed at the important points in a room. There they create focal centers to give the eyes pleasant resting places. By holding the attention at the points of interest, they simplify and unify the design of the room.

Only objects of real beauty and expressiveness are worthy of such emphasis in a home. They should not be slighted in the budget or be regarded as extravagance, for whatever is expended for them will show to excellent advantage. On the other hand, it should be remembered that they will probably be replaced in less than five years. Accessories should certainly not consist of the small odds and ends that are accumulated by the average household without premeditation if the owner wishes to achieve beauty and character in her home.

Accessories should be acquired gradually, in order to allow time to find the most effective object for the special place where it is to be used. Almost all accessories have some functional as well as esthetic value, but usually a few articles are chosen which justify their existence by their beauty and mental stimuli alone.

Variety is a source of pleasure in accessories; they might well differ in size, height, texture, color, age, period, cost, and origin. Complete sets of matching accessories for desks or dressers are usually monotonous; a collection of articles that agree in scale and feeling and are made of the same materials is more interesting than sets. Pairs of objects, however, can frequently be placed to advantage.

Expressiveness. Accessories should be chosen to express the same idea as the home itself. Indeed, it is more important for accessories to carry out the mood of a room than it is for them to have unusual beauty. For example, a room with a rustic feeling would suffer from the intrusion of a sleek Modern article, no matter how fine it might be in itself.

The personality of a family is revealed in its accessories; some of the telltale things are books, periodicals, plants, work, and hobbies. Certain hobbies, such as well-mounted groups of stamps, coins, photographs, maps, or prints, might provide distinctive notes in home decoration. Collections of interesting bottles or china could be effective in a decorative scheme, if well placed and not too extensive. See pages 60, 223, 278, and 350.

Line and Form. In line and form the accessories should conform to the general design feeling of the home. Period, Non-period, or Modern furnishings should include accessories having the same general line and form as the furniture. However, deviations from the general style are more acceptable in accessories than in other furnishings. The present vogue is to use much larger accessories than formerly.

Color. An accessory should be carefully related in color to the furnishings of the room where it is to be placed; if possible, it should be tried before being purchased. Although accessories often provide the brilliant color accents of a room, it is well to choose some accessories that have less compelling color than others. Chinese accessories which are suitable in either Modern or period rooms are often selected because of their delightful coloring.

KINDS OF ACCESSORIES

Books. Although books in open bookshelves are among the most interesting and decorative of all furnishings, it is entirely possible to have too many in one room. Books along one of the short walls are probably enough in a living room, unless there is a definite reason why the owner would feature books. Glazed bookcases should be excluded from the living room because the glass is not attractive, but they may be placed in a book room or library to hold precious books.

Built-in bookshelves are preferable to movable cases because they conform better to the lines of the room. Shelves should be adjustable to fit the height of the books, periodicals, or phonograph records holders they are to accommodate. Empty bookshelves should not be tolerated, as they can be filled temporarily with five-cent second-hand books. Figurines or pottery are sometimes effective in bookshelves. For pictures of bookshelves see pages 104, 120, 210, 346, and 348.

Books should be arranged with consideration for their size and color. The largest books belong on the lower shelves. The darkest books look well near the bottom and along the ends of the shelves. Books of the same color should usually be massed together; some might be covered with colorful paper jackets.

Clocks. Clocks are no more exempt than anything else from the rule that everything in a room should harmonize with the feeling of the room in style and in degree of simplicity or elegance. For example, a Pilgrim Colonial type of room should have a simple cottage-type clock. A mahogany grandfather clock or a Willard banjo clock is suitable for a room with eighteenth-century Colonial furnishings. With Neo-Classic furniture it would be well to consider a French brass and glass clock, or a patriotic clock decorated with a spread eagle or historical scene. Modern clocks of unusual designs and materials, such as cubes or spheres of glass, are in harmony with Modern decoration. Clocks are pictured on pages 102, 259, 347, 476, and 478.

Many of the clocks found in the average home are too large and are over-ornamented, therefore attracting more than their share of attention. A clock with plain lines and little decoration is usually the best choice for almost any room.

Fireplace Equipment. Well-designed large and plain andirons, fender, tongs, scuttle, and firescreen, matching the hardware of the room and conforming to its mood, should be chosen. For examples see pages 26, 101, 106, and 460. The wood basket, too, should be decorative and suitable. In the summertime the fireplace hole may be hidden by an attractive screen or by a large arrangement of leaves.

Mirrors. More than any other element in decoration mirrors produce a feeling of spaciousness. Entire walls of mirror are most effective and are not so costly as one would suppose from the price of small mirrors. Over the fireplace a mirror panel to the ceiling is highly decorative. In a bedroom a mirror door is essential. Permanent reflections in mirrors should be pleasing.

Attractive hanging mirrors are difficult to find. It is often advisable to have mirror frames made from appropriate picture moldings. Lucite-framed mirrors are particularly effective in Modern rooms. Unframed mirrors are suitable in some period settings and in Modern schemes. Mirrors of different types are shown on pages 26, 87, 300, 460, and 478.

Screens. A screen should be decorative, should suit its surroundings, and should be large enough to be really useful. Among recent introductions are screens decorated with greatly enlarged photographs of plants or scenery. Mirror screens are impressive; white-painted shutters are informal. Sometimes it is possible to find two inexpensive plain screens that can be fastened together, making six sections. Objectionable decorations can be painted over or covered. A carpenter or even an amateur can make wooden frames for screens and cover the center with matting, reed, bamboo, grass cloth, painted hardware cloth, fabric, plywood, composition board, or a translucent composition over screen wire. See pages 119 and 261 for utilitarian screens.

A screen may serve in a Modern living room to separate the dining area from the conversation area. In old houses screens are often needed to conceal poor architectural features. A tall screen sometimes provides a balance for a door, window, or tall piece of furniture. Screens are also useful for protection from glare or drafts. A screen adds to comfort and privacy in a bedroom occupied by two persons.

Small Sculpture. Small figures in stone, wood, metal, ivory, pottery, porcelain, plastic, or glass are suitable for home decoration. Figurines from 12 to 18 inches tall are most easily placed, as they are large enough to stand alone or in pairs. They are often effective in combination with flower arrangements. Small articles 4 inches or less in height are out of scale with room furnishings unless they are arranged in groups, preferably in cabinets. A collection might well be limited to certain subjects, certain materials, or certain types. See pages 9, 62, 88, 347, 348, 349, and 350 for some of the small sculptures pictured in this book.

Those who can afford to buy original sculpture rather than reproductions should do so, to encourage living sculptors as well as to have the satisfaction of exclusive ownership. They should become acquainted with contemporary work by attending exhibitions of sculpture. A person who wishes to be able to judge sculpture should read some of the excellent books on the subject and also the current periodicals.

One of the most important qualities of good sculpture is that it should express an *idea* that is significant to mankind. A basic human need or experience is often the inspiration for the sculptor's message. This can be communicated even in miniature sculpture.

Fine design alone is reason enough for the creation of small decorative sculptures. A few suggestions follow that may prove helpful to the amateur in judging the design of sculpture. Sculpture should be compact in design. There should usually be no protuberances that might break off if it were rolled on the floor. Decided movement in sculpture should be avoided. A figure permanently leaping induces weariness in an observer. Things delicate in texture such as chiffon, ribbons, feathers, flowers, and seafoam are not proper subjects to express in clay, stone, metal, or wood. In sculpture stylistic treatment of subjects is usually better than naturalistic treatment. Some of the best stylized figurines are Chinese or Modern.

Stone sculpture should appear compact, heavy, and stone-like. *Clay sculpture* shows its plasticity in more rounded and extended forms. *Metal sculpture* should express the fluidity of the molten medium and tensile strength. *Wood sculpture* respects the grain of the wood and is often as informal as the wood itself.

Gifts. Since accessories should express the owner's taste and personality, it is unfortunate to give them as presents. At one clever shower a bride-to-be was presented with a basket of paper flowers with peculiar green leaves which when unfolded proved to be dollar bills. This was one present that was not stored in the attic. It is said that the average home reveals the length of time since the marriage of the owners by the quantity of gifts accumulated in it. It is not a disadvantage to have many accessories, but most of them should be out of sight until they will provide exactly the right temporary decorative note. Taste and not sentiment should be the guide in the use of accessories. The art principles furnish valuable help in judging the artistic merits of gifts. Even those with beauty should be excluded unless they are consistent in style and character with the home.

Birds. Certain types of decoration would seem incomplete without birds to impart a garden feeling. Their songs, movements, and colors make them delightful additions to fixed decorations. Well-designed bird cages are procurable in various styles. Reed cages are appropriate in sun rooms, porches, dining rooms, or children's rooms. A bird enthusiast could have cages extending from floor to ceiling built into two corners of a porch. A parrot on a perch is an ornament to any garden.

Fish. Tropical fish in particular are prized for the decorative value of their colors and patterns, as well as their graceful movements. They are equally effective out of doors or indoors. Fish can be displayed in artistic fashion indoors, as public aquaria demonstrate. Perfectly plain glass containers exhibit the fish to the best advantage. Aquaria should be designed to conform to architectural lines. One effective aquarium was set into the wall between the hall and the sunroom so that it showed from both rooms. Not even in placing the aquarium may it be forgotten that things that are used together should express the same idea. Fish and fish bowls are consistent with plants and sun porches, but not with velvet carpets and mahogany furniture.

Cats and Dogs. A Siamese cat of golden color with black nose, toes, and tip of tail, large green eyes, and ever-changing graceful poses can be far more interesting than any static decorative object. A small black-and-white dog can be a lively decorative note in any color scheme.

PLACING ACCESSORIES

In any room the accessories should be placed judiciously in relation to existing groups of furniture, lamps, and pictures, and they should not disrupt but support the emphasis already there. The most important accessories in any room should be at the center of interest. The secondary centers should have less important accessories. Empty silent spaces without accessories add to the dignity and restfulness of a room.

Accessories should be arranged in original and interesting new ways. Trite groupings should be avoided, such as two candlesticks flanking a bowl of flowers on the table or a pot of stringy ivy at each end of the mantel. A new idea would be to tie together several musical instruments such as banjos and violins, in the manner of a Picasso painting, and to hang the group on a plain wall. Articles that are placed together should be made of materials that are pleasantly associated, such as pewter and wood, jade and teakwood, silver and crystal or porcelain.

In a living room in the wintertime, when the fireplace group is the center of interest, the focal point is usually the mantel shelf. If an important picture hangs over it, the articles on the shelf should be fairly inconspicuous. On the other hand, if there is no picture over the mantel, a large important accessory group belongs there. A beautiful piece of sculpture might be placed in the center with a lesser object on each end of the mantel. Three or five articles are usually sufficient for any mantel.

A desk or a living-room table should have no runner, doily, or mat on it; a lamp and possibly two small articles are sufficient. A large, low coffee table may hold a pile of two or three new periodicals, an ash tray, and a plant or cut flowers. A piano should usually have nothing on it.

The dining room is not a museum and ordinarily should not have displays of china, glass, or silver, except possibly in built-in cupboards. A bowl of fruit, flowers, or a large distinctive dish is desirable on a buffet or on a dining table. See page 10.

The most unusual articles are likely to be found in importing shops, decorators' shops, antique shops, studios of craftsmen and artists, and out-of-the-way shops. Auctions, junk yards, and storage warehouse sales are possible sources for old articles.

PROBLEMS

A sufficient number of problems are listed so that choices may be made.

1. Bring to class any small articles of good design.
2. Make interesting still-life groups of materials brought to class.
3. Arrange appropriate living-room articles on a large coffee table.
4. Cut out of paper a full-size well-shaped clock silhouette.
5. Analyze orally the articles in identical catalogs or periodicals in the hands of the class. (December periodicals usually feature accessories.) Test the articles by the art principles listed on page 49.
6. Make a box frame to hang on the wall to hold a still-life group.
7. Make up a class exhibition of articles costing 25 cents or less which are well designed. Send the exhibition to other schools, clubs, or meetings.

READING REFERENCES

DRAPER, DOROTHY. *Decorating is Fun.* Doubleday, Doran, 1939.

SOOY, L., and WOODBRIDGE, V. *Plan Your Own Home.* Stanford University Press, 1940.

Beauty has no relation to price, rarity or age

NO ARTICLE IN THIS CASE COST MORE THAN FIFTY CENTS

This exhibit was arranged and displayed at the Newark, New Jersey, Museum. Student groups should be encouraged to make such exhibits. Symmetrical balance on each shelf is usually desirable in displays. The India print in the background is good in design.

The picture above shows a small section of an exhibition of useful objects having good lines from the Museum of Modern Art in New York City. Note the curved lines of the display shelf.

Bookshelves which are depressed so that the books are flush with the wall seem a part of the architecture. A space for books on the back of a desk is desirable. A well-designed arrangement of seats and tables is shown below. *Courtesy Modernage.*

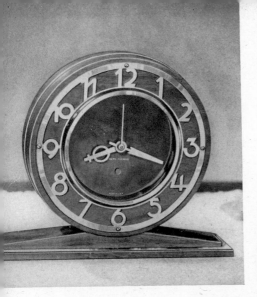

The unadorned functional clock above is suitable for a Modern room, a masculine room, a schoolroom, or an office.
Courtesy Seth Thomas.

The clock above is suitable for period rooms; it is a copy of an eighteenth-century English clock of distinction.

The symmetrical group at the right makes an effective decoration for the center of a mantel. The textures are harmonious.
Courtesy Sally Kelley.

This old Chinese jar of metal is so interesting in itself that it should not be used as a flower container. People who move their possessions often appreciate unbreakable accessories.
Courtesy Norman Rutt.

This highly stylized ceramic sculpture made for the Winnetka schools by Lilian Saarinen must be evaluated on the basis of design, not on naturalism. The pyramidal composition has strength and beauty.
Courtesy Cranbrook Academy of Art.

This coffee table with a glass-covered display space provides a novel means of showing a collection of precious small bibelots. The leather-covered furniture is attractive in design and texture. *Courtesy Rena Rosenthal, Inc.*

The mirror above right is distinctive and looks well with period or cottage furniture. The flower arrangement is casual. It needs more height in the center.

Beautiful pottery and groups of books make attractive decorations on the glass shelves beside this Modern fireplace. Note the effective fur rug on the allover tweedlike carpet. *Courtesy Georg Jensen.*

Beautiful accessories are obtainable in specialty shops of designers of recognized ability. All the objects shown in the picture above have distinction. *Courtesy Georg Jensen.*

A small home with limited wall space could have shelves for books, sculpture, and pottery on the stair well. Note the Dutch half door.

This foyer contains a space built and lighted especially for the display of a piece of sculpture. The Flexwood wall covering makes an effective background. The room is artificially lighted from behind the large ground-glass disk which is flush with the ceiling. The window sill extends forward to cover the radiators.

Glass window shelves are used here to display a collection of colorful glass bottles. The shelves coincide with the lines of the window frames. The pottery roosters are handsome. The display suits the setting, which has interesting hooked rugs. *Courtesy Carson, Pirie, Scott.*

CHAPTER 21

FLOWER ARRANGEMENT

Flower arrangement may be defined as the art of organizing flowers, other plant materials, and receptacles into compositions having harmony of form, texture, and color. Its purpose is to add cheer, life, and beauty to surroundings. The welcoming bouquet in the hall, the dining-table decoration which turns a necessity into an esthetic experience, and the children's miniature arrangements are all expressive of appreciation of beauty and love of home.

It is known that the art of flower arrangement has existed ever since the sixth century when Chinese Buddhist priests taught scholars how to arrange plant materials with reverence before the shrines in the temples. The Japanese have developed this art to a high degree through their many different schools of flower arrangement. Their influence in this field has been world wide. Early European artists painted pictures of flower arrangements; these have also affected present styles.

In the Orient the priesthood developed flower arrangement; in Europe the courts developed it; in the United States the people themselves are developing it. Art teachers and garden clubs have contributed greatly to the growth of this cultural interest. Garden club members take study courses and hold exhibitions of flower arrangements in most of the larger towns and cities in the nation.

Flower arrangement is no doubt the only field of the fine arts in which creative ability can be developed by almost anyone, through study and experience. It is a means of cultural development and consequent enrichment of life that can be learned at home without interference with home making. Financial stress is no handicap, for the weeds and grasses by the roadside and containers from the kitchen are challenging materials. Flower arrangement is a medium of consolation and escape for the person with worries or sorrows.

351

PERSONALITY

A flower arrangement should have personality as well as beauty. The arranger should often practice expressing her own moods in her compositions. When planning an arrangement, the selection of a mood, a name, or a theme helps to guide it toward a definite personality expressing one single idea.

Names, Themes, and Moods of Flower Arrangements

Spring (buds)	Deep South	Daintiness
Summer (flowers)	Mountains	Drama
Fall (fruit)	Roadside	Exuberance
Winter (dry)	Driftwood	Humor
Fourth of July	Moonlight	Luxury
Thanksgiving	Sunrise	Primness
Horn of plenty	Wind	Quaintness
Christmas	Desert	Refinement
Jewels	Seaside	Rest
Poetry	Mexico	Restraint
Music	Hawaii	Simplicity
Wonderland	Bali	Sparseness
Childhood	Dali	Strength
Rococo	Surrealism	Thrift

Inherent Characteristics of Flowers

Dignity	*Simplicity*	*Modernity*
Calla lily	Ageratum	Anthurium
Camellia	Aster	Banana blossom
Canna	Calendula	Bird-of-paradise
Canterbury bell	Centaurea	Cup-of-gold
Crinum	Dianthus	Cyclamen
Delphinium	Daisy	Hibiscus
Foxglove	Geranium	Lotus
Gladiolus	Marigold	Orchid
Iris	Nasturtium	Pitcher plant
Magnolia	Petunia	Poinsettia
Peony	Phlox	Succulents
Regal lily	Sweet pea	Tiger lily
Rose	Violet	Red-hot-poker

ELEMENTS OF ART

Line and Form. The architecture of a flower arrangement should be considered first by anyone who is creating or judging it. The basic lines are the circle (or section thereof), the triangle, and the rectangle. The basic forms are the sphere, the cone, and the cube. These lines and forms are usually modified in flower arrangements, but in Modern compositions they are often geometric. The form selected for an arrangement depends on the predominant line of the plant materials to be used. A container is chosen which carries out the same line movement, particularly that of the foliage. The finished arrangement should appear one unit.

Regardless of the forms of flower arrangements the lines of all of them may be compared to the lines of a leafless tree with its branches radiating from the trunk. In a flower arrangement the container takes the place of the trunk with lines radiating from it. Just as the tree's branches become smaller at the ends, so the plant materials should become smaller and farther apart at the extremities of the flower arrangement.

The *silhouettes* of flower arrangements should be well designed and full of variety. Most compositions require at least one void or opening in their outer boundary lines.

The forms of the plant materials are important too; three different forms and sizes make a good composition. *Large rounded forms*, like tulips, make excellent weight materials located near the centers of arrangements. *Long slender spikes*, like larkspur, provide airiness and variation. *Medium-size forms* of different shapes give pleasing transition.

Texture. The surface and the structure of plant materials determine their texture. Flowers are usually classified as *delicate*, like sweet peas, *coarse*, like zinnias, or *velvety*, like roses; however, plant materials have many other textures than these three.

Unity in texture is necessary between the flowers themselves and also between the flowers and their containers. For example, roses and columbines look well together, placed in a thin glass container, because all the components have delicacy. A metal container suits the texture of an arrangement of pussywillows, daffodils, and blue spruce.

COLOR

Color. The plant material and container constitute the color problem in flower arrangement. A *dominant* color is necessary in any arrangement for *emphasis and unity*. If three colors are used one should be first in quantity, one second, and one third. In addition only one color may be brilliant in intensity.

The *warm* colors may be combined in a flower arrangement, for they are all harmonious. They include the yellows and all the colors that contain much yellow, such as yellow-green, chartreuse, cream, buff, orange, brown, salmon, flame, and yellow-red (scarlet). The *cool* colors may be combined, for they are all harmonious. They include the blues and all the colors that contain much blue, such as blue-green, blue-violet, lavender, orchid, cool pink, magenta, gray, blue-red (crimson, beet-red), and white.

A *monochromatic harmony* consists of tints and shades in one color only. An *analogous* (neighboring, adjacent) *scheme* consists of neighboring hues on the color wheel. The analogous is the most satisfactory type of color harmony for flower arrangements in the home. A *complementary scheme* employs the greatest contrast possible, the colors that are opposite on the color wheel. It is therefore most pleasing at a distance in a large room or in dim light. *Split complements* consist of one hue and the two hues adjoining its complementary color, on the color wheel. *Paired complements* consist of two or three pairs of complements. A *triad scheme* consists of the three colors at the points of an equilateral triangle placed anywhere on the color circle. A *polychromatic scheme* employs many colors; for best results they should all be pale or subdued.

The *values* (lightness or darkness) of colors are important in arrangements. Several values of a color are preferable to one. White, near-white, or pale yellow flowers add sparkle to any dark or medium arrangement. Usually light-colored flowers look well at the upper part of an arrangement, whereas dark-colored flowers look best at the bottom, where they help to make a solid, well-balanced foundation. Very dark flowers do not usually constitute an effective focal center. Dark colors are rich and dramatic; light colors are generally lyrical and uplifting. Pale tints look better by daylight than by artificial light.

PRINCIPLES OF DESIGN

Rhythm. Every growing thing has its own rhythm or growth movement. A person should study the way a flower grows, and then select the type of rhythm to stress in arranging it. All types of rhythm are based on movement and repetition.

Radiating rhythm occurs in most flower arrangements but particularly in round or triangular compositions where the lines radiate from one place. Lanciform leaves or tall flower spikes like snap dragons and larkspur emphasize radiation in an arrangement.

Curvilinear rhythm is felt in smoothly gliding lines which lead the eyes in, through, and over a composition and container until they have seen it all, and then they rest at the point of greatest interest. This rhythm occurs naturally in the flowing lines of arrangements of wisteria, trumpet vine, nasturtiums, petunias, or verbenas. Curvilinear rhythm can be deliberately created by the arrangement of plant materials. For example, blossoms may be employed to form S or C curves against other flowers or foliage or they may help to make the curves of crescent arrangements. Curved stems, leaves, and flower stalks are useful in directing and creating continuity in curvilinear rhythm.

Diagonal rhythm is the most active type of rhythm obtainable in flower arrangements. The main line of a composition can be made dynamic by slanting it or static by placing it upright. When the leading line slants in one direction a shorter line or mass should slant in the opposite direction to halt the movement.

Proportion. The fine relationship of parts in a flower arrangement is based on proportion. A safe rule for amateurs is to have the plant material about one and a half times as high as a *medium or tall container*, although it may be very much higher, even three and a half times, in order to fit a certain background space or to secure a dramatic result. See page 379. A very tall arrangement should be narrow in form and thin at the top. Experts sometimes stress beautiful containers by using only a small proportion of plant materials in them. A *horizontal* arrangement looks well if the plant material is one and a half times as wide as the low container; however, personal taste should be the final guide. *Flat* arrangements, to be seen from above, may have one-third or two-thirds of the water covered with plant materials.

Balance. A flower arrangement that appears stable has balance. For the sake of balance the heaviest mass of plant material, the largest flowers, and the longest stems should usually be close to a line extending upward from the center of the container.

In *symmetrical or formal balance* the plant material on one side of the center of the container is approximately equal to the material on the other side, and is similarly arranged. See page 379.

In *asymmetrical or informal balance* the plant material is not similarly arranged on both sides of an imaginary line above the vertical center of the container. See page 377. One principle involved in this type of balance is the same as in the teeter-totter, a heavy weight near the center is balanced on the other side by a lighter weight farther away from the center. In a flower arrangement, weight or power to attract refers not only to quantity but also to larger size or more brilliant color than the rest of the plant material. For example, the placement of some dark begonia leaves overlapping the rim of the container on the right side only, may require the use of some taller material on the left side for balance. A small solid mass of heavy flowers on one side will balance a larger mass of filmy flowers on the other side.

An asymmetrical composition may have *self-contained balance* or *balance by placement*. The latter means that an arrangement having both weight and extended lines on one side only is balanced by placing it near one end of the area it occupies so that considerable vacant background space occurs on the same side as the lines and weight; this open space should be defined.

Emphasis. For emphasis attention is usually drawn to a center of interest or *focal point* where the flowers are largest, most numerous, and usually most contrasty or brilliant in color. For the sake of stability the focal point belongs in the lower part of the plant materials and near but not usually at the center of the container. In triangular compositions, the focal point occurs naturally at the hub where the lines converge in the container. This point must never be left open or weak.

Emphasis on a leading line is also desirable in many arrangements, with lesser lines repeating the dominating line. The emphasis of one dominating color and one dominating texture is secured by having one of the flowers dominate. Subordination of receptacle and background puts the emphasis on the flowers.

TYPES OF ARRANGEMENTS

Line Arrangements. Compositions in which the element of line is of first importance are known as line arrangements. Only a relatively small amount of plant material is used in order that the beautiful and characteristic lines of plant growth will show clearly. A favorite line arrangement consists of three sprays of different lengths that go in the same direction or suggest a triangle. Some suitable materials are: columbines, petunias, iris, ixias, tiger lilies, bleeding hearts, Japanese quince, willow, and grasses.

Americans have learned from the Japanese how to appreciate and to create line arrangements. The influence of Japanese restraint, line emphasis, asymmetrical balance, triangular composition, and use of foliage, buds, and plain containers has been extensive. Americans adapt these Oriental ideas with good results.

Mass Arrangements. Full-bodied compositions in which a comparatively large amount of plant material is employed are known as mass or massed arrangements. The grouping as a whole and the color are more important than line interest. Mass compositions may be compact, semi-compact, or airy.

Mass arrangements may be *natural, stylized,* or of a *period* type. The *natural* effects are suitable for modest flowers in informal rooms. *Stylized* contemporary mass arrangements have a center of interest, segregated colors, and sometimes linear patterns within the mass. *Period* arrangements are adaptations of those used in the palaces of Europe at historic periods. Colonial, Federal, and Victorian arrangements are described on the following page.

Combination or Line-plus-Mass Arrangements. This popular type of arranging is contemporary *American* in origin. Line-plus-mass compositions combine the best features of line arrangements and mass arrangements; the charm of a color mass is augmented by line interest. The mass should not be much more important than the line element even though it provides the focal point and weight at the base of the composition.

Design is emphasized in these arrangements; they are usually stylized, in fact they may be so severely stylized as to be entirely Modern. In such combination arrangements colors are segregated and so are the different kinds of flowers. Some popular shapes of line-plus-mass arrangements are: the triangle, pyramid, circle, upright semicircle, crescent, fan, and S curve (Hogarth).

Diminutive Arrangements. Small arrangements may be used on food trays, at individual placements at a dining table, on small end tables, or in children's playhouses. All diminutive arrangements depend largely upon proper scale for success; the size of the flowers, leaves, and container must be consistent. A shell, thimble, egg cup, or ash tray may serve as a container.

A *miniature arrangement*, according to certain garden club classifications, is one that does not exceed three inches in any dimension. This arrangement should reproduce in miniature the effect of a large flower arrangement. The classification, *small arrangements*, means one that is about six or eight inches high.

SOME STYLES IN ARRANGEMENTS

Early American. Copper or pewter pitchers. Primitive, demure, or quaint bouquets. Hardy and old-fashioned flowers, like dianthus, Sweet William, mignonette, and geraniums. Use with Early American or other cottage furniture.

Colonial or Eighteenth Century. Silver or porcelain containers with bulbous curved lines. Mass arrangements. Rich colors. Roses, lilies, and peonies. Use with Chippendale or Queen Anne furniture or any Williamsburg period furnishings.

Federal Classic. Slender alabaster urns with handles. Formal mass arrangements. Fine flowers. Light color schemes. Roses, delphinium, and white stock. Like late Georgian and French Classic. Use with Sheraton, Hepplewhite, Phyfe, or Louis XVI.

Victorian. Ornate vases, porcelain, bronze. Masses, stiffly arranged. Emphasis on heavy, rich color. Camellias, stock, tulips, fuchsias, roses, calla lilies, and petunias. No segregation, focal point, or line interest. Use with Victorian furnishings.

Japanese. Oriental or any other low, simple containers and bases. Asymmetrical balance. Line arrangements. Restraint. Sparse material. Natural growth and surroundings. Emphasis on foliage. Use with any furnishings.

Modern or Twentieth Century. Plain geometric containers. Stylized arrangements. Bold, dramatic effects. Big flowers. Solid mats of flower heads. Emphasis on clear-cut form. Omit filler material. Use with Modern furnishings.

Contemporary American. Plain containers. Flowers segregated. Designed arrangements. Use with any furnishings except casual.

PLANT MATERIALS

Plant materials vary greatly in the length of time they remain presentable in an arrangement. Flowers are the most perishable; foliage, berries, weeds, fruits, and vegetables may last from a week to a month; dried materials usually look well for a season.

FLOWERS

Preparation and Care of Flowers. Flowers are the most charming as well as the most fragile of plant materials. They can, however, be hardened by proper cutting and handling. The best results are usually obtained by cutting flowers in the evening or early in the morning, and putting them immediately in a pail of water which has been carried into the garden. Leaves, buds, and half-open and full-bloom blossoms should usually be gathered. Stems should be cut with a very sharp knife, at an angle so that stem ends will not rest flat. Foliage should be stripped off the lower part of the stems, because it fouls the water.

Bubbles of air entering the cut stems block the intake of water. Therefore, ends of stems of land plants should be burned, and ends of stems of water plants should be held in boiling water for one minute, in order to seal them. Woody stems should be slit at the end and scraped or crushed so as to allow water to enter. Certain flowers require special treatment, however. Lily stem ends should be burned and dipped in melted paraffin, hydrangea and poinsettia stem ends should be burned to charcoal, and wisteria ends should be dipped in alcohol. A hole should be pricked in the stem of the calla lily above the water line. Poppies, water lilies, iris, roses, peonies, and morning glories should be cut in the bud stage. Heliotrope, hollyhock, poppy, and dahlia stem ends should be put in boiling water. Some solid wood stem must be cut with clematis. Chrysanthemum stems should be broken under water.

After flowers have been cut, they should stand for at least three hours in a dark, cool, draftless place in deep water up to the base of the blossoms to fortify themselves with water. It is well to place flower arrangements in a cool place at night, in deep water if they are in very shallow water in daytime. In order to lengthen the life of cut flowers, stems should be trimmed daily while under water. The water should be changed every day.

Flower Combinations. Large distinctive flowers usually look best by themselves, but most flowers gain interest if arranged with others. The following list suggests some combinations that have a focal (or center of interest) material, an extending material, and a transition material, which may, however, be omitted.

Focal Material	Extending Material	Transition Material
(*Dominant*)	(*Spikes. Curves*)	(*Background*)
Tulips	bleeding hearts	
Beet-red roses	blue salvia	white daisies
Pink roses	snapdragons	gray foliage
Chrysanthemums		butterfly lilies
Magenta stock	corn flowers	
Tritomas	oats	yellow yarrow
Talisman roses	white lupine	sweet peas
Calla lilies	scarlet gladiolus	

FOLIAGE AND BERRY ARRANGEMENTS

For the average busy housewife foliage provides the best material for her semi-permanent everyday arrangements. Foliage like Chinese evergreen, huckleberry, aspidistra, citrus, pittospore, and rubber plant lasts many weeks; yew, ivy, and succulents last for months. Flowers may be added to foliage arrangements; for example, some philodendron leaves in a small round glass fish bowl are graceful and form a pleasing setting for a temporary hibiscus blossom. Arrangements of colorful croton, begonia, or leucothoe leaves welcome the addition of berries or flowers in similar hue. Bittersweet, cotoneaster, pyracantha, or pepper berries add beauty to leaf arrangements. Nandina leaves are beautiful with or without their berries.

A Modern effect is created by the use of the large central tubular leaves from the century plant, the inner white leaves providing dramatic color contrast to the darker ones. Bold effects can also be obtained in arrangements of elephant's ear, canna, or paper plant leaves or by a great pot of colorful leaves. See pages 59, 223, and 380. Interesting foliage arrangements are created by combining two or three varieties which are different in size and shape, like pittospore, iris, and yew; or hen and chickens, agave spikes, and cedar; or loquat, cycad, and pine.

WEED ARRANGEMENTS

Weed arrangements are especially creative because the materials used are without obvious beauty of their own. Children particularly should be encouraged to make weed and grass arrangements so that they learn to see beauty and grace in the lowliest plants, and, as James Russell Lowell said, "to win the secret of a weed's plain heart." Roadside materials are a boon to those who do not have flowers; some examples are plantain, Joe Pye, milkweed, moneyworth, mullein, fox tail, squirrel tail, bergamot, thistle, sandburs, and snakegrass. See page 378.

In a certain exhibition of weed arrangements one successful combination consisted of a column of crinkly dock shading from red at the base to green at the top, with some yellow fennel for variety, and grasses low at one side. Another grouping of cactus and chartreuse yellow yarrow in sand portrayed the desert.

DRIED PLANT ARRANGEMENTS

Dried plant arrangements are satisfactory particularly for fall and winter. The materials should usually be gathered in the summer or autumn and hung head downward until they are thoroughly dry. To dry leaves well first place the stems in a solution of two parts water to one part glycerine for two weeks. Branches of colorful leaves or ferns can be pressed between newspapers under a heavy board, after a light application of cooking oil.

A good collection should include dried materials of various sizes, from lotus blossom seed pods to stalks of wheat or oats. Stems and seed pods of okra, sunflowers, castor beans, poinciana, golden rain, cotton, money plant, milkweeds, thistles, teasel, date palm, and the tops of corn stalks are useful. Dry everlasting flowers, statice, and coxcomb are specially interesting in color; baby's breath, asters, yarrow, and acacia blooms can be dried successfully. A root, driftwood, lichen-covered wood, birch bark, or a small dead tree can add texture interest to some arrangements.

All the rules of good composition apply to dry arrangements. An entire arrangement may be sprayed with white paint for variety. Dry materials like gourds and seed pods may be combined into hanging decorations called charm strings. Any dry arrangement should be discarded at the end of the season.

FRUIT AND VEGETABLE ARRANGEMENTS

During the fall and winter, fruit and vegetable arrangements are freely used as decorative notes. Variety is desirable in such combinations, different shapes, different sizes, different colors, and different textures adding interest.

Leaves that are hardy, like succulents, barberry, loquat, leopardbane, rhododendron, holly, yew, magnolia, rubber, pittospore, lemon, English ivy, palmetto, cycad, pine, and cedar, are desirable in fruit and vegetable arrangements. Sprays of berries, gourds, cones, and seed pods, like okra or paulownia, are also suitable.

Compositions must be created with care to avoid suggesting a vegetable counter. It is helpful to have in mind a definite geometric form. For example, the largest or brightest article may be placed high at one side of the center to make the focal point and to form the peak of a somewhat triangular composition. Paintings of vegetables and fruits may inspire ideas. See page 381.

Appropriate containers are suggested by the surroundings as well as by the materials; however, containers may be omitted entirely. A large banana leaf, a nest of leaves, or a palm spathe placed directly on the table makes a pleasing base for an arrangement. Suitable containers include trays of wood, pewter, or tin, a steak plank, bread board, butter bowl, iron skillet, old scales, mixing bowl, pottery platter, garden hat, and a basket cut from a watermelon or pumpkin. See page 104.

A heavy pinpoint holder is useful in holding fruit, vegetables, or flowers at the angle desired. Leaf stems may be inserted into small hidden glasses or test tubes, or even into grapes to provide them with moisture. A potato or an apple punctured with an ice pick can also serve as a stem holder.

One successful combination for a table centerpiece consists of long-leaved pine and artichokes surrounded by a wreath of yellow green peppers. Pomegranates, white grapes, eggplants, and pittospore against a palmetto leaf look well together and should suggest other possibilities. A pineapple or a red cabbage is decorative enough to be the focal center in an arrangement. An attractive autumn table centerpiece can be made from red-berried barberry twigs arranged naturally with yellow chrysanthemums, fruit, and nuts. Succulents look well with fruit or vegetables.

ACCESSORIES

Any accessories that are placed in a flower arrangement should have *beauty*, should conform to the *theme* of the arrangement, and should compose into a *unit* with the flowers.

Materials. Natural materials like shells, starfish, coral, rocks, and feathers help to establish moods. For example, tropical or sea effects are obtained with coral or driftwood. The woods are suggested by a gnarled root, or a branch covered with fungi or lichens, or a small dead tree. Equal amounts of plant material and accessory material are undesirable; for example, in combining rocks and pansies one or the other must be in preponderance.

Small sculptures of people, animals, and birds may add interest to flower arrangements, but unfortunately they are often inharmonious and too small. Other materials such as candles, books, decorative boxes, tiles, glass bubbles, or fans sometimes provide the contrast of form or color that completes a composition.

Artificial materials like curls or streamers of gilt, silver, or colored paper, paper lace, and ribbons are sometimes combined with flowers to create a gay, festive mood. Outstanding examples are found in the modern interpretation of the Balinese ceremonial decorations, where a tall, slender cone is ornamented with lines of fruits, flowers, and artificial material.

Theme. A definite theme is advisable, for it prevents the combining of such unrelated materials as a pottery peasant figure, roses, and shells. A consistent idea should be maintained. For example, only water creatures should be placed in the water; land animals should stand on blocks, rocks, or other solids to help the illusion. The mood that is desired directs the relative proportion of accessory materials to plant materials.

Design. One unit of composition should result from the combining of accessories and flower arrangements. One way to accomplish this is to place a figure on one end of a raft or disk and a vase at the other end and proceed to arrange the plant material so that its lines reach towards the figure and tie all parts together. If the figure can be removed without spoiling the entire composition the arrangement is a failure. It must be admitted that compositions in which the accessories form an integral part of a flower composition are greatly outnumbered by the others.

CONTAINERS

It is impossible to arrange flowers successfully without a variety of containers of all types, sizes, and materials. Some should be bought in pairs. Containers should be acquired to fit the rooms where they are to be used. Urns are needed for formal period rooms, geometric forms for Modern surroundings, and low, squatty shapes for cottages.

Texture. The structural *material* of a container largely determines its texture. *Metals* are considered too severe in texture for many kinds of flowers; however, suitable receptacles of silver, pewter, copper, brass, lead, and tin are useful. An amateur can make a low flat lead container by bending up the edges of a sheet of plumber's lead or a round container by soldering a roll of copper. Five-gallon cans or cocoa cans or bread pans of tin can be painted or rubbed with steel wool and used for flowers. An inside coating of melted paraffin wax in the cans prevents leakage; pebbles or sand give stability. Some florists' tin containers are satisfactory for home use. A person who moves frequently appreciates unbreakable metal containers.

Glass containers range from fine crystal urns for delicate flowers to chemistry laboratory equipment and battery jars for more sturdy flowers. Large special round glass bowls should be acquired for submerged bubble bouquets. Colored water or milk can conceal holders. Glass marbles can support and also hide stems.

Pottery containers vary in texture from red earth flower pots to Victorian vases. Beautiful individual forms made in potters' studios are sometimes available. Plain kitchen mixing bowls from the dime stores are usually better than their flower containers.

Porcelain containers are procurable in old and new designs.

Wooden containers such as chopping bowls are suitable in texture for fruit or vegetable arrangements. Beautiful wooden receptacles are purchasable; however, they are not difficult to make at home. Sections of bamboo or banana tree trunks make excellent standing or hanging containers.

Plastics should eventually provide us with a variety of beautiful, indestructible containers at reasonable prices. A graceful, clear, plastic framework supporting a cornucopia surrounded by five smaller cornucopias makes an effective table centerpiece.

Form. Simplicity in design is essential in containers, as the receptacles must not compete with the flowers for attention. Anything elaborate or grotesque is wrong; ornamentation is lamentable.

A *variety of forms* in containers is essential for successful flower arrangements. Low, medium, and tall shapes in large, medium, and small sizes are all needed. *Tray or platter types* of containers may be round, oval, or rectangular; they look well with horizontal, vertical, or triangular arrangements. Low containers must be deep enough to provide water well above the height of the stem holders. Very large containers are needed for foliage arrangements.

Medium-height containers with fairly small openings require less materials and no stem holders; they are easiest for beginners and are useful for quickly made arrangements. Tall or medium-height containers that flare outward slightly at the top happily repeat the radiating lines of many flowers. Containers that function best are those that allow plenty of room for stems and for water.

Geometric forms such as the cube, oblong, pyramid, cylinder, cone, sphere, and crescent are needed for Modern flower arrangements. *Containers with stems or with two handles,* such as epergnes, cake stands, or urns, are desirable especially for symmetrical arrangements. *Asymmetrical containers* such as pitchers, spiral shells, or horns of plenty require informal arrangements. Containers of *irregular shapes,* such as an S, a kidney, or a palette, also take asymmetrical arrangements.

Color. Containers are generally subdued in color so that they will not detract from the flowers. Subtle beiges, grays, off-whites, browns, putty, clear glass, and natural colors are the most useful. Soft dull blue, foliage green, white, dull eggplant, and soft brick-red are also needed at times. Smoky colors and earthy colors suit woody material. Stimulating effects occur, however, when small, clear red-violet, turquoise-blue, jade-green, or lemon-yellow bowls hold flowers of even more vivid adjacent colors. Such sophisticated combinations must, however, be used with care. Pale blue-green which is popular for cheap containers should be avoided, for it is usable only with blue-green leaves and white or lavender flowers; however, leaf-green containers are most useful. Dark containers should be used for dark flowers; white containers should be used for white or very light flowers only.

STEM HOLDERS

Some mechanical devices are usually necessary to support stems properly in flower arrangements. Strips of plumber's lead hooked across and into the tops of bowls and around stems are useful.

Stem holders in several sizes are necessities. Needle-point stem holders, consisting of heavy metal bases bristling with points, and hairpin stem holders are especially satisfactory. A holder is fastened into a container with modeling clay; however, it will not adhere unless the holder, container, and clay are dry. Some holders come in small convenient pans that hold water.

Improvised stem holders are needed too. Each tall or medium opaque container may have in it some two-inch-mesh chicken wire crumpled and held in place with lead strips or modeling clay. Wire hardware cloth in cones, rolls, or circles is useful. Cedar or spruce foliage clippings provide sufficient support for stems in large containers and sand or bird gravel in small ones.

A holder can be made for almost any vase, which is not smaller at the top than the bottom, by greasing the vase and pouring into it a mixture of sand and melted paraffin wax, removing it before it is entirely hard, punching holes in it with a pencil, notching the edges, and making the bottom concave.

Stem holders should be concealed, but not obviously. The leaves or flowers of the arrangement provide the best screen for the holder, but material such as glass, gravel, sand, shells, moss, sticks, driftwood, fungi, or stones may be used in a natural way. Short pieces of cut stems set upright on the holder serve to conceal it and also to give support to the flower stems.

STANDS

Blocks, stands, or mats are sometimes placed under containers to improve their appearance and to protect the surfaces underneath. A stand under a container corrects a topheavy effect and also adds importance to a flower arrangement. Plain dull black Oriental stands are often used. See page 379. Many circular and rectangular slabs of wood in various colors should be acquired. They are easily made; sometimes cake or bread boards can be used. Rafts of bamboo or reed are also practical. Bases are usually needed to unify compositions of flowers and figures.

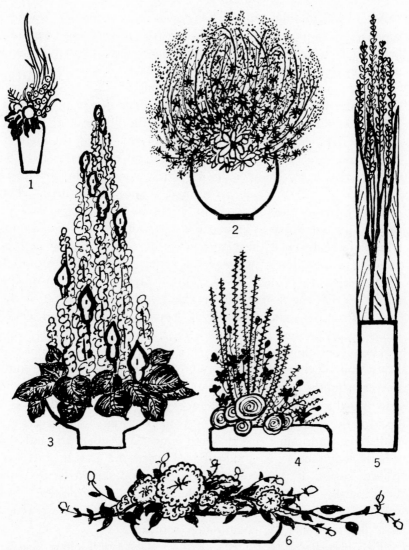

This is a page of students' drawings of arrangements of stylized flowers: 1, 4, and 6 are asymmetrical; 2 and 5 are symmetrical; and 3 is a symmetrical cone wound with an asymmetrical spiral. Agreement of container and plant material is stressed in these exercises. Some accepted rules of composition have been disregarded.

MAKING AN ARRANGEMENT

A tool kit holding snippers, long scissors, stem holders, sponge, paper napkins, pipe cleaners, florist's wire, garden tying tape, rubber bands, adhesive tape, strips of lead, wire Twist-Ems, and modeling clay is a convenience.

When making an arrangement first consider the mood and design of the setting, then the flowers and their design possibilities. Select a container to suit the setting and the flowers. If possible make the arrangement where it is to be placed, not in the kitchen.

Suppose an arrangement of calla lilies and their leaves is to be made against a narrow space in a Modern room. The characteristic lines of callas, which are curves, should be featured. The general form of the arrangement might be a tall, narrow cone, three and a half times as high as the width of the low, round container. The detail of the design could be a spiral line of flowers winding around the arrangement, carrying out the curve idea.

First select the tallest, smallest, finest lily and set it up on the holder so that the flower will be directly above the center of the bowl. Prop the stem by setting up several two-inch pieces of lily stems tightly against it on the holder.

The second flower, a trifle larger than the first, should be placed below and a little to the left or right of the first flower. The third flower, slightly larger again, should be placed to continue the downward and outward curved line which gradually winds around back of the arrangement and returns to the front. As flowers are added the continuity of the spiral must be maintained, and the whole design enlarged gradually. Finally the largest flower is placed lowest, at the center, where attention should be focused. Only perfect flowers are acceptable for this studied design. Tall stalks of a smaller and less important flower like stock are added as a filler to make the composition compact.

Two beautiful calla leaves should be placed at the base, one on each side, the smaller one higher than the larger. The horizontal leaves are a desirable balance for the perpendicularity of the whole design, and they also help to cover the stem holder. A person who makes this flower arrangement should enjoy the pure form and lovely texture of the calla lilies as well as the fine curves in the leaves and stems.

FLOWER COMPOSITION SUMMARY

1. Make a definite plan for your arrangement at the outset.
2. Restrain an arrangement to one idea only.
3. First decide on a basic form, then on details.
4. Cut all stems different, have shortest on largest flowers.
5. Arrange the tallest and widest materials first.
6. Have one leading line and some echoes of it.
7. Use upward radiating lines; avoid droopy ones.
8. Locate the focal point low and near the center.
9. Have surprises. Break some rules.
10. Let plant material cover part of rim of container.
11. Avoid regular spacing and stair step sequences.
12. Avoid an even number of flowers or stems.
13. Segregate each kind of flower in most arrangements.
14. Distinctive flowers should usually be alone.
15. Place all large flowers, such as magnolias, low.
16. Small flowers, like violets, may be in tight bunches.
17. Slender stems and buds can be extended far.
18. Obtain great variety in the silhouette of an arrangement.
19. Use large, medium, and small leaves or flowers together.
20. Combine focal, extending, and transition materials.
21. Tall containers suggest tall arrangements.
22. Medium containers invite medium or tall arrangements.
23. Low containers are suitable for all types of arrangements.
24. Circular containers suggest circular arrangements.
25. Rectangular containers are best for angular arrangements.
26. In tall arrangements use at least three stems.
27. Tall arrangements should be slender at the top.
28. A cone arrangement should be solid in feeling.
29. In a triangular arrangement stem holder may be off center.
30. A triangular arrangement requires a strong horizontal.
31. The focal point is near the hub in a radiating arrangement.
32. Place a symmetrical arrangement in the center of a container.
33. In a poor arrangement, try removing half the flowers.
34. To an insipid arrangement add lanciform material.
35. Place a base under a topheavy arrangement.
36. Study each arrangement reflected in a mirror.
37. Make an arrangement every day.

USING FLOWER ARRANGEMENTS

Personalities. Flower arrangements should suit the personalities and tastes of the family or individual who is to enjoy them. A conservative family might want to exclude contrasting colors, bold forms, or any unusual exciting ideas which would delight young experimental persons. A sophisticated personality could be expressed in a column of gladioli and calla lilies; a more domestic personality, in a loose, irregular mass of verbenas. An experienced arranger expresses her own moods in her compositions.

Occasion. Within the limits that the room itself imposes, a flower arrangement should be expressive of the occasion for which it is made. Large balanced masses in conservative, dignified color schemes are most suitable for formal affairs. Smaller casual bunches of gay flowers are in the mood of a jolly intimate occasion. Flower arrangements for the dining table can be made to express the theme of almost any party. See page 60.

Room. The *mood of a room* or the feeling it expresses determines not only the kinds of flowers which may be used therein but also the types of flower containers and the style of the flower arrangements. For example, a pair of silver urns, containing symmetrical arrangements of pale pink roses, blue delphiniums, and white sweet peas, express the refinement that suits an elegant, formal room. Calendulas put in a brown pottery bowl in a natural manner suit the intimate mood of a simple cottage. Three cycad fronds and some magnolia leaves fit well in an artist's studio.

The *style or design of a room*, too, indicates the design of the flower arrangements to be placed in it. See page 423. The angular lines of a Modern room are repeated in tight, blocklike bunches of narcissus, backed by a large, stiff palmetto leaf, which has been trimmed to a rectangle and anchored in a hollow glass brick. A period room suggests containers of the same period. For example, bulbous lines in a silver vase and bouquet conform to the lines of Colonial furnishings.

The *colors of a room* dictate the colors of the flowers for it, unless the room is largely neutral, such as beige or white. Walls colored a pale, soft, warm green, like a muted chartreuse, make a friendly background for most flowers. A colorful room usually requires flowers in the same hues as the room.

Placement. Every room should be studied to determine how many flowers it needs and where they should be placed to emphasize the design of the room. Too many arrangements lessen the effectiveness of all of them. Important arrangements in unimportant places disturb the unity of a room. When building a new house, it might be possible to make a specially lighted niche in the right place in some rooms for the main flower arrangement.

In *a living room* a large, beautiful arrangement should be placed as near as possible to the center of interest, which might be the main seating group before the fireplace. See page 282. If additional flowers are needed one or two less important secondary arrangements could be placed at the furniture groups which are next in importance, or wherever attention is to be focused. In a formal living room a pair of period vases with identical bouquets might be placed on each end of the mantel shelf; or urns could be placed on tables at each side of the fireplace. In a cottage small sprightly nosegays may be placed wherever there is a space for them.

In *a dining room* the more important arrangement is often placed on the buffet and a lower bouquet on the table so that the diners can see over it. Small identical arrangements may be grouped on the buffet or on the table or set at each place. See pages 59 and 278.

A hall should be furnished so that provision is made for a flower arrangement at the center of interest. A shelf or a table underneath a mirror is usually an advantageous location. See page 60. An uninteresting hall might be improved by the addition of two stands or pillars, perhaps from a wrecking establishment, each topped with an urn of leaves or flowers.

The *background space* where flowers are to be placed must be considered carefully, and the arrangement designed to fit it. A tall, narrow wall space prescribes a tall, slender grouping. A shelf or a buffet usually requires a horizontal arrangement with extending vine, branch, or leaves producing the lines desired. Circular arrangements and radiating lines are in harmony with low round tables.

Scale enters into the placement problem. A small bouquet seems lost on a big table; a large bouquet on a small table looks top-heavy. Small rooms suggest small arrangements; small arrangements are useless in large rooms.

SOURCES OF PLANT MATERIAL

The Fields and Woods. Wild growth, including weeds, is a plentiful source of plant material for arrangements. With wild flowers one should use foliage and grasses that are their neighbors where they grow. Branches of leaves are probably the most useful of the wild material. Dead branches bearing moss, fungi, or lichens should not be overlooked, as they are often decorative. A person who has a casual small home can use these simple, natural things.

Indiscriminate picking of wild flowers is, of course, very anti-social. Children should be taught that the flowers near the roadside must be left for the passersby to enjoy, and that those on the state conservation lists, including rare plants like the arbutus, heather, and trilliums, must never be picked. Wherever wild flowers are gathered some should be left for seed.

Gardens. In a garden, flowers should be available for cutting all through the season. Gardeners say that a dozen varieties, well chosen, will provide interesting combinations until late autumn, and also will furnish material for dried winter arrangements. Flower spikes, round target blossoms, and small flowers are needed. Those that remain in good condition after cutting should be featured. Unusual leaves or seed pods are also desirable.

In a cutting garden those flowers which fit into the colors and theme of the interior of the house should be grown. Mediterranean houses require tomato red, orange, and yellow flowers; English houses need beet-red, purple, and blue; late Colonial and French houses need light colors and white. Modern houses welcome dramatic color contrasts that suit the colors of the interior.

Flower Shops. Florists' plant materials are needed at times, although garden flowers are preferable. When selecting florists' flowers, buds as well as fully developed blossoms should be chosen to relieve monotony. Unusual foliage can often be purchased in place of the usual commonplace, smothering asparagus fern which is provided; foliage from one's garden or from a house plant is usually best. Asters, daisies, zinnias, and birds of paradise are among the florists' hardier products; certain others last only a brief time or have weak stems. The purchase of three flowers weekly gives more pleasure than a dozen each month. Florists' flower arrangements should seldom be imitated in the home.

FLOWERS AS GIFTS

Flowers are important conveyors of messages whether in times of joy, illness, or sorrow. Flowers from one's garden have a valuable personal touch. Flowers are sent as gifts in various forms, some of which are better than others.

Cut flowers for *vase arrangements* constitute the most popular floral gifts even for messages of congratulation or consolation.

Corsages should harmonize with the dress and coloring of the wearer. Choice flowers are always preferable for such personal use. Roses, camellias, dendrobiums, or orchids serve well as the dominant material; the less important lily-of-the-valley, Roman hyacinth, delphinium, or sweet peas are excellent accompanists; southernwood is desirable foliage. In making a corsage the largest flowers should be near the center or base with smaller ones and possibly delicate foliage near the outside; the ribbon should be inconspicuous.

Sprays of flowers are usually arranged by florists although they can be made by clever amateurs. Well-fortified, hardy materials should be used because sprays are not placed in water.

Wreaths of simple design are pleasing for holiday decoration. Wreaths are less desirable for use at funerals; however, they are very much preferable to elaborate *set pieces*.

Potted plants, which are in blossom, are delightful gifts, used singly or in groups.

HOUSE PLANTS

The modern feeling about potted plants is that only large plants with large leaves, such as the rubber plant, count in the decorative scheme of most living rooms. See pages 278 and 279. However, collections of potted plants of average size are in keeping with certain houses. See pages 10 and 380. A sun room in a Modern house may feature a collection of potted cacti and succulents; an old-fashioned cottage living room may have a bay window full of plants. House plants should be arranged in orderly fashion with consideration for line, color, and texture effects. Wire racks to hold plant collections may be decorative; glass shelves across windows are pleasing. Large plants should stand on the floor (page 10); hanging or drooping plants should be placed high.

EXHIBITIONS OF FLOWER ARRANGEMENTS

Staging. The staging of an exhibition of flower arrangements is an esthetic problem of importance. The factors involved are much like those present in exhibiting paintings. The ideal setting is a permanent gallery for the exhibition of flower arrangements only, with counters, stands, niches, and shadow boxes built in. The picture of such a gallery in Pasadena is shown on page 382.

Most exhibitions of flower arrangements are staged in connection with horticultural flower shows, although the two shows are very properly kept entirely separate. An empty room with suitable day and night lighting is a necessity. Plain, light walls are essential; a solarium effect is desirable.

The exhibition tables, counters, and niches should be placed so as to have wide aisles and no dead ends. Where table space is insufficient shelves may have to stand on the tables. They should be painted like the tables in color, possibly light gray, beige, or white, which are suitable background colors for flowers. Where the table tops permit, white corduroy paper, which comes in rolls, may be stood upright at the back of table tops and curved forward every yard or so to separate the flower arrangements.

Classifications. Definite limitations in the size and color allowed in each class and restriction in the number of classes help to make a flower arrangement show more beautiful. A small show may consist of six of the following classes.

1. Mass arrangement, 14 to 18 inches high.
2. Line arrangement for a card-table luncheon.
3. Small arrangement, for use with a place card.
4. Horizontal arrangement in low container for a buffet.
5. Flat arrangement of floating material, for guest table.
6. Tall arrangement in tall container, in cool colors.
7. Crescent-shaped arrangement in a 10-inch bowl.
8. Large symmetrical arrangement in a container with a stem.
9. A Modern composition in a large rectangular container.
10. A Victorian arrangement for a large wall table.
11. A medium-sized cottage-type arrangement in warm colors for an Early American room with pine walls.
12. An arrangement in cool colors in a glass container.
13. A tall weed arrangement in a metal or pottery container.

Judging. The usual procedure in judging an exhibition of flower arrangements is to award in each classification one first prize (blue ribbon), one second prize (red ribbon), one third prize (white ribbon), and possibly several honorable mentions, if they are warranted. In non-competitive classes several ribbons of each color may be awarded.

The *point system* of scoring is useful for inexperienced judges and for close decisions although it is a slow procedure. The arrangements are measured against the perfect score, and the resulting marks are added up to make the earned score. The following scale of points is satisfactory; others may be used.

	PERFECTION	THIS ARRANGEMENT
Color	20 points	? points
Texture	10 "	? "
Proportion	10 "	? "
Balance	10 "	? "
Emphasis	10 "	? "
Rhythm	5 "	? "
Container	15 "	? "
Originality	10 "	? "
Condition	10 "	? "
	100 "	Total "

Judges. The judges for flower arrangement exhibitions must have knowledge of the art elements and principles; therefore persons with art training are usually the most capable judges, provided that they have had experience in flower arrangement. Standards of taste in flower arrangement would be raised if colleges and high schools were to give more extension courses in this subject.

Garden clubs are developing accredited judges among their members. One plan is to sponsor a lecture course in arrangement and horticulture once a year for five years. The arrangement course is based on the art elements and design principles. Examinations are given on the lectures and on a prescribed reading course. Those who pass become accredited judges; however, it is recognized by the garden clubs that much experience and ability are necessary to make a good judge.

PROBLEMS

A sufficient number of problems are listed so that choices may be made.

1. Visit a flower show and report on it. Analyze the awards. Make quick useful sketches.
2. Make a flower arrangement; first sketch it.
3. Make a fruit or vegetable arrangement.
4. Make a dry material or weed arrangement.
5. Design a plain container to harmonize in form with your favorite flowers.
6. Make a large chart to hang up showing the principal shapes of flower arrangements.

READING REFERENCES

ARMS, JOHN T., and DOROTHY N. *Design in Flower Arrangement.* Macmillan, 1937.

BIDDLE, DOROTHY, and BLOM, DOROTHEA. *Flower Arrangement for Every One.* Barrows, 1947.

CARY, KATHARINE T., and MERRELL, NELLIE D. *Arranging Flowers throughout the Year.* Dodd, Mead, 1933.

CONWAY, JOHN G. *Flowers; Their Arrangement.* Knopf, 1940.

CONWAY, JOHN G., and HIATT, E. W. *Flowers: East-West. The Art of Arrangement.* Knopf, 1940.

CYPHERS, EMMA HODKINSON. *Pleasures and Problems in Flower Arrangement.* Privately printed, 1944.

DUNLOP, HAZEL P. *Let's Arrange Flowers.* Harper, 1943.

HINE, ANNABEL W. *The Arrangement of Flowers.* Scribner, 1933.

PREININGER, MARGARET. *Japanese Flower Arrangement for Modern Homes.* Little, Brown, 1936.

ROCKWELL, F. F., and GRAYSON, E. C. *The Complete Book of Flower Arrangement.* Doubleday, 1947.

SCHAEFFER, RUDOLPH. *Flower Arrangement.* R. Schaeffer, 1935.

SPENCER, EDWIN R. *Just Weeds.* Scribner, 1940.

SPRY, CONSTANCE. *Flowers in House and Garden.* Putnam, 1938.

WELCH, NELL TRUE. *Sunset's Flower Arrangement Book.* Lane, 1942.

WHITE, EDWARD A. *The Principles of Flower Arrangement.* De La Mare, 1936.

The arrangement above might well be named Autumn, Roadside, Simplicity, or Movement. The old root, weeds, seed pods, and tray are all consistent and friendly. The solidity and weight at the right side of the container are balanced by the extra length at the left side. *Courtesy Pasadena Flower Show Association.*

The triangular arrangement below has pleasing line interest. More airiness and more difference between height and width would be desirable.

Above left, a white-and-green scheme, white gladioli, lilies, and Shasta daisies are well arranged inside a hurricane glass. *Courtesy Claire Cronenwett Studio.*

Above right, a line arrangement exhibits all the beauty of the small tiger lily and the graceful stilted container, which are in perfect accord. *Courtesy Claire Cronenwett Studio.*

The arrangement below left shows grasses and fungi on a lacquered bread board. Pleasing lines and textures are employed. *Courtesy Sally Kelley.*

The natural arrangement of the trumpet vine below right has graceful lines. The highest point is over the center of the receptacle. *Courtesy Anne Plettinger.*

This beautiful vertical arrangement of roses and green wheat has contrast in form and texture. *Courtesy Claire Cronenwett Studio and Manker Pottery.*

Great variety in the shape and size of the plant materials combined makes the above right arrangement interesting. *Courtesy Pasadena Flower Show Association.*

Below left is a period type arrangement expressing charm and femininity. The plant material provides desirable contrast in size, and in dark and light. Even the stems are thoughtfully designed. *Courtesy Claire Cronenwett Studio.*

A theme of reverence is portrayed in Mrs. William Hertrick's arrangement below right. The unbroken lines of the foliage and sculpture contrast well with the flowers and driftwood.

Above is a pleasing symmetrical arrangement which should be placed in the exact center of a dining table, mantel, or shelf. The table here is much too narrow. This is a free-standing composition (both sides finished); the other side has a different focal point. The magnolia bud in the center was more effective after it had opened. The small transition flowers add a touch of femininity. This is a basic form of design for dinner-table decoration.
Courtesy Alice Westbrook arranger and A. V. Patterson photographer.

The decorative value of the collection of house plants shown below is enhanced because they are consistent in size and are arranged in an orderly manner. The turn table can be rotated between the kitchen and dining alcove. *Courtesy Armstrong Cork Company.*

The attractive container above is a carved wooden leaf. Contrasts of large and small forms and dark and light colors are pleasing. The loquat leaves are decorative, add texture contrast, and do not wilt quickly. The lines of the arrangement point toward the empty end of the container, thereby tending to balance it. *Courtesy Mabel Duffill.*

This group of ceramics by students includes a variety of well-shaped pots, some of which are decorative enough to use alone as ornaments; some are desirable for flower, foliage, or weed arrangements. *Courtesy Cranbrook Academy of Art.*

These two permanent galleries for the exhibition of flower arrangements belong to the Pasadena Flower Show Association. The wall of niches above is surfaced with grass cloth, which has pleasing texture and color.

CHAPTER 22

PICTURES

Pictures reveal the stage or esthetic development of their owners more clearly than any other articles of furnishing. Need for economy may prevent the discarding of ugly furniture, but there is no excuse for the woman who hangs pictures that she does not like, as bare wall spaces are always preferable to poor pictures.

No woman can reasonably expect to be able to select pictures that have esthetic quality unless she has seriously studied pictures. There is no such thing as natural good taste in pictures, and those who imagine that they have it are mistaken. Probably constant association with fine pictures might develop a sure taste, were it not for the fact that we are all exposed to great quantities of poor pictures in advertising and elsewhere. A dilettante could visit art exhibitions for a lifetime and still not know what to look for in pictures.

The study of pictures should include reading a comprehensive history of painting, a good recent book on the esthetics of painting, and also the contemporary art periodicals. A course in appreciation and analysis of pictures is also of great value. Those fortunate enough to be near an art museum should take the lecture courses about its pictures which are usually given there. No one can thoroughly appreciate pictures, however, unless she has had some good instruction and practice in painting in both oil and water color. Whether or not a person has talent, the experience of painting develops understanding of the problems of organization and technique that confront the artist who tries to communicate an idea by means of a painting.

In the selection of pictures for the home many phases of the subject should be considered: the artist's purpose and approach, subject-matter appeal and esthetic appeal, contemporary and non-contemporary pictures, originals and reproductions, and the different media: water colors, oils, and prints.

THE ARTIST'S PURPOSE

The purpose of an artist in painting a picture is to *express himself* and to *communicate his idea to others*. The artist does not want to make literal copies of persons or things; a camera and color film can do this far more quickly and faithfully than he.

Artists are sensitive and keen observers of man's relation to his environment. They are able to recognize man's vital experiences and to portray them in such a way that others, too, can see their significance. Artists also interpret the physical aspects of their environment, making others more aware and more appreciative of the character and beauty of their surroundings.

A picture is the means of communication between artist and observer. The artist hopes that when the observer sees his picture he will have the same feeling about it that the artist had. Some artists aim only to arouse the observer and please him; others try to convey their own thoughts to him. Some artists seek to influence the observer's opinions, possibly on social, political, or religious matters. Propaganda is a legitimate goal provided that the picture is primarily a work of art.

An exhibition of paintings showing the work of many artists usually includes a rich variety of approaches and effects. Each painter has a personal interpretation of the scene about him. He often selects subjects and experiences that are ordinarily overlooked. He emphasizes those phases of life or of painting that interest him the most. Some artists stress subject matter, others stress esthetic values; others achieve a happy blending of both.

Artists who emphasize *man and his problems* might portray, for example, the basic needs of mankind, or uncommon human experiences, or human dreams, or social injustices. Other artists might put the emphasis on man's surroundings, with pictures calling attention to unusual color or form combinations in nature or the strength of the elements or the power of growth in the soil or merely the beauty of common objects. Other artists might emphasize *esthetic problems* such as the control of movement and tension or ways to achieve the order and rhythm that are fundamental in nature. Painters of non-objective pictures have only esthetic problems to consider, for their pictures have no relation to natural objects.

THE ARTIST'S APPROACH

The layman may understand the esthetics of painting better if he is aware of the ways in which artists approach their work. The *subject matter* of a painting is often something that the artist has been considering until his feeling about it is so intense that he is inspired to paint a picture of it. On the other hand, the artist may begin by looking about him for something to take as a subject, even though he may consider nature only a point of departure and will interpret the natural material as he wishes.

Painters have the special problem of producing an *illusion of three dimensions* on a two-dimensional surface, usually paper, canvas, or plaster. Depth or space can be indicated by means of *perspective*, which is based on the fact that, to the human eye, distance makes objects appear smaller, with receding lines converging. Distance is also suggested by weak and cool colors. Third dimension can also be indicated by overlapping planes, planes graded in value, value contrasts, and texture variations.

When composing a picture a painter usually sketches with a medium such as charcoal which can be erased easily. He often experiments freely, trying many arrangements. He works with *lines, planes, and volumes*, which he organizes carefully. He locates the large objects or volumes in such relation to each other that there is a certain tension or thrust evident between them. He designs not only the solid volumes but also the negative volumes or empty spaces. The dynamic or moving quality of a picture is largely the result of the play of these opposing forces. The artist controls them so that they help to convey the message he presents.

Understanding of the *principles of design* is a valuable guide to the artist, whether the principles are applied consciously or otherwise. A few examples of their numerous applications are mentioned here. The canvas itself should be of fine *proportion;* the center of interest should receive the most *emphasis;* the theme should be strengthened by *repetition;* the dominating and supporting lines should produce *rhythm;* weight should be evenly distributed so that *balance* or equilibrium results.

The *element of color* can be almost as important as *form* in conveying the artist's meaning in a picture. Color establishes moods, vitalizes form, and suggests third dimensions.

ESTHETIC APPEAL

When selecting pictures for the home, both esthetic appeal and subject-matter appeal must be considered. Some authorities maintain that esthetic appeal is sufficient for pictures that serve primarily as part of the decorative scheme in a room. Others say that esthetic quality is, after all, only good style, and that significant content is a necessary part, and, in fact, is the aim of every worthy painting, except non-objective ones.

Esthetic appeal is fully realized only by those who can analyze a picture and see how the art elements are utilized to produce the desired results. Everyone should have some practice in the analysis of pictures, for it is possible to learn to recognize esthetic values by this experience. A questionnaire for the analysis of pictures is placed at the end of this chapter. It is well to hear expert analyses of important pictures by specialists. This should be supplemented by reading at least one good book on how to understand pictures.

From the observer's point of view esthetic appeal is chiefly concerned with color and form. In many cases the color of a picture is the sole basis for its selection, whereas composition is ignored. Neither color nor design can be disregarded, however, if the picture is to continue to hold the interest of the owners as they develop in discrimination.

In order that the reader will realize the type of information that he needs and can easily obtain by study, a few examples are given here. One of the tests of a *good composition* is to see whether there are dominating lines or planes that successfully guide the observer's eyes into the picture and around in it and finally to the center of interest. Any strong lines leading to corners are poor because they carry the attention out of the picture. One of the points to notice about the *colors* in pictures is that muddy or chalky colors are unpleasant, but these should not be confused with subtle clear grays and other neutrals which have beauty and character. A picture definitely abstract in form may also be equally abstract or unnatural in color.

The color appeal of a picture must be considered in relation to the room where it is to hang. Beautiful color in a picture may be the basis for the color scheme of a room.

SUBJECT-MATTER APPEAL

This type of appeal should always be accompanied by esthetic appeal. The most obvious kind of subject-matter appeal is present in story-telling pictures, such as one of a birthday party or of a dog saving a drowning person. Illustrations such as these have a different purpose from pictures intended to be hung on walls. Mere *story-telling pictures* are suitable for children, but they ought to be outgrown. A picture with strong subject-matter appeal combined with esthetic appeal is John Curry's *Tornado* reproduced on page 405.

Sentimental appeal bears no relation to merit in a picture. A picture of kittens is appealing but such appeal does not make a good picture. A familiar scene or one of historic importance may have subject-matter appeal but lack esthetic appeal.

Pictures for the home should have reasonably *pleasant subject matter*, since there the primary purpose is decoration. Flower paintings are universal favorites. Decorative flower paintings or careful botanical studies are often preferable to naturalistic flower paintings, although any of these types may be good or poor. A painter of landscapes usually avoids those subjects that have too obvious *pictorial appeal*, such as sunsets, the moon, panoramas, and unpaintable phenomena like the Grand Canyon. Landscapes and marine pictures, portraits, figure paintings, and animal pictures can be found which have both appealing subject matter and esthetic merit.

Subjects of great significance to mankind have been the inspiration for some of the world's most important pictures. Great pictures were painted when religion was uppermost in the minds of men. Great mural paintings, portraying the social unrest of the present generation, have been painted by Diego Rivera and José Orozco of Mexico. Subject-matter appeal and esthetic appeal are usually well blended in great pictures.

In the United States development of interest in the *American scene* has produced vital pictures. See the upper picture on page 406. Government sponsorship of murals in federal buildings all over the country has resulted in the creation of pictures of great local interest. Such subject matter is highly desirable since it appeals to and is expressive of the mass of the people.

OIL PAINTINGS

An oil painting should not be considered an impossible luxury by a family of modest means. A young artist of ability who has not yet attained recognition is usually willing to sell an original oil painting that has merit for a price below fifty dollars. Such pictures should not be confused with the commercial type of oil paintings sometimes available in ordinary department stores.

Oil paintings are usually on canvas, preferably linen. Oil paints are made from pigments of mineral or vegetable matter which are well ground and mixed with fine oil. Naturally oil paintings are more durable than water colors.

Most of the serious painting, exclusive of fresco, is done with oil paint because of its *permanence* and *flexibility*. It dries slowly; therefore it is the best medium for subjects that require deliberation. The painter has time to analyze his work, and, if he is not pleased, he can scrape off the paint on part or all of his picture. Even if the paint is dry he can remove it with paint remover. He can then repaint the picture until he is satisfied with it. Oil paintings often have a studied quality due to the consideration they have received. This is true of the author's painting of magnolias on pages 9 and 408. On the other hand, some oil paintings are done quickly and freely by artists who have an emotional approach.

A wide *variety of techniques* is possible with oil paints. Good and bad pictures are painted in all techniques. The uninitiated should not make the mistake of thinking that a smooth surface is preferable to others.

Some artists employ thin oil paint; others prefer a consistency similar to that of house paint, which can be applied in several ways. Some who use the thick paint just as it comes from the tubes apply it to the canvas so that it is ⅛ inch thick in places. Fairly thick paint may be applied all over a canvas or only in those foreground parts that receive emphasis. The size and shape and the handling of the brush are also important factors in technique.

Because of its flexibility oil paint encourages experimentation in texture, which is now receiving more attention than formerly. Texture as well as technique are only means to an end, however, and are unimportant except as they help artists to express their ideas.

WATER-COLOR PAINTINGS

Original water-color paintings should be used much more generally than they are, as they are reasonable in price and also desirable. Unframed water colors of merit are often sold for less than twenty-five dollars.

Water-color pictures are painted on paper with water-soluble paints that come in tubes or cakes. A somewhat rough paper is desired by most painters, for it adds textural interest to the otherwise flat paint. The white of the paper is often left unpainted in places throughout the picture, thereby contributing a sparkling quality.

A good water-color painting is usually highly subjective and requires a very different approach from the carefully considered oil painting. Emotional intensity is necessary for painting a water color. The artist has to work at top speed because otherwise the paint dries so quickly as to interfere with his plans.

The water colorist must place his brush strokes in a sure way, for he cannot change them or modify them. Any attempt to scrub out or touch up a water color spoils it. If a mistake is made the artist should start the picture again on another sheet of paper. Technique is so important in a water color that slight errors in drawing, in color, and even in composition should be overlooked if the technique is perfect.

Different artists handle water colors differently, however. Some use wet paper, and some dry. Others feature such characteristics as large wash areas, many separate brush strokes, delicate blotted areas, graded planes, crisp dry accents, or beautiful brush strokes. Demuth's *Begonias* on page 408 exhibits fine water-color technique.

All water-color paintings should be spontaneous and fresh. Usually they are treated broadly so that there is no niggling detail in them. Water colors are as a rule somewhat sketchy so that the observer has to exercise his own imagination in completing them. One charm of water-color painting is that the accidental effects often are better than those that are planned.

Water-color paintings are limited in size because the medium is difficult to control. A 20 by 24 inch painting is about the maximum size for home use. Water colors are most effective for quick, sparkling sketches, which are shorthand notes on nature.

PRINTS

Some print collectors say that prints belong in a portfolio and not on a wall. On the contrary, color prints and black-and-white prints large enough to be seen easily are often suitable for wall pictures. It is true, however, that about 90 per cent of the prints now hung should be in portfolios where they can be studied closely, because they are too small to be hung.

Collecting prints is a very satisfactory hobby because of its cultural benefits and its wide range of possibilities. If one begins with contemporary prints the price is moderate. Some original prints in the current print exhibitions cost only five dollars. It is only through prints that an artist's own work is available to persons of small means. Starting a print collection often leads to study that will enable one to enjoy the fine prints in the museums. Much interesting material has been written about prints, but possibilities still exist for research on special phases of the subject. True appreciation is usually developed by experimenting with print making.

Processes of Print Making. Many persons think that etchings are the only important prints made. Etchings are no doubt the favorites of the group, but lithographs, dry-points, wood engravings, mezzotints, monotypes, linoleum-block prints, screen-prints, stencils, steel engravings, aquatints, and wood blocks are also important.

Etchings are ink impressions taken from plates engraved by lines eaten out with acid. Rembrandt and Whistler were among the most important etchers of the past. Aquatints are also printed from plates roughened by acids.

Lithographing is a process of printing from a greased pencil drawing usually made on porous stone. Lithography has suffered because of its association with commercial processes.

The wood block and its substitute the linoleum block have a long history. Dürer and Holbein did wood engraving in Germany in the fifteenth and sixteenth centuries. Today interesting book illustrations are made through the use of block prints. Current exhibitions may show good block prints both in color and in black and white. These as well as steel engravings and wood engravings are printed from blocks incised by mechanical means.

ORIGINAL PICTURES

Those who can afford it should have some original pictures. Anyone whose standard of living includes a thousand-dollar automobile should have at least one original painting by an established artist. The purchaser of original paintings is helping in the creative work of her own age.

The person with a small amount of money, who wishes to buy an original picture, should buy it from the artist directly. The art dealer is, of course, necessary and should be patronized by people of means, but more people might be able to afford pictures if they could buy them from the artists.

The prospective purchaser of an original picture who does not live in a city where there are exhibitions should write to the nearest art museum for advice about buying original paintings in the price range that she can afford. It might be possible to have pictures sent on approval or to arrange a visit to some artists' studios.

REPRODUCTIONS

Reproductions of worthy pictures are much better than poor originals. *Black-and-white reproductions* of etchings and other prints are often so successful that it is impossible for an amateur to distinguish between handmade prints and machine-made copies. The person who is paying for original etchings should buy them only from the artists, exhibitions, or reliable dealers.

Commercial *reproductions in color* vary greatly in quality, the best being so faithful that they show every brush stroke of the original paintings; others are extremely poor. It is now unthinkable to hang brown or gray reproductions of paintings.

The average home could make use of several reproductions of the work of the best artists of the present or past. The pictures should be large to be effective, the minimum dimension being about 18 inches.

Reproductions of either contemporary or old pictures can be obtained from large art museums and from art stores. Department stores and other concerns that cater to public taste will have many mediocre and poor pictures of the type commonly put on calendars.

CONTEMPORARY PICTURES

The most vital pictures for the people who are living now are those that are painted today. The art periodicals are important sources of information about living artists. *Who's Who in Art*, the *Art Index*, and the *Art Periodical Index* are helpful. New books about contemporary artists are available. Every person of culture should attend current art exhibitions.

Practical consideration of contemporary pictures as home decoration divides them into two general types, conservative and Modern. Current exhibitions of paintings usually include both types and also others that do not belong in either group.

Conservative contemporary pictures are suitable in any type of home except Modern. All those pictures are here called conservative in which the artist has reproduced what he saw in nature. The poorest of these paintings are those that merely imitate nature. The best of this group are those in which the artist has interpreted nature and has practiced selection, elimination, and emphasis. The pictures on page 403 illustrate this point. The best impressionistic paintings are interpretative. The decorative pictures on page 406 show carefully organized material; such attention to order may indicate the artist's displeasure with the confusion about him.

Modern contemporary pictures are most appropriately used in Modern rooms, abstractions and distortions being best suited for the most extreme rooms. See pages 279 and 425. The term Modern painting is here meant to include all those pictures in which the objects portrayed do not appear natural. Modern artists deliberately change natural forms for various reasons, sometimes to improve the line composition, or to intensify an idea, or to heighten an emotional effect. The degree of abstraction or distortion varies from slight changes to those in which objects are not recognizable. The pictures on page 407 show interesting contrast in this respect.

Greater development in painting has occurred in recent years than at any time in the past. Since Cézanne (page 403) broke with tradition and post-impressionism began, this century has produced cubism, futurism, and surrealism, as well as many other manifestations. All these movements have benefited painting to some extent. Experimental painting should be encouraged, not ridiculed, for progress comes only through new channels.

NON-CONTEMPORARY PICTURES

Pictures painted before the twentieth century are here classified as non-contemporary; the division is merely for convenience.

The famous masterpieces of the far past are too well known to be suitable for home decoration. They no longer stimulate the imagination. Some of the pictures painted by the old masters are not well known, however, and printed color reproductions or painted copies of them might prove satisfactory. Pictures by less important artists of the past should also be considered.

In museums, period rooms usually contain pictures which were painted about the same time as the furniture was made. See page 442. Period rooms in homes need not be so accurate in style, but it is well to have some relation in idea between furnishings and pictures. Since the traditional furniture styles are combined rather freely, a wide choice in the selection of pictures is possible.

In selecting pictures for period rooms of the seventeenth century styles early pictures should be chosen. Most of the early pictures, or those painted before 1700, are in museums, and it is therefore possible to get reproductions of them. Among the most important early pictures are those painted by Giotto, Titian, Michelangelo, and Tintoretto in Italy; by Rembrandt, Rubens, Hobbema, and von Ruisdael in northern Europe; and by El Greco and Velásquez in Spain. A reproduction of a fine Rembrandt portrait appears on page 404.

With eighteenth-century furniture, which is lighter in type, the most suitable pictures are those from the eighteenth and nineteenth centuries and the conservative ones from the twentieth century. Reproductions in color of these pictures are generally obtainable. France led the world in painting during the eighteenth and nineteenth centuries. Among her important artists were Corot, Millet, Ingres, Monet, Gauguin, Renoir, Seurat, Rousseau, and Cézanne. In England, Constable, Turner, Gainsborough, and Reynolds were prominent. In the United States, Inness, Homer, Abbey, Alexander, Chase, and Whistler did outstanding painting. These lists are not complete by any means, but they are representative. Typical paintings by Cézanne and Rousseau of France and by Winslow Homer of the United States are shown on pages 403, 405, and 406.

PICTURES AND PERSONALITY

Since a picture speaks for its owner, she should be sure of what it is saying. If she is a gentle, refined person her pictures should express those qualities; if she is courageous and original her pictures ought to be the same. A person with simple tastes naturally chooses pictures very different from those selected by the person who likes complex effects. A little girl might prefer dainty pictures of dolls or flowers; a boy would probably choose Indian, animal, or cowboy pictures. A traveler might want architectural pictures from distant lands. An amateur photographer might hang his room with photographs as shown on page 121. A lover of books might collect good book illustrations, perhaps concentrating on one medium such as block printing.

RELATION OF PICTURES TO ROOMS

Pictures for the *living room* of the average family should not be too unusual in composition, color, or subject matter, because this room should be restful, and the pictures therein should not be offensive to friends or to any member of the family. Suitable living-room pictures are landscapes, marines, flower pictures, figure compositions, and portraits. Landscapes are employed on pages 221, 223, and 422; flowers on pages 9, 86, and 120; and portraits on pages 59, 88, and 314.

Dining-room pictures may be gayer because the occupants do not stay there long. Flowers, pleasant still life, and some landscapes such as blossoming trees or streams are suitable for dining rooms. A certain artistic dining room owes its charm to a row of Audubon prints of flowers and birds that form a border around the room about two-thirds of the way up the walls. The wall paper is the same dull soft blue that occurs in the mats of the pictures, so that the effect is not spotty. Page 407 shows how a valuable picture is featured; others are on pages 88, 240, and 277.

A *kitchen* of the old-fashioned type might have a place for a row of brightly colored flower prints.

In a *guest room* it is well to hang pictures with general appeal. Other *bedrooms*, however, may have very personal pictures like photographs. Having only one type of picture in a bedroom helps to unify its effect. See pages 25, 88, 421, and 422.

Children's rooms should have pictures that interest children and also have esthetic merit. It is sometimes possible to find story-telling pictures that meet these qualifications. Children's pictures should be large enough to be seen easily, and should be hung on the children's eye level. Pictures should be changed as the children grow and learn to appreciate better ones. A child's painting is hung in the room shown on page 424.

Elegant rooms provide the proper settings for valuable paintings; many distinguished rooms have been built around beautiful paintings. See the lower picture on page 121. A family portrait is suitable for a conservative room of the finer type, unless the picture is very Modern in feeling.

Simple cottage rooms should have pictures that are consistent with them in subject matter, technique, and framing. Maps, engravings, or reproductions of plain genre pictures by Millet, Breton, Jan Vermeer, Hals, Potter, and others look well in Early American and other simple rooms. Framed samplers and mottoes are also in the same spirit as these rooms.

Combining Pictures. All the pictures in one room should be friendly in texture, scale, subject matter, and color. Prints, water colors, and oils can be combined if they are equally vigorous.

It is well to have some variety in the size of the pictures in a room, without any of them being out of scale. The pictures in an ordinary-sized living room might well range from the size 14 by 18 inches to the size 20 by 24 inches, if there are only three or four pictures in the room. One picture should dominate in size and beauty, and it should have the place of honor, which is usually above the fireplace. Suitable pictures are shown on page 59.

The subject matter of the various pictures in one room should be reasonably concordant. Monotony is not desirable, but neither is great difference such as that between a picture of a forest fire and one of a small child. It is disturbing to see one picture with small houses and figures hung close to another picture with large houses and figures.

Pictures in the same room are likely to be harmonious with each other in color if they are chosen particularly for that room. Usually it is desirable to combine pictures that have different colors dominating. Probably the principal mistake to avoid in color is having some pictures too light or too dark for the others.

FRAMING PICTURES

A frame is usually desirable for any picture because it *stops the movement* in the lines of the picture. The frame also *provides the transition* between the picture and the wall on which it is hung. The size of a picture, the subject matter, movement, color, and the medium in which it is done all affect the choice of a frame.

Plain wood frames may be used for nearly all types of pictures. A variety of simple moldings is available in most art supply stores and in lumber yards. Wood frames are *finished* in their natural colors or stained or painted to suit the pictures they enclose. A frame may repeat the dominating color of the picture in a grayed tone, or it may show an opposite color. Black, white, gray, or dull silver are the usual colors for framing photographs, etchings, or other black-and-white prints; however, in certain rooms something striking like vermilion lacquer is suitable.

Unusual materials such as plastics, mirror, or metals are sometimes employed for framing pictures. Attractive frames are shown on pages 61 and 25.

Oil paintings require heavier frames than other pictures, because the canvas and the paint suggest weight. A dull gilt frame is the traditional choice for an oil painting, but painted or natural wood frames are ordinarily employed today. As a rule, neither mats nor glass are used in framing oils.

Water colors and all other pictures made on paper are usually glazed for protection. One should be careful to obtain a good quality of entirely colorless glass, as an objectionable greenish cast is common. Frames for all paper pictures are usually made from fairly narrow moldings.

Subjects that suggest strength, like buildings, peasants, men, or animals, require heavier frames than pictures of more delicate subjects such as children or flowers. Strong colors in pictures call for heavier frames than weak colors, and diagonal lines require heavier frames than placid horizontals.

Substitutes for frames are also used. A picture that does not need a frame can be fastened to the glass with special clamps at the top and bottom by which it can also be hung. Photographs or prints may be matted and put side by side behind a long glass strip which is supported by a molding nailed to the wall.

Mounts or Mats. Water colors and prints of all types are usually mounted on mats before framing. Oil paintings are sometimes mounted, but this is not a general custom. When a picture is hung against a patterned wall paper, a wide mount is usually necessary. A mat also improves a picture that is crowded with many objects and has little background, or one that has much movement and carries the eye too abruptly to the frame.

The *color* of a mat may be white, a neutral tone lighter than the frame, slightly darker than the lights in the picture, or a more uncommon color, such as dark brown, Tuscan red, black or silver, depending on the room and the picture. See pages 120 and 259.

A mat may be covered with a *fabric* drawn tightly over it and held in place on the back of the mat with quick-drying household cement procurable in tubes. The best fabrics are grass cloth, raw silk, pongee, shantung, homespun linen, and velvet. Any appropriate fabric with interesting texture can be used.

Unusual materials such as marbleized wall paper, wall board, leatherette, thin wood, cork, mirror, metal, or matting would make appropriate mats for certain pictures and certain rooms. See page 171.

The *size* of the mat depends upon the size and type of the picture, upon the space where it is to be hung, and upon the scale of the furnishing in the whole room. A picture that is a horizontal rectangle should have the narrowest margin at the top, medium margins at the sides, and the widest margin at the bottom. An upright rectangle has the medium margin at the top, the narrowest at the sides, and the widest at the bottom. A square picture usually has the same margin at the top and sides and a wider one at the bottom. A 4-inch top margin on a mat for a water color about 16 by 20 inches is reasonable. The tendency is now to use a large mat in order to increase the size of the framed picture. Since a wall is such a large area decorators consider that only large pictures have any architectural significance.

It is helpful to study the mats and frames on the pictures at contemporary exhibits, although it should be realized that the aim of the picture gallery is to display the pictures as advantageously as possible under crowded conditions. The home, on the other hand, employs pictures merely as notes in interior decoration for the purpose of enriching the total effect.

HANGING PICTURES

Pictures should not usually be hung just to fill up empty wall spaces, for unfilled areas are not undesirable. A picture should be hung over and close to some definite article or articles of furniture to build up a composition, uniting the wall and the furniture. On page 24 the upper room shows the right way of hanging pictures and the lower room shows the wrong way. Pictures are hung incorrectly if the result is a line of pictures above and a line of furniture below. However, unity is promoted if the upper lines of all the pictures are about even. Pictures should be hung low, not above the eye level of a standing person.

Small pictures are usually hung in groups so that the total effect is in scale with the furniture. For example, one or two rows of prints would look well above a long, low chest or a sofa but a single print would not be usable there. See page 421. All the pictures in a group should be related in color and subject matter. It is usually desirable to leave less space between the pictures than the width of the pictures themselves. Sometimes an inconspicuous textile or paper can serve as a background for a group of small pictures. Pictures should not be hung in step-up fashion because this makes the arrangement more noticeable than the pictures themselves. Small pictures like silhouettes are unfortunately often hung near the fireplace, which is entirely unrelated to them in scale.

Pictures should be hung as flat as possible so that they will seem like a part of the wall. If the screw eyes are placed near the top of a frame it will usually hang flat. It is best to hang pictures blind with no wire showing at all. If a picture must he hung from the molding, it is well to have two hooks, one on each end of a long wire that passes across the back of the picture through two screw eyes. In this way the picture can be easily adjusted and the triangle of wire avoided. The hooks and wires can be painted to match the wall so that they will be inconspicuous.

During the Victorian period a great many pictures of all sizes were hung in the same room; unfortunately some of the older generation even now continue this fashion, which is illustrated on page 101. Ordinarily one important picture and possibly two somewhat smaller ones are sufficient in a living room. See page 59.

QUESTIONNAIRE FOR THE STUDY OF A PICTURE

General Questions

1. What are the name and nationality of the artist?
2. When did he live?
3. Was his era a period of peace or war?
4. What were the great problems of his time?
5. What were his circumstances?
6. What is the name of this picture?
7. Is this a typical picture by the artist, and, if so, in what respects?
8. What is the artist trying to express?
9. Is the artist's idea a fundamental one?
10. Is the artist trying to further a cause?
11. Is the artist trying to stimulate and please?
12. Will this picture make the observer more appreciative of his surroundings?
13. What mood does the picture suggest?
14. What emotional effect does the picture have upon you?
15. Does the picture hold your interest, give you a new experience, challenge you?
16. Would you like to see this picture often?
17. Would you like to own this picture or a copy of it?
18. Does color or form create the mood of this picture?
19. Does the subject matter create the mood?
20. Is subject matter or design emphasized?
21. Are subject matter and design satisfactorily blended?
22. Is this picture Modern in its treatment?
23. Is it impressionistic? academic?
24. Is it primarily a decorative design?
25. Is this picture an accurate reflection of nature?
26. Has nature been modified for esthetic reasons?
27. Is there distortion of natural aspects?
28. If so, does it intensify feeling, or aid design?
29. Is this a non-objective painting?
30. Is it abstract? to what extent? in all parts?
31. Is this a water color, an oil painting, a drawing, or a print?
32. Is this an original or a reproduction?
33. What is the approximate value of this picture?

Questions Concerning the Plastic Elements

General Questions
  1. Which element is emphasized?

Line
  1. What are the main lines in the framework of the picture?
  2. Are there strong horizontal lines for a base?
  3. Are there outlining lines or accenting lines?
  4. Are there diagonals to increase movement?

Pattern
  1. Do the lights hold together in a pleasing pattern? Do the darks hold together?
  2. Is it a good pattern if the picture is turned upside down?

Volume
  1. Do the objects appear solid?
  2. Are the volumes placed with regard to tension?

Space
  1. Does the picture show deep space, shallow space, or both, with intermediate space?
  2. Is the effect of distance given by perspective lines, change of value, or change in the size of objects?
  3. Is there plenty of room for all the objects in the picture in the depth of space indicated?

Light and Shade
  1. Is there an effect of light from the sun or from a lamp? Do the shadows fall naturally?
  2. Is there a vibrating play of light all through the picture?

Color
  1. Is the color cool or warm, rich or dull, bold or timid?
  2. What is the dominating color? What is the secondary color?
  3. Is the color effect broken and impressionistic?
  4. Is there a decorative flat use of color?
  5. Does each color appear in more than one place?
  6. Are warm colors excluded from the distance?

Texture
  1. Are the natural textures copied?
  2. Is the same texture used all over the picture?
  3. Is rough texture used for emphasis?
  4. Is texture variation used to suggest space?

Questions Concerning Principles of Design

Proportion
1. Does the whole canvas have good proportion?
2. Are the main divisions of the picture well spaced?

Emphasis
1. Where is the center of interest? How is it emphasized?
2. Has anything in the picture been subordinated? by position, size, or color?
3. What line movement is emphasized? horizontals, verticals, diagonals, curves?

Rhythm
1. Is there a feeling of continuous line movement in this picture? where?
2. Has it the rhythm of regular repetition?
3. Has it radiating rhythm?

Balance
1. Is one half of the picture heavier than the other, either from side to side or from top to bottom?
2. What kind of balance is obtained? by what means?

Repetition
1. Has any line or form been repeated?
2. Have colors been repeated?

Questions Concerning Use as Home Decoration

1. What sort of home, if any, would welcome this picture?
2. What decorative idea may prevail in the room where this picture hangs?
3. Is this picture best suited to a living room, a dining room, a bedroom, or a study?
4. Would the color scheme of the picture provide a good start for the color scheme of a room?
5. What texture would you expect in the rugs, walls, furniture, and curtains in the room which contains this picture?
6. Would this picture look well in daylight? in artificial light?
7. What sort of picture would look well with this one?
8. How should this picture be framed?
9. Over what piece of furniture might this picture be hung?

PROBLEMS

A sufficient number of problems are listed so that choices may be made.

1. Visit artists' studios to see local work.
2. Visit a contemporary exhibition. Report on this experience.
3. Analyze pictures for esthetic quality according to the questionnaire in this chapter.
4. Report on an article in some current magazine about an artist and his work.
5. Select pictures suitable for certain rooms shown in photographs.
6. Select a good reproduction. Plan a room to suit it.
7. Write a criticism of the selection and hanging of pictures in a specific room. Draw a diagram to illustrate.

READING REFERENCES

BARNES, ALBERT C. *Art in Painting.* Harcourt, Brace, 1937.

BOSWELL, PEYTON, JR. *Modern American Painting.* Dodd, Mead, 1939.

CAIRNS, HUNTINGTON, and WALKER, JOHN. *Masterpieces of Painting from the National Gallery of Art.* Random House, 1944.

CHENEY, SHELDON W. *Expressionism in Art.* Liveright, 1934.

CHENEY, SHELDON W. *Primer of Modern Art.* Boni and Liveright, 1924.

CRAVEN, THOMAS. *A Treasury of Art Masterpieces.* Simon and Schuster, 1939.

DEHN, ADOLPH A. *Water Color Painting.* Studio, 1940.

GORDON, JAN. *Modern French Painters.* Lane, 1936.

KENT, ROCKWELL. *World Famous Paintings.* Wise & Co., 1939.

KISTLER, ALINE. *Understanding Prints.* Associated American Artists, 1936.

METROPOLITAN MUSEUM OF ART. *Masterpieces at the Metropolitan Museum.* Studio, 1945.

MUNRO, THOMAS. *Great Pictures of Europe.* Tudor, 1934.

PAGANO, GRACE. *Contemporary American Painting.* Duell, Sloan, and Pearce, 1945.

VELÁSQUEZ CHÁVEZ, AUGUSTÍN. *Contemporary Mexican Artists.* Covici, 1937.

Paul Cézanne, the French leader of post-impressionism, painted the picture above entitled *L'Estague*. He sought to portray fundamentals in landscape, not fleeting impressions made by changing lights and shadows. This picture is pleasing esthetically as well as in subject matter. *Courtesy the Art Institute of Chicago.*

In this oil painting of his house, Henry Lee McFee, an outstanding American painter, has attained an effect that is natural and understandable along with high esthetic value.

The *Young Girl at an Open Half-Door* was painted by Rembrandt Van Rijn, one of the great old masters. Its beauty lies partly in its composition, lighting, fine technique, and expressiveness. *Courtesy the Art Institute of Chicago.*

Eugene Speicher's modern American portrait *Lilya* has decided contrast in lines and values. The technique is effective; notice that emphasis is obtained by painting the face more clearly than the rest of the picture. *Courtesy Cincinnati Art Museum.*

Diego Rivera's *Flower Festival* shows a typical subject and typical treatment by this great Mexican painter. The distribution and balance of the light and dark masses are particularly fine. *Courtesy the Museum of Modern Art.*

Thomas Benton, a contemporary American artist, painted the strong picture *The Meal* which is shown below. Note the rhythmic curved-line movement.
Courtesy Whitney Museum of American Art.

The Gulf Stream was painted by Winslow Homer, an early American artist. This water color has interesting subject matter as well as esthetic merit.
Courtesy the Metropolitan Museum of Art.

John S. Curry's *The Tornado* is a forceful contemporary picture. The subject matter and the art elements contribute to the total effect. Episodes from the American scene constitute appropriate subject matter for American artists. For home decoration they should replace the meaningless English pictures of fox hunts. *Courtesy the Hackley Art Gallery.*

Grant Wood, an American painter of the twentieth century, painted the Iowa landscape above, in a decorative manner. The natural forms are simplified and organized into a pleasing rhythmic composition of curved lines. Interesting variety occurs in the patterns and textures employed. *Courtesy Society of Liberal Arts, Joslyn Memorial.*

In this oil painting *The Jungle* by Henri Rousseau, a French painter of the late nineteenth century, the landscape material is treated decoratively. This is the artist's conception of the lush vegetation and the law of the jungle. Every leaf is painstakingly painted, yet the composition is a unit. *Courtesy the Art Institute of Chicago.*

Lyonel Feininger, an American painter of abstractions, has a suggestion of subject matter in the dynamic *Sidewheeler* pictured above. Movement is procured with diagonals and graded planes which are organized so that there are tension and thrust among them. This is a straight-line composition except for the curves at the center of interest.
Courtesy Detroit Institute of Arts.

The room below was planned around the large semi-abstract painting by Matisse. All else is subordinate to the picture; no patterned fabrics are used. Noteworthy items are the beautiful table top, comfortable chairs, and indirect light fixture. *Courtesy Samuel Marx.*

Water-color technique is well illustrated in this painting of begonias by an American artist, Charles Demuth. Note the loose, free way the paint is handled and the sparkling contrasts. A personal variation in technique is the blotted effect in some areas in this picture.
Courtesy the Art Institute of Chicago.

The picture of magnolias below painted by the author shows a careful, studied, semi-decorative way of painting flowers with oil paints. See page 9. This picture now belongs to the Crown Princess of Norway.

CHAPTER 23

RENTED ROOMS

The purpose of this chapter is to provide handy information for those who live in dormitories, sorority houses, or in any rented rooms. Most of this material is presented in its general aspects elsewhere in this book but is here applied to the specific problems of procuring comfort, personality, and beauty in one room at small cost.

DORMITORY ROOMS

Students occupying rooms in dormitories or sorority houses should voice their opinions about their buildings and facilities to the proper authorities in order that future dormitories may meet the needs of students to the greatest extent possible. Architects should be informed that ample *daylight* and *ventilation* are more important to students than architectural style. Some features that are needed are *roof porches* for sun bathing and large *screened porches* for outdoor living. *Larger closets* containing ample shelf space are urgently needed; the supplementary wall board wardrobes that are necessary in many rooms spoil their appearance.

Most students want some kind of a *pin-up place* on their walls which they can puncture with pins and tacks at will. In building a dormitory or sorority house a strip of cork or a soft board about a foot wide can be set into the plaster at the eye level on all the walls in each room. This board should be painted the same color as the plaster. In a finished building a flat, softwood molding affixed to the walls about 6 feet from the floor would be a great improvement over the usual high picture molding, which is hard to reach.

Rooms occupied by women students should have *drying rods* on which to hang wet hose and undergarments which are too precious to hang in a common laundry room. In suite bathrooms, overhead bars above the tub or shower are advisable. See page 174. A shelf with pull-out drying apparatus underneath is convenient.

Dormitory rooms are *living rooms* as well as sleeping rooms; therefore the bedroom aspects should be minimized. This is easily done if beds without visible frames are used. See page 422. In dormitories or sorority houses where the usual conspicuous bed frames are supplied, a petition to the authorities may accomplish the substitution of hidden bed frames known as Hollywood beds. Beds on such frames look like couches and can be placed parallel to walls, covered with a medium or dark spread, and supplied with large box cushions, thereby creating a sitting-room effect. A washable wall finish or a 4-foot band or dado is desirable where couch or sofa beds are used.

Personality in the appearance of an institutional room is desirable. Individuality is expressed by personal possessions and hobbies, which must be arranged to look orderly, uncluttered, and clean. Since there is usually no place in a dormitory room to hang up trophies, pictures, and souvenirs except on a high picture molding ingenuity should be exercised in providing a place. Small bulletin boards are usually inadequate. Large composition board, obtainable at lumber yards, can be cut to fit a wall space and hung from the picture molding. A tennis net can be hung from the picture molding to hold photographs. Hanging shelves are useful for books and hobbies where floor space is limited.

Students should usually decorate their rooms as soon as they are definitely located before study and activities take all their time. They should not, however, buy their furnishings until they reach the campus and see their rooms.

A woman student should consider her college room a valuable opportunity to gain experience in expressing herself and achieving a good-looking home-like effect. She should be willing to take the time and effort to do a thoughtful job, because this experience is valuable for a potential home maker.

Planning the Room

Consider the *architecture* and *decoration* of the dormitory.
Consider the *style* of the furniture in your room.
Select the *theme or mood* to express in your room.
Plan the *color scheme* to suit the room as well as yourself.
Determine *what articles* of furnishings are needed.
Make a tentative *budget* of costs.

When planning the limited decoration that is possible in a dormitory room, the *style* of the furniture which it contains sometimes affects the choice. For example, with Early American furniture, fabrics and accessories of the same period should usually be employed. If the furniture is of no definite style, the theme selected for the room and the future use of the articles purchased should determine their character.

The following terms may suggest some *theme* for the room decorations which could be adopted if it suits the personality of the owner: art, photography, cinema, drama, dance, sports, fashions, travel, stamps, aeronautics, army, navy, China, South Pacific Islands, tropics, gardens, or flower arrangement.

The *color* of the walls, wood trim, and furniture of a dormitory room contribute the fixed elements in the color scheme. In a small room it is not well to add more than one color to those already there, but several values and intensities of the chosen color may be used to give variety. For example, the rugs, curtains, and bedspread may be related blues. In the small accessories, however, other bright colors are possible. In a larger room occupied by several persons, a two-color or a three-color scheme of related or contrasting colors would be suitable. One student's bedspread, curtain, and scatter rug might be green and across the room the other student's might be yellow.

Interesting variation in *texture* can be secured, since several fabrics will be used. The texture of the wall and the furnishing should affect the choice of textures in fabrics. Whereas with mahogany furniture a silk or satin bedspread might be appropriate, with maple, oak, or pine furniture, a corduroy, novelty cloth, desert cloth, Osnaburg, or other cotton bedspread would be more suitable. A duplicate of the bedspread could be split for window draperies, if desired. See page 422.

Not more than one *patterned fabric* should be used in a small room. Plaids and stripes are safe and usually interesting. Since opportunities for originality in dormitory decoration are few, it is important to do something striking with the draperies, such as overlapping very full ones or hanging them from ceiling to floor. Possible substitutes for draperies are Venetian blinds or porch blinds of bamboo or split reed; however, drapery may be used with such blinds.

Room 1

For two modern art students who are gay and daring.
Rug. Grass or fiber in natural color.
Curtains. Venetian blinds or bamboo roller blinds.
Bedspreads. One vermilion and one chartreuse corduroy.
Beds. Frames discarded, box springs on hidden frames.
Chairs. Two colorless plastic chairs with webbing seats.
Accessories. Small abstract sculpture. A rubber plant.
Pictures. Reproductions of abstract paintings. Cartoons.
Lamps. Modern geometric shapes.
Waste basket. Plastic cylinder.

Room 2

For a demure student with an interest in ancestors.
Curtains. Full ruffled Swiss criss-crossed, hung to floor.
Bedspread. Quilt, white, green, and rose-red, family tree pat-
  tern featuring black sheep among branches.
Slip cover for chair. Calico with white dots on rose-red.
Ottoman or footstool. Like the chair.
Pictures. Groups of old costume plate pictures framed in white.
  Family coat of arms.
Reproductions of very old family photographs in old-fashioned
  frames. Miniatures.
Dressing table. Ruffled skirt of white dotted Swiss.
Flower. A rose-red geranium plant.

Room 3

For a blonde who has an interest in motor travel.
Rug. Plain, dark blue rough woven cotton, or Klearflax.
Draperies. Cretonne, hanging from ceiling to floor, landscape
  motifs in white and yellow on a turquoise background.
Bedspread and cushions. Turquoise material of rough texture.
Slip cover for chair. Turquoise material, white welting.
Ottoman. Same as chair.
Pictures. Travel posters and maps. Windshield stickers pasted
  on the mirror. Groups of framed photographs taken on her
  trips perhaps including some national parks foresters.
Accessories. Travel souvenirs.

Room 4

For a girl from Texas who likes rodeos.

Rugs. Mexican saddle blankets in gray and red.

Windows. Loose hanging red-and-white hand-woven Mexican bands, shorter ones over center of windows.

Bedspread. Plain red, textured, novelty cotton cloth.

Chairs. Mexican maguey and cowhide.

Wall decorations. Lariats tied in fancy knots. A cow skull.

Lamps. Hanging lanterns electrified.

Plants. Cacti and succulents.

Sculptures. Cowboys, cattle, or horses. *The End of the Trail.*

Picture. Rodeo photographs.

Room 5

For a belle from the deep South.

Rug. Victorian pattern or plain rose-red velvet.

Draperies and bedspread. A flowery chintz in rose, violet, and white, edged with white ball fringe.

Slip cover. Pencil stripes in pink and pale violet.

Furnishings. A whatnot for holding shells, feathers, souvenirs.

Wall decorations. A hanging shadow box for bouquets. A poster board for photographs of pin-up boys.

Accessories. Incense burner and candlesticks.

Pictures. Sketches of court yards in New Orleans.

Lamp. Old-fashioned glass base, flattering pale pink shade.

Room 6

For a girl whose fiancé is at the U. S. Naval Academy.

Rug. Plain navy blue fiber and wool.

Venetian blinds topped with loops of nautical heavy white rope cord ending with tassels.

Bedspread and deck chairs. Blue and white stripes.

Pillows. Firecracker-red cotton fabric.

Wall decorations. Large framed photo of the cadet. United States flag. Map of the world.

Bulletin board for snapshots of Him and photographs of the fleet.

Waste basket. Dark blue with white anchors.

Lamp base, converted shell case. Shade, white plastic.

Room 7

For a girl with friends in the South Pacific.

Rugs. Hawaiian fiber mats.

Bedspread and draperies. Cretonne with tropical island motifs in blue, green, and yellow.

Accessories. Bamboo screen. Black-and-white toy bear.

Wall decoration. A large poster board for a collection of stamps and interesting envelopes.

Picture. Reproduction of a Gauguin painting of Tahiti.

Fabrics. Woven mats, batiks, tie-dyes, and India prints.

Waste basket. Woven grass basket.

Room 8

For a somewhat dramatic music student.

Rugs. Off-white string rugs.

Bedspread. Lime colored, highly textured rayon.

Draperies. Lime, black-and-white rayon plaid.

Screen. White frame, center covered with sheet music.

Furnishings. White radio, phonograph, and bedside table combination.

Wall decorations. A row of old phonograph records around the wall mirror. Musical instruments hung in a cluster on wall.

Waste basket. White lacquered metal decorated with staff and clef with notes of favorite melody.

Sculpture. A 12-inch figure of a young musician.

Room 9

For a zoology major who likes a laboratory effect.

No rug. No curtains. Venetian blinds.

Bedspread and cushions. Green-and-white striped awning.

Chair. Folding camp chair with same awning.

Wall decorations. A butterfly collection. A large photomural of undersea life and plants, printed in green.

Accessories. Aquarium of tropical fish.

Pictures. A row of reproduction of Audubon bird pictures or a reproduction of Rousseau's *Jungle*.

Sculpture. A collection of small sculptured animals.

Lamp. Adjustable student gooseneck lamp.

Room 10

For an ultra-modern girl from New York City.

Rugs. Rectangular rug of white sheep or goat fur.

Draperies. Yellow taffeta with large white leaf motif.

Bedspread. Plain yellow taffeta with large white monogram.

Hassock. Deeply tufted jade-green velvet.

Pictures. Reproductions of Matisse's *Odalisque* and a Georgia O'Keeffe flower picture, both framed in white.

Accessories. Hanging shelf of beautiful containers for Modern flower arrangements.

Waste basket. White plastic.

Lamp. Jade-green pottery base, white plastic shade.

Sculpture. Brancusi figures or other Modern sculptures.

Room 11

For two girls who are physical-education majors.

Rugs. Strips of pile carpeting the same color as the floor.

Draperies. Kelly-green with large white polka dots.

Bedspread and cushions. Kelly-green rough cotton fabric.

Stools. Hassocks, brown leatherette seats.

Sculptures. *Discus Thrower* or other athletes.

Picture. Reproduction of Bellows' *Skaters* or *Kids Swimming*.

Wall decoration. A tennis net suspended from the picture molding all around the room, hung with photographs.

Accessories. Hanging shelves containing sports trophies.

Room 12

For two home-economics students.

Rugs. Natural-color rush squares or matting.

Drapery. Pleated natural-colored sheer fabric from ceiling molding to floor.

Wall treatment. Natural-colored coarse-textured fabric hung from ceiling to floor to cover one or two windowless walls.

Beds. Brilliant electric-blue corduroy covers and pillows.

Chairs. Natural-colored reed or wicker chairs of good lines.

Furnishings. Hanging shelves with colorful collection of beautiful glass, china, and pottery and a few hopeful pieces in the selected silver patterns. Special table containing electric grill.

AN INEXPENSIVE UNFURNISHED ROOM
FOR TWO WOMEN

Selection of Room

General considerations in the selection of a room are price, nearness to transportation and a shopping center, kind of neighborhood, quiet, laundering facilities, and safety from fire and intrusion. Considerations that apply to specific rooms are the location of the bathroom, adequate heat, hot water, ventilation, daylight, and closet space. The condition and colors of the ceiling, walls, wood trim, floor, and light fixtures should be noted; if their condition is poor and the landlord refuses to improve them permission to redecorate should be obtained from him.

Planning the Decorating and Furnishing

Survey the possibilities of the room.

Decide on a theme to fit the room and the personalities of the occupants, such as gay, demure, artistic, or professional.

Select a furnishing plan to fit the theme and the room.

Make a budget, estimating probable costs.

Visit stores, collect samples, and check the budget.

Select a color scheme to fit the room, theme, and occupants. For example, a desirable color scheme for an east room occupied by two young brunette stenographers might consist of dusty-pink walls, ceiling, wood trim, and doors, with dark brown floors and white or natural cotton string rugs, striped or plaid brown-and-white couch covers and slip covers, two white side chairs, a pink or white chest of drawers, and accents of periwinkle blue.

Decorating (Possible for Amateurs)

Ceiling. If the ceiling is not satisfactory, paint it with hot- or cold-water paint over any kind of surface.

Wood Trim and Doors. Paint them with special water paint or with the more durable oil paint in dull or semi-gloss finish if they are not satisfactory. Only one coat of oil paint is necessary if a medium color is chosen, and a quart of paint is usually sufficient. Sub-turpentine can be used to thin oil paint if it gets too thick. Kerosene or gasoline will clean oil-paint brushes. A 2-inch brush from the dime store is usually adequate.

Walls. If the walls are not satisfactory they can be improved by means of paint or wall paper. Paint dealers give directions for preparing walls and applying the paint or wall paper. Either one can be applied by amateurs with surpisingly good results. Certain hot- or cold-water paints can be applied over wall paper, paint, or wood, and they are comparatively inexpensive. Flat oil paint is more durable but it costs more and cannot be applied so quickly.

Wall paper for a small room can be obtained for a few dollars. Solid colors are easiest to use but they show imperfect surfaces more than patterned wall papers. A flowery bedroom type of design should be avoided; one stronger in character with stripes, plaids, or dots is preferable. Prepasted wall papers and washable wall papers are now obtainable.

Floor. First the floor should be well cleaned. If it is unsatisfactory it should be painted with a good floor enamel. With a large rug, naturally only the edges need be painted.

Furnishings

In the low price range the choice is usually limited to unpainted new furniture or to second-hand furniture. In the *unpainted furniture* two types are available now, simple Modern or the turned-leg cottage style. One or the other of these styles should be used exclusively.

With second-hand furniture a period effect can often be created. Neo-classic, Victorian, and Empire reproductions and adaptations are not uncommon in second-hand stores. Interesting old-fashioned pieces can sometimes be found; others can frequently be cut down or simplified. The old finish can be removed with paint remover or with household ammonia and steel wool; however, it is often possible to apply oil paint over the old finish.

A new bed or beds suitable for a sitting room should be purchased first. The latest forms of folding spring-mattress combinations should be investigated. One model can be converted into a seat by raising one end somewhat like a hospital bed. Double day beds are also available. Some studio couches consist of two separate single mattresses which are combined into a sofa for the daytime. A standard twin-size mattress-and-box-spring on legs is desirable. Some box springs and mattresses are upholstered in good-looking fabrics at the factory so that they may be left uncovered.

An old dresser can be used, for the legs and mirror can be removed and the mirror hung separately. Painting them light improves them. A table should be selected to fit the size and feeling of the room. A kitchen table and two kitchen chairs, painted to suit, are satisfactory. Two comfortable chairs are also necessary.

A large grass, fiber, cotton, or felt rug is inexpensive and satisfactory. New offerings in rugs should be examined. String and other small rugs, even carpet remnants, may be used.

Fabrics should be chosen which carry out the theme and add life, cheer, and color. For practical purposes the couch cover may be darker and heavier than the curtains. Draperies may be made from fabrics like denim, desert cloth, gingham, or men's shirting which are dense enough for draw curtains, making roller shades unnecessary. Plain, unbleached muslin may be decorated with many tassels sewed in rows.

Two plain, adjustable floor or table lamps are needed. If a plain white shade, such as a plastic, is not obtainable, a decorated shade can be simplified by painting it all over with oil paint or covering it with fabric.

Desirable table equipment is sometimes procurable at the dime stores. For constant use it is best to buy plain white dishes and plain clear or white glassware and provide bright colored linens. However, Chinese dishes or undecorated colorful dishes may be added for salads and desserts and colorful glasses are festive. Knives, forks, and spoons may well be plain plated silver or may be steel with bone handles if they fit the theme. No table cover is ever necessary if the table top is good looking; if it is not, fiber place mats, or strips of brightly colored cotton or linens are desirable at meal times. See page 104.

Pictures which have personal significance can be framed inexpensively by inserting them into the frames of pictures from the dime stores. If the pictures are small, several of similar subjects should be hung together over a piece of furniture. See page 421. For flower containers fish bowls, mixing bowls, and tin dishes intended for the kitchen are often more desirable than regular flower vases. The person who does not live in a permanent home should buy some containers and other accessories of metal rather than the breakable pottery or glass. A blossoming house plant is delightful in a one-room apartment.

AN INEXPENSIVE ALL-PURPOSE FURNISHED ROOM

Planning the Decorating and Furnishing

Evaluate the furnishings, itemizing good and bad points.

Consider the background, walls, ceiling, wood trim, floors.

Decide on a theme to express your own personality.

Select a color scheme.

Plan the means of concealing the kitchen area.

The *kitchen area* must be concealed or the appearance of the room will be hopeless. If possible, plan one entire end or one side of the room for utility, the corner nearest the closet or bathroom for the dressing table, and the corner nearest the sink or bowl for the cooking equipment. Several suggestions for concealing the utility area from the living area follow. Hang two large natural-colored bamboo roller porch shades on screw hooks from the ceiling. Porch shades can also be hung so that the slats are vertical.

Hang a strong fabric in a plain color from the ceiling to the floor on a thick wooden pole or a solid metal rod.

Use a rolling bamboo screen like the one on page 172. Use two triple folding screens about 6 feet high with enough width to conceal the utility area. These screens may be made of Celotex, sized, painted, and nailed to a frame made of 1-inch-by-2-inch strips of wood. Reversible hinges should connect the sections.

Place book shelves 5 or 6 feet high as a semi-partition to hide the utility area.

In selecting a *color scheme* consider the color already in the room. Build a scheme around the colors that are good. For example, if the curtains are a plaid of cream and navy blue, then the entire scheme chosen might be:

Walls, wood trim, and ceiling—cream.

Couch cover—medium-blue denim.

Floor—navy-blue enamel.

Small rugs—cream colored.

Screen—natural bamboo.

Dishes—cream without decoration.

Table linen—dark shrimp-pink.

Two chair slip covers—shrimp-pink glazed chintz.

Whether the room has single or double beds discard the entire bed frame. See pages 9 and 422. Buy or make for each bed a simple stand to support the spring. This frame can be easily made from finished pine 1 inch thick and 4 inches wide to fit the measurements of the spring. Two side pieces, two end pieces, two long pieces for the tops, and four or six pieces of 2 inches by 4 inches by 9 inches for legs are needed. Fasten together with screws, not nails, if possible. Put a metal disk under each leg as a glider. Cover the spring, mattress, and frame with a couch cover to the floor.

If there is a nondescript overstuffed chair, it should have a slip cover. If the straight chairs are ugly, either make quilted slip covers which conceal their backs and seats, or discard them and buy some folding card-table chairs, or porch chairs of simple, good design, or stools.

If there is an ordinary dresser in the room, unscrew the mirror and frame from the dresser and hang the mirror directly on the wall. Try to persuade your landlady to let you saw the legs off the dresser so that it becomes a chest of drawers. A dressing table is obviously not a living-room piece, so put it out of sight. If you need bookshelves buy a few dozen bricks or hollow tiles and several boards as wide as the bricks, paint them all white, and set up the shelves with the bricks as supports; no nails are needed. If the table is ugly, small and inadequate, put it in the cooking area or discard it, and buy a card table or a kitchen table. Have several end tables for comfort. For a coffee table substitute a folding luggage rack and a large tray.

If the rug is ugly in pattern, discard it; perhaps leave the floor bare or paint it a positive color. Otherwise look for remnants of plain carpeting, or grass, matting, string, or American Indian rugs, or any odd rugs that suit the purse and the theme selected.

If the lamp shade is poor, try painting it; however, inexpensive plain new ones are procurable. Use candlelight for conversation and meal time. If the ceiling light fixture is ugly, and the landlord will not remove it, conceal it entirely with a huge inverted drum-shaped shade, made for that purpose.

Everyone should acquire gradually a few accessories of beautiful design expressive of her own personality. They can sometimes be found in Chinese shops, in antique shops, or in gift shops.

Personal taste is evident here, at least in fruit. Such treatment is interesting but is probably somewhat temporary. The padded side and head boards beside the beds are procurable without beds in some shops. Matching chests, cabinets, or dressers should usually stand side by side like these to save space. *Courtesy Rich's.*

The scalloped cornice, the stenciled decoration, and the dark panel behind the desk can be used in almost any room to give additional interest. Note the white rugs, dark floor, dark mesh curtains, novel window shade, and suitable lamps. *Courtesy Celotex Products.*

Above left, a man student's room in International House is expressive of its purpose. It needs well-chosen personal accessories. *Courtesy University of Chicago.*

Above right, a Modern dormitory room for two men gains character by featuring bold texture and bold pattern. The same material for draperies and bedspreads is desirable.

The dormitory room below is occupied by an art student. The student's personal additions do not suit the room, however. Her radio, which was improved by having its legs amputated, is period in character, and her chair is Modern, whereas the desk and other furniture in the room are Early American. The bed corner functions well; the student can recline in bed against the large cushion and control the radio, or read by the adjustable lamp or by daylight. Curtains like the couch cover would have been better. Four cushions are desirable for this couch so that several persons can sit on it. The water colors are suitable in size and well hung. The floor of asphalt tile is easily kept clean; it would have been better without pattern. *Courtesy Louisiana State University.*

In dormitories where it is not permissible to put tacks in walls, broad tape or webbing like the above can be suspended from the molding to hold pictures or other decoration. *Courtesy Lord and Taylor.*

This dormitory has provided good, conservative, period-type furniture; the absence of conspicuous head and foot boards on the bed is desirable. The curtains and rug are pleasing. However, the student has made a poor furniture arrangement. The desk should be at the windows; the bed should not cut off the windows, the most attractive feature of the room. The bed may be pushed into a corner and supplied with four box cushions to make a conversation center. Bed and cushions should have an interesting textured fabric. The two tiny pictures in this room are too small to hang. Evidence of the student's personality is lacking here. *Courtesy University of Chicago.*

This guest room, designed by Dan Cooper, has several ideas which may be borrowed for inexpensive furnishing. Instead of the customary curtains, buy enough fabric to cover an entire wall, windows and all. All the fabrics used here are beautiful, with emphasis on texture. A bench like this one is a useful substitute for a chair in any room. The lamp by the sofa is a desirable size and shape. The cornice board on the window wall effectively conceals the source of artificial light. *Courtesy Rich's, Atlanta.*

The accessories in this room reveal the personality of the owner and his interest in the Southwest. A college student could bring such articles as the sculpture, stool, picture, and Indian blanket to decorate a dormitory room. *Courtesy Sternberg-Davis.*

Corner shelves like these are useful in dividing a room into various functional areas. The living-room area is indicated by the large oval rug. Notice the plants in the dining corner. *Courtesy Congoleum-Nairn Company.*

This all-purpose room or one-room apartment has a niche for the beds and one for the cooking equipment. They can be shut off with folding partitions, which are functional and good looking, particularly with Modern furniture. The composition floor covering too suggests the Modern style. The furniture is arranged in definite groups. The Duncan Phyfe table is well placed at the window; the Chinese nest of tables is consistent. The conversation group is concentrated around one of the white rugs. The chair and hassock in the foreground are well tailored and comfortable. The study or writing group is separate. A living-room atmosphere prevails. *Courtesy Newcastle Products.*

Dan Cooper has designed the Pakto furniture in the two pictures above, which can be readily demounted and made into a pack. It can be combined into units of different sizes and shapes depending upon available space. Even the packing boxes become part of pieces of furniture when not on the move. This furniture is a boon for those whose work requires them to move constantly. *Courtesy Dan Cooper.*

Gilbert Rohde designed the group below at the left. It includes the most compact folding table yet devised, which is only 8 inches wide when closed. Those who live in small apartments appreciate such space-saving furniture. The bentwood chairs are light, comfortable, low priced, and remarkably strong, for there are no joints to come unglued at the back of the seats. The flower arrangement should have been tall, dramatic, and Modern. *Courtesy Kroehler Manufacturing Company.*

A dormitory room for a Service woman pictured below at the right fortunately has walls of composition board on which thumbtacks can be freely used. The furniture is well designed, the bedspread and picture well chosen. With such a plain background, lively colorful curtains and a patterned rug are desirable. *Courtesy Federal Housing Authority.*

PART FIVE

HISTORY OF DECORATIVE MOVEMENTS

CHAPTER 24

THE RENAISSANCE MOVEMENT

Those decorative movements will be considered here that have had the most effect on European and American furnishings. The oldest influence, but an unimportant one, is the ancient *Egyptian*, which goes back to 4000 B.C. Tomb excavations and mural paintings have revealed beautiful, well-made furniture decorated with motifs of lotus, palms, swans, animals, and the sun.

The most important decorative influence that the world has known is the *Classic style* which originated in *Greece* and reached its height there during the fifth century B.C. This style is the basis for the traditional architecture and decoration of western Europe. The Greeks sought to express divinity through beauty and succeeded in creating the finest sculpture and architecture of all time. Their decorative arts, including their furniture and pottery, were also beautiful in form and ornamentation. The Classic style was continued in the *Roman Empire*, which conquered Greece in the second century B.C. and endured until A.D. 500.

During the Middle Ages (the Dark Ages), Byzantine, Oriental, and Romanesque influences existed but were far less important than the *Gothic style*, which culminated in the magnificent cathedrals of France and spread all over Europe. The Gothic castles were sparsely furnished with large oak furniture and tapestries.

Between the fifteenth and eighteenth centuries inclusive three great decorative movements spread over Europe. Since all are based on the Classic styles of Greece and Rome some writers consider them all *Renaissance*, but in this book the *Baroque*, *Rococo*, and *Neo-Classic* styles are treated separately. Each movement is considered in its international aspects.

427

THE GREAT DECORATIVE MOVEMENTS

HISTORICAL SUMMARY

	RENAISSANCE	BAROQUE	ROCOCO
	1400–1600, *originated in Italy,* *based on the Classic*	*1550–1750,* *developed in Italy,* *based on Renaissance*	*1715–1775,* *developed in France,* *based on Baroque*
Italy.........	Began in Florence...........	Michelangelo, Bernini,.........	Copied from French, Venice the center
France.......	Francis I, 1515–1547,.......	Louis XIV, 1643–1715,.........	Régence, 1715–1723,
	to Louis XIII, 1610–1643	Charles Lebrun, artist	Louis XV, 1723–1774
Spain........	From Italy about 1500,......	From Italy about 1600,........	French influence
	Moorish influence	Oriental influence	
England.......	Tudor....................	Restoration..................	Chippendale, 1718–1779
	Henry VIII, 1509–1547;	Charles II, 1660–1685;	(Later-Victorian-Rococo
	Elizabeth, 1558–1603	James II, 1685–1688	
	Jacobean:	Dutch influence:	
	James I, 1603–1625;	Wm. and Mary, 1688–1702;	
	Charles I, 1625–1649	Anne, 1702–1714;	
	Commonwealth, 1649–1660	Chippendale, 1718–1779	
United States	Early American, 1620–1700,.. influenced by English provinical furniture	Colonial, 1700–1780:.......... Am. William and Mary; American Queen Anne; Wm. Savery, Philadelphia; John Townsend, Newport; John Goddard, Newport	American Chippendale, American Louis XV (Later-Victorian-Rococo)

NEO-CLASSIC

	POMPEIIAN	EMPIRE
	1775–1800, *inspired by excavations* *at Pompeii and Herculaneum*	*1800–1830,* *originated in France,* *dictated by Napoleon*
Italy..........	Influenced by French........	Copied from French
France........	Louis XVI, 1774–1793.......	The Directory, 1795–1804; Empire (Napoleon), 1804–1815; Jacques Louis David, artist
Spain.........	Influenced by French.......	Influenced by French
England.......	Late Georgian.............. George III, 1760–1810; Adam; Sheraton; Hepplewhite	Regency period, 1810–1820; George IV, 1820–1837
United States	Federal, 1780–1840......... American Louis XVI; American Hepplewhite; American Sheraton	American Directory, American Empire, 1810–1840; Duncan Phyfe, 1768–1854

THE GREAT DECORATIVE MOVEMENTS
DESCRIPTIVE SUMMARY

RENAISSANCE	BAROQUE	ROCOCO
Large (monumental).	Large.	Small.
Symmetrical.	Symmetrical.	Asymmetrical.
Straight lines.	Straight and curved lines.	Only curved lines.
Straight or turned legs, low heavy stretchers.	Cabriole legs. Ball and claw feet.	Cabriole legs. No stretchers. No angles.
Architectural motifs, acanthus, humans, animals.	Classic motifs, shells, lions, acanthus, etc.	Nature motifs, rock and shell, ribbons, Chinese.
Turning, carving, painting.	Carving, veneer, lacquer, ormulu.	Gilding, lacquer, caning, marquetry, ormulu.
Oak, walnut.	Walnut, mahogany, ebony, marble tops.	Walnut, mahogany, fruitwood, rosewood.
Velvets, brocades, damasks, cloth of gold. Tapestries.	Damasks, brocatelles, velvets, needlepoint, leather, Gobelin tapestries. Oriental and French rugs.	Damasks, brocades, satins, taffetas, moirés. Toiles de Jouy. French rugs.
Crimson, gold, green, blue.	Red, yellow, blue, green.	Soft, light neutral colors.
Chests, cabinets, refectory tables, beds, chairs, stools.	Cabinets, tables, chairs, four-poster beds, clocks.	Commodes, desks, tables, consoles, beds, sofas, chairs.
Formal dignity, sincerity, strength, repose,	Massive grandeur, elegance, elaboration, variety.	Luxurious ease, intimacy, femininity, gaiety.

NEO-CLASSIC

POMPEIIAN	EMPIRE
Small.	Large (architectural).
Symmetrical.	Symmetrical.
Straight lines and ovals.	Straight or flaring lines.
Straight tapering legs.	Straight or flaring legs.
Ovals, urns, cupids.	Classic and military motifs.
Fluting, painting, inlay.	Veneering, metal appliqués, carving.
Mahogany and satinwood.	Mahogany, satinwood, fruitwoods.
Silk, cotton, needlework.	Hard-textured fabrics. Leather.
Delicate, gay, pastel colors.	Deep, rich, primary colors.
Cabinets, consoles, sideboards, four-poster beds.	Round pedestal tables, boat beds, Récamier sofas, Greek chairs.
Dignity, delicacy, femininity, comfort.	Massive grandeur, solidity, masculinity, discomfort.

THE RENAISSANCE

Italy. Fifteenth and sixteenth centuries.

Spain. Sixteenth century.

France. 1500–1643.

England. 1509–1660.

Tudor. {Henry VIII. 1509–1547.
       {Elizabeth.   1558–1603.

Jacobean. {James I.   1603–1625.
          {Charles I. 1625–1649.

Commonwealth. 1649–1660.

United States. 1625–1700.

English Colonial. (Early American.) 1625–1700.

Spanish Colonial. Seventeenth and eighteenth centuries.

The Renaissance was a revival of Classic civilization, after Greek and Roman art, literature, and science had been neglected during the thousand years of the Middle Ages. It was one of the world's outstanding periods in the development of thought, as Man emerged from a long period of misery and subjugation and understood his right to earthly pleasure. The new interest in humanism and realism was integrated with art consciousness and was expressed in the architecture, sculpture, painting, and minor arts of the time.

There were several reasons for this rebirth, the most immediate being the flight of the Byzantine Greek scholars to Italy when Constantinople fell in 1453. Their veneration of Classic art inspired others to study the philosophy and government of the Greeks and Romans so they learned that the ancients had lived better and happier lives than they. Other important causes of the Renaissance were the Crusades, the invention of printing, the art patronage of wealthy Italian families, and the cultural activity of the Church of Rome under Pope Nicholas V.

The Renaissance was not alone a rebirth of the classicism of *Greece* and *Rome*, for *Oriental* and *Gothic* influences were also factors in its development. The Renaissance began in Italy and achieved its highest development there, but it spread to all western Europe, where it had a strong effect on France, Germany, Spain, and England and prevailed for more than a century. Most of the period houses and the period furniture that are used today are descendants of the Renaissance.

ITALY

Historical Background.   Italy became prosperous because the trade between the Orient and western Europe passed through its northern cities.   Prosperity, contact with the Orient, and the decrease of religious fervor contributed to the change in thought known as the Renaissance, which began in Florence in 1400 and spread to other Italian cities.   During the Renaissance, Italy was the home of the greatest sculptors, painters, and architects in the world.   Such masters as Michelangelo, Titian, Botticelli, da Vinci, and Bramante did their incomparable work during this time. Powerful Italian families, such as the Medici, Pitti, Borgia, and Vendrimini, employed many architects and artists to build and furnish their magnificent palaces.   The common people of Italy, too, appreciated art and created artistic products for their own use.

Furniture.   As it is only about four hundred years since the height of the Renaissance, we can still study the beautiful furnishings of the time in museums and also in their original settings. Renaissance furnishings were designed by artists to harmonize with the architecture.   Beautiful design and fine workmanship were required by the guilds as well as by the patrons.

The furniture of the height of the Renaissance was massive, stately, and rectangular in contour.   Classic proportions were sought, and many architectural features such as columns, capitals, and cornices were employed.   Usually there were low stretchers near the floor, bracing the legs, which had bracket, scroll, or paw feet.   This furniture was generally decorated with well-designed and well-executed carving.   Characteristic motifs were shields, scrolls, masks, cupids, rosettes, and the acanthus.   Carved furniture was commonly made from walnut, but chestnut and other woods were also used.   See page 441.

The furniture in the very early Renaissance was somewhat primitive.   The chest or cassone was the principal article of furniture in the early part of the period.   It served many different purposes—as a storage box, couch, chair, bench, or trunk when traveling.   Sometimes chests were beautifully decorated by great artists. Several pieces of furniture evolved from chests.   First a drawer was inserted at the bottom of the chest next to the floor.   Then two drawers were made, and doors were substituted for the lid.

Cabinets and chests of drawers developed when legs were added to the low chests. The credenza, or domestic cupboard, is an elevated chest with doors—the forerunner of the modern sideboard. The armoire is another interesting cabinet.

The earliest tables were simple trestle tables; they were followed by refectory tables. Small pedestal tables and wall tables with drawers were also used.

Beds were often placed on platforms. They had high paneled head boards and low foot boards in the earlier stage. Later four posts were added, and finally the posts were made high enough to support testers, from which hung rich fabrics.

Well into the fifteenth century benches, stools, and chests were generally used to sit on. At first chairs were only for the dignitaries, but by the sixteenth century they were in general use. There are several distinct types of chairs. The sgabelli chair, which developed from the simple wooden stool, was used in northern Italy and its neighboring countries. The cross-legged or curule Roman chair developed into the Savonarola chair, which sometimes had many ribs, and also into the ribless Dante chair. These chairs were often covered with tooled leather. The outstanding chair of this period, however, was high-backed and of rectangular structure. It had fine proportions, restrained carved decoration, and beautiful upholstery edged with fringe.

Fabrics. In the earlier Renaissance fabrics the small Byzantine patterns were used. When Italian weavers made their own designs they kept the ogee plan of arrangement but used large patterns of urns and conventionalized flowers. Many of these were made in rich red and gold velvet which was used with gold galloon. Later in the period came a change in design, Venetian cut velvets being made in small geometric or floral all-over patterns in two-color effects. Velvets, brocades, damasks, and cloth of gold were used throughout the Renaissance.

Minor Arts. All articles, utilitarian or decorative, were well designed and perfectly made at this time. Cellini was the master goldsmith and jeweler working in Florence and Rome. The Della Robbia family of sculptors made their famous enameled terra cottas in Florence, and in Venice glassware for service and for decoration was produced and exported.

SPAIN

Historical Background. The Renaissance in Spain began about 1500. It derived from several sources besides the Italian Renaissance. The Moorish masters of the country from A.D. 711 until their conquest in 1492 and their expulsion in 1609 exerted a powerful influence on Spanish art. Characteristics of the Moorish work are colored tile, fine inlay, fine ironwork, geometric design, and rich effects. The Portuguese brought Oriental influences to Spain. Charles V came to Spain from Flanders as ruler of the Holy Roman Empire, bringing with him Flemish workmen, as well as embroideries, tapestries, and other rich furnishings. All these helped to shape the Spanish Renaissance.

Furniture. The Spanish had only a small amount of furniture in their homes. Their early furniture was of a very simple type, with a native flavor which was diminished later when it was combined with Renaissance forms. In this early furniture some oak and chestnut were used, but later the finer pieces were of walnut. The legs of tables, benches, and chairs were straight, spool turned, or spiral turned and splayed, and joined with iron bands. The feet were usually splayed, curled inward, or rounded.

The best furniture was decorated with turning, carving, inlay, polychrome, painting, and gilding. Italian Renaissance motifs and Flemish scrolls were combined with Moorish patterns. Since the Moors were not allowed to use animal or human figures in their designs, they developed geometric motifs to an amazing degree of beauty. It is said that among the Moors in Spain were some of the greatest draughtsmen in the world; their designs continued in use there after the Moors were expelled. Decorative nail heads were sometimes parts of the designs employed on Spanish furniture.

The most common pieces of furniture were tables, benches, chairs, beds, chests, and cabinets. The vargueno was the most characteristic Spanish piece, as it was different from anything produced elsewhere. It consisted of a cabinet on high legs, and had a front that lowered, showing an arrangement of drawers of various shapes, beautifully decorated with inlay, for holding jewelry and valuables. There were handles at either end, so that the cabinet could be taken along in traveling.

Long chests served many purposes, even to hold food. The common chests were placed together and covered with pads to form beds. The marriage chests containing the bride's possessions were greatly prized as they were beautifully decorated, often covered with tooled leather showing the coats-of-arms of both families.

The refectory tables were plain, with planklike tops resting upon plain or carved end pieces. Folding-top tables supported the extra leaf with two pegs that were pulled out. Two small tables were typical—the Moorish taboret, and a metal table with a tile top that was used either outdoors or in.

Benches, stools, ottomans, and chairs of different types were common. A typical Spanish armchair resembled the best Italian chair. It had a rectangular form, with a high back arched at the top and bottom, a high, elaborate front stretcher, and turned posts and side stretchers; it was covered with tooled leather or brocade held in place with large-headed nails. Some chairs had arcaded backs. The Catalonian chair was a simple rush-seated chair, with framework composed entirely of turned spindles; it was painted in bright colors, often vermilion. The scissors chair was the seat of dignity of the Moors.

Beds at first were only mattresses placed on raised platforms; later some heavily draped four-posters were produced.

A peculiarly Moorish development was the use of stamped, painted, gilded leather for upholstery, screens, chests, floor coverings, curtains, cushions, and table covers in the homes, and for wall hangings in palaces and cathedrals. The city of Córdova became famous for its tooled leather, which other communities imitated but could not equal. The Moors had a secret way of treating leather which they had learned from the Egyptians.

Fabrics. The early fabrics of the Spanish Renaissance were Moorish in design, but later the large, florid Italian designs appeared in upholstery and drapery. A certain quilted effect is typically Spanish. Tapestry, brocade, velvet, silk, and cloth of gold were used in various ways.

Ceramics. Tiles were used for floors, dadoes, door and window facings, stairs, niches, and fountains. Heavy earthenware dishes of Spanish majolica combined utility with decorative merit.

FRANCE

Historical Background. The Gothic movement dominated the art expression of France for nearly four centuries. By 1500, however, France was ready to accept a new influence, the Renaissance, which arrived through various agencies. Charles VIII invaded Italy and brought back with him the fashionable style of the Italian Renaissance. Francis I (1515–1547) invited the best Italian architects and artists to France. Two queens of France from the famous Medici family of Florence, and Charles IX, Henry III, and Henry IV (1574–1610), who were princes of Italian and French extraction, helped to introduce the Italian style. The French Renaissance lasted until 1643, the end of the reign of Louis XIII.

Furniture. Changes in the furniture style came quickly although architectural changes were slow. French furniture became somewhat smaller and more domestic, comfortable, varied, and plentiful in the Renaissance period. Walnut took the place of the Gothic oak. The decoration was principally carving, inlay, and gilding. The perfection in the carving was due to the Gothic influence, although the motifs were largely Italian. Columns, cornices, scrolls, acanthus, swags, shields, masks, cartouches, oak and laurel leaves, claws, and fruit were used, but few flowers.

The furniture was very much like the Italian, particularly in southern France. Cupboards began to displace chests. The chairs were particularly good in design at the time of Henry II. The armchairs resembled the Italian, but there were also small chairs with spiraled turnings and upholstered half backs. The tables were long and supported by carved under-sections at the ends. The cabinets were massive and much decorated. The beds, also large, were enshrouded in rich hangings of damask or velvet.

Fabrics. The fabrics, mostly brocades, taffetas, brocatelles, damasks, and velvets, were decorated with large Italian designs, consisting mostly of conventionalized urns and flowers arranged in ogee patterns. Like the designs, the colors of the textiles were bold—red, yellow, green, and blue. Italian weavers settled at Lyons and made it the most important textile center in France. World leadership in the manufacturing of fine fabrics was permanently established by France at this early date.

ENGLAND

Since Renaissance art came to England through Flanders, Spain, France, and the Netherlands, its Classicism arrived there as modified by those countries. The English Gothic also affected the new movement, so that in England a distinct transitional stage preceded the Renaissance. See pages 441 and 442.

The Tudor Period

Renaissance ideas affected King Henry VIII so that he withdrew the Church of England from the Papal Authority and introduced the Renaissance thought and architectural style to England. He hired architects and craftsmen from Italy, France, Flanders, and Germany to build and decorate in the new style. The Italian influence became very prominent at this time, showing particularly in the high, paneled, carved walls, the cornices, the ceilings, and the chimney pieces. Queen Elizabeth enjoyed peace and prosperity and further development of the Renaissance. She imported many German craftsmen, who were responsible for the ungainly bulbous adornments on the table legs and bedposts. See page 85.

The rooms of the Tudor period were large and bare. The furniture was also large, and architectural in line, but it lacked the good proportion, excellent design, and finish of Italian furniture. The native craftsmen had neither the fine taste of the southerners nor their technical ability, and moreover they used the less flexible oak instead of walnut. There were, however, freshness, vigor, and naïveté in the English work.

Carving, of a rather coarse character, was the principal mode of decoration. Gothic motifs such as the linen fold, pointed arch, wheel, grapevine, and Tudor rose continued in use; but the most popular motifs were the acanthus, masks, grotesques, dolphins, human figures, guilloches, strapwork, scrolls, cartouches, geometric figures, columns, and pilasters.

The pieces of furniture were few and of limited variety, as chests served many purposes. The most highly decorated objects were the enormous bedsteads built to accommodate many persons. The elaborate head boards and two great posts at the foot of the beds supported the testers and roofs from which curtains extended to the floor. Mattresses were supported by ropes.

The wood carver gave almost as much attention to carving cupboards as bedsteads. The court cupboard, meaning in French the
short cupboard, was originally a small affair that stood on a side
table. The two pieces were finally joined together, making the
true court cupboard, one of the most interesting types. The court
cupboard held dry food, wine, and candles for the family; the
livery cupboard held such food as bread, butter, and cheese, which
was to be given out as servants' wages. The low hutch or dole
cupboard also held food and was therefore ventilated by means
of an open spindle front. "Hanging" cupboards were not themselves hung, but clothes were hung in them.

Trestle boards were often used instead of the long, narrow
refectory tables. Draw tables were large oblong affairs supported
by heavy legs decorated with enormous melon bulbs. Low
stretchers connected the legs of the tables as foot rests to keep the
diners' feet off the cold, filthy, rush-covered floors. Servants'
tables were lower than other tables.

Backless benches and joint stools were used to sit on. Chairs
were owned only by the rich, as they were regarded somewhat as
thrones. The wainscot chairs had solid wooden backs and seats
and were exceedingly uncomfortable. Dante chairs from Italy
and three-cornered spindle chairs from Scandinavia came into use.

Metals. There was very little hardware on Tudor furniture,
but simple wrought-iron hinges, key plates, and pulls were employed. Wrought-iron lighting fixtures were prevalent. Silver,
pewter, and pottery platters and bowls were receptacles for food.

Fabrics. As England's trade expanded, fabrics were imported
from the Orient. Painted cottons from East India were popular,
the favorite design being the tree of life with its branches, leaves,
flowers, and birds. This motif was copied in crewel embroidery
and block-printed fabrics. Crewel embroideries done by hand in
wool or silk, on cotton or linen, served as curtains and bed hangings. Loose cushions were made for seating furniture, as practically no upholstering was done. Great wall tapestries, highly
prized for warmth as well as for colorful decoration, were imported or were made in England. Henry VIII is said to have had
twenty-six hundred tapestries in his palaces. Richly colored rugs
decorated with conventionalized and abstract forms were imported
from Turkey for the royalty and nobility.

The Jacobean or Stuart Period

The term Jacobean is derived from the Latin form of the name James. Jacobean here refers to the reigns of James I (1603–1625) and Charles I (1625–1649), although it sometimes includes the Commonwealth period (1649–1659) and the Restoration (1660–1689).

The furniture of the Jacobean period was more English than that of the preceding or following periods. Like the Tudor it was made of oak in rather squat, sturdy forms, but it was more plentiful. Turning, both spiral and plain, paneling, carving, painting, marquetry, the application of split turned ornaments such as balusters and lozenges, and applied moldings provided the decoration. The motifs on the furniture were about the same as the Tudor and resembled those of the interior architecture. The melon bulb had now become elongated and was used as part of a balustrade.

The pieces of furniture in use during this period were cupboards, cabinets, Bible boxes, buffets, dressers, chests, hutches, bedsteads, day beds, tables, settles and settees, chairs, forms, stools, and footstools. See pages 441 and 442. The small gate-leg tables were interesting; chairs were lighter and had upholstered seats and backs.

Needlework, the chief occupation of women of leisure, was produced in enormous quantities, particularly the hand-embroidered linens which were employed as bed draperies. Weaving factories were encouraged also. James I established the Mortlake tapestry manufactory with the help of Flemish weavers.

The Commonwealth

The inefficient rule and unpopularity of the Stuart kings and the rise of Puritanism brought about a civil war and the execution of Charles I. Oliver Cromwell, the new director of the Commonwealth, and his followers, the Puritans, hated the luxurious surroundings of the aristocracy, so the contents of the nineteen palaces of Charles I were sold abroad. Cromwellian furniture was chiefly oak and was a severely simplified version of Jacobean furniture without any decoration except turned supports. Although this period was brief (1649–1660) it is particularly interesting to us because it produced the type of furniture that was brought to New England by the Puritan colonists.

UNITED STATES

The English Colonial (Early American)

Historical Background. (1620–1700.) Many of the first settlers in New England came from the lower middle classes of the provinces of England; consequently their homes were like those in rural England. Houses and furniture of this period are called *Early American.* The furniture was modified Renaissance in style and was copied from provincial English Jacobean and Cromwellian furniture. See pages 94, 101, 102, 104, and 441.

Furniture. The furniture was usually rectangular with turned, flat-carved, or molded decoration. Oak, pine, and many other native woods were used. Often the furniture was painted or stained black or red.

The furniture pieces consisted mainly of chests, cupboards, beds, desks, stools, forms, benches, and tables. The early wainscot chair with a solid back was discontinued because of its weight, but the turned spindle type was satisfactory and developed into the so-called Carver, Brewster, and Windsor types. The most common tables were the rectangular, gate-leg, butterfly, and chair tables. Beds were usually of the four-poster type, with trundle beds and cradles for the children.

Fabrics. Textiles were very important in the early Colonial houses and many were imported. The women wove and wrought table carpets, cupboard cloths, chair and stool pads, and curtains. Turkeywork, petit point, stumpwork, and crewelwork decorated the fabrics. Beds that stood in the parlors often displayed beautiful coverlets, valances, and curtains.

Metals. The early inventories list a great many silver, pewter, brass, and ironwork articles, although very few of them have survived. Wrought iron was generally used for kitchen utensils, irons, firedogs, firebacks, firepans, tongs, and pokers.

Dishes. For the first half century dishes were made of wood. Later common pottery was obtained from England, and porcelains and glass were imported from the Orient.

The Spanish Colonial

This furnishing is described in the section on American provincial types on page 95. It is based on Renaissance forms.

PROBLEMS

A sufficient number of problems are listed so that choices may be made.

(When tracing pictures from books or periodicals always trace through a sheet of celluloid, to protect the book or periodical.)

1. Trace pictures of Renaissance chests from Italy, France, Spain, England, and the United States, and arrange on a chart.
2. Visit a museum to study Renaissance and related furniture.
3. Draw or trace a costume of this period, in order to observe the relationship between clothing and furnishings.
4. Identify Early American furniture in a store or catalog.

READING REFERENCES

Aronson, Joseph. *The Encyclopedia of Furniture.* Crown, 1938.

Eberlein, H. D., and Ramsdell, R. W. *Practical Book of Italian, Spanish, and Portugese Furniture.* Lippincott, 1927.

Kimerly, W'm. L. *How to Know Period Styles in Furniture.* Periodical Publishing Co., 1931.

Nutting, Wallace. *Furniture of the Pilgrim Century.* Old America Co., 1924.

Schottmueller, Frieda. *Furniture and Interior Decoration of the Italian Renaissance.* Brentano, 1921.

Speltz, Alexander. *Styles of Ornament.* Grosset and Dunlap, 1936.

RENAISSANCE FURNITURE
Courtesy of the Metropolitan Museum of Art

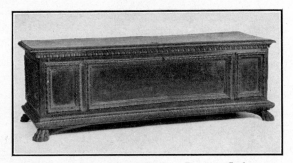

A fifteenth-century chest from Florence, Italy.

An American chest of drawers in Jacobean style.

A sixteenth-century chair
from Spain.

An American trestle table of oak and pine dated about 1650.

American and Dutch interpretations of Renaissance transition furniture are shown in the alcove above. The costumes and background as well as the furniture are dated about 1700. *Courtesy Museum of the City of New York.*

The Early English furniture below shows Renaissance influence. The oak paneling is from a seventeenth-century English house. *Courtesy Eaton's, Toronto.*

CHAPTER 25

THE BAROQUE AND ROCOCO MOVEMENTS

Italy. Seventeenth and eighteenth centuries.
Spain. Seventeenth and eighteenth centuries.
France. 1643–1774.
    Baroque. Louis XIV. 1643–1715.
    Rococo. Louis XV. 1715–1774.
England. 1660–1765.

Transition. ⎰ Carolean or Restoration. ⎰ Charles II. 1660–1685.
                             ⎱   ⎱ James II. 1685–1689.
                   William and Mary. 1689–1702.

Baroque and Rococo. ⎰ Queen Anne. 1702–1714.
                           ⎱ Thomas Chippendale.
United States. 1700–1780.
    Transition Period. 1700–1725.
    Baroque and Rococo (Colonial). 1725–1780.

The term *Baroque* was originally a Portuguese word used by jewelers to indicate unevenness, particularly in the surface of pearls. The word is now applied to a great art movement that began in Italy in the late sixteenth century and spread over Europe. The Baroque developed gradually out of the Renaissance, and in fact some authorities designate the period as late Renaissance. The Baroque movement differed from the Renaissance, however, in that it was largely an expression of the romantic spirit as opposed to the Classic. A description of the Baroque movement follows under the heading Italy.

The term *Rococo* came from the rock and shell motifs, *rocaille et coquille*, which were featured in its ornamentation. The Rococo style was a further elaboration of the Baroque style. It is described in detail in this chapter in connection with the Louis XV period of France.

ITALY

The Baroque Movement

At about the middle of the seventeenth century the Baroque style reached its height in Italy. Changed social and political conditions had fostered the development of this idea. The simple Classic style no longer sufficed to express the new spirit. The period was one of great prosperity, and magnificent display was desired by the higher classes. It was also a time of religious disquiet. The church was influential in the development of the Baroque, as it was attempting to reach the spirit through the senses.

The art of the day expressed the agitation of the period, with its contorted columns, disturbed horizontal lines, awkward forms, and confused and excessive ornamentation, all contriving to produce an effect of unreal grandeur. The aim was to achieve the exceptional in all forms of art. Palaces were splendid, home furnishings were magnificent, and clothing was gorgeous.

The Baroque was a dynamic style expressing movement as opposed to the classical idea of repose. Curved lines replaced straight. Large curves, reversed curves, short, vigorous, stopped curves that usually ended in tight scrolls, and cyma curves were characteristic. Broken pediments and tall finials were typical forms. Rich sculpture was carved on articles made of wood. An important development was that decoration no longer followed structural lines but was meant to provide esthetic satisfaction in itself, regardless of the object decorated.

The greatest artists that the world has ever known also helped to develop the Baroque movement. The master Michelangelo was not to be bound by the traditions and restrictions of the Classic style. His genius helped to produce this new, exuberant, and powerful style. In architecture, sculpture, and painting he created new forms expressive of the age. Vignolia and Palladio also helped to develop this movement; Bernini carried it on.

Sad to say, Michelangelo's less-talented followers sometimes used the new forms as a means of decorative over-display, consistent nevertheless with the time. Some classicists consider the Baroque style decadent. It was, however, a bold, vigorous, masculine expression as contrasted with the feminine Rococo that followed.

Some of the *furniture* of this period was much like Renaissance furniture except that the decorations were far more restless. Twisted columns were used as furniture supports, because Bernini had used them in the high altar in St. Peter's. Rome in fact led the country in the Baroque style.

The chairs were very different from earlier ones. Lower backs, exaggerated finials, rich coverings, twisted stretchers, carved foliage forms, and sometimes a carved coat-of-arms on the front stretcher were typical of these well-proportioned chairs.

The armoires were typically Baroque, with heavy carving of curved motifs for their cresting. The credenza remained in general use. Beds were of carved walnut, with or without the canopy, and sometimes had elaborately carved head boards. Stone tables, narrow and long, were used, often inlaid with colored marble. At this time large candelabra, candlesticks, sconces, and large mirrors with carved and gilded frames were made in great numbers. Pedestals of elaborate design were built to carry sculptures.

The Rococo Movement

Invaded by France, conquered by her enemies, and politically divided, Italy now declined in creative power. But the French Rococo influence spread from the north through Italy, transforming the art and the lives of the Italians, and bringing gaiety and frivolity as an antidote for wars and defeats. Venice became the capital of the world's pleasure-seekers. Italy was now so poor that inferior materials were used in producing pretentious effects. Furnishings and ornamentation in Rome became more and more decadent as one invader followed another. Florence, as always, showed better taste than the other cities. The Italian middle classes were still serious, however, and their furnishings remained simple.

The Rococo *furniture* became less architectural, more decorated, and smaller in scale. Marquetry was again employed in decoration. Cabinets, credenzas, and armoires were used. Tables still rested on stretchers. Commodes often had marble tops and bulging fronts, with decoration running fancy free and not according to structure. The Venetian painted furniture of this and the following period was famous for its beauty, especially of color. Reproductions of Venetian chairs are successful.

SPAIN

The Baroque Movement

The Baroque influence in Spain, occurring in the seventeenth and eighteenth centuries, was absorbed first from Italy, which it dominated at the time, and later from France. More color appeared in the tiling, painting, and textiles. The Baroque furniture of Spain retained the contours of the Renaissance. The chests and cabinets especially were unusual and excellent in design. The motifs that decorated the furniture were Italian combined with Moorish and other Oriental forms.

The Rococo Movement

The Rococo movement in Spain was a reflection of the French. The religion of the Spanish prevented their responding quickly or completely to the gay, frivolous influence of the Rococo.

FRANCE

The Baroque Movement

Historical Background. The Baroque style in France developed during the long reign of Louis XIV (1643–1715). It was derived from the Baroque style of Rome, modified by Flemish and Chinese influence and by French national taste. The French people were susceptible to new ideas, which they were able to absorb and present again in an interpretation of their own. Although the Renaissance had remained Italian after being transplanted into France, the Baroque idea became decidedly French.

Louis XIV was king for seventy-two years and exerted a powerful influence on all the arts. He selected great architects, decorators, and painters to direct the work in the arts, and he built the Louvre, a palace where they could live and work. Charles Lebrun was put in charge of the art of France, including the Gobelin factory and the furnishings for Versailles. The architect Mansart designed the great palace of Versailles, and Lenôte designed its beautiful gardens. The court of Louis XIV at Versailles was the envy of the other rulers for its magnificence and its size. Louis XIV had planned it to be the heart of the social and cultural life of Europe.

Characteristics. The typical qualities of the Louis XIV style were heroic scale, magnificence, and military formality. In all these respects the style merely reflected the characteristics of the people of that time, who expressed themselves in elaborate over-decoration, astonishing but not charming. Costumes and background were but a pageant for the pleasure of Louis the Grand. The style was also affected by the taste of the women who were the favorite companions of the king.

Decoration. The period exhibited conflicts in decorative ideas. For example, the typical chair was rectangular, large, and formal, but its decoration was playful and confused in line. During some of the period, chair and table legs were generally square and tapering, although at the last they were curved. Motifs were of three kinds: Classic borders, shell and scroll, and naturalistic flowers. The king's own symbol was a head encircled by the rays of the sun.

Decoration included carving, enamel, gold or silver leaf, and solid silver. Chiseled ormolu mounts of bronze were used in decorating the furniture, particularly cabinets, commodes, consoles, tables, and desks. Metal hinges, pulls, rosettes, beadings, and foot tips were prominent.

Furniture. Baroque furniture was usually made of walnut, oak, or ebony. The most important pieces were the great cupboards, the sideboard cupboards, the bookcases, and the commodes. Upholstered sofas and chairs had high rectangular backs in the Italian style. See page 459. The bergère type of chair with visible wooden framework appeared, followed by caned chairs with cabriole legs. Commodes with bombé fronts, secretaries, and writing desks were very elaborate and impressive. Beds were large and ornate with richly carved posts and testers and heavy draperies. Armoires and prie-dieu were among the most interesting bedroom pieces. Side tables and consoles usually had marble tops and were elaborately carved and gilded.

Fabrics. Elegant textiles were used, such as velvet, damask, tapestry, brocade, taffeta, cloth of gold, silk, and satin. The large, naturalistic designs, which became smaller and less realistic at the end of the period, were combined with scrolls and latticework. Rather deep, rich colors were popular at this time, particularly green, blue, and gold, with white accents.

The Rococo Movement

The French Regency. The Regency was a brief period from about 1715 to 1725 during which the Duke of Orléans, an uncle of Louis XV, ruled. This term promoted the gradual transition from the massive angular forms of the Baroque style to the light, graceful, curved forms of the Rococo style. The chief characteristics of the Régence style were *exquisite decoration* employing *symmetrical balance* and *curved lines* contained within a *rectangular framework*.

Historical Background. The Rococo movement developed in France during the reign of Louis XV, 1725 to 1744; therefore this style is also known as Louis Quinze. The Rococo style is definitely French and is in fact the highest achievement of the French period styles, although it deteriorated because of excessive ornamentation. Its influence was very important in all northern European countries, where it persisted for a long time.

The Rococo style was the joyous expression of a people who were glad that Louis XIV was dead as they were tired of his pomp and his costly wars. When Louis XV became king, the stiff formality of the previous regime was entirely gone. Louis XV was ruled by the women of the court, who favored smaller houses and rooms and smaller, comfortable furniture. The aim was no longer to be impressive and grand, but to be gay and luxurious.

Source. The source of the Rococo style was the Baroque, modified by Flemish, Oriental, and naturalistic influences. The Rococo style was definitely romantic with a studied defiance of Classicism. Originality and novelty took the place of formal decoration.

Interior Architecture. Although the buildings of this period were Classic in design the interior decorations were Rococo. See page 460. Panels on interior walls were often outlined by delicate moldings, broken by Rococo scrolls. In the panels were mirrors, fine textiles, or painted decorations. Sometimes the pictorial decorations were paintings by the best artists of the period such as Watteau, Fragonard, and Boucher. One of the most delightful features of the style of Louis XV was the unity between the wall decorations and the furnishings. This unity was achieved because one single total impression resulted from harmonious lines, colors, and textures.

Line and Form. The most distinguishing trait of the Rococo style was the dominance of the curved line, a double curve being considered especially beautiful. The legs of all furniture were curved, and even basic rectangular forms were camouflaged by curvilinear ornamentation. See page 86. Another outstanding characteristic of the Rococo period was asymmetrical balance, not only in the lines of decorations, but also in the contour of small articles like mirrors.

Motifs. One of the amazing features of the Rococo style was the variety of subject matter for decorative material. Any subject was acceptable as long as it was handled in a smart, spirited fashion with a finished technique. Scale was often mischievously violated; for example, a tiny monkey might be sheltered by a blossom much larger than himself.

Scenes of social activities and pastoral joys were the vogue. The shell was the favorite motif; others were stalactites, festoons, pendants, vases, ribbons, lace, cupids, flames, wreaths, flowers, plumes, wings, birds, satyrs, figures, Chinese dragons, pagodas, and scenery. Beautiful irregular rhythms of curved lines were produced by the intertwining of leaves, flowers, rocks, and shells copied from nature.

Color. For the first time colors were light and also bright. Gilt, ivory, gray, soft rose, and light green were the most popular.

Furniture. Furniture was made from fruitwood, walnut, and mahogany with precious woods for inlay, marquetry, and veneer. Elaborate carving, gilding, lacquering, ormolu, inlay, and marquetry decorated the furniture. The most important lacquerwork was the greenish vernis Martin, created by Martin to protect the pictures painted on the furniture. Ormolu or metal ornamentation was very common during this period. Furniture was trimmed with gay metal forms serving as drawer pulls, corner mounts, hinges, key plates, feet, or merely as design elements. Tables, bureaus, and commodes had marble tops. The intimate life of the period encouraged new articles like the chaise longue, bergère (padded armchair), and fire screen.

Textiles. Damask, brocade, brocatelle, satin, velvet, printed cotton and linen, tapestry, and needlework were used. Slip covers of heavy taffeta were sometimes employed in the summer time. French carpets or Oriental rugs of thick pile covered the floors.

ENGLAND

The Restoration

Historical Background. Shortly after the death of the Lord Protector Cromwell in 1659, the Stuarts were restored to the throne. Charles II and his followers returned from the court of Louis XIV of France and brought with them the elaborate Baroque style. Italian, Spanish, and Flemish furniture was also imported into England and reproduced.

Characteristics. The Restoration style in England was transitional, because, though it usually retained the rectangular structural line of the Renaissance, it added the curved lines of the Baroque in its decoration. The new style affected the movable furniture but not the architecture.

Furniture. The new way of arranging furniture with symmetrical balance gave the rooms an orderly feeling. Furniture was now designed to fit the body and was therefore more comfortable. The backs of large chairs were slanted. Leather and fabrics were employed in upholstering, and many loose cushions were common.

Furniture was more richly ornamented than formerly because walnut, largely used for furniture, lent itself to more elaborate carving than oak. Carving, the favorite method of decoration, was modeled, flat, or incised. The flat type was made by gouging out the background slightly; the incised work consisted of deep-scratched outlines. Other forms of decoration were inlay, paint, lacquer, veneer, and applied ornament.

Many additional items of furniture were employed in the Restoration period. The most interesting piece was the Carolean chair of Flemish influence, which had a tall, narrow, ornamental back surrounding a section of caning. See page 85. Grandfather chairs, love seats, day beds, large four-poster beds, tallboys, court cupboards, and long buffets with cupboards above were used. Gate-leg and many odd tables became common, as it was highly fashionable to play cards and drink tea, coffee, and cocoa.

Fabrics. Draperies became important in the Restoration period. Splendid Italian and English fabrics were hung. Colored linens and calicoes in Oriental designs sufficed for simpler homes. Wall tapestries were not used in the new Classic interiors.

The William and Mary Period

Historical Background.   At the death of his brother Charles II, James II became king, but he was so much disliked that he abdicated and fled to France.   His daughter Mary and her husband William, Prince of Orange in Holland, occupied the throne of England from 1689 to 1702.   They brought with them shiploads of furniture and many workmen.   The entire attitude of the English people toward home furnishings was changed by this new influence, and they wholeheartedly adopted the domestic attitude of the Dutch, whose object was to obtain a comfortable, convenient, private home life.   The Elizabethan ideal had been to obtain splendid though crude effects; the Cromwellian, to endure harsh discomfort for the sake of the soul.   The Carolean ideal of extravagance and display had only irritated the English people.

Furniture.   In its form the furniture of this period was a pleasing transition between the rectangular Renaissance furniture and the curvilinear Baroque.   Some pieces employed both kinds of lines.   The furniture was lighter in weight than formerly, and decorated with veneer, marquetry, and lacquer.   The height of the *age of walnut* began in the William and Mary period.

Some typical pieces of this period were the flat-top cabinets or highboys with cornices.   See page 459.   They had six or eight legs, which had inverted bell, cup, or trumpet turning, ending with bun or ball feet.   Their flat, curved, and tied or crossed stretchers were close to the floor.   The aprons were sometimes shaped in the ogee form.   Desks became common at this time; they were often beautifully decorated with intricate seaweed patterns in marquetry. The high, rectangular chair of Italian style with elaborate crest and front stretcher, the wing chair, the love seat, and the sofa were used.   Tables of all sizes and shapes were common.   The hardware on the furniture was simple, teardrop and ball handles and plain pierced shields being most popular.

Fabrics.   Shortly before this period, the Edict of Nantes, which had given religious liberty to Protestants, was revoked by Louis XIV.   As a result, forty thousand families emigrated to England, among them many skilful Huguenot weavers.   Colorful silk, velvet, brocade, damask, printed linen, and cotton were made at the factories.   Queen Mary set the fashion for doing needlework.

The Queen Anne Period

Furniture. In this period (1702–1714) the Dutch influence continued to grow and comfortable furniture became common. Straight lines had practically disappeared, and furniture was built on curved lines to fit the shape of the body. The Baroque and Rococo furniture of France influenced this period, but the English furniture was much simpler and stronger. Walnut, which was used either in solid form or in veneering, was the favorite wood, but others were also utilized. Simpler woods were sometimes finished with brilliant-colored lacquer decorated with gold. The turned leg went completely out of fashion, and the shaped stretcher was replaced by a simple one which also soon disappeared. The cabriole leg had now arrived and was often carved with a shell motif on the knee, ending with a club, spoon, or scroll foot. Even the case furniture had curved legs and sometimes double hoods to repeat the curved lines. See pages 90 and 460.

For the decoration of furniture, turning, carving, lacquering, gilding, and veneering were used rather sparingly, and marquetry had almost gone out of fashion. The beauty of the grain of the wood was preferred to carving, gilding, or ormolu. Shells and sun rays were carved on cabinet furniture; sphinxes, griffins, eagles, flowers, and human and animal figures were carved on table bases. Chinese motifs were used on furniture and wall paper.

The typical chair of the period had a hoop back, spooned to fit the body, with a solid fiddle- or vase-shaped splat down the center and a slight dip in the middle of the top rail often filled in with a carved shell ornament. The comfortable upholstered wing chair of this period is still a favorite. The ever-popular day bed was graceful, having three or four cabriole legs on either side and a rolled head rest.

Very fine secretaries were made with broken pediments at the top and cabriole legs. Sometimes they were lacquered a brilliant color such as vermilion, green, or black. Cupboards, called dressers, with open shelves above and drawers below, appeared at this time. Sideboard tables had marble tops. Corner cupboards and cabinets were numerous because collections of porcelain were fashionable. Chests on stands, tallboys or highboys, and knee-hole desks, as well as many small desks, were made.

Small tables were common, the gate-leg and drop-leaf types being very popular. Many new tea tables, bedside tables, and gaming tables were created. The tilt-top variety had a round top with a pie-crust edge and was supported by a single pedestal standing on three short cabriole legs. Some card tables also had fold-over tops with projecting corners to hold candles.

The bedposts continued to be absurdly high, and the framework was entirely covered with a rich material which was also made into drapery and bed covering. Beds became simpler late in the period. Round-top mirrors, in lacquered or partly gilded walnut frames, were very popular at this time. Small mirrors with small drawers below sometimes stood on dressing tables.

Fabrics. Among the popular fabrics were velvets, damasks, brocades, and petit-point needlework. Oriental chintzes and printed cottons were very fashionable. Bright colors were popular, particularly the primary colors and black and gold.

Thomas Chippendale

English furniture styles immediately after the period of Queen Anne are named for the designers of the furniture rather than for the rulers. Thomas Chippendale (1705–1779) was the first of a famous group of English cabinet makers who worked in the second half of the eighteenth century, a time which is called the golden age of furniture making. He designed, made, and carved furniture, adapting foreign designs with skill. He followed the Rococo style in most of his work, but Chinese and Gothic designs were also included in his book, *The Gentlemen's and Cabinet-Maker's Director*, published in 1754. Although cabriole legs were the fashion he used straight legs on some of his furniture.

Chippendale was fearless in attempting to make other ideas fit the life of his time. By encouraging his clients to have their own opinions and to avoid aping the royalty, and through his willingness to work in a variety of styles, he helped to develop a period of individual taste. Unlike his contemporaries Chippendale preferred to work in the Baroque and Rococo styles of the preceding period rather than in the new Neo-Classic style. He opened a cabinet-making shop in London about 1705. He was a good salesman as well as a craftsman, serving both tea and gossip to his prospective customers in his display rooms in St. Martin's Lane.

Chippendale preferred mahogany to other woods. With it he was able to make his furniture strong even though light; and, most important of all, he found it excellent material to carve.

There were three typical Chippendale chairs. The most-used type resembled the Queen Anne, but it had the following differences: the shoulders were square, and the top of the back formed a graceful bow shape; the splat was pierced in ribbon and scroll shapes and always reached to the seat; the cabriole front legs were carved with scrolls and acanthus; ball and claw feet were usual. His ladder-back chairs, which had four or five pierced and curved slats, straight legs, stretchers, and a saddle seat, were his best. His Chinese chairs and other articles were light and rectangular, and decorated with open fretwork and lattice ornament.

Chippendale upholstered very little except the seats of his chairs. He generally employed the lighter-weight upholstery materials, among them silk, damask, and brocade, but he sometimes used red leather and horsehair.

Chippendale originated a cumulative dining table in four parts, two ends and two center pieces, that could be adjusted to fit various needs. He made tilt-top card tables, pedestal pie-crust tea tables, small tables with fretwork galleries around them, and many other whimsical small affairs. His secretary bookcases were among his best productions, as their charm depended upon fine proportion and beautiful finish rather than on ornament. His bombé serpentine-shaped commodes and desks were modeled after the French but had distinct Chippendale characteristics. Interesting accessories came from his shops. His Chinese mirrors were fine in workmanship, as were also little pieces of tripod furniture such as pole screens and table stands. For examples of Chippendale furniture see pages 85, 90, 459, and 477.

Opinions vary greatly as to the beauty of Chippendale furniture. Although much of it is excellent in design and technique, some articles are not well-organized units of design. For example, the typical side chairs have curved cabriole legs in conjunction with backs of unrelated lines. Some highboys appear top-heavy and not well supported on their cabriole legs. Many Chinese pieces and nearly all the pseudo-Gothic articles are very ugly. In general the best Chippendale pieces are simple in their structural lines.

UNITED STATES

The home furnishings of the period from 1700 to 1725 passed through a transitional stage copied from England. From 1725 to 1780 occurred a Baroque and Rococo period influenced by England, Holland, France, and China. These periods are usually called Colonial; the preceding period is called Early American.

Transition Period

By the end of the seventeenth century many of the colonists had prospered enough so that they could afford much of the equipment for comfortable living. The furniture of the transition period had rectangular contours, but curved lines had begun to appear in its decoration. The furniture was smaller, better finished, more refined, and built of better wood than in the early seventeenth century. This was largely the result of the influence brought to the colonies by craftsmen and by the furniture imported from England. Transitional furniture in the Colonial period included the furniture copied from the Carolean or Restoration period and the William and Mary period in England. Some of its foreign features were Flemish scrolls, Spanish feet, and caning from Portugal.

Baroque and Rococo Periods

By 1725 the merchants living along the seaboard had become wealthy through extensive trading. In the South, especially in Maryland and Virginia, the large grants of fertile land enabled the privileged owners to live in fine style, as landed gentry. A fashionable social life centered around the King's representatives.

By 1750 many beautiful Colonial houses had been built here. Books of architecture were guides for colonial builders. The exteriors and interiors of Colonial houses were symmetrical in plan. The interior architecture was a robust interpretation of Classic design. The furnishings were Baroque in style; Queen Anne and Chippendale furniture were in high favor. Constantly changing fashions and originality helped to produce elegant, sophisticated decoration. The restoration of Colonial Williamsburg has focused attention on this brilliant period. See page 86.

Furniture. In the less elaborate earlier phase of the Colonial period, furniture was made of walnut in the Queen Anne style. At the height of the period it was made of mahogany usually from Chippendale designs. See pages 86, 90, and 460.

The most easily recognized feature of the Baroque style is the cabriole leg, which has a high knee curve. These curved legs appeared on chairs, tables, beds, desks, highboys, lowboys, and chests of drawers. Cabinet makers had become skilful enough to make these legs so strong that they did not need stretchers to support them. They were finished with Dutch, Spanish, Flemish, snake, slipper, or ball-and-claw feet. Sometimes bracket feet were used on case furniture.

Another important design feature of the Baroque style was the broken curve. Some of the decorative motifs were the acanthus, lions' heads and feet, satyrs' masks, scrolls, frets, egg and dart, shell, honeysuckle, fuchsia, and Chinese motifs.

The chief method of decoration was carving, but imitation of Chinese lacquer was also fashionable. The flat surface of case furniture was broken by the block front, the bow front, and the serpentine front. The block front, an American development from Rhode Island, featured by John Townsend and John Goddard, was particularly handsome. It consisted of a raised portion on each side of a similar sunken portion. The shell motif was sometimes used at the top of the three sections of the block front. See page 459.

The chairs were of many types, including the typical Queen Anne chair of walnut with rounded shoulders, solid central splat, and horseshoe seat, and the typical Chippendale chair, of mahogany with a bow-shaped top rail resting on back posts, an openwork splat, and a seat with straight sides. There were also upholstered easy chairs with or without arms. The Windsor was a provincial chair of this period.

Tables were of many varieties. Side tables were made the same height as the drop-leaf dining tables so that they could be combined when necessary. The card table with a hinged flap was popular. Tea tables were very important to the colonial dames because much of the social activity occurred at tea time. Tilt-top pedestal tea tables of a number of sizes, many kettle stands, and various tray tables were found in both parlors and bedrooms.

Highboys made by William Savery were particularly elaborate and beautifully carved. In the bedrooms were chests of drawers and also chests on chests. Slant-topped desks, with or without book case tops, were used. Beds commonly had four tall posts and a tester hung with curtains. In the early part of the period cupboards were frequently built in, often in pairs.

The tall clocks of this period were designed like the furniture. They often had block fronts, scrolled pediments with finials, columns, bracket feet, or fretwork for decoration. They were frequently carved or japanned in an elaborate manner. Clocks and mirrors were new at this period and received more ornamentation than was desirable.

Fabrics. Many kinds of fabrics were used. Damasks, silks, mohair, needlework, haircloth, linen, woolens, and cottons such as calico and chintz were common. Walls were often hung with papers or textiles. Chinese, Classical, and other papers were advertised at this time. Painted canvases found favor both as floor and as wall covering. Persian and Turkish rugs were used, and also Scotch carpets.

Metals, Pottery, and Dishes. The designs in metalwork were often copied from the furniture decoration. Iron, brass, silver, and pewter were used. The fireplace tools were made of iron or brass. The Franklin stove was very popular during the eighteenth century. Candlestands were made of iron or brass; chandeliers and sconces were commonly of brass.

Imported and domestic pewter was generally used. Silver utensils were designed in the Rococo manner, often showing the same decorative motifs as the furniture. The contours of silver pieces had now become bulbous, even the lids being domed. Feet were constructed on some of the hollow ware. There were many fine silversmiths in the colonies, among them Paul Revere of Revolutionary fame. Sheffield plate was imported and later manufactured by the colonists.

Henry Stiegel manufactured glass of high quality in Pennsylvania. The potters, however, were less active than the metal, glass, and wood workers, for their pottery consisted mostly of a crude type of stoneware and glazed earthenware. Much of the table porcelain was imported from England, Holland, and China.

PROBLEMS

A sufficient number of problems are listed so that choices may be made.

1. Trace pictures of Baroque chairs from all the countries named in this chapter, and arrange on a chart.
2. Visit a museum or a home to study this period.
3. Identify Baroque and Rococo furniture in a store or in a catalog.
4. Draw or trace a costume of this period.

READING REFERENCES

ARONSON, JOSEPH. *The Book of Furniture and Decoration.* Crown, 1936.

BINSTEAD, HERBERT E. *Furniture Styles.* Pitman, 1929.

McCLELLAND, NANCY. *Furnishing the Colonial and Federal House.* Lippincott, 1936.

MILLER, GLADYS. *Decoratively Speaking.* Doubleday, Doran, 1940.

ODOM, WILLIAM M. *A History of Italian Furniture.* Doubleday, Doran, 1918.

ORMSBEE, T. H. *Story of American Furniture.* Macmillan, 1940.

BAROQUE FURNITURE

Courtesy of the Metropolitan Museum of Art

An eighteenth - century chair in the English style known as Chippendale.

An eighteenth-century American chest of drawers of the block front type.

The William and Mary highboy at the right is an example of the transitional style in England at the beginning of the Baroque period.

The Louis XIV chair below shows restraint in its design.

Baroque furniture of English derivation is shown in the alcove of 1760 pictured above. The seated figure occupies a Chippendale chair; the other pieces are Queen Anne. The curves are repeated in the andirons and mirror. The furniture of this period is large and strong. The decorated tiles are a Dutch feature. *Courtesy Museum of the City of New York.*

The palatial Rococo interior below shows background and furniture in the style of Louis XV. Notice that no straight lines are used in the chair designs. The entire effect is delicate and feminine. *Courtesy Philadelphia Museum of Art.*

CHAPTER 26

THE NEO-CLASSIC MOVEMENT

POMPEIIAN. 1760–1800

Italy. Late 18th century.
Spain. Late 18th century.
France. 1774–1793.
   Louis XVI. 1774–1793.

England. 1765–1793.
   Robert Adam. 1728–1792.
   George Hepplewhite. ?–1786.
   Thomas Sheraton. 1750–1806.
United States. 1780–1810.
   Federal. 1780–1810.

EMPIRE. 1800–1830

Italy. Most of 19th century.
Spain. Early 19th century.
France. 1795–1815.
   Directoire. 1795–1804.
   Empire. 1804–1815.
England. 1793–1837.
   Regency. 1810–1837.
United States. 1810–1840.
   Directoire and Empire. 1810–
      1840.
   Duncan Phyfe. 1768–1854.

POMPEIIAN

The Neo-Classic movement was a welcome reaction against a romantic style. Baroque and Rococo ideas had been carried to such extremes that the furniture was often queer and absurd as well as unstructural in design. People were tired of the romantic style; it was time for a change. The discovery of the buried city of *Herculaneum* in 1709 and the successful excavations there and in *Pompeii* were by 1750 the inspiration for a revolution in taste. All over Europe it became the fashion to study the late Roman Classic work. In the short space of ten years the slender, straight structural lines of the Neo-Classic style had replaced the curved Baroque and Rococo forms. The new style was brought to England by the architect Robert Adam, and from there it came to the United States. In France it inspired the style known as Louis XVI, which spread across the frontiers into Italy and Spain and also across the ocean to the new republic, the United States.

461

FRANCE

Louis XVI

Historical Background. A return to greater simplicity in living and in art forms in this period was a natural reaction from the extravagances and superficialities of Louis XV. The nobility preferred the change; the taxpayers demanded it. Furthermore, the young queen, Marie Antoinette, had simple tastes.

Although the Neo-Classic revival had begun in the time of Louis XV it reached its height under Louis XVI (1774–1793). A delicate feminine interpretation of the Classic evolved. The Petit Trianon, a small palace in the gardens of Versailles, is the outstanding example of the architecture, decoration, and furnishing of this period. It was designed by Jacques-Ange Gabriel and was a favorite abode of Marie Antoinette. See page 477.

Characteristics. This period produced some of the most refined interiors and furnishings ever made. Although modeled on the antique, the Neo-Classic style was adapted to the needs of the time. The symmetry of the style gave it dignity, which was modified, however, by the light French interpretation. Restraint in line and decoration was an element in its beauty.

Decoration. Carving, painting, inlay, caning, marquetry, lacquering, porcelain insets, and metal mounting were the methods of decoration most in favor. Ornamentation was Classical, Pompeiian, or floral. Typical motifs and decorations were fine beadings and bandings, urns, the acanthus, the guilloche, medallions, caryatids, lyres, laurel, swags, rosettes, heads, busts, human figures, cherubs diaperwork, arabesques, love knots, fluting, reeding, and galleries.

Furniture. Curves had been discontinued, and the furniture was straight lined and small in scale. See page 86. The legs were slender, round or square, plain, reeded, fluted, laced, or spiraled, and always tapered. Furniture was made in sets, especially for drawing rooms and bedrooms. Upholstered or caned chairs had square, oval, or round backs. Sofas were shorter than they had been in the preceding periods, with rather high backs and from five to eight legs. Beds were smaller, with identical high head and foot boards, and were usually curtained. Commodes, armoires, consoles, cabinets, and numerous tables were popular.

Mahogany, walnut, rosewood, fruitwoods, and also precious woods of many kinds were used for furniture. Graining was appreciated and was sometimes featured. The usual finishes were enamel or paint in delicate tints and gold.

Fabrics. The most popular fabrics were damasks, velvets, Persian and Indian brocades, figured silks and satins, needlework, linens, and printed cottons called toiles de Jouy. Stripes were so common that in 1788 Mercier wrote, "Everybody in the King's cabinet looks like a zebra." The popular colors were generally delicate ones like pink, rose, blue, yellow, green, lavender, gray, and white. The most important carpets of the time were the Aubusson and Savonnerie.

ITALY

The revival of Classicism about the middle of the eighteenth century renewed the pride of the Italians in their Classical heritage. The Italian cabinet makers again produced articles of artistic merit in contrast to the commonplace work done in the preceding period.

Furniture was commonly made of walnut, although mahogany and other woods were also used. The decorative processes in fashion were inlay (especially bone), lacquer, polychrome, painting, gilding, paper appliqué, canvas paneling, and carving. Motifs were mostly Classic. Some of the more usual pieces of furniture were bookcases, secretaries, wardrobes, chests of drawers, chests, cabinets, cupboards, chairs, sofas, and tables. Others with more of a native flavor were the corner cabinets, both standing and hanging, Venetian credenzas, sets of consoles, prie-dieu, writing tables, bedside tables, and spinet cases.

To this period belong the most colorful productions of a nation that understands and loves color, Venice particularly showing originality and brilliance in its use of the Neo-Classic style.

SPAIN

The eighteenth century in Spain was lacking in creative decorative art. The Neo-Classic period produced chiefly imitations of the furniture of France, Italy, and England, but the proportions were usually larger and the structures heavier. Fortunately the native custom of covering furniture with fabrics and decorating with mounts continued.

ENGLAND

Robert Adam

England, like France, was inspired by the excavations at Pompeii. As previously noted, it was the architect Robert Adam (1728–1792) who brought the Classic revival to England and who eventually became the king's architect. He had made a careful study of the ancient buildings in Italy, fully appreciating their beauty and their adaptability to contemporary usage. His brothers, James, John, and William, were associated with him in architectural work, their trade mark being the Adelphi (brothers).

The Adam brothers realized keenly that Baroque furniture was unsuitable for Neo-Classic backgrounds, and therefore they designed all the furnishings for the houses that they built. This furniture was fine, graceful, and delicate to the point of fragility. See page 475. The contours were straight, although curves occasionally appeared in such articles as chairs and consoles. The Adam brothers did not actually make this furniture, however, but engaged others to do it. Thus they gave impetus to as notable a group of furniture makers as the world has known, among them Hepplewhite and Sheraton.

George Hepplewhite

"To unite elegance and utility, and blend the useful with the agreeable" was the aim of the Hepplewhite shop as stated in its catalog, *The Cabinet-Maker and Upholsterer's Guide*, published in 1788, two years after Hepplewhite's death. This aim was achieved in most of the furniture that Hepplewhite designed, for it was generally excellent in contour and decoration, as well as original in conception. At different periods he worked for Adam and others, copied French styles, and originated his own designs.

During Hepplewhite's time mahogany was still used to a great extent in making furniture; but the delicacy of Neo-Classic designs made lighter-colored wood desirable, so satinwood, chestnut, and sycamore were also employed in their natural colors. Beautiful veneers or inlays of colored wood were also in fashion. Sometimes panels painted by Angelica Kaufman or Wedgwood medallions were used to decorate furniture. Painted pieces were usually finished in light colors or gilt and decorated with floral motifs.

Hepplewhite used curved lines more freely than his contemporaries. In chairbacks, seat frames, arms of chairs, tambour writing desks, French sofas, tables, the serpentine fronts of sideboards, and other wall pieces the lines were nearly always curved. The plain, reeded, or fluted legs of his furniture were straight and tapered, more often square than round, and usually had spade or thimble feet, or none at all.

Hepplewhite concentrated his ornament on chairbacks, which were often shield-shaped hollows broken in a great variety of ways, with motifs such as the Prince of Wales' plumes, a sheaf of wheat, or the draped urn and lyre. Other shapes for chairbacks were interlaced hearts, ovals, hoops, or ladders. Since the central part of the chairback did not reach to the seat rail but was supported by two curved members, some designers feel that his chairs are weak at that point. His armchairs are notable for the graceful line extending from the back leg or the front leg into the arm. The wing chair was a Hepplewhite favorite. See pages 87, 90, and 476.

It is said that Hepplewhite was not at his best when making larger case furniture, but his smaller objects were exquisite. Pole screens, washstands, and small tables were among his best creations. Hepplewhite or Shearer was responsible for the modern sideboard. It was one of these men who first joined together the three-part arrangement that Adam designed; however, both Sheraton and Hepplewhite improved the original sideboard design. It is possible to distinguish between the sideboards of these two men, because the fronts of Hepplewhite's sideboards were concave towards the corners, whereas the fronts of Sheraton's were convex, giving more room inside. Hepplewhite designed fine sofas upholstered in horsehair cloth of subtle colors, striped or checked. These sofas had six or eight legs, with bowed or arched backs, or chairbacks. Hepplewhite also made the following pieces with beauty and variety in size and design: chests of drawers with tall French feet, long bookcases in three sections, secretaries, tambour writing desks, wardrobes, dressers, cases for grandfather clocks, and slender four-poster beds.

The fabrics which he favored most were horsehair cloth, moiré, and damasks for upholstering; printed cottons, linens, and delicate silks for hangings. The colors were usually rather delicate.

Thomas Sheraton

Many critics consider that Sheraton, who lived from 1750 to 1806, was the greatest of the English cabinet makers. He had a fine sense of proportion and perfect taste in ornamentation. That he was influenced by the style of Louis XVI, Hepplewhite, and Adam shows in his *The Cabinet-Maker and Upholsterer's Drawing Book.*

Sheraton used mahogany and satinwood, with beech and pine as a foundation for veneer or painting. He decorated chiefly with inlay but also employed painting, gilding, lacquering, reeding, fluting, turning, and carving. His favorite decorative motifs were inconspicuous swags of flowers, drapery, urns, lyres, or shells.

Sheraton's furniture was slender and rather small in scale. His furniture had no stretchers, but fine craftsmanship made it durable. It usually had straight, square, tapering legs, although sometimes they were round, and reeded or fluted. For upholstering Sheraton preferred finely woven horsehair, brocades, damasks, printed linens, and cottons in light colors. See pages 87 and 475.

Among Sheraton's most beautiful pieces of furniture were his secretary bookcases with glass doors above and panels below, tall secretaries with cylindrical fronts, sideboards with serpentine fronts, chests of drawers, wardrobes, and highboys. Undraped beds were just coming into fashion, so Sheraton beds were sometimes built without any top framing on the slender posts. His chairbacks varied in design, but nearly all had a broken or slightly curved top line. The central splat usually rested on a cross piece a little above the seat and was decorated with a lyre, an urn, or several narrow slats. Caned chairs and settees were common and were made more comfortable by cushions. Upholstered sofas had straight backs. Sheraton tables were of many varieties, like extension tables, and game, sewing, dressing, and writing tables.

Sheraton was not only a designer of furniture, but also a drawing teacher, a preacher, and a publisher of religious tracts. Unfortunately his rather short life was spent in poverty and misery. It should be stated here that although Hepplewhite and Sheraton published design books, there were many other cabinet makers in England who were almost as important as these two in developing the particular styles which they used.

UNITED STATES

Federal Style

Historical Background. The Federal style, which lasted from 1792 to 1825, is known also as Early Republican, or Post-Revolutionary. During this period both France and England influenced the style of furnishings in the United States.

After the Revolutionary War, Americans were much interested in their ally France, and ambassadors were exchanged, Benjamin Franklin going to France and Lafayette coming to the United States. Lafayette made the Louis XVI style so fashionable in this country that for many years interiors of southern houses were of this character, Mount Vernon for example showing its strong influence. New England too was affected by the style of Louis XVI, for Marie Antoinette sent a shipload of furniture to Maine, to which state she had meant to flee. This furniture was later distributed and had a softening effect on New England furnishings. Moreover, because of the French Revolution many French families entered the United States about this time, bringing with them their household possessions and spreading the Louis XVI style.

American domestic architecture and furnishings of the Federal period were influenced by the English too, although that influence came later when more cordial relations were established between the United States and England. Samuel McIntyre of Salem, who was one of the first professional architects in America, built houses in the best Adam tradition. They were supplied with furniture made from Adam, Sheraton, or Hepplewhite designs. Furniture was imported from England, too, and was extensively copied in the United States. Furthermore, English cabinet makers were numerous here. English and French furnitures were combined with pleasing results for they were compatible in all the art elements—line, form, texture, pattern, and color.

Color. The tendency of this period was towards light, cheerful color schemes because the lighter scale and attenuated motifs of the Neo-Classic period required the use of light colors. Not only was the furniture made of light-colored wood or painted in light colors, but also the walls, ceilings, and woodwork were painted some light, cool color such as fawn, gray, white, blue, or green. Sometimes Pompeiian color schemes were employed.

Decoration.   The motifs of the Louis XVI style and also of the English Neo-Classic style decorated the American furniture of this period.   In addition, after the inauguration of the first president, the American eagle became a popular motif.   The spread eagle was used on tavern signs, was inlaid in mirror frames, secretaries, tables, chests, desks, cabinets, and clocks, and was cut in metal articles.   See pages 477 and 478.   The number of stars in the spread-eagle design changed as additional states came into the union.   Three-dimensional eagles perched on mirror frames, picture frames, and clocks.   The eagle was also made to support pedestal tables and wall brackets.   So great was patriotic fervor that historic scenes were painted on clocks and mirrors.

Furniture.   The furniture of this period was more refined and smaller in scale than that of the romantic style that preceded it. Baroque and Rococo curves became passé, and straight structural lines were preferred again.   Sheraton models were copied more extensively than Hepplewhite.   See page 476.

Variety was displayed in the design of the furniture.   Tables of various shapes and sizes were made for many purposes.   Buffets, sideboards, desks, and chests of drawers of excellent design were constructed.   Comfortable sofas, settees, and high four-poster beds were produced.   Many good designs were made for wooden and upholstered chairs; the "fancy chair" was an adaptation of a Sheraton chair, having a rush or cane seat and an open back of slats or spindles.   Architectural tall clocks and mirror frames were fashionable.

Finer and lighter woods, like cherry, apple, pear, curly maple, and satinwood, were made into furniture.   Mahogany was still a favorite.   Fine veneering was done by some cabinet makers.

Miscellaneous.   The fabrics of the period were mostly imported.   Damasks, brocades, satins, velvets, taffetas, horsehair, cottons, and linens were used for upholstery and drapery.   The metalwork for the fireplace was brass, designed and executed with delicacy.   Silver and plate were made in Classic forms, such as urns, with engraving the accepted decoration.   Much of the table porcelain came from France and England, Wedgwood ware being very popular.   Chinese Lowestoft was favored, sometimes decorated with the spread-eagle design.   Miniature painting was one of the important forms of art in this period.

NEO-CLASSIC EMPIRE

FRANCE

Directoire

Historical Background. The Directoire (1795–1799) and the Consulate (1799–1804) followed the French Revolution, during which Louis XVI and Marie Antoinette were executed. The complete change in the form of the government inspired a change in the decorative style also. The Directoire style was considered to be a revolt against the hated Louis XVI style; however, some of the features of the previous style were retained. A rather indefinite transitional style evolved during this brief period.

Characteristics. Designers turned to the pure Classic forms of Greece and Rome for inspiration. Graceful Greek chairs with concave curving legs were models for new chairs, sofas, and other furniture. The symbols of the Revolution, such as liberty caps, spears, arrows, drums, trumpets, triangles, stars, and clasped hands, were used for ornamentation during this period. Light-colored native fruitwood, oak, and walnut were usually employed, since very little mahogany could be imported.

Although the Directoire style had delicacy, simplicity, charm, and beauty it was without the original light French touches present in the previous styles. See page 88.

Empire

Historical Background. While Napoleon was emperor from 1804 to 1814, the furniture reflected his taste, which inclined toward the imperial, military, and brutal modified by majestic splendor. As his campaigns in Egypt and Italy made him an admirer of the ancient world, Egyptian, Greek, and Roman forms were copied for him. David, the court painter, and two architects, Percier and Fontaine, developed the Empire style.

Characteristics. The Empire style is based on ancient Classic forms which were copied with archeological exactness and applied whole to buildings, interiors, and furniture. In Empire rooms the walls, which usually had a dado and cornice, were often hung with fabrics or wall paper, or painted in Pompeiian fashion. Floors were usually made of contrasting tile, marble, or oak blocks.

Furniture. The few existing designs of ancient furniture were models for Empire furniture whenever possible. The forms were generally large, heavy, and rectangular. However, the Grecian concave curve was employed, particularly on seating furniture.

Cabinet furniture resembled architecture, often displaying miniature columns. Such furniture included chests of drawers, wardrobes, bureaus, secretaries, buffets, and cabinets, all of which were ostentatious in size. Most of the tables were round, with pedestal or tripod bases. Boat, gondola, or sleigh beds with scrolled head and foot boards of the same height were most popular. However, beds with corner pillars were also used. Sofas with straight rolls over backs and arms were typical of the period, although sofas and daybeds with one end higher than the other were frequently made. The pleasing curved lines in the legs and arms of sofas and chairs and in the circular backs of some chairs were copied from antique Grecian chairs. Rush-seated chairs, stools, curule chairs, cross-legged chairs, and short settees were used. Most of the seating furniture was uncomfortable.

Mahogany was preferred for furniture, but ebony and rosewood were employed occasionally. Large plain surfaces, sometimes veneered, were left undecorated to show the grain of the wood. The chief form of decoration was the application of metal ornaments, although some heavy carving, painting, gilding, inlay, and turning were done. Upholstery materials were hard textured, such as leather, tapestry, and silks, in rich primary colors.

Decoration. Decorative motifs of the Empire were often related to Napoleon. The letter N enclosed in a wreath was a favorite; the honeybee, the emblem of an Athenian queen, was applied also to Bonaparte. Egyptian motifs such as pyramids, sphinxes, lotus blossoms, and palm leaves were used. Pineapple, acanthus, honeysuckle, laurel, wreaths, military trophies, cornucopias, eagles, swans, griffins, lion heads, twisted rope carving, vases, torches, and crowns were other popular motifs. See page 87 for a modern interpretation of the Empire style.

Although this furniture had a tendency to be pompous and artificial it was usually impressive, but at the end of the period it became quite awkward and ugly. The influence of this period spread over Europe and America and helped to produce the hundred-year era of bad taste.

ITALY

Italian Directoire furniture was copied from the French, for France set the standards of taste in Europe at this time. However, the Italian designers employed the Classic motifs such as the lyre, acanthus, scrolls, and flutings in a more lavish manner than the French. *Italian Empire* furniture faithfully copied the French. In fact, this style was so pleasing to upper-class Italians that it continued in fashion during most of the nineteenth century, although Napoleon fell in 1814. The furniture was chiefly walnut, which was the most plentiful wood in Italy.

SPAIN

Spanish Directoire and Empire furniture was made for palaces; provincial products were not affected by this French style. Exquisite metalwork, decorative nail heads, and inlay were the decoration. Upholstery materials were heavy and richly colored.

ENGLAND

The *English Regency* is the period when George IV was regent for his insane father, George III. However, the Regency style began about 1793 and continued to the beginning of Victoria's reign in 1837. Although the English disliked France and French politics, their furniture designers copied the *French Directoire and Empire styles*. By this time original furniture designing had ceased in England. The furniture was interesting, however, in the early part of the period, but at the end it was coarse, grotesque, and ugly, lacking proportion and comfort.

Regency furniture was dark mahogany or rosewood, or painted black and touched with gold paint. The fret and the Prince of Wales feathers were favorite motifs in ornamentation. Typical Regency pieces were sofas with flaring curved lines in legs and backs, cross-legged stools, chaises longues, four-legged console tables mounted on very thick bases, three- or four-legged pedestals holding urns or marble busts, and huge sideboards and bookcases with temple façades. See page 88 for a modern Regency room.

The walls were of plain, lively colors. Broad pilasters, wide flat cornices, flat arches over doors and recesses, and black-and-white marble floors in important rooms were typical features.

UNITED STATES

As natural sympathy with France disposed the United States to follow French styles in dress and furnishings, an American Empire period existed here from about 1810 to 1830. The French Empire style was unpleasantly massive and elaborate, but American modifications of it were lighter and simpler. It had large, undecorated, veneered surfaces, but there was also considerable bold effective carving, like pineapple finials. Pillars on the fronts of case furniture, table pedestals, and bedposts were plain, spiraled, or decorated with carving.

Duncan Phyfe

The most important exponent of Directoire and Empire styles in America was Duncan Phyfe. He was born in Scotland in 1768, was brought to the United States by his parents in 1784, and lived here until his death in 1854. His cabinet-making shops in New York City occupied 168, 170, and 172 Fulton Street.

Phyfe's work was as good in design as that of the great English cabinet makers of the eighteenth century. He showed fine judgment in the proportions of his furniture, in its graceful, flaring, spirited lines, and in its restrained decoration. He used such subtly curved lines that sometimes they appeared straight. His favorite motifs were acanthus leaves, dogs' feet, lions' feet, lion-mask handles, carved leaves, fluting, cornucopias, rosettes, drapery, wheat, and indeed all Classical motifs.

Since Phyfe required wood that had lightness and strength he chose mahogany. The typical Phyfe chair had a low, open back with an ornamental slat, lyre, or half hoop, scrolled arms, a broad seat, and legs with concave curves. His sofas and settees had pleasing but rather formal lines. Phyfe's tables were of three kinds: with legs at the corners, with a center pedestal on three short legs, or with end supports of lyre design.

In his early work Phyfe copied Louis XVI, Adam, Hepplewhite, and Sheraton styles for his customers. His most important contribution, however, was the beautiful style that he created from the Directoire and Empire styles of France. Excellent examples of Phyfe's work are in the Metropolitan Museum of Art in New York City. For illustrations see pages 90, 475, and 478.

THE VICTORIAN OR NINETEENTH-CENTURY PERIOD

Following the Neo-Classic period came the so-called Victorian period, named for Queen Victoria, who reigned in England from 1837 to 1901. A description of the Victorian period does not exactly belong in the chapter on Neo-Classic styles. It is inserted here because it is chronological and is not important enough to comprise a separate chapter.

The nineteenth century is sometimes called the era of bad taste. Among the causes for the ugliness of many of its products were their manufacture by machinery, including the jig saw, the confusing variety of its styles, and the lack of taste of the newly rich classes in Europe and America.

The *English Victorian* period showed the influences of the Empire, the Regency, Chippendale, Sheraton, Rococo, Biedermeier, Neo-Greek, Gothic, and some Chinese. The large English homes were profusely and vulgarly furnished.

The *French* of this period of Napoleon III revived the Rococo, Gothic, Greek, and other styles but still featured the Empire with a resulting confusion and ugliness. The newly prosperous class refused the hated style of Louis XVI.

The *American Victorian* furnishings were very much like the English and French but somewhat lighter in weight, smaller, and simpler. In general, however, the furniture was heavy and substantial. It was well made although too ornate. Short, broad legs and massiveness were typical of wall pieces such as sideboards and bureaus. Victorian rocking chairs, mirrors, side chairs, and sofas usually showed strong curves but lacked fine proportions.

Rosewood, mahogany, and walnut were used in Victorian furniture. Papier-mâché furniture and accessories painted black or dark green and decorated with colorful flower and fruit designs were common. Black walnut and horsehair were featured. Needlework was popular for chair cushions and foot-stool covers.

Draperies were voluminous and complicated. Among the fashionable colors in fabrics and elsewhere were purple, mauve, lavender, pink, baby blue, brown, dark green, dark rose, crimson, and gold. Patterns were large, contrasting, and freely used. The whole effect was restless, romantic, and over-elaborate. See page 88 for an illustration of Victorian decoration.

PROBLEMS

A sufficient number of problems are listed so that choices may be made.

1. Trace pictures of Neo-Classic tables from all the countries named in this chapter, and arrange on a chart.
2. Visit a museum, home, or store to study the furniture of this period.
3. Report on the Neo-Classic articles in your home or dormitory.
4. Draw one straight and one flaring chair leg of this period.
5. Draw or trace a costume of this period.

READING REFERENCES

ARONSON, JOSEPH. *The Encyclopedia of Furniture.* Crown, 1938.

BOLTON, ARTHUR T. *The Architecture of Robert and James Adam.* 2 vols. Charles Scribner's, 1922.

CESCINSKY, HERBERT. *English Furniture of the 18th Century.* Funk & Wagnalls, 1915.

EBERLEIN, H. D., and McCLURE, A. *The Practical Book of Period Furniture.* Lippincott, 1914.

HALSEY, R. T. H., and CORNELIUS, C. O. *Handbook of the American Wing. Metropolitan Museum*, 1938.

MAU, AUGUST. *Pompeii: Its Life and Art.* Macmillan, 1899.

McCLELLAND, NANCY. *Duncan Phyfe and the English Regency.* Scott, 1939.

NEO-CLASSIC FURNITURE

Courtesy of the Metropolitan Museum of Art and the Art Institute of Chicago

A B

A. An eighteenth-century American chair, in the style of Sheraton.
B. An inlaid English table dated 1790, in the style of Hepplewhite.
C. An American chair made by Duncan Phyfe.
D. An English satinwood desk designed by Sheraton.
E. A painted satinwood cabinet designed by Robert Adam.

C

D E

Neo-Classic furniture of the type designed by Sheraton (English) is shown in the room above. The oval motif appears in the woodwork and in the shape of the table. This straight-line furniture is rather delicate in scale. *Courtesy the Metropolitan Museum of Art.*

Neo-Classic furniture designed by Hepplewhite (English) is shown in the gallery below. This straight and slender-legged furniture is also refined in scale and in ornamentation. *Courtesy Philadelphia Museum of Art.*

Louis XVI furniture at its best is exhibited in the room above, which is a reproduction of the boudoir of Marie Antoinette. Straight lines, restrained decoration, and small scale are features of the Pompeian Neo-Classic style. *Courtesy Eaton's, Toronto.*

In this room at Mount Vernon, a sofa, two chairs, and a console table are straight-legged Neo-Classic; the three Chippendale chairs, mirror, and pedestal are Baroque. Notice the beautiful carpet with an adaptation of the United States seal as a central motif. *Courtesy Mount Vernon Ladies Association.*

American Empire furniture is shown in the gallery above. The chairs are the most acceptable of these designs. *Courtesy Philadelphia Museum of Art.*

Duncan Phyfe furniture is exhibited in the room below; the chair by the window is the most typical piece. Straight-legged and flaring-legged pieces of furniture are combined. Notice the patriotic eagles over the girandoles. *Courtesy Museum of the City of New York.*

PART SIX

CHAPTER 27

SUGGESTIONS FOR HOME-FURNISHING PROBLEMS

Some of the problems below may be preferred to those listed at the end of each chapter in this book. It would be highly preferable if actual problems could replace these that are theoretical.

1. A girl's dormitory room.
2. A women's study and rest room.
3. A demonstration apartment.
4. A classroom.
5. A cafeteria.
6. A women's club room.
7. A men's club room.
8. A youth center.
9. A dormitory lounge room.
10. A boy's bedroom and study in a former chicken house.
11. A girl's combination bedroom and sitting room in her home.
12. An attic studio for an art student.
13. A basement game room for the family.
14. A one-room apartment for a couple with an income of $150 a month.
15. A small apartment for a couple with an income of $250 a month.
16. An old apartment to be furnished with second-hand furniture.
17. An old house to be remodeled, and a mixed collection of furnishings to be reorganized and replenished.
18. A farm house.
19. A summer cottage to be furnished as inexpensively as possible with new furniture.
20. A small house in a suburb or town for a couple with two children and an income of $300 a month.

PLANNING, DECORATING, AND FURNISHING MY FIRST HOUSE

For Students Who Paint

This work may be carried on throughout a semester or a term along with study of the textbook material. Sufficient plates have been suggested so that the instructor or student may choose those which she prefers.

PLATE

1. A typed statement of the project, including a description of the family, the idea to be expressed in the home, the income, and the total cost of the lot, landscaping, and furnishings.
2. A scale drawing of the plot plan, showing landscape design. See page 134.
3. A scale drawing of the floor plans of the entire house. See page 155.
4. A colored drawing of the front view of the house (without perspective).
5. A colored drawing of the rear view of the house.
6. A color scheme (in paint) for every room in the house.
7. A scale drawing of a furniture-arrangement floor plan. See pages 230, 234, 237.
8. A furnishing budget for the house, stating where each article can be procured.
9. A fabric chart for the house, with samples and prices.
10. A painted elevation for a living-room wall.
11. A painted elevation for a dining-alcove wall.
12. A painted elevation for a kitchen wall.
13. A painted elevation for a bedroom wall.
14. A painted elevation for a bathroom wall.
15. A painted elevation showing the outdoor living room.
16. Drawings of lamps suitable for the house.
17. Drawings of accessories suitable for the house.
18. Drawings of table equipment for the house.
19. Design for a painted decoration for a child's room in the house.
20. List of books and periodicals consulted in the research for this project.

PLANNING, DECORATING, AND FURNISHING MY FIRST HOUSE

For Students Who Do Not Paint

Since much of this material consists of clippings and circulars it is advisable for each student to have a durable paper file about eight inches by ten inches, consisting of at least twenty attached compartments labeled like the envelopes listed below. Only the material that applies directly to this one specific house and its complete furnishings should be mounted; additional clippings may be kept in the file, however. Such a file usually becomes a permanent acquisition.

ENVELOPE

1. Statements and written reports. Index. A typed statement of the project, including a description of the family, the idea to be expressed in the home, income, and the total cost of the lot, landscaping, house, and furnishings. Reports of trips. Bibliography of books and periodicals consulted.
2. Sites and landscaping. A scale drawing on squared paper of the plot plan, showing the house and landscape gardening.
3. Floor plans. A scale drawing of the floor plans.
4. House exteriors. Clippings and photographs.
5. Color schemes. Chart of colors for every room.
6. Furniture arrangement. Scale drawings. See page 230.
7. Furnishing budgets and shopping reports. Actual budgets with local prices.
8. Fabrics. Chart of fabric samples for the house.
9. Rugs and carpets. Chart of clippings for the house.
10. Living-room furniture. Chart of clippings or tracings.
11. Dining-room furniture. Chart of clippings or tracings.
12. Kitchens. Mounted pictures of kitchen and equipment.
13. Bedroom furniture. Chart of clippings or tracings.
14. Bathroom furnishings. Chart of clippings or tracings.
15. Outdoor living areas. Chart of garden furniture.
16. Lamps and lighting. Chart of lamps. Catalogs.
17. Table equipment. Chart of china, glass, and silver.
18. Accessories. Chart of suitable accessories. Catalogs.
19. Flower arrangements. Chart of arrangements.
20. Pictures. Chart of clippings or small reproductions.

BIBLIOGRAPHY

See other lists at the chapter endings.

The classroom should contain an illustrated Encyclopedia of Furniture or Ornament or Decoration so that students can look up unfamiliar terms.

BOOKS

Aronson, Joseph. *The Encyclopedia of Furniture.* Crown, 1938.

Aronson, Joseph. *The Book of Furniture and Decoration.* Crown, 1941.

Draper, Dorothy. *Decorating is Fun.* Doubleday, Doran, 1940.

Gardner, Helen. *Art Through the Ages.* Harcourt, Brace, 1926.

Gillies, Mary D. *Popular Home Decoration.* Wise, 1940.

Miller, Gladys. *Decoratively Speaking.* Doubleday, Doran, 1939.

Sooy, L., and Woodbridge, V. *Plan Your Own Home.* Stanford Press, 1940.

Spears, Ruth W. *Home Decoration.* M. Barrows & Co., 1940.

Whiton, Sherrill. *Elements of Interior Decoration.* Lippincott, 1937.

Wright, Richardson. *Interior Decoration (House and Garden).* Simon and Schuster, 1942.

PERIODICALS

The American Home
Antiques
The Architectural Forum
The Architectural Record
Arts and Architecture (California)
Better Homes and Gardens
House Beautiful
House and Garden

INDEXES

The Art Index
The Industrial Arts Index
The International Index to Periodical Literature
The Readers' Guide to Periodical Literature
Who's Who in American Art
Who's Who in Art

INDEX

Note: Italicized page numbers indicate important discussion of topic.

483